Principles of Knowledge Auditing

Principles of Knowledge Auditing

Foundations for Knowledge Management Implementation

Patrick Lambe

The MIT Press
Cambridge, Massachusetts
London, England

The MIT Press would like to thank the anonymous peer reviewers who provided comments on drafts of this book. The generous work of academic experts is essential for establishing the authority and quality of our publications. We acknowledge with gratitude the contributions of these otherwise uncredited readers.

This book was set in Stone Serif and Stone Sans by Westchester Publishing Services. Printed and bound in the United States of America.

Library of Congress Cataloging-in-Publication Data

Names: Lambe, Patrick, 1960– author.
Title: Principles of knowledge auditing : foundations for knowledge management implementation / Patrick Lambe.
Description: Cambridge, Massachusetts : The MIT Press, [2023] | Includes bibliographical references and index.
Identifiers: LCCN 2022015397 (print) | LCCN 2022015398 (ebook) | ISBN 9780262545037 (paperback) | ISBN 9780262373159 (epub) | ISBN 9780262373166 (pdf)
Subjects: LCSH: Knowledge management. | Organizational learning. | Organizational change.
Classification: LCC HD30.2 .L362 2022 (print) | LCC HD30.2 (ebook) | DDC 658.4/038—dc23/eng/20220718
LC record available at https://lccn.loc.gov/2022015397
LC ebook record available at https://lccn.loc.gov/2022015398

10 9 8 7 6 5 4 3 2 1

For my dear colleagues Edgar Tan and Ng Wai Kong, who have generously tolerated both my absences and my presences.

Contents

Introduction

The spotlight on KM theory reveals, at first sight, a somewhat chaotic landscape.
—Crane (2016, p. 3)

Knowledge management (KM) is a profoundly important, a profoundly aspirational, and a profoundly disappointing discipline (Lambe, 2011a, pp. 192–194). Here is an illustration.

Getting Knowledge Management Right

Paul McDowall tells the story of a robust, successful, and sustained KM initiative at the Treasury Board of Canada Secretariat (TBS) between 2000 and 2006. The TBS is the agency that advises and supports the federal government's Treasury Board on government administration, policies, and expenditures. Paul's case study is a tale of doing everything right and of enjoying significant success for a number of years, only to have a few simple decisions doom the program by inadvertently undercutting the ground on which it was founded (McDowall, 2014).

Paul followed a common pattern in KM practice. He started small and close to the business, embedded within an operational unit where he had clear visibility into needs and capabilities. He focused on an issue of widespread and pressing concern: high staff turnover in a very expertise-intensive environment. He assisted new officers in getting up to speed quickly in their areas of greatest need, thereby reducing stress, generating a great deal of appreciation, and increasing the staff's speed to effectiveness in a critical function of the organization. He ran his program skillfully, learning to tune it according to evolving needs. Success reinforced success.

Paul used this achievement and the senior support it generated to conduct an organization-wide assessment. He drafted a framework from what he had learned in the initial stages and from his experience in KM, and he deployed this framework in a series of workshops across the organization in order to gather input on needs and opportunities. The framework provided a scaffolding against which to collect, organize, and synthesize valuable evidence on working contexts as well as KM needs.

This is a common, and necessary, step when it comes to scaling up KM. Individual pilots in specific operational areas do not easily scale well because the conditions they are based on and tuned to do not apply equally across the whole organization. We must learn about the variety of contexts and their commonalities and differences. In Paul's case this was a comprehensive scan within a common sensemaking framework, learning from people on the ground, to balance and weigh needs and opportunities and to

(a) extract broad-based needs for large-scale action,

(b) generate local action plans based on localized needs, and

(c) align the various centers of power in the organization (leadership, technology owners, people process owners, strategy, operations and planning owners).

This is essentially what a knowledge audit or KM assessment seeks to achieve. It comprises a specific set of activities to learn about conditions, needs, and opportunities in order to develop and maintain KM programs on any large scale.

At the TBS, the task of alignment did not go perfectly. Paul had the support of leadership, but the support service teams (e.g., human resources [HR], information technology [IT], information management, communications, library services) had little appetite for transforming the way they were working in order to align with a "knowledge management" action plan.

This is not uncommon in KM, particularly when KM is branded as a distinct functional area. "Back office" support functions such as HR, IT, finance, and library services are heavily proceduralized and mandated to staff and deliver a stable portfolio of highly structured services—upon which they are measured. They are not generally organized for agility in their service configuration. If KM is business focused and they are service focused, there is often a disconnect.

Depending on the KM needs and the personal buy-in of the management in those service domains, this can hamper the speed and extent of KM rollouts. In these cases a systematic partnering approach and a means of monitoring the health of the partnering relationships can help (Milton & Lambe, 2020, chap.10). This implies that any knowledge audit or KM assessment must also assess the levers for change in those service areas where KM has dependencies, and there must be mechanisms in place to detect changes in those levers.

Paul and his team did the sensible and pragmatic thing. They focused on what they could achieve with the support they had, and they did a pretty good job. They continued to find, and build upon, success, extending their programs incrementally based on what worked and was delivering value. Paul's team was frequently asked to assist in tricky organizational problems involving cross-functional collaboration or complex problem-solving.

Then two things happened. The head of the TBS decided to relocate the KM function to a more strategy-focused business unit so that it could serve the whole organization. This was a politicized unit oriented toward strategy, not the tactical-operational focus that had previously driven the KM team. This isolated the KM team from the operational business units, and they started losing the contextual richness and the immediate feedback loops of the operational environment. With a broader mandate, they conducted another organizational assessment, this time through a series of interviews with the senior leadership team on the organizational problems to be solved from their perspective. The recommendations had the support of the Executive Board members but not of the chair of the board, who had not been interviewed. The proposals were not taken any further, and KM became a function that facilitated corporate events and executive retreats.

The decision to relocate the KM function may have seemed to make sense at the time, but it cut off the KM function from its roots in the business and from intimate, day-to-day knowledge of the business. Had the decision-maker consulted the KM team to determine the best way to transition the KM function to a larger context, the outcome could have been very different (P. McDowall, personal communication, August 27, 2021).

This, again, is what a knowledge audit or KM assessment seeks to provide: an intimate knowledge of the needs of the business, an "at-a-glance" view of the landscape of needs and opportunities so that priorities can be identified and accepted by all the actors involved. It should provide a way of monitoring the environment so that KM efforts can (a) learn as they go from their effects on the ground and (b) pick up signals of new needs and opportunities. If this kind of mechanism or framework is in place, then the KM program will be less fragile.

Why Knowledge Management Is Challenging

Where KM works, it can have enormously positive effects on the organizations and communities it serves. It helps us work together effectively in large-scale groups and when separated in time and space. It mitigates our natural tendencies to

- work based on limited and local knowledge,
- improvise rather than systematize,
- act without reflection, and
- favor our localized silos over broader interests and goals.

But more often than we care to admit, we do not produce our intended effects in KM. Even when we do, it is challenging to sustain these positive effects over time. There are several reasons for this; some of them are simply part of the territory, and some of them are our own fault. Here is what comes with the territory:

1. Most KM initiatives at any large scale require the orchestration of different parties, whether they be partners in HR or IT, or different layers of management and staff, or the stakeholders who provide input to or need support from our knowledge services. As we saw in the TBS case, the agendas and priorities of all these parties are not necessarily aligned, and we may not have the political clout to align them.

2. Because KM is needs driven and because needs change according to context, all KM initiatives are highly context sensitive and need to be tuned constantly to changes in the environment.

3. Because knowledge use is partly visible (consumption and application of recorded knowledge) and partly invisible (how people gain and apply knowledge in their decisions and actions), it is sometimes difficult to steer without mishap, and KM must negotiate ingrained (and often invisible) habits of thought and action, whether in individuals or in processes and infrastructure, particularly in support service areas (Lambe, 2006).

The need to orchestrate, the context sensitivity, and the lack of full visibility into the habits embedded in the landscape have a further consequence—that for KM at any large scale, it can take a number of years of consistent effort and tuning to see significant progress and impact (cf. Milton & Lambe, 2020, pp. 80–82). This, of course, makes it vulnerable to shifts in support, to leadership whims, and to discontinuities in staffing, even when, as in Paul McDowall's case, the program is well framed, successful, and ostensibly well supported.

This is what comes with the territory of KM. Most experienced knowledge managers will be prepared for this, and we have a pretty good idea now of how to address these challenges (Milton & Lambe, 2020).

We have a lot more work ahead of us to address the factors that are our own fault. Before getting into them, I want to be clear that our weaknesses are collective, not individual. Knowledge management as a discipline is typically peopled by professionals who are aspirational, ethically driven, skilled, persistent, entrepreneurial, and highly committed. Behind the KM success stories we learn from and the many disappointments and failures we do not hear about are remarkable people engaging in innovative effort and sheer hard work. They are often unrecognized and inadequately rewarded in their organizations, but they persist nonetheless because they believe what they do is important and because they are committed to making a positive difference in the organizations and communities they serve. They are among the toughest and most resilient people I know.

Collectively, however, we are not very good at taking our own medicine. There is lots of networking and sharing, but it is too often focused on our short-term operational needs and issues. This surfaces in three big weaknesses:

- KM theory and KM practice do not interface well (Ragab & Arisha, 2013, p. 890; Lambe, 2014; Hislop et al., 2018). There appears to be little appetite among practitioners for learning from academic research or for building and contributing to a stable body of theory to underpin our practices, and a great deal of KM research focuses on micro issues with very little synthesis to improve practice, or to support widespread application by practitioners. We tend to adopt practices and approaches based on personal affinity and exposure rather than appropriacy and legitimacy.

- There appears to be little appetite for understanding the disciplinary and theoretical roots of the practices we have adopted. We learn very slowly as a profession because we have no structured mechanisms for learning collectively. We share "good" practices easily but not to common standards, often omitting crucial contextual factors that do not transfer well. We do not easily share information about failures, which is where most of our learning happens. Consequently, we encounter the same problems and issues over and over again, and we reinvent the same wheels over and over again. Collectively, we are forgetful and inattentive to anything beyond the immediate problem or quick fix (Lambe, 2011a).

- We are not good at building common ground. In chapter 9 we trace the tumultuous and often rancorous history of attempts to develop standards in KM over a quarter of a century. It is scandalous that this effort took so long to reach fruition, and it is poor testimony to our collective ability to share and synthesize diverse sources of knowledge, experience, and expertise.

There are good reasons for all this. The orchestration, context sensitivity, and visibility challenges that are endemic to KM consume our energies and leave little room for broader discipline-wide efforts. Knowledge management professionals come from a wide variety of backgrounds and disciplines, so we are also hampered by a lack of common language about the origins and nature of our various practices (cf. Serenko, 2021). Our discourse, as we shall see, is rife with unacknowledged imprecision, ambiguities, and flat-out contradictions. The field of knowledge auditing exemplifies these problems vividly.

In this book I intend to focus on the areas that are our own fault—that is, a lack of coherence in the way we describe and communicate our practices and our partial understandings of the origins and affordances of our practices. If we improve at these, then the challenges that come with the territory should become easier to deal with because we will be better at planning, learning, and communicating as a professional community, and we may become more sophisticated in adapting our practices to different contexts and changing needs.

To address these areas, this book is partly an exercise in semantics and partly an exercise in archaeology—most especially, an archaeology of ideas and practices related to knowledge auditing. If we can clean up our semantics, we can start to think about having a coherent body of theory. If we know our archaeology of practice, we can better adopt, adapt, and apply a wide variety of practices in appropriate ways according to our needs.

Because knowledge auditing shapes the way that KM is framed and defined in organizations, getting better at both these things has wider implications for knowledge management as well. If we can clarify the semantics of knowledge auditing (in particular, how we describe and measure knowledge use in organizations) and if we can better understand the evolution of our knowledge-auditing practices over time, we will be better equipped to observe, plan, practice, share, and learn in the broader field of knowledge management.

Why Knowledge Audits Are Important

We conduct knowledge audits, KM assessments, and knowledge-mapping exercises because we espouse a theory of change. We believe we can improve the effectiveness of the organizations or communities we serve by better understanding the dynamics and levers of knowledge production, access, and use. If we acquire that understanding, we believe, we can undertake management actions to bring about important improvements and create value. So the family of activities involved in a knowledge audit underpins much of what we plan and do in KM.

However, we also believe that the determination of what needs to change and what can change should not rely on individual intuitions, hunches, or belief systems. We believe there should be a reliable, robust, and replicable audit process through which any suitably qualified and experienced auditor, whether internal or external, would reach broadly similar conclusions or, at the very least, recommendations of equivalent usefulness and effectiveness.

In the broader usage of the term *audit* beyond knowledge management, not all audit types espouse a theory of change. Some forms of audit are focused on *maintaining* a desired standard or behavior or status quo. Examples might be financial audits, quality audits, or ecosystem audits. The point of the audit is to uncover divergence from a perceived norm, validate "good" practices, and detect and mitigate deficiencies where they exist. To be sure, a "maintenance" audit of this type may recommend changes to practices based on its findings, but these changes represent a return to a desired standard.

In KM we usually focus on moving *from* the current status quo, not on reverting *to* a status quo. We generally believe that the way we work in our organizations can and should be improved to become more effective, and we believe there will be constant improvement opportunities as the environment changes. Even when there are maintenance aspects to what we do (e.g., to preserve what is working well), our primary focus is usually one of change (O'Riordan, 2005, p. 17; Milton & Lambe, 2020, p. 41). This is especially true of our motivation to conduct a knowledge audit. Indeed, the knowledge audit is specifically intended to inform the way that change is framed.

This simple distinction in what an audit is intended to achieve (to maintain or to change) is an important one. We should keep the change-focus in mind throughout this book as a guiding principle. It will prevent us from being misled by "maintenance" models of audit.

It is not sufficient for a theory of change to have an end goal or vision in mind. We also need to have a deep knowledge of our starting point—our current environment, our needs and opportunities, the capabilities we have to work with, our levers for action, and the potential obstacles in our path. By understanding the starting point, we understand the nature and character of the journey that is required. This is what a knowledge audit or KM assessment should provide. It is fundamental to planning any change journey in KM.

Moreover, as Paul McDowall's case study illustrates, shifting conditions in terms of organizational structure, degree and level of support, access to operational knowledge, or the nature of the external challenges can dramatically shift the assumptions upon which the original improvement plan was founded. In the case of the TBS, the significant and unexpected organizational change required a very different approach. If they are to guide the KM programs on a continuing basis, the methods and approaches used in knowledge auditing must be sufficiently accessible and flexible, and sensitive enough to unanticipated events. Successful change is steered more than planned.

Knowledge audits and their underpinning methods are foundational for any realistic goal-setting exercise in KM and for an effective but responsive execution.

Why Knowledge Audits Are Challenging

The practice of knowledge auditing is subject to much more variation than the simple distinction between a maintenance audit or an improvement audit would suggest. The general term *audit* is itself subject to a wide variety of meanings, and audits can encompass a wide variety of practices and methodologies (Tourish & Hargie, 2000b, p. 23). "The topic of knowledge audits in the knowledge management world is not sufficiently rigorous to be a trusted and practical executive-level tool" (Handa et al., 2019, p. xiii).

There is also a great deal of variety and inconsistency in the ways that knowledge is described in organizations. Part IV of this book catalogs a dizzying array of different, and competing, typologies of knowledge. The term *knowledge* needs to be pinned down just like the term *audit* so that we can be precise about the phenomena we are investigating and mapping in a knowledge audit.

This is where our collective weaknesses as a discipline come into play. The literature from both academics and practitioners is rife with competing definitions of *audit*, types of audits, and even the knowledge phenomena we examine in our audits (Pa et al., 2012, p. 1).

When the vocabularies of audit or of knowledge are used uncritically, without explicit definition and carrying implicit assumptions that are rarely made clear, it becomes difficult for the novice to detect where competing or contradictory meanings are being used under cover of a superficially consistent language. Poor language produces poor practice.

The original book I had planned to write was a practitioner's guide to knowledge audits and knowledge mapping. When I started, I felt I had a stable and well-informed practice, drawn from the discipline of information auditing, and substantial experience under my belt. However, the more I looked at the broader knowledge-auditing practice, the research literature behind it, and the divergent traditions behind both, the more I discovered that I was myself within an insulated and limited pipeline of practice conditioned by my own background, and that there were parallel (noncommunicating) and equally valid practices originating in quite different disciplines.

I realized that a practitioner's guide would do little to advance the practice without first resolving some of these key ambiguities and inconsistencies and integrating these scattered traditions. I believe that we must first establish a firm foundation upon which to build a common and authoritative practice, and we need to build common ground out of which professional sharing and learning can begin to make sense, instead of adding to the present confusion of voices.

When we talk about a *knowledge audit*, what is it that we say we are auditing? Knowledge assets? Knowledge resources? Knowledge processes? Knowledge flows? Knowledge management enablers? Outcomes of knowledge use? How does a knowledge audit relate to intellectual capital measurement and accounting? The literature and practice give no coherent guidance on these questions.

The Handa et al. book, (2019) book *Knowledge Assets and Knowledge Audits* and *Organizational Network Analysis: Auditing Intangible Resources* by Anna Ujwary-Gil (2020) are examples of recent attempts to provide a comprehensive and integrated view (in very different ways), but they are isolated examples. Across the broader field of research and practice, the failure to answer these questions is a key source of confusion (cf. Ayinde et al., 2021).

The same problem exists in relation to the subdiscipline of knowledge mapping. We are faced with an array of very different knowledge-mapping forms and mapping techniques, with little guidance on which forms or techniques are most suitable for which purposes (cf. Čavalić & Erkan, 2012). There is a disturbing lack of any underpinning theory of mapping that could assist us in determining the differences between (a) good and useful maps, or (b) constructs that are more expressive of the dispositions and perceptions of the cartographer than of the reality on the ground.

In summary, there is a great deal of uncertainty and ambiguity about what a knowledge audit entails and how it should be conducted. This frustrates our desire for a reasonably scientific, robust, reliable, and replicable process. It also leaves us vulnerable to individualistic perspectives, very diverse views on what counts as audit evidence, persuasive and unsubstantiated quackery, or wishful thinking. It leaves us mired in a knowledge management that is founded on personality and rhetoric, not evidence. It means that as a profession we are unable to compare our practices and our results in a meaningful manner, which in turn leaves us unable to learn across regions, organizations, and practitioners.

And that in turn undermines our projects of change. We set KM goals based on imperfect knowledge of our starting points and with few mechanisms that enable us to remain sensitive to the changes that will have an impact on our purpose, and giving ourselves enough time to anticipate and respond to them. For those of us who are new to knowledge auditing, how can we be assured that our process is sufficient and appropriate to the need? How can we become better and more focused in our orchestration, tuning, and change activities?

How This Book Aims to Help

Our first goal in this book is to tease apart the different senses and models of audit and then reintegrate them in a meaningful and useful way. In so doing, we can find the operating model that makes the most sense in a KM context so that we can find clear, consistent, and transparent ways of planning, communicating, and learning from what we do as a professional community. That is the semantic approach I mentioned earlier, which you will see most especially in parts II and IV of this book, where we will try to establish a consistent and coherent framework for how we speak about audits and for how we speak about knowledge, and knowledge use, in organizations.

This does not mean that we have to impose a standard set of meanings and definitions. Despite the challenges it poses, the diversity of language and practice in our discipline is also a great source of richness. I do not believe that semantic standardization alone is a practical or useful solution. I believe the answer to the challenges we face lies in greater clarity about the language we use, common awareness of critical distinctions and sources of ambiguity, and greater precision in the way we use the language of our discipline. We should certainly be aware of conceptual confusions that get in the way of good practice. This does imply the need to think harder about the way in which we describe, frame, and communicate what we do.

This is another way of saying that we need a common frame of reference more than we need a standard. Standards have their uses, including as aids to building common ground, but they only provide markers and signposts, and they are certainly not good representations of the richness of the landscape.

I also said that my endeavor is partly archaeological. This is because within knowledge management and specifically within knowledge auditing, we have inherited various portmanteaus of methods and approaches, together with their underpinning theories, from a variety of sources at different times. I myself inherited an information management set of assumptions and concerns and origin myths. Others have come out of an organizational communications or social networks background. Others have come out of compliance or quality management or technology management backgrounds.

These originating contexts, and the drivers that gave them shape and meaning, generate specific assumptions about the appropriate methods and approaches we should use. The rationales and assumptions behind these approaches are rarely visible to the practitioners who adopt them because we take them for granted—they are just part of our disciplinary "wallpaper." Furthermore, all of us have only partial views of the landscape, and none of us are fully aware of the alternatives that are available to us elsewhere. This means that we are not very sophisticated or modulated in our practice, so we either communicate at high levels of abstraction or, on matters of detail, at cross-purposes. This also makes it very difficult for collective learning to take place.

So solving the semantics problem only addresses half of the challenge. The other half is the archaeological challenge, which is to understand the origins, the tools, and the affordances of the several disciplines that have struggled for the past eighty years or more with problems of understanding and improving the ways that organizations work with information and knowledge flows and knowledge resources. Parts I and III of this book deal with the origins and evolution of practices and methods related to knowledge auditing.

If we succeed, we should improve the way we communicate across our disciplinary boundaries, and we should be able to enlarge our portfolios of practice by borrowing from each other. If we have a coherent and consistent language and approach, we will be able to meaningfully share and combine data as a broad professional community and build upon that, rather than talking past each other and perpetuating our endless cycles of improvisation.

I hope that this book will help to bring greater clarity to knowledge audits and to the task of planning and selecting audit methods. I hope it will help us communicate better about what we are doing and why with our sponsors, stakeholders, and peers.

And if we are successful, perhaps a helpful book on knowledge audit practices and methods might then be possible after all.

Recovering Our Past

1 Seeking to Understand Knowledge in Organizations

Is there a thing of which it is said, "See, this is new"?

It has been already in the ages before us.

There is no remembrance of former things, nor will there be any remembrance of later things yet to be among those who come after.

—Ecclesiastes 1:10–11

Case Study: An Early Communication Audit

Over a period of several months in the early summer of 1960, Charles "Chuck" Connaghan traveled to a sawmill just outside Vancouver to interview eighty hourly paid workers there about company communications and information flows. He was working on his master's dissertation in psychology at the University of British Columbia. (Connaghan 1960).

It was a cool, rainy start to the summer that year, and Connaghan conducted his interviews in the workers' lunchroom during their lunch hours. It was noisy and distracting. There were three shifts, so he would catch three workers per day for interviews lasting up to forty-five minutes each. He must have been a personable young man because almost all of the workers he approached agreed to give up their precious lunchtimes despite, as it turned out, their suspicion and hostility toward their management and their foremen. Connaghan had been preparing for several weeks. He had spent time at the mill to understand its workings, he had gotten permission from the mill owners and management with no restrictions on what he could ask, and he had procured the consent of the union, provided the men agreed to speak to him.

Photographs of the time show him as an open-faced, friendly, but somewhat serious-looking young man. He looked the part of a white-collar manager—which he later became. At twenty-eight and fresh out of his bachelor degree program, he was a relatively mature student. He had served in the British Army before emigrating from Ireland. He was obviously both an ambitious and an attractive personality. He had served as president of the university's student association and in this role had spent a day in March in full academic dress accompanying Mrs. Eleanor Roosevelt on an official visit to the university. Now he was sitting in a canteen keeping hourly paid manual laborers away from their lunch and asking them how they felt about their employers.

Connaghan reported that the men seemed "relaxed" in the interviews. The challenge of bridging differences seems to have appealed to him, both then, and in his subsequent career.

Two things jump out of his findings at the Vancouver sawmill. The first we have already alluded to. Connaghan (1960) concluded that the workers, across types and age ranges, were mistrustful, hostile to their employer, and demotivated. In particular, they mistrusted their foremen, whom they felt could not "be depended upon to give accurate, objective information. . . . In the opinion of the workers the foreman is a block to communication in that he withholds information, giving only that which he deems necessary for them to receive. He is also suspected of distorting for his own benefit, the information he passes along" (p. 82).

The first observation is clearly what preoccupied Connaghan and his contemporaries. The relatively recent experience of the Second World War had focused attention on the importance of morale and motivation for productivity and effectiveness. The new field of communications studies had been influenced by techniques developed for propaganda work during the war. In parallel, the immediate postwar period was marked by almost full employment for the first time in living memory, accompanied by increasing union activism and power. There was competition for labor; the balance of power between labor and employers had shifted. Industrial relations, and the role of information and communication flows in improving both morale and cooperative behavior, became major areas of interest and study.

The second observation from Charles Connaghan's findings is more pertinent to us, though Connaghan himself does not remark on it. In the interviews, Connaghan asked his interviewees to indicate which of twenty-six types of information they would find useful. The information types fell into three broad classes:

(A) Information related to the company's performance (costs, profits, productivity, competitors, new products, layoffs, and new job prospects)

(B) Information related to terms and conditions of employment (policies on job transfers, promotions, sick leave, insurance, pension plan, complaints procedure)

(C) Information related to work improvements (better ways of doing the job, changes in the job, how the job relates to the overall production process)

Class C is interesting to us, because it is the closest information type cited in the interview that touches on job knowledge and learning issues. It was universally ranked lowest in the responses of Connaghan's interviewees. Less than a third of the workers said they were interested in it. The most in-demand class of information was class A, relating to company performance (Connaghan, 1960, p. 34).

It is impossible to tell whether Connaghan's respondents had been coached to reply from a union-influenced playbook—class A represents, after all, the information types most useful in a collective-bargaining process. The responses were remarkably consistent, but Connaghan had no mechanisms in place to control for potential bias. Whether spontaneous or not, however, it is striking that when given the choice between job knowledge and bargaining knowledge, the workers said they would rather go for the latter.

Connaghan's research is interesting, not so much for its findings but for the vivid snapshot it gives of a knowledge and information needs picture from a specific workplace and at a specific time. It is interesting for what people said they were most concerned with. Connaghan's research was typical of hundreds of such studies undertaken by personable young men and women across North America throughout the 1950s and 1960s, in a frenetic attempt to understand how communications and information flow could improve the lot of business and of labor. The method he used, a simple, unstandardized investigation driven by a series of personal interviews and analyses conducted by the auditor, with all its shortcomings, exemplifies an all-too-common model still in common use with knowledge audits today. For all the intervening years, we have not come far in our basic methods.

Communications as Information Systems

It is critical for our understanding of this period to know that *organizational communication* originally meant systems of information flow. Only later would our contemporary, narrower connotation emerge of corporate communications as a set of processes and techniques for exerting external and internal influence.

Charles Connaghan's account contrasts in its specifics with the generalized and commonsensical abstractions of management and organizational theorists from the same period. Let us take this contemporary passage from Herbert Simon's famous book *Administrative Behavior*:

> The information and knowledge that has a bearing on decisions arises at various points in the organization. Sometimes the organization has its own "sensory organs"—the intelligence unit of a military organization, or the market analysis section of a business firm. Sometimes individuals are recruited and installed in positions for the knowledge they are presumed already to possess—a legal division. Sometimes the knowledge develops on the job itself—the lathe operator is the first to know when his machine breaks down. Sometimes the knowledge is knowledge of other decisions that have been made—the executive turns down one request for the expenditure of funds because he knows that he has already committed these funds to another use.
>
> In all these cases particular individuals in the organization are possessed of information that is relevant to particular decisions that have to be made. An apparently simple way to allocate the function of decision-making would be to assign to each member of the organization those decisions for which he possesses the relevant information. The basic difficulty in this is that not all the information relevant to a particular decision is possessed by a single individual. If the decision is then dismembered into its component premises and these allocated to separate individuals, a communication process must be set up for transmitting these components from the separate centers to some point where they can be combined and transmitted, in turn, to those members in the organization who will have to carry them out. (Simon, 1957, p.155)

Simon's interest in communication is as a mechanism for moving pieces of information and knowledge to the points where they can assist in the making of decisions. This fits with his concept of an organization as a complex decision-making machine. It also appears pretty relevant to knowledge management (KM) today. Morale and motivation do not enter into his calculus except as possible disrupters of the authority mechanisms that drive decision responsibilities and instructions arising from decisions.

Flipping from Connaghan to Simon gives us wildly different perceptions of the concept, functions, content, and mechanisms of organizational communication. Simon's account has a rigorously worked out connection between communication and an organization's ability to deploy the information and knowledge at its disposal (as we would expect from a management theorist). Connaghan's account stops short of any theorizing but also implies that in the naturalistic world he was exploring is a hierarchy of needs well beyond the rationalistic model proposed by Simon and other management thinkers.

This tension exemplifies perfectly the dilemma of management researchers in the 1950s and 1960s. On the one hand was a strong, emerging theoretical framework on the role of information and information flow in organizational effectiveness. On the other hand were empirical difficulties in (a) harnessing and coordinating the energy and efforts of workforces that were often antagonistic to managers and owners and (b) understanding the dynamics of the different influences upon performance within increasingly complex organizational structures.

There was also a strongly felt shortfall in analytical frameworks that could help to marry theory with the practical realities on the ground. Edith Penrose (1959) characterized this problem as the "uncomfortable no-man's-land between the high and dry plateaus of 'pure theory' and the tangled forests of 'empiric-realistic' research" (p. 9).

Out of this sense of shortfall, systematic audit methodologies eventually emerged, initially in more sophisticated communication audit models than that deployed by Connaghan, and later on in information and knowledge audits. However, we have inherited a tangled thicket of methodologies largely disconnected from a coherent body of theory and practice.

Parallels with Knowledge Management

Largely because of this sense of a gulf between theory and ground reality, there was an explosion of literature on organizational communication in the 1950s, not dissimilar in many ways to the explosion of KM literature in the late 1990s.

The kind of disparity we see between Connaghan and Simon is represented in the literature at large. Writers and practitioners were keenly aware of the lack of a solid evidence base for how communications actually contributed to organizational life and performance. For example, George Odiorne (1954) wrote critically of "excursions . . . and numerous speculations" flooding the trade and technical literature (p. 235).

Charles Connaghan (1960) himself wrote of the need to systematize the "hunches and prejudices" that governed how decisions on communications were managed in organizations (p. 1). There is an unmistakable parallel with Victoria Ward's (2010) harsh characterization of knowledge management, when she referred to "sloppinesses, assumptions, half-baked metaphors and undigested analogies" (p. 7). Dennis Tourish's (2019) comment on the broader field of management studies is equally applicable to knowledge management research and practice: ". . . rogue findings or poorly designed studies often go unchallenged, and can become conventional wisdom" (p. 198).

In the 1950s and 1960s, this sense of shortfall fueled a strong interest in developing systematic ways of studying communications in organizations. As with KM in the 1990s, in the 1950s there were several independent lines of research and professional interest converging on the umbrella concept of organizational communications. As with KM, it was often hard to tell where information management ended and where communications research began.

As with KM, the field of communication studies was largely made up of—in J.-C. Spender's (1996b) somewhat sardonic phrase—"concepts in search of a theory." As late as 1980, communications theorists Brown and Schaefermeyer (1980) appeared to despair of communication studies as a legitimate social science:

> Still without a dominant paradigm for their research, students of human communication practice a diversity of methodologies premised on mid-range models or on none at all. Some have despaired of theory building in their generation and have become antitheoretical in bias, busying themselves in descriptive studies; others, atheoretical in orientation, have involved themselves in social betterment efforts, sharing information with others on what seems to work; others, having committed to one of several mid-range theoretical models such as attitude change, construct theory, or symbolic interactionism, continue with field and laboratory studies, abstracting and measuring the interaction of source-message-receiver-context variables. (p. 37)

The parallels with knowledge management could hardly be more obvious:

- An early period of speculation and hypothesizing
- A period of intense but fragmented publishing in research and trade literatures stimulated by the economic and industrial pressures of the time
- The co-option of several and sometimes competing research disciplines under a common umbrella
- A tendency to tribalism between competing schools of thought
- Tools and methodologies taking precedence over development of an overarching, integrating theory (Lambe, 2011a).

There was one crucial difference between the birth of communications research and the birth of knowledge management, however. The post–World War II period saw the aggressive institutionalization of the social sciences in Western higher education. Part of this effort was to establish the credibility of the social sciences as "scientific." There was enormous pressure to develop tools and methodologies that were robust, stood the tests of reproducibility and peer review, and "felt" scientific.

This pressure was partly self-imposed, with social scientists lobbying for the funds and resources to open institutes, laboratories, and research centers. It was partly economic, fueled by industry's and government's increasing consumption of social science research, beginning in the Second World War and accelerating after it (Schramm, 1980, p. 81; Chandler, 1977, pp. 476–483).

World War II had provided a context in which social instability and chaos were being consciously addressed through new social scientific approaches. There was a growing confidence in the *calculability* of social phenomena, whether for influencing (propaganda) purposes or for analytical and predictive purposes. This new sense of confidence was pervasive. It found its way into science fiction as well, most famously in Isaac Asimov's concept of a branch of predictive mathematics called *psychohistory* in his famous Foundation series, beginning in 1942. John W. Campbell was the influential editor of the science fiction magazine *Astounding Science Fiction*. He was an active promoter of the idea of the future exactness of the social sciences (Nevala-Lee, 2018), whether it be Asimov's "psychohistory" or Wyman Guin's (1952) story about *psychostatistics*. Guin, not unrelatedly, was an advertising executive. The ideas of science fiction, of the social sciences, and of a "scientific" approach to organizational communications did not seem so far apart.

Organizational communications research was front and center in this incredible expansion of interest in the social sciences *as an applied science*. Resources were poured into the social sciences, tightly coupled with an expectation of "scientific" measurement and rigor. Colleges, institutes, and research programs were established and funded. The level of confidence can be measured in the sheer amount of money poured into the postwar expansion of the social sciences.

Knowledge management also had strong economic drivers behind its adoption and promotion in the 1990s, but it has never been held to account with the same degree of rigor as communications research in the 1950s and 1960s. For that reason we can learn a lot from that first wave of interest and how it played out.

By contrast with communications research and practice, knowledge management has been characterized by its lack of rigor, self-reflection, and mindfulness in its adoption of methodologies and theories (Lambe, 2011a). Communications research had an expectation of measurability built into it from the start, and this is what lay behind the eventual blossoming of systematic audit techniques, techniques that we can still learn from today. The field produced a range of sophisticated methodologies of audit, all of which might (but often do not) exist today in the knowledge auditor's portfolio.

Too often, the knowledge manager's modern portfolio of auditing methods is as meager as Charles Connaghan's, comprising questionnaires and interviews with an overdependence on direct reporting using limited instruments and with few controls for bias.

The history of communication audits can provide the knowledge auditor with a formidable armory of techniques to deploy.

*   *   *

Summary

It is often assumed that knowledge audits are a recent phenomenon. In this chapter we used the example of a communication audit from 1960 to show that the concerns we face now, as well as the ways we approach knowledge audits today, have strong similarities to the environment of the 1960s. In this book we will take a broad view of knowledge auditing so that we can access a wider range of insight and experience in building a robust and reliable methodology.

2 The History of Knowledge Audits

As far as I remember
I have not ever estranged myself from You,
nor does my conscience prick me for it.
—Dante, *Purgatorio* XXXIII

In the verse above, Dante claims to have no memory of sin. However, his lover Beatrice then reminds him—somewhat sharply—that he has just drunk from the river Lethe, whose water brings forgetfulness. In Greek mythology the goddess Lethe, who brought (sometimes convenient) oblivion, was the counterpart of the goddess Mnemosyne, who brought perfect memory and with it, omniscience. Perhaps also guilt.

For a discipline that promotes the reuse of existing knowledge, knowledge management (KM) is tremendously forgetful. It is not just that we repeatedly invent the same things over and over again (we do). It is that we reframe older practices as if they are entirely original and new. We preach the virtues of Mnemosyne but are addicted to the waters of Lethe.

Elsewhere I have documented the tendency of KM to forget or ignore its theoretical and methodological antecedents. The dominant foundation myth of KM is that it began in the early 1990s, but we can trace clear antecedents going back to the 1960s (Lambe, 2011a). This is not unique to knowledge management, by the way. It is a feature of many management fads and several academic disciplines. The sociologist Robert Merton (1965) described this phenomenon as "obliteration by incorporation," whereby older ideas and practices are adopted and reframed as new knowledge, concealing their origins.

More specifically, we see the same phenomenon in knowledge auditing and knowledge mapping. Let us take this statement from Wesley Vestal, in a 2005 book on knowledge mapping published by the American Productivity and Quality Center (APQC): "Prior to 1995, few tools existed to understand what knowledge was embedded in organizations, and any methodologies for improving flow and use were miles away from materialization." There is clearly a vested interest in the waters of Lethe here (pardon the pun) because Vestal (2005) continues: "For more than a decade [since then], APQC has worked on establishing methods and conducting benchmarking studies that have refined the practice of knowledge management" (p. 2; cf. Ermine et al., 2006, p. 130).

Vested interest aside, even a cursory glance at the literature shows that the claim of novelty is manifestly untrue. We intend to demonstrate that fact.

Precursors of Knowledge Audits

Before there were knowledge audits, there were information audits. And before that, as we have seen, there were communication audits. These audit types bear strong family resemblances to each other. They were all grappling with different aspects of the same question: How can we observe, measure, and improve the quality of information and knowledge flow and utilization in large, complex organizations?

Only very rarely, however, is an explicit genealogy recognized where the precedent audit type is acknowledged as an influence. Even where it is recognized, the implication is that the successor audit type in some way goes further in scale and scope than its predecessor. This may have been partly political, as the Vestal example suggests: the 1990s and 2000s were periods of strong management fads, and appeals to inventiveness may have been more attractive than appeals to past authority. It may have been laziness, or lack of awareness, or wishful thinking. It is hard to say. But we will not fully understand what knowledge audits are capable of if we do not understand where they come from.

Knowledge audits started to gain traction in the late 1990s, just as information audits reached their peak. Despite this, only 10 percent or so of the writers on knowledge audits made the connection back to information audits. Similarly, when information audits began to grow in the 1980s, only a very small minority of writers (I have estimated some 2 percent of the literature) made the connection to communication audits.

Yet, as we have seen, the genesis of communication audits (in the 1950s) was focused on information flows to support decision-making and organizational control. Communication audits also became interested in how the knowledge of workers got deployed in support of enterprise effectiveness. There are striking connections here with the aims of information audits and, later on, knowledge audits. As knowledge audits blossomed in the 2000s, the link back to communication audits had been all but forgotten. Based on my review, only 0.5 percent of the total literature on knowledge audits traces its lineage back to communication audits.

Even today, each audit type has its professional "tribe"—communications managers, information managers, and knowledge managers—each maintaining and developing its own audit practices within strict disciplinary silos and only rarely looking above the parapets at what their colleagues (often in the same organization) are doing (Lambe, 2011b; P. Griffiths, 2012, p. 40; cf. Raub & Rüling, 2001; Becher & Trowler, 2001).

Figure 2.1 shows an analysis of the literature covering communication audits, information audits, and knowledge audits from the 1950s to the end of the 2000s. The counts are from articles, dissertations, and citations found on Google Scholar in 2014, reviewed and vetted for false positives.

The diagram shows that communication audits had a slow start, with a handful of articles each decade in the 1950s and 1960s focused on auditing and measuring organizational communications (although the general literature on organizational communications was booming in the post–World War II era). In the 1970s, communication audits began to take off, with several sophisticated audit instruments being developed

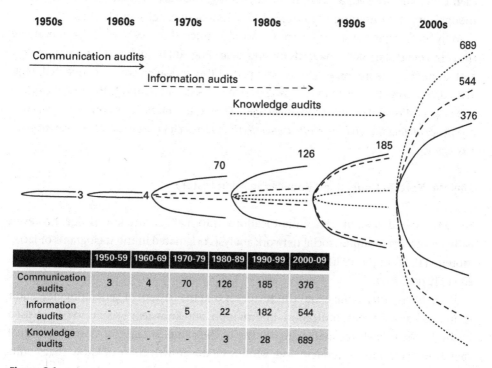

	1950-59	1960-69	1970-79	1980-89	1990-99	2000-09
Communication audits	3	4	70	126	185	376
Information audits	-	-	5	22	182	544
Knowledge audits	-	-	-	3	28	689

Figure 2.1
Growth of literature on communication audits, information audits, and knowledge audits, 1950–2009, taken from an analysis of Google Scholar, August 2014.

and tested, and by the 1980s they were becoming solidly entrenched. They continue to grow today.

References to information audits did not begin until the 1970s and had a similarly slow start, but by the 1990s they were matching the volume of communication audit literature and by the 2000s had outstripped it. Information auditors do occasionally try to connect what they do to KM, but as a collective they also maintain their own independent course. Information audits and communication audits continue to maintain parallel existences alongside knowledge audits. Knowledge audits began—again, slowly—in the 1980s but followed a similar pattern of expansion as their predecessors and by the 2000s had outstripped both of them in the volume of articles produced.

This representation is important because it shows two things: (a) a similar "pulse" pattern of audit methodologies being developed in successive decades, focused on similar organizational capabilities, and (b) each outstripping the others on ever-accelerating growth curves. In many cases these audit methodologies developed independently of each other and seemed, at least at the beginning, unaware of their predecessors even though they were attempting to address very similar questions and problems.

Why is this prehistory interesting? Because since the 1950s we have repeatedly sought to build systematic methods for understanding and influencing information flow and knowledge use in organizations. As a part of this endeavor, we have invented, reinvented, and forgotten or ignored a wide range of tools and methods for understanding our organizational lives around knowledge. *There is a substantial history of learning and experience around this endeavor, often imperfectly understood or accessed by knowledge auditors today.*

Why We Need to Understand Knowledge Audit History

Some tools used in audits of communications, information, and knowledge, had even earlier roots. For example, social network analysis originated in the sociograms of Jacob Moreno (1934) in the 1930s. Many of these tools are today poorly understood or inadequately deployed.

What is also interesting about this history is that the pattern of generating new audit techniques around communication, information, and knowledge seems to have ceased in the 1990s. Knowledge audits are the last in their line, at least for now. Intellectual capital audits and measurement closely followed the growth curve of knowledge audits and can be subsumed within the same pattern of activity. We seem to have stopped inventing "new" audit forms. Perhaps the time for consolidation and collective sensemaking has arrived. In my introduction I mentioned the recent books by Handa et al.

(2019) and by Ujwary-Gil (2020). These are examples of an increasing sense of the need to integrate a fragmented landscape.

However, as we will see, while knowledge audits are widespread and the knowledge audit literature continues to grow, knowledge audits take multiple forms, generally lack methodological and theoretical consistency or stability, and are understood in widely varying ways.

What does this actually mean? It implies that we have multiplied our ways of working, with increasing imprecision of meaning, and with decreasing coherence in what we do. As David Snowden and Peter Stanbridge (2004) put it, "part of the confusion and frustration associated with the knowledge management domain is linked to this overgeneralization of approaches and missing understanding of the diverse theoretical backgrounds that have led to them" (p. 141).

Whatever the mystery behind this "pulse" pattern of repeated and forgetful reinvention, the pattern reminds us—as sharply as Beatrice did Dante—that we have a history. Knowledge audits were not the beginning of a new trend. They were a manifestation of a longer-term trend that started in the 1950s.

To understand how to frame a productive knowledge audit, we will need to follow the trail back to the post–World War II interest in communication as a management and organizational discipline, through to the identification of information as a strategic resource in the 1980s and then into an expansion of focus on knowledge as an asset, and beyond that to an appreciation of a systematic approach to knowledge practices as an organizational capability.

But first we need to clarify the concept of *knowledge auditing*, and we will start by focusing on the concept of auditing in general.

*   *   *

Summary

This chapter showed that we have, if we wish, access to a significant tradition of knowledge-related auditing that began in the 1950s, along with the attendant methodologies, rationales, and lessons learned.

II Speaking Clearly about Audits

3 What Is an Audit? A Definitional Approach

> On the first day of an official audit, the audit team arrives at the agency in question, to be greeted by the management team. The chief auditor says, "Good morning. We are here to help." The head of agency replies, "Good morning. You're very welcome." In fact, neither of us believes the other.
> —Auditor-General's Officer

The anecdote above, told many years ago to a colleague of mine, points up the tensions inherent in the practice of auditing. An audit is supposed to ensure excellence of processes and operations. It is supposed to result in validation of a status quo or recommendations for improvements. To this extent, it is supposed to be helpful.

But it is also troublesome. It is difficult, as an operational manager, not to feel defensive when you have strangers poring through your records, looking, you might feel, for evidence of your mistakes. You are conscious that you and your team may have developed unsanctioned ways of working that will take time and effort to defend and validate, even though you may be convinced they are in the best interests of the business (cf. Niang, 2020, p. 17). Auditors interfere. You tell yourself you are not a robot mindlessly following procedures, especially when they are contrary to common sense. Auditors, perhaps, are enforcers of robotic behavior.

In this chapter we examine "tight" models of audit, focused on compliance, and consider how they can inform knowledge audits.

Connotations of *Audit*

The term *audit* has a variety of connotations. Here is a list of attributes frequently associated with the term when I ask workshop participants what auditing means to them:

- Conducted by a qualified person
- Systematic

- Has a rigorous methodology
- Precise and measurable
- Compliance oriented
- Quality oriented
- Checking
- Monitoring
- Accountability
- Evidence based
- Ensuring value for money

At face value, the conjunction of *knowledge* with *audit* seems like a conjunction of opposites. *Knowledge* as a term in common use is vague and unspecific, difficult to measure and define—in fact, you might think it the antithesis of all that is auditable. If the concept of *knowledge auditing* inspires interest, it may be because of the mystery and implicit challenge that the phrase entails. How do you audit something as imprecise as knowledge?

As it turns out in the real world, however, this perception is a complete illusion. The connotations of rigor and systematics that accompany the term *audit* evaporate when we look at the use of the term in practice. In fact, once we peel away the associations with financial and internal audits, there is a wide spectrum of implied rigor in practices labeled as audits, from the loosest sense of paying systematic attention to something and giving an account of it, to creating inventories for various purposes, to evidence-based evaluation, to checking practices systematically against standards, to valuation of assets and the exploitation of those assets.

As management communications experts Dennis Tourish and Owen Hargie (2000b) put it, "The term 'audit' has by now been applied to an enormous range of activities. Its very ubiquity often generates confusion" (p. 23; cf. Baker, 1999, p. 1).

In this and the next chapter, we examine the notion of auditing. Our goal is to identify a typology of audits that we can then use in thinking more systematically about how we frame knowledge audits.

Tight Models of Audit: Financial and Operational Audits

As we have seen, *auditing* is a surprisingly imprecise umbrella term covering a multitude of very different practices, from very loose to very tight. The association with the tightest connotation (compliance and checking) often carries over in the popular mind into the looser sense of *systematic evaluation*. This is problematic because the tight connotation can give a loose methodology an authority it does not always deserve.

If many different practices could be implied, our first step should be to figure out what type of audit we intend to conduct, and this should then drive the methods deployed. These will in turn have an impact on the robustness of the findings and the authority of the recommendations.

Oxford Dictionaries now covers their bases by including both ends of the spectrum, tight and loose, in their definition of *audit*:

Audit

1. An official inspection of an organization's accounts, typically by an independent body: *audits can't be expected to detect every fraud*
2. A systematic review or assessment of something: *a complete audit of flora and fauna at the site*

Perhaps the tightest definition (and the one that brings with it the strongest sense of rigor) comes from the field of financial audits. Here is what Maire Loughran (2010) says: "Auditing is the process of investigating information that's prepared by someone else to determine whether the information is fairly stated. . . . you investigate the assertions that a company makes on its financial statements" (p. 9).

Two elements are of interest to us here. First, the audit is an examination of records or evidence, and second, it is a validation check on the assertions made in those records. The *examination* component of an audit also explains the root of the term, from the Latin *audire*, meaning "to listen." Both academic examinations and statements of account in the Middle Ages were delivered and quizzed orally. Did the auditees stand up to scrutiny?

Crucially, the audit in this tightest sense is a purely *descriptive* exercise. Its output is an opinion, not a set of recommendations. The auditor takes no responsibility for ensuing actions. Regulatory mechanisms external to the auditor and to the client take care of that. The auditor is an impartial, uninvolved third party whose sole role is to assess the validity of the assertions made as to the accuracy of the client's financial accounts.

A descriptive audit involves

(a) a critical examination of evidence, and

(b) a check as to the validity of assertions made about the business.

So while the notion of a systematic review of evidence might make sense to us as knowledge auditors, the passivity of a financial audit might not make sense if

- we do espouse a theory of change,
- we have been engaged to seek out opportunities for change, and
- we want to see actionable recommendations coming from the audit.

For us, by contrast, knowledge auditing is more about "accurately appraising what we now do, in order to establish what we must do tomorrow" (Tourish & Hargie, 2000a, p. 4).

There is no external regulatory framework in knowledge management (KM) to take care of ensuing actions for us, as there is in accounting. Even the International Organization for Standardization (ISO) 30401 standard does not aim to serve in that role. What is the utility of assessing the accuracy of our statements on our KM practices without some guidance on follow-through? The financial audit may communicate rigor, but it provides little in the way of a model for a productive knowledge audit.

The field of internal audit, often described as operational auditing, provides a no less tight, but a richer and more expansive, understanding of the practice of auditing. Here, an audit is an examination of an organization's mechanisms of control, that long-standing preoccupation of modern management. And it is here, more than with the financial audit, that we find an affinity with the knowledge audit's ancestor, the communication audit.

> An effective tool of managerial control is the internal audit, or, as it is now coming to be called, the operational audit. . . . Although often limited to the auditing of accounts, in its most useful aspect operational auditing involves appraisal of operations generally. . . . Thus operational auditors, in addition to assuring themselves that accounts properly reflect the facts, also appraise policies, procedures, use of authority, quality of management, effectiveness of methods, special problems, and other phases of operations. (Koontz et al., 1976, pp. 670–671; cf. Chambers & Rand, 2010, p. 4)

It is also in the practice of operational audits that we encounter the *prescriptive audit*, where findings lead to recommendations and specific guidance on potential improvements.

> Internal auditing is an independent, objective assurance and consulting activity designed to add value and improve an organization's operations. It helps an organization accomplish its objectives by bringing a systematic, disciplined approach to evaluate and improve the effectiveness of risk management, control, and governance processes. (Institute of Internal Auditors, 2021; cf. Chambers & Rand, 2010, p. 5)

Operational audits start their work by looking at specific operational areas—that is, the business functions of the organization. They examine the extent to which risk, control, and governance are addressed in the service of management objectives.

However, while they are functionally oriented, they cannot take a completely functional view. All organizations are systems of interlocking and interconnected functions. As Chambers and Rand point out, "Whereas the control processes operating within a function or department may be well defined and applied, there is the potential for control weaknesses at the point of interface with other related functions."

They therefore stress the importance of an *audit universe* approach, organized around cross-organizational business processes. Department-oriented audits have the advantage of being tightly scoped and relatively easy to conduct. Business processes are more difficult to assess because they cross business functions and reporting lines, and for that very reason, they are more prone to failures in control, risk, and governance. This makes them more worthy of an auditor's attention (Chambers & Rand, 2010, pp. 11–12, 28–30).

What can the knowledge auditor gain from this audit model? First, the operational audit approach is more organically related to the organization's context and objectives than the financial audit approach. While more difficult to implement and more demanding of an auditor's skills, it is richer in its coverage and more likely to pick up actionable insights for management to consider.

Second, the functional orientation supplemented by the "audit universe" perspective, is a particularly useful concept for a knowledge management agenda—it is not enough to examine specific functional silos for their knowledge and information management practices and potentialities. KM is often concerned with how the organization as a whole exploits and leverages its knowledge.

Third, the operational audit espouses a theory of change: insight without action is limited in value. The operational audit is oriented toward empowering managerial decision-making in a way that the financial audit is not.

Thus far, operational audits would appear to contribute more toward a useful model to guide knowledge audits than do financial audits.

Prescriptive audits

(a) are grounded in an organization's context and objectives,

(b) combine functional perspectives with whole-of-organization perspectives,

(c) seek to generate *actionable* insights and recommendations for improvement and change.

Operational audits do have specific areas of focus and measurement: "They are looking for opportunities for business processes to be done differently so as to improve their effectiveness, efficiency and economy" (Chambers & Rand, 2010, pp. 15–16).

- Effectiveness means doing the right things—it measures the extent to which planned objectives and outcomes are met.
- Efficiency means doing things well—it measures the smoothness of the systems and processes that produce the outcomes and is particularly concerned with reducing wastage, effort, mistakes, and rework.
- Economy means doing things cheaply—it measures the cost of actual effort versus planned effort.

In more recent years, three additional elements have been added to the operational auditor's scope that are less easy to measure as positive phenomena but certainly amenable to evidence gathering (Chambers & Rand, 2010, p. 16):

- Equity—avoidance of discrimination and unfairness and recognition of the value of diversity
- Environment—behaving in an environmentally responsible way
- Ethics—the conduct of staff and management is ethical in both moral and legal senses

Thus far, the operational audit model looks sound and reasonable. However, the application of this model in detail is problematic when it comes to knowledge management.

What is an effectiveness measure for KM? Is it the extent to which an organization has carried out its KM objectives? Or is it the extent to which KM can be shown to contribute toward the overall business objectives of the organization? The former would seem easier to appraise and establish than the latter. But the former just says that KM has done what it said it would do, not that it has done anything useful.

While easier to audit, a focus on the objectives of KM isolated from the organization's overall business objectives runs the risk of viewing KM as a functional silo isolated from the goals of its parent organization. In principle an audit of a KM function could reach a finding of effectiveness, efficiency, economy, equity, environment, and ethics without any assurance that it has contributed in a meaningful way to an organization's overall performance.

The trouble is that as long as KM's contribution to an organization's performance is poorly understood (it is often based more on anecdote and intuition than reproducible evidence), a traditional operational audit approach does not have the levers required to give actionable insights.

And indeed, when we look at the Chambers and Rand suggested approach to knowledge auditing, their measures for KM effectiveness, efficiency, economy, equity, environment, or ethics seem insubstantial. Their proposed audit observations (and, presumably, recommendations) are guided by an understanding of generic good practices in KM without any foundational understanding of why they are supposed to be "good" and how they are connected to organizational performance. They lack a mechanism contextualized to the organization for assessing their relative importance in changing circumstances.

For example, the knowledge auditor is invited to find evidence that an "appropriate cultural tone" has been set for KM, without any guidance on what *appropriate* means. An auditor may find that "active steps have been taken to capture and record elements of tacit knowledge" (Chambers & Rand, 2010, pp. 551–552). However, without any more specific guidance on what tacit knowledge is at play and how it relates to the overall business capabilities, it is quite possible to have a positive audit finding with a negligible or distracting impact on organizational performance. Not all elements of tacit knowledge are equally beneficial to the effectiveness of the business, nor is it clear from the audit instruction how the auditor is to establish such a linkage, if at all.

It is assumed, rather safely, that management needs to take action to ensure that the organization recognizes the importance and value of knowledge and its effective management, *but there is no guidance on how specifically that should be measured, nor even what it might look like in practice.* It would be quite possible to have the appearance of positive behaviors without being able to verify the impact on the organization's effectiveness.

This is a problem intrinsic to the use of objectivist models of audit when we come to "soft" management systems, where not all elements of the system are measurable or observable to the same degree of ease. In that case, observation and measurement frequently retreat to the most easily observable, but the resulting incompleteness and partiality of the audit are never acknowledged.

In a landmark 1977 paper, organizational theorists John Meyer and Brian Rowan referred to this phenomenon as a *decoupling* of a measurement system from the actual effects of management practice. In decoupling, the ceremonies of measurement deflect us from addressing the more problematic areas of *performance*, by substituting for them the simpler measures of *activity*. This avoidance happens because of the uncomfortable questions about effectiveness and legitimacy surfaced by the difficulty of performance measurement. "Goals are made ambiguous or vacuous, and categorical ends are substituted for technical ends" (Meyer & Rowan, 1977, p. 357).

The marks of a decoupled measurement system are (a) the use of general categories (or *motherhood* statements) in place of granular defined outcomes, (b) the use of ambiguous language that is capable of supporting multiple interpretations, and (c) an insistence on measurement and documentation of observed behaviors, regardless of how well they reflect the underlying activity of the system.

This practice is deliberately maintained as a ritual that is unquestioned, in order to conceal the difficulties in measuring the effectiveness of complex human systems, and to conceal the lack of clarity about how effectiveness is actually to be achieved. It is a masterpiece of misdirection.

The result is to create an illusion of measurement while ensuring that the actual practice of interpretation and audit is amenable to informal negotiations and is dependent on constant recourse to the skills of "specialist" (but opaque) expertise on the part of the auditors. This is a problem endemic to knowledge auditing. We will return to the problematic phenomenon of decoupling between actual effects and observable behaviors when we discuss KM standards in chapter 9.

In the Chambers and Rand operational audit model, what started out as a set of apparently rigorous measures—which may well work for more easily observable organizational functions—ends up as a series of generic, hard-to-measure motherhood statements based on widely acknowledged generic practices. Without specific contextual guidance, the operational auditing approach may well achieve positive findings about the knowledge management environment without establishing any direct connection to the organization's performance. At the same time, decoupling provides an illusion of confidence and certainty.

Conversely, some of the generic desired indicators of "good KM" *may not* be present, yet the organization's performance may still be benefiting from KM practices. For example, an audit objective could be to establish that there is senior management commitment and buy-in for KM (Chambers & Rand, 2010, p. 550). In chapter 9 we will look at the possibility of a positive impact from "under the radar" KM, in which senior-level buy-in is not present. On the other hand, senior-level buy-in can be nominally present from an auditor's perspective without assuring any substantial business benefits or real sustainability in KM practices. Where appearances and realities diverge, audit findings do not support an actionable framing of change.

The same assumptions behind the operational audit model appear in a slightly different guise in the 2018 update to ISO 19011, *Guidelines for Auditing Management Systems* (ISO, 2018a). Similar to an operational audit, the ISO guidelines follow a process model of audit in which a systematic cycle of audit steps and activities gives an impression of specificity and control. In the case of ISO 19011, the *audit universe* is a management system or a bundle of management systems, defined as a "set of interrelated or interacting elements of an organization to establish policies and objectives, and processes . . . to achieve those objectives" (ISO, 2018a, p. 4). Examples of management systems are systems for risk management, quality management, innovation management, and knowledge management.

This represents a key differentiation from an operational audit because the primary focus of the audit is on the elements of the management system itself, as distinct from primary business functions, and the links to how that system supports organizational effectiveness now sit at one remove of analysis. It is true that all of the ISO management system standards stipulate the requirement that the management system should be evaluated on its ability to support organizational goals and effectiveness. While this technically checks the box for the validity of a management system, when you look at the specifics of some of the management system standards, the vulnerability to the decoupling effect becomes visible again.

The first clue is in the espoused objectivism within the ISO 19011 guidelines, which sits strangely counterpoised against a deference to individual auditor experience and judgment (one of the signals of decoupling). Let us look at some of the key definitions (ISO, 2018a, pp. 1–6):

- **Audit:** systematic, independent, and documented process for obtaining objective evidence and evaluating it objectively to determine the extent to which the *audit criteria* are fulfilled.

- **Audit criteria:** a set of requirements used as a reference against which objective evidence is compared [e.g., the requirements of the system against which conformity is to be assessed].

- **Objective evidence:** data supporting the existence or verity of something; Note 1 to entry: *Objective evidence can be obtained through observation, measurement, test, or by other means.*

- **Audit evidence:** records, statements of fact, or other information, which are relevant to the audit criteria and verifiable.

- **Evidence-based approach:** the rational method for reaching reliable and reproducible audit conclusions in a systematic audit process.

So far, so good. Then the facade starts to crack. We begin to see how fragile is the dependence on "objective" documented information when it comes to verifying the compliance of a soft management system against a normative standard. The standard repeatedly acknowledges the limitations of documented information and has repeated recourse to the notion of "professional judgment," wherever the immeasurability of action pushes the auditor back upon informal interpretation and negotiation.

> Only information that can be subject to some degree of verification should be accepted as audit evidence. Where the degree of verification is low the auditor should use their professional judgment to determine the degree of reliance that can be placed on it as evidence. (ISO, 2018a, p. 24)

> Auditors should apply professional judgment during the audit process and avoid concentrating on the specific requirements of each clause of the standard at the expense of achieving the

intended outcome of the management system. *Some ISO management system standard clauses do not readily lend themselves to audit in terms of comparison between a set of criteria and the content of a procedure or work instruction.* In these situations, auditors should use their professional judgment to determine whether the intent of the clause has been met. (ISO, 2018a, p. 36; italics mine)

Auditors should have relevant sector-specific knowledge and understanding of the management tools that organizations can use in order to make a judgment regarding the effectiveness of the processes used to determine context [implication: the extent to which the organization has adequately considered the needs of its business context in developing its management system is *not* amenable to "objective" fact-based verification]. (ISO, 2018a, p. 39)

The organization's treatment of its risk and opportunities, including the level of risk it wishes to accept and how it is controlled, will require the application of professional judgment by the auditor. (ISO, 2018a, p. 40)

This reliance on the "professional judgment" of the auditor, without specifying how that professional judgment is or should be constituted, is what Meyer and Rowan (1977) refer to as "the logic of confidence and good faith," which accompanies decoupling. "Participants not only commit themselves to supporting an organization's ceremonial facade but also commit themselves to making things work out backstage." Roles such as the auditor are ritualized and professionalized, and they are underpinned by an assumption of competence and good faith. In this way they are themselves made impervious to inspection. The auditor's professional judgment is a black box (Meyer & Rowan, 1977, pp. 357–359).

Now this is fine if the assumptions of competence and good faith are accurate. What happens if competence is absent or cannot be measured, and/or when good faith is compromised by conflicting motives and counterproductive measures of performance? When we consider the development of KM standards in chapter 9, we will see the concerns raised in relation to the commercial interests of cash-strapped standards bodies and commercial certification agencies, and whether these commercial interests have had an impact on the development and application of standards.

Even in a general compliance audit against a standard, respondents can tend to incline toward the generous in their self-reporting (cf. Niang, 2020, p. 17). When this happens with standards that contain ambiguity, such as the ISO 30401 standard, the verification process can become either adversarial, without adequate means of objective resolution, or superficial.

So much for the general auditing guidelines. The management system standards themselves demonstrate the same superficial clarity and objectivity combined with deep pockets of uncertainty. We will examine the ISO 30401 management system standard for knowledge management in greater depth in chapter 9. However, even a cursory glance at some of the requirements of that standard reveal the same concerns about the ability to make an authoritative, objective audit finding across all of the audit requirements. Now, the ISO 30401 standard does not fall prey to the same degree of generalized motherhood statement as the category descriptors in Chambers and Rand. But not all its requirements are equally and evenly susceptible to objective, verifiable observation and measurement. They can still fall prey to the decoupling effect. Take the following, for example (ISO, 2018b, p. 5):

> The organization shall determine:
>
> —the interested parties that are relevant to the knowledge management system;
> —the relevant requirements of these interested parties.
>
> These requirements shall be analysed, prioritizing the main areas and contexts relevant to the organization and the knowledge management system.

This is a very difficult requirement to audit consistently and thoroughly. The *visible, documented evidence* of compliance with this requirement (that an organization has conducted such an exercise and reached some conclusions) does not in itself provide evidence of effectiveness. It is quite possible to conduct such an exercise incompletely and badly, and it is quite possible that the "objective evidence" of the exercise would not reveal the effectiveness gap. To assess effectiveness would often require quite a deep familiarity with the organization and its context on the part of the auditor, to a degree that may not always be present. And it is not clear that conclusions would be incontestable or reproducible by different auditors.

> The operational audit's overt focus on observability and documented conformity against requirements can create an illusion of performance where it does not necessarily exist, and it can suffer from a decoupling between documented practice and how things actually happen in real life.
>
> The gaps between the "hard" requirement of the prescribed standard and the ability of an auditor to verify whether the purpose of the requirement is met, can result either in a retreat to "paper" compliance that does not match reality, or a dependency on the "black box" of auditor judgment without clear criteria as to how that judgment is to be reached and supported.

The operational audit model gives us some useful ideas of how a knowledge audit might function and contribute, but it contributes little in the way of specifics. It is all very well to lay claim to "systematic, disciplined processes" covering risk management, control, and governance, and we can see that these things would matter in a knowledge context. However, achieving that goal depends on having credible, measurable factors of observation and reporting, together with clear causal linkages to organizational performance, and this is where the operational audit model falls short.

The model must fall back on the unspecified "experience and judgment" of the auditor, and the aspiration toward reliable and reproducible results looks more rhetorical than real. The workings of knowledge in enterprises just do not look as tangible as other purely function-based or business process–oriented audits.

So while the tight definitions of *audit* give us some useful grounding in what an audit should look like and what it can achieve, they do not fully account for what we need in the context of knowledge audits.

As David Williams (2014, p. 89) notes, an effective model must be functional (meet our needs), make sense (be clear and easy to understand), and be accurate (be measurable and evidence based). Both financial and operational audits make sense in general, but within the domain of KM, they neither fully meet our needs nor provide actionable, measurable evidence for reliable and reproducible results. They look as if they have shortfalls in functionality and accuracy.

*   *   *

Summary

There are two sets of ambiguities to unravel in the term *knowledge audit*: the ambiguities in the term *knowledge* and the ambiguities in the term *audit*. We dealt with *audit* first.

We started with precedents in financial and operational audits and examined the differences between tight senses of audit (e.g., a prescriptive audit for compliance) and loose senses of audit (e.g., a descriptive review of evidence). Each has implications for the authoritativeness of the audit itself and expectations for legitimate follow-up actions.

The main points can be summarized as follows:

1. A descriptive audit involves

   (a) a critical examination of evidence and

   (b) a check as to the validity of assertions made about the business.

2. Prescriptive audits

   (a) are grounded in an organization's context and objectives,

   (b) combine functional perspectives with whole-of-organization perspectives, and

   (c) seek to generate actionable insights and recommendations for improvement and change.

3. The most interesting uses of knowledge in organizations are hard to observe and measure. Prescriptive audit models look reasonable on paper but are difficult to implement in practice.

4 What Kind of Audit Is a Knowledge Audit? A Naturalistic Approach

... in the absence of ... agreed standards there is no minimum level of acceptable information audit performance. Because of this, discussion tends to be theoretical and stakeholders and shareholders have no real idea of what information auditors actually do.

—P. Griffiths (2012, p. 40)

We have seen that financial and operational audits may drive popular perceptions of what an audit is, but neither of them fully meet the needs of knowledge managers. If the tight definitions of *audit* do not meet our needs, what about the looser definitions? Perhaps the best place to start is naturalistically, with what knowledge managers themselves understand by the term.

What Do Knowledge Management Practitioners Mean by the Term *Audit*?

The variability of meaning we see in general usage also manifests itself in how knowledge management (KM) practitioners understand the term *audit*. There is little consistency or clarity of understanding. This introduces a great deal of potential for confusion in an activity that is intended to be a foundation for KM strategy development and planning.

Here are some examples of how KM practitioners have asked and answered questions about KM-related audits on some of the major online forums between 2008 and 2012.

October 2008 (SIKM Leaders Forum)

Subject: Knowledge Culture Audit—How To?

Do you know of anyone who could conduct an assessment of department to summarize how well its culture supports knowledge sharing?

Summarized Replies

- Conduct an organizational network analysis (ONA) or social network analysis (SNA).
- Conduct a knowledge architecture audit involving interviews, ethnographic studies and survey.
- Collect hundreds of stories from employees and visualize them in a quantitative way.
- Conduct a KM Capability Assessment using an online survey tool against a reference framework and with peer benchmarking capability
- Determine human information processing preferences of employees using a short individual survey.

September 2009 (ActKM Discussion List)

Subject: Performing an Audit Using the Australian KM Standard

I am doing some work with an organization who wish to perform an audit of their KM programme in the future (which is mostly information management at the moment) using the Australian KM Standard.

I don't see there's any reason why they can't compare what they are doing with the advice in the KM Standard but as it's an advisory not a prescriptive standard so measuring "compliance" is not really what the standard is about. This may just be a language issue as "audit" can mean many things.

Summarized Replies:

- Use guiding questions: "What do I want to find out?"; "Why do I want to know?"; "How will I conduct the audit?"; "What is the business problem/opportunity I can help to solve using the audit?"; "How will I use the information from the audit to make that happen?"
- Use guiding questions: "What are the organization's knowledge needs?"; "What knowledge assets does it have and where are they?"; "What gaps exist in its knowledge?"; "How does knowledge flow around the organization?"; "What blockages are there to that flow?"
- My first question is "Why?"—"What is the problem they are trying to solve?"
- We used the framework of People, Technology, Process, Content used in the Standard and enquired from a sample population via email and focus groups how knowledge use

fell into those areas—participants said they learnt a lot from the process but not sure if the resulting tables had direct application.

- We use the KM Standard to guide our KM activities and run a regular survey using the four parts of the framework and a Knowledge Continuum ranging from basic to fully integrated.

- Managers want to be able to say they are complying with a national standard to reduce perceived risk, and they want to review their progress over time.

November 2012 (KM4Dev Listserv)

Subject: Your Advice on Stocktaking/Knowledge Audit

We are doing a stocktaking of how far we got in implementing our 2007 KM strategy for better KM/KS /L as part of our business processes, people and technology. This should be an input to our efforts to define a way forward and implementation plan for the next three years. . . . We seek your advice/practical tips in particular in how to undertake a stocktaking (knowledge audit).

Summarized Replies

- Conduct a survey and then focus group discussions, both face-to-face and through Skype. Once the survey results are analyzed and you have some key messages coming out of it, you can also follow-up with a short online discussion to validate those main findings.

- Surveys throw up a set of core issues, which then inform the focus groups/ workshops and interviews. We tend then to interview around events and critical decisions to see what knowledge and information is important in the organization.

- I use a questionnaire to collect data on existing learning practices (and sources), knowledge generation (products), and knowledge sharing (question flows); I map the data and analyze the content to determine the learning and knowledge types.

- Examine the way people actually work as well as information artefacts and communication channels; I prefer the interview method to generate rich meaning and discovery but I also use surveys where applicable. But even in the survey, I allow for qualitative discovery and analysis.

- We ask people to give personal illustrations (stories) as examples to illustrate their replies to survey questions.

- In knowledge audits I include the multiple knowledges: biophysical, social, ethical, aesthetic and sympathetic. I don't use those technical words of course. I ask everyone involved to share, first their ideals, then their experiences, then their ideas for change then their ideas for action. In whatever action they choose we check against their ideals as we go. That way the audit is mutual, which allows for collective learning and captures change.

December 2012 (ActKM Discussion List)

Subject: Knowledge Audit Questions

It has been suggested to me that knowledge audits have been reduced to templates (i.e., a pre-existing set of questions). If true, that strikes me on the one hand as an indictment of knowledge audits and on the other hand as a sign that knowledge audits have been routinized. . . . I'm also interested in your favourite knowledge audit questions.

Summarized Replies

- There's a difference between knowledge audits (which use workshops to map knowledge assets and knowledge flows) and KM audits (which use surveys and interviews to uncover KM practices, processes, enablers, etc.).
- I think the knowledge audit would be most helpful in identifying what knowledge they need now and in the future, taking stock of what they currently have, and then identifying and addressing the gaps.
- I don't know that I've ever heard of a Knowledge Audit, in the sense of someone coming in and "measuring" some level of Knowledge Achievement, as (even to this date) there is no one globally accepted definition for what Knowledge even represents. However, I do know that there are Knowledge Assessments that are very much like audits that take things like a Knowledge Capability Inventory, and measure its components against things like a Knowledge Strategy.
- I've always thought a "knowledge audit" mainly pertained to identifying specific areas of explicit knowledge in the form of content (primarily) although it also could identify knowledge at risk or possessors of rare and valuable knowledge in the organization.
- Our knowledge assessment / audit poses these questions: "How do we find information?"; "How do we find our experts?"; "How do we retain critical knowledge?"; "How do we learn and share across the organization to create new knowledge?"; "How do we learn and share publicly to create new knowledge?"
- An effective knowledge audit or assessment must recognize both living knowledge in people's heads, the tools for assessing this, and mechanisms for accessing and sharing it when and where it is needed for organizational needs, as well as explicit forms of knowledge.
- Knowledge management audits without a preceding knowledge assets audit tend to be very general and based on abstract notions of "best practice"—the knowledge assets audit grounds KM practices in real organizational knowledge requirements, and helps to prioritize and focus on practices that count.
- It occurs to me that a "knowledge at risk" assessment qualifies as a knowledge audit too.

These discussions express a variety of understandings of KM-related audits. Table 4.1 shows clearly that there are three different drivers of variation in how KM-related audits are understood. They can vary widely in terms of *scope* (what the audit is examining), *operating model* (the audit approach), and *methods* used (how the audit is conducted).

Table 4.1
Variant understandings of KM-related audits among KM practitioners

Audit scope	Operating model	Methods utilized
Knowledge behaviors	Organizational climate assessment (presupposes presence of positive and negative factors and ability to identify them)	Network maps (knowledge flows)
KM practices	Discovery review (combines internal opinion-seeking with external insight)	Interviews, ethnographic study, survey
Knowledge behaviors	Discovery review (collective self-representation)	Story collection, content analysis, coding and analytics
KM capabilities and practices	Capability, maturity, and benchmarking assessment	Survey following reference framework (KM capabilities and maturity), peer benchmarking
Individual information-processing preferences	Discovery review (involves aligning individual preferences)	Survey
KM program	Standards-based self-assessment	Assessment against business problems/opportunities Surveys and focus groups to facilitate a learning conversation around the standards framework
Knowledge stocks	Inventory of knowledge stocks, gaps, flows	Knowledge-mapping workshops
KM program	Standards-based self-assessment and maturity assessment	Surveys
KM program	Standards-based self-assessment and progress stocktake	KM standards
KM program	Progress stocktake (implies reference to previous goals)	Survey, focus groups, interviews, discussion to validate findings
KM program	Discovery review (multiple factors of analysis)	Survey, mapping of survey data on knowledge flows and content analysis of knowledge types
KM program	Discovery review (multiple factors of analysis)	Observation, mapping of information assets and communication channels
KM program	Discovery review (multiple factors of analysis)	Story collection and surveys
KM program	Participative goal setting, matching actions to ideals	Facilitated sharing sessions
Knowledge stocks	Inventory of knowledge stocks, gaps, flows	Knowledge-mapping workshops

(*continued*)

Table 4.1
(continued)

Audit scope	Operating model	Methods utilized
KM program	Discovery review	Survey and interviews
Knowledge stocks	Discovery review and stock-take of knowledge stocks and knowledge gaps	Knowledge-mapping workshops
KM program	Capability, maturity, and content inventory	Survey and interviews, content inventory
Knowledge stocks	Inventory of knowledge stocks, knowledge risks, owners	Knowledge-mapping workshops
KM practices	Discovery review	Survey and interviews
Knowledge stocks and KM practices	Inventory of knowledge stocks, tools, processes	Assessment against business problems/opportunities
Knowledge stocks	Discovery review	Knowledge-mapping workshops
Knowledge stocks	Risk assessment	Knowledge-mapping workshops

Figure 4.1 summarizes the findings from the KM practitioner discussions in visual form. I believe it provides a useful framework for analyzing and planning knowledge audits, including

- audit models (what we mean by *audit*, the type of audit we need to conduct),
- audit phenomena (what we are auditing), and
- audit methods (how we audit).

The framework makes it clear that there are interdependencies between the three dimensions. How we audit (methods) should flow from what we are auditing (scope) and the audit model we are using. This model simply represents what we have picked up from our examination of practitioner discussions. We will need to do some further tuning on this framework before we can use it in planning because it omits important insights from the research literature and from other forms of knowledge-related audits. However, the three dimensions of the model-phenomena-method (MPM) framework give us a good start.

We can see that from the KM practitioners' point of view, there are at least four distinct operating models for a knowledge-related audit. We will consider the target phenomena of an audit in chapter 5. We will see how some of the major methods in knowledge auditing have emerged from the history of communications, information, and knowledge audits. For the rest of this chapter, we will look at fleshing out the models of audit.

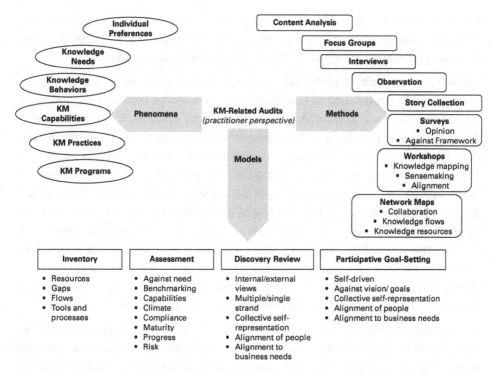

Figure 4.1

The model-phenomena-method framework for scoping a knowledge audit.

Inventory audit In this kind of audit, we are concerned mainly with creating an inventory of stocks, gaps, flows, tools, and processes related to the knowledge that an organization uses and may need. There is very little value judgment involved in this type of audit, and what we should do with the results of the audit is left open. The audit itself is primarily descriptive, although it would commonly be followed by an analysis and prescription phase; that is, it will be combined with one of the other audit models. This meaning of the term *audit* is also in common usage. *Oxford Dictionaries* gives the following example: "A complete audit of flora and fauna at the site." Inventory audits can be used in conjunction with any of the other audit types below.

Assessment audit There are a number of different types of assessment audit, but they all involve evaluation and prescription of some kind. The reference model for the evaluation can vary in strictness, from standards, to guidelines, to benchmarking factors, to a "best practice" framework, to expert external assessment, to measurement of needs versus supply, or to internal authoritative opinions gathered through instruments such as surveys and methods such as interviews. An assessment audit is highly prescriptive, often appealing to an external authority. In common usage, *Oxford Dictionaries* gives this example: "the situation will then be reviewed after a safety audit."

Discovery review audit   The discovery audit is much more open-ended. It seeks to gather evidence of any combination of knowledge stocks, knowledge behaviors and use, issues around knowledge use, knowledge gaps, and knowledge priorities. It often follows multiple lines of inquiry, examining the organization's environment from multiple perspectives. It typically has an analysis and sensemaking phase that makes some reference to the organization's espoused strategy and needs. The main difference between the assessment audit and the discovery audit is that the assessment audit tends to take a deductive "authority-based" approach, evaluating an organization against an external reference model. By contrast the discovery audit tends to take an inductive approach, gathering an evidence base first and then drawing conclusions from the findings against an internally generated set of priorities. This type of audit is also implied in common usage. *Oxford Dictionaries* has this example: "Start by completing an audit of the existing lighting systems, assessing both the condition and the performance of all components in the system."

Participative goal-setting audit   This is probably the most open form of audit we encountered in the practitioner discussions. It is an approach that has been emerging for some decades and is influenced by, among others, Weick's (1969) work on organizational behavior and the work of David Bohm (1996) on dialogue. In this form of audit, there is a facilitated process and a loose framework to guide an organization or a group through self-reflection, mutual understanding, and alignment. To be effective, this kind of audit also needs to close with a prescriptive phase leading to decisions on action, but the point is that the goal setting, the audit design and conduct, and the follow-through are entirely self-driven. This type of audit is not obviously represented in common usage for the term *audit* but is implicit in some representations of audit. As we will see, the participatory, self-driven approach has particular interest for KM because of the diffuse and intangible ways in which knowledge work is conducted in organizations and groups. It would often make sense to deploy an audit approach that is driven by the knowledge agents themselves, especially where it is important that the agents are empowered to direct their own change.

What Does the Research Literature Tell Us about Models of Audit?

Thus far we have derived our models of audit from a review of practitioner discussions. What does the research literature tell us?

While the literature on knowledge audits is fairly new (dating mainly from the 1990s), we saw in chapter 2 that knowledge audits have strong family resemblances to their predecessors, information audits and communication audits, which together go back to the 1950s. Looking at the collective literature of communication, information, and knowledge audits provides us with a larger sample within which to discern different models of information and knowledge-related audits at work.

In fact, a review of the literature on communication, information, and knowledge audits from the 1950s onward finds all four types of audits represented, with two significant additions that are not obvious in the KM practitioner discussions we looked at in the framework above. These additions are *value audits* and *learning audits*. They are not so obvious in the knowledge manager discussions we reviewed because they have been exploited more extensively in communication audits and information audits. However, both have strong validity in the KM context.

Value audits originated largely in the information audit literature, though they have earlier roots in records management and have strong associations with the resource-based view of the firm, the knowledge-based view of the firm, and the intellectual capital movement. We will explore these associations in greater depth in chapters 12–14.

Value audits focus on assessing the value or the value creation potential of the information or knowledge resources, processes, and systems being examined. In the information audit tradition, these value audits originally focused on cost-benefit analysis for information management services, but in some cases they also looked at how to create new value from information or knowledge resources, so they have an important connection to the KM literature on intellectual capital and the literature on knowledge capitalization. Knowledge capitalization, also known in a public policy context as knowledge mobilization, refers to the creation of productive value from knowledge and/or knowledge management processes (Matta et al., 2002; Renaud et al., 2004; Levin, 2008).

Learning audits originated in the analysis of medical records and data to find statistically based insights on more or less effective courses of treatment. While they have their roots in nineteenth-century medical research, they are today often referred to as clinical audits or medical records audits (Lembcke, 1956, p. 646; Fraser, 1982; Baker, 1999, p. 2) This form of audit seeks to uncover insights from records of past practices in order to provide learning for improved practices in the future. In the late 1990s, this form of audit began to be taken up in the communication audit literature, largely because of the pressure within the communication audit discipline to strengthen its orientation toward evidence-based prescriptions for improvement and change (Hargie & Tourish, 2000, p. 181).

While they belong to the family of prescriptive audits, because of their focus on learning from records of past activity, learning audits are quite distinct from the more broad-based and open-ended *discovery review* audit, and from the *assessment audit* (whether it is assessment against an external standard or against benchmarking data from other organizations). However, to the extent that clinical audits can be used to establish professional standards of care, they can also be closely connected to assessment audits.

Figure 4.2 summarizes the types of audits that emerge from a combined analysis of KM practitioner discussions and the research literature. The *inventory audit* is the only one that is purely descriptive, although it is often used as a foundational step for the other audit types. All the other audit types have some form of prescriptive power of varying authority, depending on their structure, on their warrant, and on whether they are purely internally oriented and driven or take reference from some external data or standards.

Each audit type has dependencies. The *discovery review audit* is the most open, but for its findings to be effective, it depends on clear, agreed-upon audit scope, methodology,

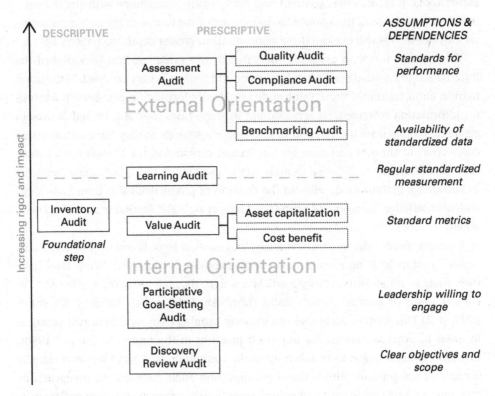

Figure 4.2
A typology of audits.

and objectives. The *participative goal-setting audit* depends on a readiness by the organization's senior leadership team to take ownership for the learning and decision-making process arising from the audit. Both types of audits tend to have an internal orientation: they depend largely on goals set from within and on data and evidence gathered from within.

As we move up the vertical axis, the level of perceived rigor and impact rises. *Value audits* depend on agreed or standardized ways of measuring value or projecting value, whether they are accounting driven (e.g., a cost-benefit analysis of knowledge, of knowledge services, or of KM processes) or strategy driven (an assessment of the extent to which knowledge or KM processes deliver strategic value to the organization). With a focus on value and valuation, it is often expected that these standards for measuring and assessing value should be capable of being shared with other organizations. We will see in chapters 12–14 that articulating the value of knowledge is an unresolved challenge in KM for a number of reasons.

Learning audits depend on standardized ways of collecting data on regular actions and outcomes; otherwise, the data will not be amenable to aggregated analysis and sensemaking. Learning audits can be purely internal, or if data are collected in standardized ways across multiple organizations, they can also be combined and applied over a wider landscape of activity. This is an underexploited area of knowledge auditing, largely because of the lack of standard ways of describing knowledge, collecting knowledge audit data, and associating KM practices with organizational outcomes. Most "learning audit" work in KM is more focused on lesson learning from individual programs than on the large-scale aggregated data analysis that would be typical of a clinical records audit.

Thus far, the scope of data gathering relies on a mostly internal orientation. As we move up the "increasing rigor" axis, we start to compare internal performance against external reference points.

Assessment audits rely on generic instruments and/or data, shared across organizations. They depend on the availability of interorganizational data collected in standardized ways (for benchmarking audits) or on the availability of widely accepted standards for performance (for compliance or quality audits).

Already, we can see that knowing the dependencies will be able to help us identify

- the audit type(s) most appropriate to our situation,
- the level of authority we can claim for the audit results and the reasonable expectations that can be made of it, and
- what we need for a proper conduct of the audit.

Note that this typology by no means exhausts the types of audits that exist out there in the world. For example, we do not include here the verification audit that we know from accounting practice (although the concept of verification is also used in assessment audits). The typology presented here is only for those audit types that we see evidence for in knowledge-, information-, and communication-related practices in organizations.

A Typology Approach or Integrative Metaconstruct Approach?

When faced with a bewildering array of divergent understandings and definitions, one can

(a) take an integrative approach and build a metaconstruct to attempt integration of the commonalities (e.g., Handzic & Zhou, 2005; Griffiths & Evans, 2010) or

(b) find a categorization or a typology that the reader can navigate and use.

The *integrative metaconstruct approach* assumes that contradictions and divergences can be resolved into a common model. This may not be feasible where radically different worldviews are at play in generating the differences. And while this approach may provide a useful methodology for pattern detection, when we force fit divergences into a common framework, we run the risk of ironing out discrepancies that represent valid outliers. The average dominates the picture, and significant outliers can be ignored. In the real world, averages are often only statistical realities, not actual realities.

Here is an example. Todd Rose (2016) begins his book *The End of Average* with a story from the 1940s about the design of cockpits for fighter pilots in the US. Pilots were crashing their planes with unusual frequency, and pilot error did not seem to be a satisfactory explanation. They eventually discovered that the cockpit designs were based on a study of the average physical dimensions of pilots as measured in 1926. Dimensions had evidently changed and so had the gender balance. So they commissioned a new study, intending to find a new, updated average. To their surprise they found that there was no such thing in the real world as an "average-sized pilot." Out of over four thousand pilots, and looking at any combination of just three measurement dimensions out of the ten they measured, they found that just 3.5 percent would be average-sized on all three dimensions (Rose, 2016, pp. 1–5).

As an example of the problems that the metaconstruct "averaging-out" approach can cause in KM, in 2015 John and JoAnn Girard used a metaconstruct approach for the task of defining *knowledge management*. It is based on a word frequency count from more than one hundred definitions of KM. Here are the two variants that emerged (Girard & Girard, 2015, p. 14):

- Knowledge management is the process of creating, sharing, using, and managing the knowledge and information of an organization.

- Knowledge management is the management process of creating, sharing, and using organizational information and knowledge.

These definitions, based on frequency of word use, restrict the scope of knowledge management to the organizational context alone, excluding interorganizational, societal/community, and personal/team-level KM. Unsurprisingly, there will be some concern from professionals working in the fields of KM and public policy and KM for development, as well as from people interested in interfirm knowledge transfer.

This kind of "common denominator" approach is what the metaconstruct approach to definitions of KM can end up with. Pluralities win; significant outliers are concealed. "By only looking for common themes, researchers can only discover common answers" (Dumay, 2010, p. 58).

Integrative averaging-out approaches are useful for some things and not for others. Their virtue is in presenting a landscape view and in identifying common features of the landscape. Their vice is that they can deprecate and often conceal significant variations in the landscape.

Peter Heisig (2009) used an integrative metaconstruct model to develop a harmonized KM enablers framework. It is the nature of enabler frameworks to need to represent an ecosystem, and in that respect, comprehensiveness is a virtue. However, to apply the insights from this to a specific case, we need a way of characterizing types of situations and not averaged-out commonalities. David Griffiths and Peter Evans (2010) showed that it was possible to combine an integrative analysis with the identification of significant outliers. Again, this is useful for a comprehensive landscape or ecosystem view, but it is not likely, on its own, to provide rich descriptions of particular types of situation.

In relation to knowledge auditing, there have been brave attempts at the formation of an integrated conspectus using a metaconstruct approach (e.g., Handzic et al., 2008; Levantakis et al., 2008; Ganasan & Dominic, 2011). However, these attempts tend to fall between two hard places: they either appear too complex to apply with versatility or they retreat to a generic series of audit cycle steps, evading the hard questions on audit type, choice of phenomena, or methods to use.

My own belief is that there are so many divergent origins, influences, and motivations behind the use of audits in the KM space that to attempt the metaconstruct approach is both futile and misleading.

A *typology approach* differs from the metaconstruct approach by starting bottom-up, clustering and dividing known entities by relative similarity to each other, and relative difference between clusters. The features or characteristics of each cluster are abstracted into a descriptive label for the "type."

That is the inductive phase. Then there is a deductive phase. Each type comes with a set of attributes that can be used to sort other entities in the world into that type. Placing attributes of types along structured dimensions, as we did in figure 4.2 (such as levels of formality, descriptive vs. prescriptive, degree of effort involved, internal to the organization vs. external to the organization, top-down vs. bottom-up), allows us to imagine viable combinations of attributes that we may not have encountered yet (Bailey, 1994; Lambe, 2007, pp. 25–26; Eppler, 2008, pp. 60–65).

A good typology is both pragmatic (it helps to explain and organize things in useful ways that match our understanding of the world) and predictive (it is hospitable to new entities that we may not have encountered yet). Unlike the metaconstruct approach, it is not limited by the data we have available. More to our purpose, by giving us multiple dimensions to describe the types, it helps us to represent the distinctive features of any given phenomenon rather than flattening them out in an averaging exercise. It provides us with a series of memorable *prototypes* against which to compare real-world phenomena (Eppler, 2008, p. 61).

This "nonflattening" feature is very important in knowledge management because KM is so context sensitive. The scoping of a knowledge audit is itself a situated exercise, driven by specific circumstances. In this case there is little point in using an averaged-out model of audit.

My own view in this book is that a typology of knowledge audits is the most useful approach to take. Let us look at how this works in practice.

The Knowledge Audit Typology in Practice

In 2017 I tested the typology of the audits represented in figure 4.2 against a global survey of 150 KM practitioners (Lambe, 2017). The survey asked respondents to indicate whether they had experience with knowledge audits and how much. In this way we were able to differentiate between the perceptions of KM practitioners who were inexperienced in knowledge audits and those who had some experience of conducting them. Experienced practitioners comprised 69 percent of the respondents.

Respondents were able to select any number of definitions evidenced in the literature of knowledge audits, framed largely by the analysis above. We also compared the overall responses against what the experienced practitioners reported.

The descriptions I gave to participants for the types of knowledge audit are given below, labeled according to their types:

- An inventory of knowledge stocks and flows in an organization (inventory audit)
- A discovery exercise using an external facilitator looking for ways to improve the way that knowledge is managed in an organization (discovery review audit)
- An internal review of the way that knowledge is managed in the organization, supported by management, with the goal of developing a KM plan or strategy (participative goal-setting audit)
- A cost-benefit analysis of the way that knowledge and information are exploited in an organization (value audit: cost-benefit)
- An analysis of the way that knowledge creates value for the organization (value audit: asset capitalization)
- An assessment to measure compliance with an external knowledge management standard (assessment audit: compliance)
- A review of records and/or data in a specific practice domain with the goal of identifying lessons and improvements in that domain (learning audit)
- An assessment to review the quality of KM practices against an external standard or framework (assessment audit: quality)
- A way to benchmark the way an organization manages knowledge against other organizations (assessment audit: benchmarking)

All of the knowledge audit types were recognized, but in different frequencies. Figure 4.3 shows the relative recognition and use of audit types among survey respondents. Inventory audits and participative goal-setting audits were by far the most commonly recognized types of knowledge audits, at 74 percent and 66 percent, respectively, followed by value audits: asset capitalization at 49 percent.

Compliance audits and value audits: cost-benefit were the least commonly recognized, at 26 percent and 23 percent, respectively. Externally driven audits sat in the middle, in the 30–40 percent range. It would seem that knowledge audits at the time of the study were driven primarily by internal parties and criteria. This may shift as the ISO 30401 standard becomes more widely accepted, but this has not happened yet.

Undoubtedly, this spread is due to a lack of consistency in audit methodology and in ways of describing knowledge in use in organizations. We can imagine, for example, that greater consistency across organizations in inventorying knowledge stocks and flows, and in value-creation practices, should lead to greater adoption of benchmarking audits and learning audits.

Experienced knowledge auditors seemed even more skeptical about compliance audits than the sample as a whole (10 percent), but they were more intensive users of

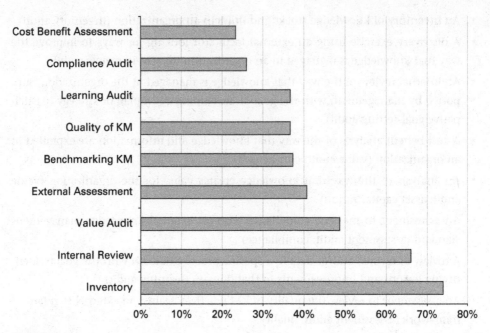

Figure 4.3
Frequency of recognition of knowledge audit types in practice.
Source: Lambe, 2017.

the inventory audit and the participative goal-setting audit (79 percent and 71 percent, respectively).

Knowledge Audits Should Be Compound Activities

The second insight from this survey was that knowledge audits very rarely use just one model of audit. The most common approach is to combine models of audit, usually an inventory audit together with a participative goal-setting audit or a value audit: asset capitalization.

It is clear that knowledge audits are seen as compound activities, blending a number of audit types and multiple data-gathering methods into the same overall program of investigation and analysis. The respondents with some experience of knowledge audits usually saw about three audit types being combined in an audit exercise.

There are good reasons why multiple audit models are necessary. A great deal of knowledge use in organizations happens inside people's heads and in the interactions between people. It is not easily observed. The broader field of organization studies within which knowledge management sits is a complex one, and organizations present "complex, variable-rich phenomena that can be studied from multiple perspectives" (Daft & Lewin 1990, p. 2).

This means that audit instruments interested in what goes on within an organization's life, as knowledge audits are, must apply techniques that capture, and are capable of modeling, the equivocations, ambiguities, and gaps in understanding that we find in organizational knowledge use (Daft & Lewin 1990, pp. 5–6). This is why Charles Connaghan's approach to a communication audit, based on a single audit model (discovery review) and a single opinion-gathering methodology (survey+interview), fell short and why its many modern knowledge audit successors also fall short.

The need for a multidimensional, multi-instrument approach has been recognized from the birth of the study of modern organizational life. In the famous "Hawthorne Studies" begun in 1927 at the Chicago plant of the Western Electric Company and led by the Harvard Graduate School of Business Administration, surveys and interviews were used to gather employee reactions and opinions, alongside observations and other objective data-gathering methods, to assess the effects of a number of experimental variations in working conditions (Mayo, 1933; Roethlisberger & Dickson, 1943).

The University of Minnesota Industrial Relations Center conducted a series of long-term "Triple-Audit" studies on factors affecting industrial relations throughout the 1940s, analyzing economic indicators of employing companies, benchmarking of industrial relations and employment/union practices, and employee opinions and reactions. Again, opinion gathering was an adjunct to the audit technique, not a primary vehicle (Yoder et al., 1951). The espoused goal, as with communication auditing, was to move from the sphere of managing on the basis of "untried hunches" to more evidence-based industrial relations practices (Yoder, 1952).

In the 1970s the most sophisticated approach to communication audits yet developed, the International Communication Association (ICA) communication audit, also used a multimodel, multi-instrument approach (Goldhaber, 1976, pp. 9–11).

In the opaque world of organizational knowledge, the challenge for auditors is *a problem of triangulation*. We seek to form a series of independent perspectives on a multidimensional phenomenon that cannot be wholly directly observed, in order to reach more reliable conclusions about it. "A decision based on the combination of critically appraised evidence from multiple sources yields better outcomes than a decision based on a single source of evidence" (Barends & Rousseau, 2018, p. 17).

On the other hand, the more audit models and techniques that we deploy, the more complex the audit becomes to administer and analyze. As we will see a little later, too much complexity led to the ultimate downfall of the ICA communication audit. Less experienced KM practitioners tend either to combine more models of audit (rendering it more complex) or to apply a single audit type conducted alone (rendering it too simplistic). More experienced knowledge auditors tend to use two to three models and no more, typically creating inventories, evaluating needs, and assessing contribution and value (Lambe, 2017).

Our task then is to find the right balance between models and instruments of audit that are

(a) sufficiently compound and complex to isolate diverse features of knowledge use and knowledge work in organizations;

(b) sufficiently independent of each other that data gathered from one instrument can reliably illuminate data gathered from another; but

(c) not so complex that the burden of administration and analysis is too heavy for achieving productive, cost-effective outcomes and ongoing monitoring and control.

Figure 4.4 numbers the most common combinations of knowledge audit types: inventory audits are most often combined with participative goal-setting audits, then with value audits (asset capitalization), and then with discovery review audits. Perhaps in such a confused domain, the openness of discovery review audits is intimidating.

Which Audit Types Should We Adopt?

This brings us to our first main decision in scoping a knowledge audit. Which combination of audit types should we adopt? Aside from audit types, there are a number of other scoping decisions we have not covered; for example, we have not yet looked at considerations governing

- the *phenomena* we need to audit,
- the *drivers* underpinning our desire to conduct an audit in the first place,
- how we set *goals* for our audit,
- how we can reliably and consistently *characterize knowledge* and knowledge use, or
- how we judiciously select *methods* for evidence collection, depending on what we want to achieve.

However, we already have some important guiding considerations:

1. A comprehensive inventory audit is very likely to form a useful foundational step unless we have very limited resources and time.

2. We have a choice to weigh between an internally driven participative goal-setting audit or a much more open discovery review audit. This choice will be influenced

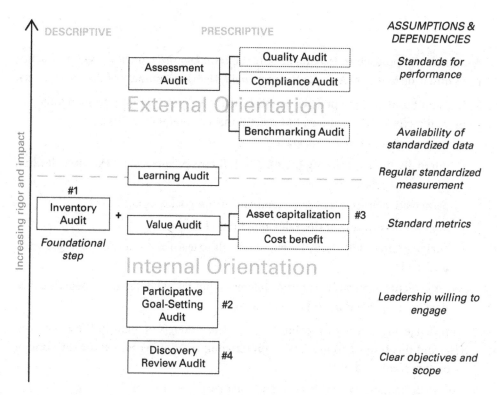

Figure 4.4
The four most common types of knowledge audit.

in part by the degree of internal support at senior and middle management levels to engage in a participative process and in part by whether we have the internal competencies in facilitating such a process.

3. We know there will be some pressure to characterize the productive value of knowledge and of knowledge management in the organization but that this is not likely to be helpful if it is focused simply on cost-benefit analysis. We will want to assess what value is created from our knowledge.

4. We know that the various forms of assessment audit will be more challenging to conduct because of their dependence on robust external standards and data sets.

5. We know that a learning audit in the strict sense will also be challenging unless we are focused on standardized, repeatable processes for which we have large amounts of transactional and outcome data.

*   *   *

Summary

A naturalistic approach to looking at how the term *knowledge audit* is used in practice picks up a wide range of senses for the term *audit*. Here is a summary of the main points:

1. In common speech and practice, audits can take a variety of forms, some tighter and more prescriptive than others. KM practitioners can refer to audits as
   - inventory-gathering or stocktakes;
   - internally driven, learning-oriented self-discovery and review exercises, leading to recommendations;
   - participative processes of self-examination and goal setting;
   - assessments of value or the value potential of assets;
   - analyses (often statistically based) of records to learn and improve on target activities; and
   - assessments against an external reference model, whether it be benchmarked data or an agreed standard of performance.

2. Knowledge audits usually combine two or three models of audit in the same exercise, and this is most commonly a combination of an inventory audit with one or two other forms of audit.

3. Knowledge-auditing practitioners must balance
   (a) having sufficient complexity in the audit approach to enable a useful triangulation of knowledge use in an organization while
   (b) not being so complex that the audit becomes a logistical burden out of proportion to its value.

5 What Are We Auditing?

All the food was simple. And I don't mean easy, or dumb. I mean that for the first time, I saw how three or four ingredients, as long as they are of the highest and freshest quality, can be combined in a straightforward way to make a truly excellent and occasionally wondrous product.
—Bourdain (2007, p. 165)

In the previous chapter, we saw that knowledge management (KM) practitioners may have many different things in mind when they discuss knowledge-related audits. When they think about the scope of a knowledge audit, they may be thinking about auditing

- KM programs,
- KM practices,
- KM capabilities,
- knowledge behaviors,
- knowledge stocks, or
- individual preferences for working with knowledge.

Moreover, what exactly somebody intends by the target of the audit is often not made explicit when the term *knowledge audit* is used, multiplying the confusion and ambiguities with which the discourse about knowledge audits is fraught. Yet more confusion arises from the tendency to slip between the term *knowledge audit* (which suggests a focus on knowledge) and *knowledge management audit* (which suggests a focus on processes), as if these were interchangeable (e.g., Lauer & Tanniru, 2001; cf. Lee et al., 2021, p. 72).

The goal of this chapter is to establish some clarity on how the scope of the knowledge audit is defined and on how to be clear about whether our focus is on knowledge or on knowledge processes. In many respects the scoping of an audit is similar to the chef's marshaling of ingredients for a meal. The quality of an audit, like the quality of a meal, depends on the ways in which the ingredients complement and enhance (and do not compete with) each other (cf. Collison et al., 2019).

The Target Phenomena for Knowledge Audits

The model-phenomena-method (MPM) framework that I presented in figure 4.1 suggests a number of target phenomena for a knowledge audit as cited by KM practitioners. They included

- KM programs,
- KM practices,
- KM capabilities,
- knowledge behaviors,
- knowledge stocks, and
- individual preferences.

This is obviously a limited list, based on just a few discussions. It also has some apparent overlaps (e.g., knowledge behaviors and individual preferences, as well as KM practices and KM programs). We need to systematize this and check for comprehensiveness.

Handzic et al. (2008) provided a useful framework for analyzing the target phenomena of KM audits, compiled through a review of the KM literature. They identified six potential areas of interest for an audit, each derived from particular ways of approaching KM implementations:

- Knowledge *stocks* (including the intellectual capital approach as well as other knowledge asset-oriented approaches)
- Knowledge *processes* (including the Nonaka SECI model)
- Social and technological *enablers* of KM
- The extent to which KM addresses *contingencies* arising from the context and environment
- An *evolutionary* model for KM which has close relationships with KM maturity models
- The extent to which KM activities result in positive *outcomes* for the organization

There are some obvious parallels with the target phenomena of information audits cataloged by Peter Griffiths (2010), which we will look at in chapter 8. Handzic et al. (2008) proposed integrating these perspectives into a single holistic framework for conducting KM audits. However, this implies that there is "one right way" to conduct knowledge audits, and we have seen so far that there are many possible ways to approach a knowledge audit, depending on our goals and resources.

For our purposes we will simply adapt their proposed list and use it as a framework for thinking about the scoping of knowledge audits. To their list we add one further area that they omitted, the audit of knowledge flows and knowledge networks, one of the two main foci of knowledge-mapping activities (Alavi & Leidner, 2001; Cross & Parker, 2004; Dattero et al., 2007). This is also a key point of similarity with early communication audits (Davis, 1953). Figure 5.1 summarizes the framework.

The right-hand side of the framework has more in common with inventory, discovery review, and participative goal-setting audits. Here, the audit is typically aimed at understanding the strengths and weaknesses of an organization in relation to its needs. As we move down toward the bottom of the framework, we see a greater association with value audits.

The left-hand side of the framework suggests that it is useful to assess the way in which KM is being conducted in the organization. This approach has more in common with various forms of assessment audit.

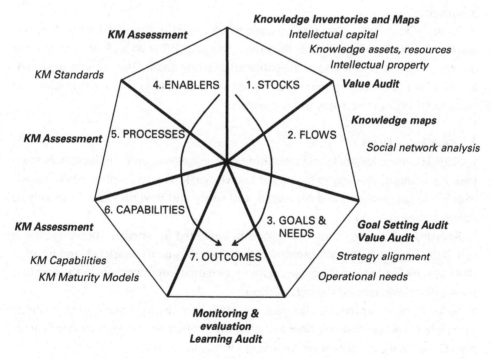

Figure 5.1

A framework for scoping the target phenomena of knowledge audits. Adapted from Handzic et al., 2008.

Both sides of the framework converge on the ultimate goal of contributing to positive outcomes for the organization. A focus on tracking outcomes, together with some standard and consistent ways of describing KM enablers, processes, and capabilities, may also imply an opportunity for a learning audit.

1. Knowledge Stocks

There are many ways of looking at knowledge stocks, whether

- by knowledge type (from more tacit to more explicit),
- from the perspective of intellectual capital (capabilities of the organization that need to be valued and leveraged), or
- even from the perspective of intellectual property (an explicitly valued and protected form of asset).

Chapters 15–20 will examine in detail the different ways of characterizing knowledge stocks and will attempt to create some clarity around how they can be described and inventoried.

Audits of knowledge stocks are frequently referenced in the practitioner discourse and have particular affinities with the inventory audit (What do we have and where is it?), the discovery review and participative goal-setting audits (How can we make better use of our knowledge resources?), and the value audit (How are we exploiting and creating value from our assets and resources?).

2. Knowledge Flows

Looking at knowledge stocks and examining knowledge flows are complementary activities. For example, one way of looking at knowledge flows is to examine where knowledge stocks get produced and consumed, and where and how they travel throughout the organization.

Knowledge flow audits may be especially interested in whether knowledge use is being optimized, whether accessibility of knowledge is unduly restricted, and whether there are any bottlenecks, blockages, gaps, or potential improvements to the way that knowledge moves around the organization.

Social network analysis techniques are often used in inventorying or mapping knowledge flows. Knowledge flow inventorying is often described as *knowledge mapping*. Confusingly, so is the inventorying of knowledge stocks.

Audits of stocks and flows must first begin with a descriptive, inventorying, or mapping phase (inventory audit), typically leading to a more prescriptive discovery review or participative goal-setting audit. It is less common to see a knowledge flow audit connected to a value audit.

3. Knowledge Needs

This category is especially friendly to the line of thinking that there is no universalized ideal form of KM, and that KM should address the contingent demands of the host organization's context and environment (Handzic et al., 2008). These demands can exist at both *operational levels* (Do people have access to the knowledge they need to be effective in their roles?) and *strategic levels* (Does the organization have the capabilities it needs to respond to the demands of the environment—that is, the contextual drivers behind the impetus for knowledge management?; Probst et al., 2000; Handzic et al., 2008). Chapters 16, 19, and 20 will examine the different characteristics of strategic and operational knowledge.

Audits of knowledge needs have particular affinities with discovery review audits and participative goal-setting audits. However, they may depend on inventory audits for their baseline data (What do we already have, and when we consider our needs, where are the gaps?). Particularly when directed toward strategic needs, an audit focused on knowledge needs in relation to strategic capabilities may be applicable within a value audit model. In this case it will be oriented toward creating strategic value for the organization.

Now we examine the left-hand side of the model, which focuses more on KM practices or drivers for KM than on the knowledge itself. In this sense, the left-hand side of the diagram is an *indirect* form of auditing, relying for the quality of its findings on the validity of the assumptions it can make about what is "good" practice. It observes practices within the organization and compares them to what are believed to be good practices in general or to KM standards. They are, by and large, assessment audits. This is in contrast to the right-hand side of the diagram, which represents *direct* auditing approaches, focused on identifiable phenomena and drivers within the organization itself.

The need to rely on externally verified assumptions is perhaps why assessment audits were less commonly cited in our survey of KM practitioners. On the one hand, there is a fairly stable body of beliefs as to what constitutes "good" KM practice, but on the other hand, the applicability of that practice to the contextually driven specifics of a given organization at a given point in time is less obvious (cf. Snowden, 2002; Becerra-Fernandez & Sabherwal, 2010, pp. 27, 258–268).

KM assessment audits of this type will rely on a combination of methods and instruments:

- By *methods* we mean processes such as interviews, survey exercises, facilitated workshops, and content analysis.
- By *instruments* we mean prestructured frameworks or collecting mechanisms, such as interview protocols, survey questionnaires, standards, or structured collections of "recognition" indicators around cultural behaviors, pain points, KM enablers, processes, capabilities, and so on.

4. KM Enablers

Knowledge enablers (or KM enablers) refer to the elements in an organizational ecosystem that enable or support the productive use and deployment of knowledge to serve organizational goals. These are both social and technical, and a KM framework approach is the most common approach against which to identify, categorize, and evaluate enablers. Typical elements of a KM enablers framework would be the following (Milton & Lambe, 2020, pp. 126–133):

- **Governance:** To what extent do leadership, policy, and planning support or inhibit the productive use of knowledge?
- **Process:** To what extent do established organizational processes support or inhibit the productive use of knowledge?
- **People:** To what extent do the organizational culture, the resourcing of staff, and their competencies and skill sets support or inhibit the productive use of knowledge?
- **Infrastructure:** To what extent do technology platforms and physical environments support or inhibit the productive use of knowledge?

The International Organization for Standardization (ISO) 30401 standard on knowledge management systems (by which is meant management systems, not technology systems), in common with all newer ISO management systems standards, also takes an enablers approach. Enablers here include (ISO, 2018b):

- Leadership
- Policy
- Roles and responsibilities
- Resources
- Competence
- Awareness

If we truly subscribe to an ecosystem view of how these enablers combine and interact to support productive knowledge use, then we must also look at the interactions between these enablers and their compound effects (Davenport, 1997, pp. 28–45; Nardi & O'Day, 1999, pp. 51–54).

This is where it gets complicated. With a pure enablers approach and using an assessment audit model alone, we have to make assumptions about what "good" looks like for these enablers and what "good" looks like for their interactions, and then assess our own organization against those assumptions.

Assessment audits, with their built-in prescriptiveness, their need to generalize to accepted "good practice," and their attendant deficiencies around context blindness, are still the dominant operating model for examining KM enablers and their interactions, as well as for the auditing of KM processes (Chambers & Rand, 2010, pp. 542–553). They are rooted conceptually in the operational auditing model. We critiqued the assumptions behind this approach in chapter 3.

The assessment audit model, taken on its own, presents two problems:

1. If we look externally for data on what "good" looks like and use that data prescriptively, then we risk applying standards that do not match our specific situation and needs.

2. If we simply take the enablers as generic principles without specific examples or scenarios attached to them (i.e., using them descriptively), then they basically function as "motherhood" statements that look good on paper and in audit reports but have little real traction for driving the transformation and change we desire.

However, it is also possible to use a KM framework of enablers as a *nonprescriptive* prompt to guide a participative goal-setting audit or a discovery review audit. For example, the question "To what extent is our leadership supportive of and engaged in the direction of our KM efforts?" can stimulate productive conversations without making arbitrary value judgments. In this approach, a framework of enablers can be used as a reference point to probe our own practices.

This is the approach Paul McDowall used in his KM assessment of the Treasury Board of Canada Secretariat. This can be particularly useful when combined with an audit of organizational goals and needs if our practices are set into the context of goals and needs. We will look at this approach in chapter 7, when we look at discovery review and participative goal-setting audits, and in chapter 9, when we look at KM standards.

5. KM Processes

In a KM processes-focused audit, we are looking at the presence and robustness of knowledge-related processes. KM processes are typically organized on a *knowledge life cycle* model and might include the following (Chambers & Rand, 2010, pp. 544–545; Milton & Lambe, 2020, pp. 130–132; ISO, 2018b, pp. 6–7):

- Knowledge creation
- Knowledge capture
- Knowledge storage
- Knowledge organization
- Knowledge discovery
- Knowledge sharing or discussion

- Knowledge acquisition
- Knowledge synthesis
- Knowledge representation
- Knowledge application
- Knowledge curation
- Knowledge retention
- Knowledge internalization or learning
- KM process improvement

There is also a growing literature on end-of-life-cycle processes—that is, the need for managed unlearning or "forgetting" processes in situations where existing knowledge may act as a brake on agility or a constraint on adaptation, or where poor control of intentional forgetting leads to accidental loss of critical knowledge (Nystrom & Starbuck, 1984; Benkard, 2000; Martin de Holan & Phillips, 2004; Martin de Holan, 2011; cf. ISO, 2018b, p. 6).

The ISO 30401 standard also lists key *management processes* (ISO, 2018b, p. 7):

- Alignment with organizational needs and goals
- Monitoring and evaluation
- KM planning
- Knowledge risk management
- KM communications

Taken by themselves, KM process audits, like audits of KM enablers, tend to give rise to an assumption that if found absent, these processes must be created and accounted for. If this is done without attending to the specific needs and characteristics of the organization, this can lead to a "checkbox mindset" focused exclusively on observable phenomena (such as the existence and documentation of the process), which can be blind to less observable but no less critical factors (such as which specific knowledge work the process is supposed to be supporting and why).

It also implies that completeness trumps partial coverage, and this can result in KM efforts being diffused over multiple "required" processes when it might be more appropriate to focus on fewer processes for greater depth and impact. This is the risk of a "checkbox" mentality in the prescriptive operational audit model more generally when a model is applied too unthinkingly to knowledge management and fails to meet actual business needs. A KM processes audit on its own can suffer from the same deficiencies as a KM enablers audit in failing to engage with the specific context and needs of an organization. We present a case study illustrating this risk in chapter 9 when we look at KM standards in greater depth.

6. KM Capabilities

Capabilities are closely associated with enablers and processes, but they are slightly more complex to review. We can say that an organization's KM capabilities are compound effects of the KM enablers it has in place, and of the KM processes it has in place.

However, the concept is worth calling out separately because a capability is more than the sum of its enablers and processes. In organization theory, *an organizational capability is both a capacity and an ability to learn, respond, and innovate in specific competence areas*— that is, in its key product or service offerings (Collis, 1996). It follows from this that KM capabilities *represent an organization's capacity and ability to learn, respond, and innovate in the way it deploys knowledge to support organizational goals.* It depends on enablers and supporting processes, but it is not the sum of those things. We will examine capabilities in greater depth in chapter 19 as a way of looking at strategic organizational knowledge.

Unless they are anchored in the specific organizational context, assessments of KM capabilities fall prey to the same recipe-based prescriptivist problems surrounding a simplistic "perfect-world" view of KM enablers and processes. Standardized capability maturity models represent one manifestation of this.

Capability maturity models presuppose a linear, progressive series of maturity lifecycle stages, typically covering some combination of the following stages (cf. Gibson & Nolan, 1974; Paulk et al., 1993):

- **Initiation**—awareness and limited and isolated initiatives
- **Expansion**—scaling out of repeatable systems and processes
- **Formalization**—definition and stabilization
- **Maturity**—managing, integrating, connecting, and adapting systems and processes, establishing consistency and control
- **Optimization**—improving and innovating to create organizational value

While the notion of KM capabilities in general makes sense, capability maturity models, developed initially for specific applications in information systems and software development, have a number of flaws in relation to KM assessments. They make a number of assumptions that do not apply consistently to all aspects of knowledge use in organizations. They assume that

- all aspects of knowledge use can be observed and measured consistently;
- reliable, objective indicators for each stage can be derived;
- all organizations will start in the same place and progress through the same stages in the same sequence;
- organizations can be represented by a single "averaged" maturity profile as distinct from containing a number of different profiles.

Suffice it to say that KM capability assessments *on their own* can suffer from the same limitations as KM enabler and KM process audits, particularly if they are tightly associated with a maturity framework:

- They can direct attention to observable features and ignore difficult to observe but important features of KM capabilities.
- They carry assumptions about a single *correct* way of doing KM and a single correct *sequence* for progressing through a KM journey despite many counterexamples in practice.
- They do not easily accommodate the context-specific circumstances that organizations find themselves in.

However, if a KM capabilities audit is combined with other forms of audit that pick up the particularities of your organization's knowledge resources, needs, enablers, and processes and if the audit does not assume a prescriptive dependency on external best-practice standards, a capabilities audit can provide useful insight and help to focus attention on key priorities.

We have used a standard KM capabilities framework to describe known good practices in a range of KM enabler areas, at different levels of maturity, and then asked, "In relation to the goals of your organizational unit, where is this capability now, and where does it need to be to support what you want to do?" This approach localizes the assessment and contextualizes it to present needs (cf. Handa et al., 2019, chap 3).

This entire discussion implies that assessments on the left side of our diagram should never be conducted in isolation from the evidence-gathering audit activities on the right side of our diagram. The right side of the diagram provides the context-specific particularities of the organization we are studying. The left side of the diagram provides models against which to compare, have important discussions, and make informed decisions about how these particularities should be addressed and shaped in the future.

KM enabler audits, KM process audits, and KM capability audits should not be used and applied in isolation as "pure" assessment audits:

- They should always be combined with inventory audits (Which knowledge stocks and flows need to be supported through which enablers and processes?).
- They should be aligned with an audit of needs and goals (participative goal-setting, discovery review, and/or value audits).

Otherwise, they can become abstract exercises without any real grounding in the organization's specific situation, goals, needs, and resources.

7. KM Outcomes

Our discussion on the different elements of this framework reinforces the argument presented in chapter 4 that a knowledge audit is a compound and multidimensional activity.

We do not only deploy different models of audit in combination (e.g., an inventory audit + a participative goal-setting audit + a value audit) but also want to focus our attention on any combination of target phenomena *depending on what it is that we want to achieve through the knowledge audit and in KM.* We will develop an appreciation of the potential drivers and motivations for an audit in the next section of this book.

If knowledge auditing and KM are underpinned by a theory of change, we need indicators that we can reaudit and review periodically to ensure that the change we intend to bring about is actually happening. So our mechanisms and approaches need to be lightweight and easy to apply.

Therefore the final step in an audit-scoping activity will be to determine *which KM outcomes* we want to monitor and evaluate over time. Depending on what it is that we are auditing and why, it can be any combination of knowledge stocks, flows, needs and goals met, enablers, processes, or capabilities. This framework is, then, less a selection framework from which to choose individual items and more a portfolio of possible combinations to consider in scoping a knowledge audit.

*   *   *

Summary

In this chapter we examined the first important decision in scoping a knowledge audit—the types of phenomena we might want to review. Here is a summary of the main points:

1. The scoping of a knowledge audit involves identifying the combinations of the target phenomena we are interested in, as well as the types of audit we want to employ.
2. The target phenomena for a knowledge audit can be any combination of
   - knowledge stocks,
   - knowledge flows,
   - knowledge needs and goals,
   - KM enablers,
   - KM processes,
   - KM capabilities, and
   - KM outcomes (usually dependent on the preceding phenomena).

3. Inventory audits focus on stocks and flows.

4. Discovery review and participative goal-setting audits will usually look at knowledge goals and needs and will take in a wide range of other phenomena.

5. The target phenomena for KM assessment audits are KM enablers, KM processes, and KM capabilities.

6. The risk of conducting KM assessments on their own is that they can be driven by an idealized, prescriptive view of what "good" KM looks like. This is unlikely to match the specific context and needs of the organization conducting the audit.

7. KM assessment audits should always be conducted with some combination of an audit of stocks, flows, needs, and goals to avoid becoming detached from the specific contexts and needs of the organization.

III Drivers and Motivations

6 What Stimulated the Emergence of Knowledge-Related Audits?

... the social system is an organization like the individual. . . . it is bound together by a system of communication, and . . . it has a dynamics in which circular processes of a feedback nature play a prominent part.
—Wiener (1961, p. 24)

We have seen that the term *audit* is highly ambiguous. Ambiguity creates an uncertain conceptual space in which different interpreters are free to draw their own conclusions in indeterminate ways that are difficult to contest. If we want to improve the reliability and robustness of a knowledge audit process, then we need to reduce this ambiguity.

We have taken the line that different types of audits evolved for different legitimate purposes and reasons. It makes more sense to build a typology of knowledge audit operating models together with a clear understanding of the rationale, purpose, strengths, and weaknesses of each type so that practitioners can make their own decisions and choices as to which audit model they want to adopt, and how, and why.

In chapter 4 we identified six different models or types of audits deployed in knowledge-related audits. Notwithstanding some of their family resemblances, these models of audits are quite distinct from each other and have quite different implications for their authority and methodological rigor. These distinctions matter. Any kind of ambiguity opens up the knowledge-auditing process to individual bias and hence reduces our assurance of reliability. If I mean a looser sense of audit but you understand a tighter sense of audit, I can use my audit methodology to persuade you of things that have less intrinsic authority than you think.

Different models of audit imply different sources of evidence. If I conduct an inventory audit of intellectual property assets and combine it with a participative goal-setting audit (to set goals) and a value audit (to determine value creation), I have three distinct kinds of evidence with differing degrees of authority and reliability:

(a) A relatively high degree of observability and objectivity in my inventory

(b) A qualitative but collectively derived and validated assessment in my goal setting

(c) A target value creation goal that can only be realized by actual exploitation in the future.

The scoping of a knowledge audit will depend on our purpose and the drivers and motivations for conducting the knowledge audit in the first place. We need to establish where our interests lie and create appropriate audit focus questions, and this will help determine the target phenomena we are interested in and the types of audits we should adopt.

> The types of audits we adopt, and the combination of types, depend on what we want to achieve, the resources available to us, and the level of commitment in our host organization.

In chapter 5 we identified the different phenomena that an audit might be interested in, from knowledge stocks, to flows, to goals, to enablers, to processes, to capabilities. In fact, as we saw, our audit models can be applied (in combination) to gain an understanding of any combination of these phenomena.

> Which phenomena we are interested in, and why, should flow from the drivers for conducting the audit in the first place.

The Drivers for the Knowledge Audit Determine Our Audit-Scoping Choices

Our choices flow directly from a consideration of goals and needs. Here are three different examples of how circumstances drive choice:

1. If I am concerned about the risk of tacit knowledge loss because of an upcoming increase in retirements of experienced staff, I would want to make an inventory of the types of tacit knowledge that were important to my business, I would want to understand the knowledge flows that need to be in place to assure continuity, and I would want to understand the enablers and the processes that directly affect those flows and that continuity. I would probably *not* want to conduct a comprehensive assessment and audit.

2. If, on the other hand, my industry is in a period of turmoil and change and we need to take a fresh look at how we are equipped to respond to it but are not sure exactly

how, I would probably want to start with a strategic knowledge inventory, assessed against strategic goals and needs, and an assessment of my knowledge management (KM) capabilities to support these needs. I may then drill down to a midlevel operational knowledge inventory and mapping exercise to understand my current resources, flows, and capabilities. Only when I have a view of what I want to achieve in terms of knowledge building and reequipping would I then look at things like the enablers and processes that need to support my new direction.

3. If I already have a clear strategic direction but want to know how to optimize my KM practices to support it, then I would probably want to take a "middle-out" approach, inventorying my knowledge resources and flows across the organization. I would want to understand resources, flows, goals, needs, and pain points at the operational level. I would then want to align any insights gained with my strategic view. Each strategic goal will be translated into a capabilities statement that characterizes the strategic knowledge capabilities I need to be in command of, if we are to go where we want to go. I would conduct a gap analysis between what we have at an operational level, and what we need to have at a strategic level. Then, again, I would look at the enablers and processes that need to be adjusted to serve the transformation that is required.

These are just three examples. There are many more. Context is everything. Drivers are everything. How I compile and scope my audit in terms of model and target phenomena can be very different depending on my circumstances.

Only once the audit model and target phenomena are identified can we then choose appropriate methods for evidence gathering. The model-phenomena-method (MPM) audit framework we presented in chapter 4 represents an initial framework for making decisions about a knowledge audit's scope that is appropriate to an organization's goals and needs. In that framework, choice of audit methods comes last.

The aim of the next few chapters is to discuss the way that larger environmental drivers have influenced the development and application of audit models, target phenomena, and methods. We will begin with a historical review of the principal drivers behind knowledge-related audit practices since the 1950s.

In covering this ground, we can begin to remove the lack of clarity and the ambiguity from discussions of knowledge audits among KM practitioners so that when we speak to colleagues and stakeholders about our knowledge audits, we have a way of explaining and discovering exactly what each of us intends. In the process we will also uncover a rich portfolio of tools and methodologies for audit-based learning and insight.

So much for the semantics. Now let us look at the archaeology and see what we can extract for current knowledge audit practice.

The Roots of Knowledge Audit Methodology in Communications Research

There were four distinct strands of communications research in the 1950s, each of which contributed to the literature on organizational communications and by extension to the information and knowledge vibrancy of an organization. This proliferation of attention contributed to the sense

(a) that the field was blossoming,

(b) but that it was fragmented, and therefore

(c) that the time for systematic study and measurement was at hand.

Each strand produced auditing and measurement methodologies that continue to have high relevance for KM and for knowledge audits. Their underlying drivers continue to be relevant to KM in organizations today. The four strands were

1. communications for control,

2. communications for a productive organizational climate,

3. communications for influence, and

4. communications for effects.

In the sections that follow, I will present the drivers behind each of these strands, the practices and methods they developed, and the illustrations of the contributions they can make to the practice of knowledge audits today.

1.   Communications for Control

With the growth of the telegraph and the railroads in the mid-nineteenth century, the shape of the business landscape started to shift. From the mid-nineteenth century to the great crash of 1929, the industrializing economies, particularly in North America, saw the slow but steady growth of large distributed enterprises serving multiple markets and connected by rail, postal services, and telegraph communications.

The ad hoc management techniques used by small, owner-operated businesses serving local markets would no longer suffice to serve large hierarchical organizations run by professional managers with offices in different geographic locations, and competing with other businesses for customers and suppliers.

These pressures combined to drive the evolution of what came to be known as *systematic management*, at the core of which was the notion of *managerial control*: the ability to collect information from the various operations, ensuring regular flows *upward* to decision-makers who would make decisions and issue instructions, which would then be communicated *downward* to the employees in various parts.

Detailed record keeping and regular reporting systems would provide the capability to analyze the performance of the business system over time and make adjustments to optimize its performance. Here lies an ancient progenitor of knowledge management.

Among the first examples of this trend were the railroads themselves. In the early days of low-density rail networks, timetabling communications and instruction giving were still rather ad hoc. As the traffic density (and competition) increased, particularly on single-track systems, the need for more systematic coordination and control became more pressing.

A series of accidents on the Western Railroad in Massachusetts in 1841 resulted in a much more disciplined system of timetabling, decision-making, and instruction giving. It was supplemented by a system of record keeping and vertical reporting to enable managers to learn from the network performance so they could adjust the system accordingly. The companies developed techniques of cost accounting to enable the optimization of the system (Yates, 1989).

This was an early example of the communication and information management systems that propagated first across the railway industry and then, from the 1890s onwards, through large distributed manufacturing and engineering companies (Yates, 1989; Beniger, 1986).

The culmination of this trend was Herbert Simon's (1957) vision, cited in chapter 1, of an administrative system as a decision-making machine enabled by communications—which meant efficient and effective flows of relevant information and knowledge to decision-makers.

By 1958 Simon, in collaboration with James March and Harold Guetzkow, had refined his understanding of the different types of communications in organizations beyond the simple *directive*, or control-oriented, communications. They added three *informational* communication types. The five types of communications March and Simon (1958, p. 161) identified were

(a) communication for coordination of nonprogrammed activity (directive),

(b) communication to establish, initiate, and coordinate programs of work (directive),

(c) communication to provide data for the execution of programmed work (informational),

(d) communication to direct attention to problems or opportunities (informational), and

(e) communication to provide information on the results of activities (informational).

It is worth noting that although the repertoire of organizational communications had expanded beyond directive communications to include informational communications, even the informational communications were still ultimately responsible for influencing decision-making and control.

What is of interest to us from a measurement and audit point of view is the way March and Simon discovered the distinctions between the informational communication types. They achieved this through an empirical analysis of how accounting data were used in the operational units in manufacturing firms, specifically at the functional and task levels. Accounting data were being used as a window into understanding how information influenced the control and coordination of tasks and functions.

They noted that data were being used to address questions regarding appropriate courses of action (type *c* above), attention-directing questions on which problems should be addressed (type *d*), and "scorecard" questions on how well they were doing (type *e*; March & Simon, 1958, pp. 161–162).

Underpinning this analysis were techniques for analyzing documentation and content, analyzing functions and tasks and their informational dependencies, and observing how functions and tasks were performed in practice. Let us translate this to a modern setting using table 6.1 to do so. How can this past experience inform our knowledge audits today?

Table 6.1
Audit focus: Knowledge management for control

Sample knowledge audit focus questions	Models of audit	Phenomena to audit	Methods of audit contributed
How does KM contribute toward processes for the control and coordination of standard processes, including risk management, process management, and quality management?	Inventory	Knowledge stocks and flows	Function and task analysis Content analysis—process knowledge Observation
What knowledge and information resources and flows are necessary to perform our core functions and activities?	Participative goal setting	Needs and goals	
How does KM contribute to learning and adaptation so that operational processes can be adjusted and improved based on organizational and team learning?	Value: capitalization	KM processes	
What knowledge and information flows are necessary to alert us to emerging problems and faults in our processes?			
How should knowledge management support effective and timely decision-making?			

2. Communications for a Productive Climate

One of the consequences of systematic management, and the *communication for control* movement was a perception of increasing depersonalization and bureaucratization of relations between

- managers and employees,
- managers and managers, and
- employees and their (nonmanager) supervisors.

This became a significant sociological concern as well as a practical concern. Already in 1893, sociologist Emile Durkheim was writing about *anomie* as a breakdown in mutual familiarity and a sense of interdependency among workers, and he wrote of the pathological loss of coordination and healthy functioning that followed: "Rules do not themselves create the state of mutual dependence typical of an organic body, they can only express what to do in tightly defined, predicted situations" (1893, p. 410. My translation of the original: "La règle ne crée donc pas l'état de dépendance mutuelle où sont les organes solidaires, mais ne fait que l'exprimer d'une manière sensible et définie, en fonction d'une situation donnée.").

The imposition of depersonalized communication and control systems could, on the one hand, lead to active resistance, thereby compromising the objectives of coordination and control (Yates, 1989). On the other hand, it could lead to poor mutual familiarity and poor adaptiveness in response to variations in the environment, thereby compromising the organization's ability to respond swiftly to a competitive environment (Durkheim, 1893, pp. 412–413).

The "control revolution" (Beniger, 1986) was irreversible, but management systems began to try to mitigate its negative, depersonalizing effects. The *welfare capitalism* movement of the late nineteenth and early twentieth centuries, with social clubs, worker accommodations, libraries, education, health care, and other corporate welfare programs, was one attempt. In an employment climate that had seen increasing labor hostility and activism, this movement worked at humanizing the management-employee relationship, albeit in a heavily paternalistic way (Yates, 1989, p. 16; Brandes, 1976).

Alongside the regulation of communication and information flows for control, which, as markets and economies grew, increased in rigor and intensity, there emerged a new internal corporate communications function. It followed the paternalistic lead of the welfare capitalism movement. In 1959 the manager of Employee Communications at the General Electric Company, C. J. "Mickey" Dover, characterized this style of corporate communications, typical of the period leading up to World War II, as "the era of entertainment":

> Company publications thus dealt largely with choice items of gossip, social chit-chat about employees, notices of birthdays and anniversaries, jokes, notices of local recreation and entertainment opportunities, etc. . . . There were occasional exhortations to lead clean, moral, and thrifty lives, some attacks on the evils of "demon rum," some attacks on the "bolsheviks," and some printed resistance to early attempts at unionization. (Dover, 1959, p. 169)

Dover (1959) used content analysis of internal communications to identify two subsequent phases of development in communications practice:

(a) The "era of information" (the 1940s) to inform employees of company operations and make them feel part of a single organization

(b) The "era of persuasion" (the 1950s) to attempt to win employees to the management's point of view

There were more sophisticated attempts to study the problems raised by Durkheim and others. The German psychologist Kurt Lewin fled Hitler's Germany in 1933 and migrated to the US, where he was influential in founding the field of group dynamics, to study interactions, communications, and behaviors in social collectives. He founded the MIT Group Dynamics Research Center in 1945, shortly before his premature death at the age of fifty-seven.

Lewin was not, by all accounts, a good lecturer. He was unstructured and would pick a problem at random to talk about, thinking up his words as he went along. He preferred problem-solving and methodology development to systematic theory building. Yet he inspired very innovative work and great loyalty. His students' most memorable learning took place at his Saturday morning informal meetings open to all of his students. In Berlin he had called these sessions *Quasselstrippe*: in German *quassel* means "to ramble on." Today we would call them knowledge cafés (Schramm, 1980).

Lewin and his group contributed several key concepts and associated techniques to what would later become integrated into systems thinking: action research, force-field analysis, change management, and the concept of leadership climate. *Organizational climate* studies are a direct descendant of Lewin's work (Jablin, 1980).

Lewin and his students were the first to introduce analysis of group behaviors into communications psychology and research and to analyze the influence of communications on social change. Lewin was responsible for the concept of the "gatekeeper" in communication networks, which became a keystone of communications theory and of social network analysis (Schramm, 1980). Table 6.2 suggests how we can learn from this strand of development.

Table 6.2

Audit focus: Knowledge management for a productive climate

Sample knowledge audit focus questions	Models of audit	Phenomena to audit	Methods of audit contributed
How does KM contribute toward a positive and productive organizational climate where behaviors are helpful, knowledge is shared when needed, individuals and teams align and share common objectives, and there is openness to learning and change?	Inventory	Knowledge flows	Social network analysis Content analysis—coordination-related communications Observation
	Participative goal setting	Needs and goals	
What information and knowledge flows need to be in place to keep individuals, teams, and organizations aligned?	Assessment	KM enablers KM processes KM capabilities	Climate survey
How do we enhance knowledge flows by discovering and cultivating the knowledge brokers in our organization? How do we identify and overcome bottlenecks and blockages in knowledge flows?	Value: capitalization	Outcomes	Change management Action research
How does KM contribute toward a positive leadership climate that supports and does not inhibit a productive organizational climate?			
What enablers need to be in place to support a productive organizational climate and organizational agility and adaptiveness?			
How do we learn to become more effective in working together on scale, especially when developing new capabilities?			
How do we know that our knowledge, information, and communication flows are effective in keeping us aligned?			
How do we overcome silo-based working and resistance to learning and change?			
How do we overcome the demotivating and alienating effects of restructuring, downsizing, mergers and acquisitions, rapid growth, and rapid change?			

3. Communications for Influence

The exhortatory types of corporate communications described in C. J. Dover's account of "entertainment-era" communications were symptomatic of a newly emerging strand of theory building from the 1930s onward—the study of how communications could influence behaviors, through persuasion or other means.

In part this grew out of a sense of the limitations of communication for control, and in part it extended the insight that organizational climate was more than a system of transactions and authority relations. Influence and persuasion were at least as important as control.

Midcentury America was awash in the idea of communicating for personal influence after the wild success of Dale Carnegie's (1936) public-speaking courses and his long-running bestseller *How to Win Friends and Influence People*. Carnegie is credited with popularizing the connection between communication skills and managerial success (Sanborn, 1964, p. 5).

The Second World War brought investment into more systematic research into mass persuasion and propaganda techniques, specifically to aid the war effort. The experimental psychologist Carl Hovlund was hired by the US War Department in 1942 to investigate the nature and influences of communications upon morale. This quickly morphed into a scientific study of the effects and characteristics of successful propaganda and attitude change, and the implications for learning, teaching, and instructional design.

Hovlund had a great impact on the understanding of successful messaging, the persuadability of audiences, and the cognitive effects of persuasive communications (Schramm, 1980). By the 1950s it was considered an article of faith that good communications alone in an industrial setting would bring about high morale. Communication audits and other forms of industrial relations audits helped to dispel this simplistic belief (Yoder, 1952; Perry & Mahoney, 1955).

Nevertheless, propaganda and morale were fertile areas of research in the postwar period and were responsible for several methodological innovations. Harold Lasswell spent his entire career (he received his doctorate in 1926 and died in 1978) studying and writing about propaganda. He was a pioneer in techniques of content analysis, the study of elites and leadership, and the idea of probable futures, scenarios, and future options—key ideas in measuring the impact of propaganda communications. He was also interested in the use of symbolism in communications and how symbolism connected to common cultural roots. This would prefigure the use of narrative in understanding organizational cultures and behaviors pioneered by Dave Snowden (1999).

Perhaps inevitably for a student of propaganda, Lasswell was guided by a conviction that it was not enough to have skills and techniques for measuring, describing, and analyzing communications. To become a genuine profession, communications research needed to be able to project and guide interactions to desired outcomes. Measurement precedes enlightenment and enlightenment implies the ability to accomplish specific goals (Schramm, 1980).

If we translate this into a theory of audit, it is not enough to analyze and understand; we must be able to influence a human system toward desired outcomes. Or, to put it much more succinctly, following Charles D. Shaw in writing about clinical audits, "Change is the measure of audit" (Baker et al., 1999, p. ix).

It is easy to understand why morale and propaganda were two key themes in communication studies in the war years and how they might then be converted to a postwar industrial setting where there was competition for labor and a great deal of mistrust between employers and unions, and between managers and employees.

An associated strand of research with a more commercial orientation was the emerging study of mass communications. Paul Lazarsfeld was Austrian, studied mathematics, and spent his early career in the field of community studies and social psychology. He was a pioneer in combining mathematical and statistical analysis with survey research.

Offered a traveling fellowship to the US in the early 1930s, he became interested in radio research. In 1935 he was hired by CBS to establish the Bureau of Applied Social Research to develop and apply systematic methods for studying the effects of mass communications. He brought together some of the leading social science scholars of his day to study audiences and the effects of radio (and later other mass media) on them.

The bureau developed new methods for audience research, including surveys, focus groups, and reaction analyzers (buttons that studio audience members pressed to record their reactions to what they were observing). In the 1940s his team studied the effects of the mass media on two presidential elections. They discovered that mass media did not have direct persuasive effects but tended to reinforce existing affiliations and positions (Schramm, 1980). This is a lesson we are relearning today in the concept of filter bubbles on the internet (Pariser, 2011).

The techniques developed by Lazarsfeld and others fed into opinion research related to business communications. They also generated a new appreciation of the importance of semantics in content analysis and in understanding the importance of matching the languages of broadcasters and audiences.

In 1961 Verne Burnett, a public relations specialist and younger brother to the advertising genius Leo Burnett, reported:

> The fact that management often fails to get through with its messages was emphasized during the recent steel strike, when the steel companies came to the realization that their communications to employees, plant communities, and the general public contained words and phrases

that didn't register with their listeners, resulted in confusion, and sometimes caused irrita-
tion and resentment. This unhappy fact was confirmed by surveys of the steelworkers, which
revealed that they considered management's messages complex, stilted, abstruse, confusing,
and irritating. (Burnett, 1961, p. 5)

In knowledge management this insight would later reemerge in the guiding principles
behind taxonomy design (Lambe, 2007, chap. 8) and in the factors inhibiting knowledge
transfer, including arduous relationships between knowledge holder and recipient, the
cognitive or social distance between knowledge holder and recipient, and the absorp-
tive capacity in the recipient (Szulanski, 2003, pp. 29–31; Rogers, 2003, pp. 240–246).

Communication style also became a focus of attention. It took a management professor, Douglas MacGregor, to crystallize the emerging sense of polarization between
communications for control and communications for influence. In his famous book
The Human Side of Enterprise, MacGregor charted the gradual decline of top-down
dependency and authoritarian control, succeeded by a sense of interdependency and
the need for new forms of influencing and alignment in the American workplace. He
told the story of a new manager in a textile mill:

> The manager came into the weave room the day he arrived. He walked directly to the agent
> and said, "Are you Belloc?" The agent acknowledged that he was. The manager said, "I am the
> new manager here. When I manage a mill, I run it. Do you understand?" The agent nodded,
> and then waved his hand. The workers, intently watching this encounter, shut down every
> loom in the room immediately. The agent turned to the manager and said, "All right, go ahead
> and run it." (MacGregor, 1960, p. 23)

MacGregor (1960) had started from the assumption that "effective prediction and
control are as central to the task of management as they are to the task of engineering or
of medicine" (p. 11). However, efforts at predicting and controlling human beings in the
enterprise are at best "spotty," resulting in unrealized potential in terms of how human
resources are utilized in the service of organizational effectiveness (p. 4).

MacGregor argued that there were two types of assumption implicit in managerial behaviors in the organizations he had studied. The first set of assumptions (those
implicit in his textile mill manager) he characterized as *Theory X*—the traditional,
authoritarian view of direction and control. A student of Maslow, MacGregor thought
Theory X might be effective in conditions of high top-down dependency and a high
degree of influence over a worker's basic physiological and security needs. Here, the
style of communication is authoritarian and instruction laden.

We are reminded, again, of Durkheim's warning about the impact of *anomie* from
the alienation this approach produces, and the striking loss of organizational adaptiveness it induces. MacGregor made the point that the contemporary labor market (in the
late 1950s) was no longer constrained by those conditions of control and dependency.

The second set of assumptions MacGregor labeled *Theory Y*. In Theory Y, self-actualization through work is a motivating factor. Employees can be trusted to employ a high degree of initiative, responsibility, and creativity in the service of their employing organization if they understand and can be persuaded to commit to the goals of the organization.

In the crudest form of this view of influence, communications become "selling" interactions—but MacGregor points out that in a true sales relationship the salesman does not, as in the enterprise, have the capacity to fall back on authority and instruction giving. Salesmanship and power relations make uneasy partners (MacGregor, 1960, p. 19). The boundaries between control and influence are sensitive and tricky to interpret and navigate in a corporate context.

True Theory Y communications become invitational in style, involving the sharing of information on the organization and its goals, the sharing of feedback on how people are motivated and how they see their jobs, and dialogue about how employees can best contribute. In a discussion of a case example, MacGregor (1960) observes:

> Evans succeeded, by his manner more than by his specific words, in conveying to Harrison the essential point that he did not want to occupy the conventional role of boss, but rather, to the fullest extent possible, the role of a consultant who was putting all of his knowledge and experience at Harrison's disposal in the conviction that they had a genuine common interest in Harrison's doing an outstanding job. (p. 65)

4. Communications for Effect

The Burnetts of organizational communications were interested in the semantics of communications largely from the perspective of successful influencing. Another strand of research focused on the efficacy of message transfer—that is, whether the information carried in the communication had been transmitted and received accurately and produced the intended effects.

There were practical investigations of this within organizational contexts, but there was also substantial theoretical work done, and this took place in the intersection between communications theory and information theory. In this latter domain, the theme of communications and information transfer for control returned to prominence. However, there was also substantial interest in feedback loops, learning, and the development of adaptive capabilities. It was an extraordinarily rich and generative period.

As good a place to start as any is with Norbert Wiener, child prodigy, ballistics expert turned pacifist, famously absentminded professor, inveterate traveler and collaborator (Hardesty, 2011). Wiener was a mathematician, but he was a passionate believer in multidisciplinary collaboration on interdisciplinary problems regarding what he called the "blank spaces" in the boundary regions between disciplines (Wiener, 1961, pp. 2–3).

Table 6.3
Audit focus: Knowledge management for influence

Sample knowledge audit focus questions	Models of audit	Phenomena to audit	Methods of audit contributed
How do our KM processes and communications influence behaviors toward positive outcomes for the organization?	Inventory	Knowledge stocks	Content analysis (KM communications and key knowledge artifacts)
How do we know what our people are really thinking and how they really feel? How do we discriminate the real needs and desires that will affect behaviors from opinions that do not affect behaviors?	Participative goal detting	Needs and goals	Communications for change Change management
How do we make sense of the complex and often contradictory signals that our people give us about what their needs and pain points are?	Assessment and/or discovery review	KM enablers KM processes KM capabilities	Opinion surveys Focus groups Instant reaction surveys Cultural analysis Observation of interactions Boundary conditions for control vs. influence Invitational comms
How do we define observable and measurable outcomes for our change initiatives so that we know we are achieving our change goals?			
Are our codified knowledge artifacts, information artifacts, and communications framed in a way that is suitable to our audiences, their contexts, and their needs?	Value: capitalization	Outcomes	Outcomes measurement
How can we better understand, and at a deeper level, our organizational culture and our people's values, attitudes, and behaviors, including through the interpretation of workplace stories and the use of symbols?			
How can we better understand the boundary conditions between management for control and management for influence, particularly in relation to encouraging knowledge-sharing behaviors?			
What is the best communication style to use for managing knowledge by influence rather than by control? How do we make KM "invitational" where it needs to be and policy driven where it needs to be, with clarity on where the boundaries lie?			

In his time he helped to apply mathematical techniques in physiology, electrical engineering, computing, ballistics, control and communications, information science, statistical mechanics, psychology, sociology, economics, and anthropology. He worked with Kurt Lewin on techniques for opinion sampling and modeling opinion diffusion.

Wiener, through his collaborations, was a leader in developing the post–World War II field of cybernetics. His 1961 book on cybernetics caused a sensation. As Wiener explains it, the term was coined from the Greek for *steersman*, but our modern pronunciation of *cyber* conceals its etymological links with the English term *governance* (κυβερνητική). Crucially, it was meant to refer to the ways in which biological, social, and mechanical systems are governed, adjusted, and controlled through communication and information flows.

The link with *steersman* is suggestive. In the field of cybernetics, governance, as in steering a craft, is reflexive; it depends on feedback about how we are positioned relative to our goals, and it is responsive to our own movement as well as changes in the environment that affect how we reach our goals. Feedback and learning are central concepts in cybernetics.

So in Wiener's work, the notions of communication, information flow, and control were tightly linked, but they were linked with a specific focus on determining *effective outcomes*. Wiener (1961) was an intensely practical man, interested in the applications of his theory in the real world:

- Does the antiaircraft missile succeed in shooting down the moving plane by predicting its future position?
- Does the hand successfully pick up the cup by using observational feedback for fine motor control?
- Does the signalman successfully route a series of trains using feedback from signaling systems and the instructions he has been given?
- Does an organization successfully exploit and act upon the information held by its members through effective exchange of communications?
- Can a system filter out distortions in message accuracy caused by background noise?
- Can a large organization or society act purposively as a single entity through control of "the means for the acquisition, use, retention, and transmission of information"?

Three seminal concepts in this strand of communications research subsequently had an impact on information and knowledge management:

1. The concept of feedback for adaptation and fine control
2. The concept of noise
3. The concept of an organization as a system

1. Feedback for adaptation and fine control   One of the central concepts in cybernetics is that of feedback on purposeful behaviors, where information from observations on the goal is constantly adjusting the actions on the goal, until the goal is reached. This was elegantly summarized by Wiener and his colleagues as "a continuous feed-back from the goal that modifies and guides the behaving object" (Rosenblueth et al., 1943, pp. 19–20).

Although feedback was a well-known concept in mechanical and control engineering, Wiener's work on modeling feedback and applying it to information and communications theory had a strong influence on the emergence of *management information systems to support decision-making* in the 1950s and 1960s (Leavitt & Whisler, 1958; Dickson, 1981). As Stafford Beer (1966) put it, "Management is the sentient filter of the feedback loop" (p. 443).

The concept of feedback was also important in developing the idea of *learning cycles*. The statistician Walter Shewhart observed in 1939 that statistical measures for quality control in manufacturing could only be achieved incrementally through increasing cycles of precision. He described a three-stage cycle, from specification, to production, to inspection and measurement, leading to a refinement of specification and production, which was then reinspected, and so on, until a fine degree of quality control had been reached (Shewhart, 1939, pp. 45–46). This is a classic use of feedback for control.

It was W. Edwards Deming (1982) who, in 1950, transformed the cycle into a learning cycle, adding a fourth stage: "What did we learn, what can we predict?" (p. 88).

Beginning in the 1960s, US Air Force colonel John Boyd (1964, 1976) began to think about the use of learning cycles to make sense of shifting and uncertain environments (in his case military combat environments) and to create adaptive capacity as well as speed and effectiveness of decision-making *while simultaneously interfering with the sensemaking capabilities of adversaries.*

By the mid-1990s, Boyd (2018, pp. 384–385) had condensed his ideas into the *OODA loop* (observe, orient, decide, act), in which he distinguished between (a) insights from observations that "feed forward" to decisions and actions and (b) learning and insights that "feed back" from decisions and actions to frame new ways of sensing and orienting.

As early as 1963, Richard Cyert and James March (1963, pp. 100–102) had characterized the firm as a learning entity, where learning and subsequent decision-making was driven by both short-term feedback from the environment and longer-term feedback taking larger perspectives.

This would eventually bloom into a body of theory on *organizational learning* from the 1990s onward and which has interacted with KM in a curious blend of familiarity and standoffishness (Spender, 2008).

A central concept in organizational learning, reflecting the short- and long-term perspectives of Cyert and March, is that of *double-loop learning*, popularized by Chris Argyris.

In single-loop learning, feedback and reflection are used to solve problems and learn in relation to the matter at hand; for example, how do I solve a specific production quality problem?

In double-loop learning, feedback and reflection from encountering problems are used to question and learn in relation to the underlying objectives, policies, and processes of the organization; for example, if we fix all our accumulated production problems with this product, the manufacturing costs will exceed revenue from sales, so should we be making this product at all? Double-loop learning is much more expansive, and hence it is often more difficult to perform effectively because to take effect it must also overcome cultural barriers, assumed norms, and vested interests (Argyris, 1977; cf. Stacey & Mowles, 2016, p. 117).

2. Noise and the effectiveness of information transfer   Another of Wiener's concerns was the corruption of messages through the interference of background noise. Wiener's treatment of noise and his subsequent development of noise filters were applied in the technical domains of communications and audio engineering. Claude Shannon (1949) established a vocabulary for analyzing communications and noise that became prominent in communications research: the triple construct of transmitter-message-receiver. Shannon, with Warren Weaver (1964, p. 4) identified three classes of communication problems arising from this:

LEVEL A. How accurately can the symbols of communication be transmitted? (The technical problem).

LEVEL B. How precisely do the transmitted symbols convey the desired meaning? (The semantic problem).

LEVEL C. How effectively does the received meaning affect conduct in the desired way? (The effectiveness problem).

While initially driven by a technical engineering concept scheme, the underlying concept goes to this intensely practical social question: How do we know that the information in a communication we have received is the same as that which was transmitted and that its effects are as desired? Human systems use feedback mechanisms and checking processes to deal with this problem (Wiener, 1961, p. 96; Thayer, 1961, p. 132).

Communications researchers took up the Shannon and Weaver concept scheme enthusiastically because it gave them a handle on methods of measurement (e.g., Redding, 1964). Norbert Wiener's cautions (1961, p. 164) on the limits to the statistical reliability of communications measures in social systems, and the consequent deficiencies of quantitative measurement regimes, went largely ignored.

From the 1950s onwards, communications researchers were devising techniques to *measure the effectiveness of communications*, and by the 1970s there was a growing literature on detection and measurement of distortion in communications reception and interpretation (Dahle, 1954; Sussman, 1974).

Power relations and cultural norms are a major factor in the distortion of communications messaging upward and downward in organizational hierarchies. This insight established a direct link between measures of communication effectiveness and the capacity of an organization to perform double-loop learning (Argyris, 1977, pp. 116–117).

Argyris and his colleague Donald Schon developed a facilitated method for *two-column journaling* to help organizations overcome message distortion and filtering and to support double-loop learning. In this method, different stakeholders in a given process, problem, or function write the elements of their formal analysis of the situation in the right-hand column. In the left-hand column, they write for each of these elements what they are thinking or feeling about the situation but would not usually communicate formally to colleagues. This method reveals the hidden assumptions and drivers for action that would not normally be visible to others.

In a facilitated session, the two-column technique helps participants make collective sense of the dynamics at play across the organization, and learn collectively to move toward a larger solution (Argyris, 1977, pp. 119–120). Argyris and Schon showed that techniques to facilitate *group sensemaking* can be an important part of overcoming distortions in information and knowledge flows.

In the late 1990s, the US military was formulating its concept of network-centric warfare, centered on the ability of teams to flexibly interpret military plans based on variations in local conditions, and to adapt to events that could not be predicted at the planning stage (Cebrowski & Garstka, 1998).

Network-centric warfare marked a shift from centralized control to distributed communications. This implied a new approach to the notion of *commander's intent*—the idea that an intended goal could be clearly articulated by the commander and understood in such a way that local actors could adopt the most appropriate means to achieve that goal. While clear in its intent, it needed to be framed in a sufficiently general way to allow for flexibility in how the intent should be met, based on local conditions.

But sensitivity to local conditions only satisfied the need for flexibility. Larger-scale coordination was also required, so the third ingredient was the mutual updating of teams on *situation awareness* so that all the teams would have a common operational picture.

These three interlocking concepts (commander's intent, adaptiveness to local conditions, common situation awareness) depend upon the accurate transmission of commander's intent and the availability of methods to evaluate how effectively teams actually interpret commander's intent and develop situational awareness in variable situations (Shattuck & Woods, 2000; Thomas et al., 2007).

More interestingly, this framework has clear implications for KM, where clarity of high-level direction, accurate understanding, local flexibility of response, a common situational picture, and coordination of activity over large organizational structures are also important capabilities to maintain (Barth, 2001; Storlie, 2010).

These criteria are all dependent on effective knowledge and information flows within and between teams. The effectiveness of knowledge transfer does not stand alone. It depends upon supporting capabilities in coordination effectiveness and situation awareness, so that effectiveness can combine with adaptiveness and be sustained through time and changing conditions. It also depends on consistency of operation, so that teams can anticipate how their peers will respond to changes in the environment. This comes from a shared set of capabilities and methods.

3. Organizations as information-processing systems Wiener (1961) and his collaborators became interested in social groups as information-processing systems, where the flow of information can be modeled to provide insights about the boundaries and capabilities of the group:

> Properly speaking, the community extends only so far as there extends an effectual transmission of information. It is possible to give a sort of measure to this by comparing the number of decisions entering a group from outside with the number of decisions made in the group. We can thus measure the autonomy of the group. (pp. 157–158)

The idea that you can model the information and knowledge characteristics of a social group by analyzing its information flows and transformations gave direct impetus to the adoption of *social network analysis* techniques in communications research and later on in information and knowledge management. For example, an early communication audit technique measured the diffusion of messages through an organization's social network to assess the quality and effectiveness of information flows for coordination and governance (Davis, 1953).

The postwar period saw a general rise in interest in the interdisciplinary study of systems and their characteristics, principally deriving from early twentieth-century advances in the study of biological systems but undoubtedly also influenced by sociological interest in mass movements and their impact in the period leading up to the Second World War.

Elias Canetti's (1962) masterpiece *Crowds and Power* was a response to his experience of fascism in Italy. It is a sophisticated examination of the behavior of a social system as entirely distinct from the individual motivations and behaviors of its constituent parts. Social systems have distinct grammars of behavior that are not simply composites of the behaviors of their members. This was a theme picked up by the anthropologist Mary Douglas (1986) in her book *How Institutions Think*. Social behaviors can have the *appearance* of purpose (e.g., concerted action toward the overthrow of a leader), but they are what economist and complexity theorist Andy Clark (1997) calls *ensemble effects*— distinct effects of a system that cannot be decomposed to the actions or motivations of its components (pp. 103–111).

The scientific study of how systems behave *as systems* underpinned Wiener's work and was represented in a number of other thinkers from diverse disciplines, including Kenneth Boulding, William Ashby, and Talcott Parsons. However, the early enthusiasm for applying insights and methods from mechanical and biological systems to organizations and societies was qualified by Norbert Wiener (1961), who pointed out:

> . . . in the social sciences we have to deal with short statistical runs, [and] nor can we be sure that a considerable part of what we observe is not an artifact of our own creation. An investigation of the stock market is likely to upset the stock market. We are too much in tune with the objects of our investigation to be good probes. In short, whether our investigations in the social sciences be statistical or dynamic—and they should participate in the nature of both—they can never be good to more than a very few decimal places, and, in short, can never furnish us with a quantity of verifiable, significant information which begins to compare with that which we have learned to expect in the natural sciences. We cannot afford to neglect them; neither should we build exaggerated expectations of their possibilities. There is much which we must leave, whether we like it or not, to the un-"scientific" narrative method of the professional historian. (p. 164)

The self-referential elusiveness of "hard-scientific" measurement methods in the field of social systems research prompted a new wave of approaches to measurement and analysis.

Peter Checkland, the British management professor who pioneered the development of *soft systems* theory to characterize the human interactions and motivations surrounding technical systems, observed rather sharply that systems thinkers tended to slip "promiscuously" between using *system* as a precise term for a bounded and measurable entity and as a loose and figurative metaphor for "something complex that has connected parts." He believed that a great deal of the confusion surrounding the design and evaluation of management information systems (MIS) arose from this ambiguity (Checkland, 1999).

The soft systems approach moved the focus *from measurement to representation*, to aid collective sensemaking, problem-solving, and change management. Without such methods, overengineered "systems" designed on a "hard systems" mental model would simply not work when implemented in real human contexts. Checkland and his collaborators employed and developed a number of methods for characterizing the human soft systems surrounding "hard" technical systems. These were methods that were comparable to the two-column method of Argyris and Schon and the narrative methods advocated by Wiener. They included *action research, rich pictures, and activity model building* (Checkland & Poulter, 2007). Dave Snowden's (1999) work on narrative approaches to "organic" knowledge management is a descendant of this work.

The idea of an organization as a system for processing feedback, learning, and sensemaking was also pioneered by Karl Weick, beginning in the late 1960s. Weick's (1969) book *The Social Psychology of Organizing* presents organizations as communication and feedback systems that are dynamic and reflexive. The phenomenon of organizing is an emergent response to informational complexity and ambiguity in the environment (Weick, 1969). The work of organizing is never complete. The central question is: How *responsive* is the organizing activity to emerging needs?

In consequence you could make inferences about an organization's capacity to adapt to (that is, reorganize for) ambiguity and uncertainty in the environment by measuring the interconnectedness of the internal communication relationships (Kreps, 1980). This is an indirect measure but a measure nevertheless, and it prompted fresh interest in novel applications for social network analysis, tracing communication networks as indicators of adaptive (and learning) capacity (Cross & Parker, 2004; Burt, 2005).

Weick would go on to create a self-auditing instrument for developing the characteristics of a high-resilience organization. The audit leads organizations through a self-examination to promote *mindfulness* of the important features necessary for rapid learning across an organization, for sensemaking, and for dealing with uncertainty (Weick & Sutcliffe, 2001, pp. 85–115). In our typology this would be closest to a discovery review audit focused on capabilities or, to the extent that the sensemaking process is wholly owned and self-directed by the decision-makers themselves, a participative goal-setting audit.

*   *   *

Summary

In this chapter we took a historical view of investigation questions pursued in communications research and organization studies since the 1950s. These questions are, still relevant today and can be reframed to help us direct our knowledge audit choices. They also suggest a broad array of audit methods.

Table 6.4
Audit focus: Knowledge management for effects

Sample knowledge audit focus questions	Models of audit	Phenomena to audit	Methods of audit contributed
Do our management information systems present timely, accurate, and pertinent data to assist in leadership decision-making?	Inventory	Knowledge stocks Knowledge flows	MIS design Social network analysis Comms diffusion mapping
How adaptive are our organizational governance processes based on learning and feedback from the environment?	Participative goal setting	Needs and goals	Soft systems methodology Collective sensemaking Goal alignment Narrative methods
Do we practice regular learning cycles at all levels in the organization to ensure continuous improvement and adaptive planning?	Assessment and/or discovery review	KM enablers KM processes KM capabilities	Learning review processes Double-loop learning processes Communications effectiveness checking Collective learning methods Soft systems methodology Self-examination for mindfulness Narrative methods
How good are we at facilitating collective sensemaking and leveraging the diverse insights and knowledge of our people?			
Do we have effective processes for organizational learning, and specifically, how good are we at exploiting double-loop learning to become more effective?	Value: capitalization	Outcomes	Change management Two-column method Situation awareness methods Outcomes measurement
How well are our people and operating units aligned around common goals, policies, and values? Do we have check mechanisms in place to ensure that we maintain common ground and common situation awareness?			
Do we have processes or methods to identify and mitigate distortions and filtering in information flows arising from power relations or trust issues?			
Do we have an accurate understanding of how information actually flows in our organization and where the bottlenecks, blockages, or gaps are?			
Do we have methods for discovering, representing, and sharing the human perceptions, motivators, and drivers surrounding our technical and formal managerial systems?			
How good are we at getting our people to sense-make, solve problems, and learn together across organizational and hierarchical boundaries?			

1. The types of audits we adopt, and the combination of types, depend on what we want to learn, what we want to achieve, the resources available to us, and the level of commitment in our host organization.

2. Which phenomena we are interested in, and why, should flow from the drivers for conducting the audit in the first place.

3. An understanding of our drivers and motivations can be framed into a series of audit focus questions, and this will help us frame our audit-scoping choices, as well as our supporting methods.

7 Beginnings and Improvisations: Discovery Review, Inventory, and Participative Goal-Setting Audits

The law of chaos is the law of ideas,
Of improvisations, and seasons of belief.
—Stevens (1942, p. 134)

Our review of communications research from the 1950s onward reveals a complex set of strands awash with emerging measurement, representational, and analytical techniques. While the *soft systems* approach urged caution on exact translation of measurement methods from "hard" to "soft" systems, there was at the same time a confidence in the value of measurement and analytical methods for modeling, understanding, and influencing the behavior of human communication systems. The social sciences in general were under pressure to establish measurement techniques on a par with the natural sciences.

And yet when the first communication audits began to emerge, they were driven by a sense of curiosity, improvisation, and invention more than by the spirit of scientific measurement. Communication auditors, with rare exceptions, did not heavily exploit the range of technical methods being invented by their colleagues in communications research. It was only later that methodological sophistication began to develop. This methodological naïveté carried over into information and knowledge auditing.

In this chapter I will cover the earliest forms of knowledge-related audit that appeared—the discovery review audit, the inventory audit, and the participative goal-setting audit. I will trace the history of these three types of audits through communication audits and into information audits and knowledge audits, and consider the drivers behind the adoption and use of these forms of audit.

Emergence of the Communication Audit as an Opinion-Based Approach

Given the wide array of methods available in the broader communications research field, it has always been a mystery to me why, when seeking reliable, actionable insights about and from a complex and multidimensional environment, the staple instruments in the information and knowledge auditor's tool kit are survey questionnaires and their face-to-face equivalents, structured interviews (cf. Webb, 1998, pp. 21–23; Liebowitz et al., 2000, pp. 5–6; Hylton, 2004; Dube, 2011, p. 9; Lambe, 2017, p. 12). This is despite the shortcomings of these particular instruments (e.g., limited perspectives, risk of subjectivity and bias) and despite an early lead on the need for multiple methods from knowledge management (KM) pioneers such as Karl Wiig (1995, pp. 97–239).

As I argued in chapter 4, if knowledge auditing is meant to render reliable and useful insights, we need multimethod approaches, more sophisticated methods, and ways of controlling for bias. We saw this in Charles Connaghan's sawmill study in chapter 1.

Despite this, in our global survey of knowledge audit practices, even among experienced practitioners, we found that interviews were more likely to be used than any other method (Lambe, 2017). It was encouraging that interviews were relatively frequently being used in combination with workshops (47 percent of responses). In workshops, at least, collective sensemaking and self-representation can moderate the bias from individual opinions. However, interviews in combination with surveys were still quite common (representing 38 percent of responses). This combination is problematic if there are no additional methods being used to control for undue bias or purely individualistic perspectives, or to resolve disagreements.

This narrowness of practice seems characteristic of KM at large. Alexander Serenko (2021, p. 1905) found that KM research in general relies heavily on case studies, surveys, and interviews, with little recourse to a broader palette of methods such as ethnography, action research, or content/data analysis.

We can already see from our review of the audit methodologies deriving from communications research that a very rich range of methods is—in principle—available.

In other audit traditions, particularly those stemming from the industrial relations and organization effectiveness audit tradition, opinion-gathering methods (such as interviews and surveys) were used as *adjuncts to an evidence-based analysis* of documented fact, *but they were not used as the principal instrument of choice*. As we saw in chapter 4, this was the case in the Hawthorne Studies at Western Electric and in the longitudinal Triple Audit studies at the University of Minnesota.

By contrast, the communication audit, when it began, had an unusual dependence on opinion-based methods and used a limited range of methods. The origins of the communication audit may offer some explanation of how this unusual dependency came about and why it seems to have carried over into information and knowledge audits. Two factors seem to have been at play here:

- First, the pioneers of communication audits were field practitioners who seemed largely unaware of, and uninterested in, the range of methods being developed within the rapidly developing field of communications research—a dichotomy between research and practice that persists in KM today.
- Second, initial practice seems to have been patterned on the limited approaches of early pioneers.

When we begin a new endeavor and have no sense of history, everything is an improvisation. We take whatever methods are at hand, and those improvisations, however imperfect, can act as a pattern for the practices that follow. We see this time and again in the development of communications, information, and knowledge audits.

In 1952 the US-based National Society of Professional Engineers (NSPE) began a series of industry-wide research studies on topics of interest to its membership base. Over the next thirty years or so, these studies would cover topics like training and education, pension plans, unionization, salary scales, and professional ethics.

The NSPE early research typically took a two-pronged approach. The first was a survey of members asking a series of questions, and the second involved convening an expert panel. A variation of this approach (engaging with expert panels iteratively to make sense of a complex domain) eventually emerged in the Delphi method in the late 1950s and early 1960s (Linstone & Turoff, 1975, pp. 10–11).

In 1952 the first topic selected to launch the program (reflecting a major concern of the day) was "How to Improve Engineering-Management Communications" (NSPE, 1952). The survey consisted of a series of sixteen questions on issues such as whether members were involved in management planning, whether they felt informed about long-range plans, how they felt about the adequacy of communication channels, the effectiveness of meetings, and so on.

As a mechanism for gaining insights from a wide membership base, the survey method made sense. The report's authors note that the survey findings broadly agreed with the views of their expert panel. In their enthusiasm the authors recommended that similar surveys be conducted by organizations wishing to improve their communications systems, or failing that, they might simply take the findings of the research report and act on those.

However, conducting a survey across a broad population is quite different from conducting a survey among closed, possibly partisan groups in the same organization, especially where power relationships between groups might be an issue of concern (Roethlisberger & Dickson, 1943, p. 292; Odiorne, 1954, p. 237). In the latter case, the potential for undue bias is much stronger.

But the die was cast. Even the doubters adopted the survey method, and only where they were especially conscientious did they attempt to control for possible bias.

Surveys have other problems, especially if you want to get at an understanding of the organization as a complex, multidimensional system. Allen Barton (1968) complained that

> ... the survey is a sociological meatgrinder, tearing the individual from his social context and guaranteeing that nobody in the study interacts with anyone else in it. It is a little like a biologist putting his experimental animals through a hamburger machine and looking at every hundredth cell through a microscope; anatomy and physiology get lost, structure and function disappear, and one is left with cell biology. (p. 1)

To be fair, Barton was not complaining about the problem of controlling for bias in surveys—he was thinking about general population surveys, where sampling was supposed to take care of bias. His issue was the abstraction of individual responses from their social context. Without an understanding of social context and how social affiliations and social structures help form and reinforce our values, attitudes and behaviors, survey responses give a radically sparse set of data. Indeed, random sampling does not just protect against bias, it also systematically removes any insight that might emerge from an understanding of the context from which the responses come. This is the same objection we had to "averaged-out" characterizations of KM capabilities.

The NSPE report is useful, as far as it goes. It illustrates the concerns about employee-management relations that we see in Connaghan's research almost a decade later, but unlike Connaghan's study, and possibly because it was an industry-wide survey, it clearly connects the issues of industrial relations with morale and organization effectiveness.

It is, however, the first-known explicit instance of the communication audit, and it provided a model for its successors. Here are some of its key insights:

> Managements which wish to check the effectiveness of their programs and the level of understanding of their engineers should conduct an audit. (NSPE, 1952, p. 43)

> Answers to these questions, and others in a like vein, will give management a useful appraisal of the state of morale of its engineers and the suitability of its communications system. The statistical findings of the audit will disclose the major gaps in communication and the comments and suggestions of individuals may give management an entirely new outlook on its relations with its professional employees. (NSPE, 1952, p. 38)

> This interest of management is not entirely altruistic. In most cases it is a well conceived plan to improve company operations by creating a climate in which management's aims will be pursued vigorously by engineers who understand those aims and identify themselves closely with management and successful company operation. (NSPE, 1952, p. 35)

To summarize, the NSPE report is interesting in three respects:

- For the connections it draws between industrial relations, morale, and organization effectiveness
- For modeling the use of the survey format as the primary model for conducting an audit of communications
- For the implicit (not fully developed) idea of a "communications system" that would later lead to analyses of communication flows and tests of completeness and accuracy of information transmission

The supposed originator of the communication audit as a distinct activity is George Odiorne, a professor at Rutgers University, who wrote the first-known journal article on the communication audit in 1954. But Odiorne (1954) took the idea—and the survey-based approach—from the NSPE study, largely unaltered.

When communication audits took off in the 1960s, Odiorne would become the standard reference in the myth of origins for the communication audit. Despite his own misgivings about the subjectivity of the survey method when applied in the closed population of a single organization, he adopted it wholesale from the NSPE precedent, and his approach then provided the model for the large-scale communication audits that developed in the 1960s and 1970s.

In his own first audit, Odiorne investigated an engineering company that had undergone rapid growth in the postwar years. There were known problems in that company around failures of coordination, lack of mutual understanding and cooperation among key groups, and high turnover of staff. He, and the company's management, felt that it might be helpful to conduct a "careful analysis of communication, both vertical and horizontal," and the NSPE report looked like a helpful starting point (Odiorne 1954, p. 236). At the very least, it could perform a useful reference function.

Odiorne (1954, p. 237) stipulated that he was interested in two things: (a) employee views of the effectiveness of the communications and (b) a test of whether information from upper echelons had reached lower echelons and gained acceptance, and whether or not it got there through formal communication channels.

In the event, his use of the survey method really only tested his first concern. It would take several years before information-flow-mapping methodologies would be available to support his second proposed test. Over time the communication audit and its successors did introduce additional audit methods, but the dominant role of the opinion-based approach was set.

Discovery Review Audits

As we have seen, the first communication audits were essentially improvisations, in which researchers and auditors had questions of concern but no real sense of the wide array of methodological resources available to them. They picked up methods that were readily at hand or became visible to them through their practice or the background disciplines they were framed in.

If you have broad questions or concerns about a complex environment that you have little insight into and you are not quite sure how to go about investigating it, then your model of audit, almost by definition, is going to be discovery review. You try to figure out what is going on in your area of concern and match it to organizational needs. So it should not be surprising that this was the earliest model deployed in the communication audits of the 1950s.

While there had been earlier attempts to measure discrete aspects of organizational communications (e.g., Bavelas, 1950; Jacobson & Seashore, 1951; Leavitt, 1951), the 1952 NSPE study was the first comprehensive communication audit. It was constructed as an exploratory study based on no known standards or precedent but was intended to come through exploration and dialogue to an internally generated consensus on what "improvement" might look like (NSPE, 1952).

The discovery review model also appeared among the earliest information audits. In 1979, Ann Quinn listed one of the goals of an information audit as determining "whether the company's system for supplying information reflects corporate goals and serves real needs" (1979, p. 18). While her language is, on the surface, very assessment oriented, the reference points (corporate goals and user needs) are highly contextual to the organization; that is, they are endogenously, not exogenously, generated, as in a pure assessment audit. And the comparison against high-level goals and needs happens after the insights from the audit have been collected.

This was very likely also influenced by the prevailing thinking on operational auditing in the late 1970s and early 1980s, which focused on evaluating whether the audited system was aligned with the purpose and goals of the organization and whether the information systems of the organization supported those goals (Gruber, 1983, pp. 39–41).

The clearest early reference to a discovery review audit model in knowledge management appeared in 1997 in the inaugural issue of the *Journal of Knowledge Management*. This was a case study of a KM implementation in a business-consulting unit of the UK's Royal Mail (Baker et al., 1997, pp. 67–68).

A knowledge audit was used to discover what knowledge stocks existed in the business (inventory audit) and what knowledge practices existed in relation to key processes, including an exploration of the cultural inhibitors to the adoption of new information technology. The findings were then used to build out a KM framework, covering people, process, and technology as complementary mechanisms, with communications processes figuring large.

This is a classic form of discovery review, where the investigation is not predetermined and where the findings can inform the design of the next stage. In fact, this is one of the main advantages of the discovery review audit when dealing with an environment that you do not understand well. Depending upon what you discover along the way, you can adapt your approach and add new investigation activities to find out more about, clarify, or validate the insights.

Inventory Audits

Inventory audits have a much more complex history than discovery review audits. They also tended to appear relatively quickly in the communication, information, and knowledge audit literature. This makes a lot of sense. If you are undertaking an exploratory discovery review audit, it makes sense to try to understand what you are dealing with through inventories and catalogs, whether they are of the instruments and channels by which communications are delivered, or the knowledge and information resources you are interested in.

For example, George Haas and Hermine Zagat (1957) surveyed the typical communication instruments relating to labor relations, including labor relations policies, contract clause books, union contracts, strike manuals, records of grievances, employee magazines, special bulletins, and publicity releases. This kind of inventory served as a benchmarking precedent for subsequent communication audits and was used to measure the range of communication channels being actively used across a variety of organizations.

Inventory audits were used as a prelude to a discovery review audit. In a particularly innovative 1953 communication audit study, Keith Davis of Indiana University used the identification of information items as a first step in tracing the information and knowledge flows through an organization.

Each information item, along with its medium of transmission, was coded into a short questionnaire, which was then administered to all employees to record whether they had received it and when and how they had received it. This enabled researchers to trace the speed and effectiveness of information transfer through the organization and then make inferences on factors impeding information flows and on interventions to improve them (Davis, 1953).

This methodology, termed ECCO analysis (episodic communication channels in organizations) was to become a relatively common component in communication audits, and it prefigures the development of knowledge-flow maps. Insights from the ECCO analysis could then be incorporated into the exploratory phase of the discovery review audit.

When the information audit emerged in the 1970s, it very quickly took on the characteristics of an inventory audit. It had its own roots, independent of the communication audit. Although taking stock of communications channels had become a standard component of communication audits by the 1970s, information auditors did not become widely aware of their communication audit predecessors until the 1990s, when scholars started to trace the development of their discipline. And while communication auditors were more interested in inventorying communication *channels* (i.e., a flow perspective), information auditors were, initially, at least, more interested in inventorying information *resources* (i.e., a stocks perspective).

It is likely that the inventory focus within information auditing emerged independently and was influenced by a long tradition of inventorying records as part of the discipline of records management and its predecessor, archives administration. The concerns and drivers behind archives and records management would also shape the ways in which information auditing would develop. The methods and perspectives at hand were the ones most easily adopted.

Inventorying in archives administration was initially driven by the need to provide access to the growing volume of records to be administered. As early as 1915, the public archives of Iowa were boasting of their method for inventorying and classifying some seven hundred thousand documents in a systematic fashion: "One of the main objects aimed at in the classification of the documents is the reduction to the minimum of the time and labor required to find a certain document, by any one seeking information" (Stiles, 1915, p. 15).

By the late 1940s, the burden of managing volume had shifted from people who managed collections of *historical* records (archives) to people who were managing *current* records, especially in government agencies and very large corporations such as DuPont, Standard Oil, and Westinghouse Electric. The administrative burden added the new consideration of cost control—*what is the cost versus the benefit of enabling access to current records to support effective decision-making and coordination*?

In short, the modern discipline of records management was initially shaped by information management problems. There were two main concerns:

• Maintaining speedy access to records for operational purposes
• Controlling the cost of storage and administration of records

Some practices and methods were preserved; others were new. Inventory audits were an old practice, repurposed to new needs.

Writing for *The American Archivist* in 1949, Emmett Leahy of the National Records Management Council spelled out three strands of expertise required in "modern" records management (Leahy, 1949, p. 232):

1. Management's engineering in the mechanization, specialization, and duplication of record making and record keeping

2. The archivist's modern science in selective records preservation, planning, equipping, and administering large-scale and specialized facilities for the maintenance of and access to records and the development of new techniques in finding media

3. The historian's science in organizing, evaluating, and interpreting recorded experience

There is a discernible shift here. Records inventories were no longer simply in the service of accessibility. They were about discriminating records of value from those that could safely be discarded. There was a foretaste of early knowledge management here too. As Leahy (1949) put it, "the experience contained in records must be drawn upon and put to work" (p. 232).

As it eventually transpired, the knowledge reuse element in Leahy's early take on records management eventually took a back seat to the managerial focus on accessibility, efficiency, and cost control.

When the first annual conference on records management was held in New York in 1954, knowledge reuse and corporate memory were still explicitly part of the new records management agenda. In that conference Robert Shiff's (1955a, 1955b) "records management credo" proclaimed a dual emphasis on "scientific controls on record making and record keeping with a very positive policy of ensuring the preservation of recorded experience." Yet already Leahy's active "putting to work" of recorded experience had begun to fall back into the historian's more passive "preservation of recorded experience."

Knowledge was swiftly deprecated further. Within industry, the ideals of efficiency and streamlining in scientific management had begun to be extended to clerical (i.e., information) work (Stopford, 1954), and by the 1960s, the general stock in trade of the records manager had stabilized into a core set of administrative disciplines:

- Inventory and appraisal (Blegen, 1965)
- Scheduling (Dockens, 1968)
- Identification of vital records (Derry, 1967; Hambelton, 1969)
- Disaster planning (Shiff, 1965)
- Storage (Kish & Morris, 1966; Rye, 1967; Tarrant, 1969).

When James Leonard (1971, pp. 79–81) presented his master of business administration dissertation to the Fairleigh Dickinson Graduate School of Business on the benefits of records management, the dominant narrative was on savings and cost control.

These developments meant that when information audits began to emerge in the mid-1970s, they had a strong and confident precedent in the inventory-based procedures of records management.

The orientation of information managers was more complex than that of records managers: where records managers were artifact oriented (the records in their care), information managers began to focus on the systems and flows of information to decision-makers or on the curation of collections of information in corporate libraries. There is an intrinsic tension here between methods that are meant to inventory artifacts (records or information items) and methods that are meant to inventory flows (information flows to decision-makers). This tension was not always clearly identified (as it was not in knowledge management later on).

Despite this difference, records managers and information managers were really looking at the same landscape through different lenses. Arguably, in fact, the growth of information management in the 1970s and 1980s was a reaction to the failure of records management to live up to its initial promise of enabling management information flows, after the energies of the profession had become preoccupied by the systematic proceduralization of records administration.

Whatever the case, the newly emerging information management discipline in the mid-1970s found convenient models of operation and self-justification at hand in its records management older cousin. In one of the earliest articles about the information audit, Riley (1976) focused on an audit as an aid to the cost-benefit analysis of information products and services, and Quinn (1979) combined an inventory approach with a cost-benefit analysis. A narrative that had formed in the records management discipline (inventory + cost benefit analysis) carried over into the information management discipline.

This mental model would later contaminate information resource management with an operationally focused cost accounting perspective, and it would inhibit the recognition of information management and knowledge management as strategic disciplines.

Sometimes the inventory approach would appear as a negative audit—that is, as an audit of needs and gaps. In 1992 a newly reorganized Regional Health Authority belonging to the UK's National Health Service (NHS) conducted an information management review. It first reviewed its new corporate objectives and determined what information would be required to meet them. Then it conducted an inventory audit (via questionnaire) to find out whether the information existed and how it was currently used. This flipped the typical sequence of inventory audits preceding discovery review audits and had the benefit of focusing inventorying effort on what was believed to be strategically important. However, on the downside, it would not discover any existing resources in the organization that the original team had not anticipated as important (Booth & Haines, 1993).

The inventory audit model also emerged early on in the history of knowledge audits. In 1988 Maris Martinsons published a paper on developing tenable technology strategies, in which knowledge audits were a means of determining which knowledge resources already existed to support key activities. These audits were meant to be precursors to the development of a business strategy, but were essentially descriptive exercises that did not in themselves embed prescriptive recommendations (Martinsons, 1988).

The concept of the knowledge audit as a discovery review exercise seems at the very beginning to have evolved independently of the information and records management tradition. However, the associations with information audits were picked up quite early on, and with them came the practice of inventorying. Jean Graef (1998) referenced both information and knowledge audits in the same article but did not discuss their differences. The terms were used interchangeably.

The prior practice of information auditing introduced the possibility of assimilating the information-focused inventory audit into knowledge management. There was more enthusiasm than clarity about this.

By 2000, as the hype around KM began to grow, Susan Henczel (2000), who had written widely on information auditing, was touting the information audit as a step toward knowledge management and a potential vehicle for career progression by special librarians and information managers.

Henczel (2000) described a situation "where many information units are being closed or downsized and organizations are encouraging information users to acquire, control and manage their own resources that support knowledge creation and development" (p. 210). There was a slightly opportunistic flavor to the repurposing of information management practices to knowledge management, and Henczel's distinction between an information audit and a knowledge audit was not entirely clear.

Influenced by her background in information auditing, Henczel's (2000) initial definition of a knowledge audit still had a distinctly inventory-oriented flavor. "A knowledge audit is conducted to identify an organization's knowledge assets, how they are produced and by whom" (p. 215).

She attempted to preserve intact the information audit methodology and yet at the same time make sense of the differences between an information audit and a knowledge audit, but her narrative is not entirely consistent. Henczel's (2000) disproportionately brief description of the knowledge audit at the end of her paper focuses more on the knowledge audit as a needs analysis following on from an inventory—that is, as a discovery review audit:

> A knowledge audit has two main objectives, with the first being to identify the "people" issues that impact on knowledge creation, transfer and sharing. These include the communication issues that enable or prevent knowledge transfer, and the cultural and political issues that impact on the success of knowledge management strategies. The second objective of a knowledge audit is to identify which knowledge can be captured, where it is needed and can be reused, and to determine the most efficient and effective methods to store, facilitate access to and transfer of the knowledge. (p. 225)

It sounds as if the information audit provides the inventory, and the knowledge audit provides the discovery review. Others in the library and information science space agreed that the information audit provides the basis upon which to conduct a knowledge audit (Webb, 2003, p. 252). However, in this period the clarity and specificity about what an information audit was, contrasted sharply with a lack of specificity about knowledge audits. The information audit's operating model was still clearly an alien import not yet organically connected to other KM practices.

By the late 2000s, practitioners and researchers were attempting to make sense of the differing audit models and methods available but, in doing so, sometimes papered over the evident fault lines in approaches, originating disciplines, operating models, and methods deployed. Ambiguity proliferated.

For example, one group of researchers, attempting to resolve the apparent overlaps between the two competing disciplines of information and knowledge management, made a distinction based on types of knowledge resource. They claimed that a knowledge audit is focused on tacit knowledge, while an information audit is focused on explicit knowledge (Gourova et al., 2009, p. 607; cf. Schopflin & Walsh, 2019, pp. 101–103).

This was a convenient distinction that allowed for an inventory approach to both (as well as the retention of an information audit methodology as a baseline), but the methodological implications were not clearly explained. Clearly, they should be. We know that the more explicit and tacit forms of knowledge are used in tight concert within the conduct of work, so it seems odd to have different audit methodologies for each. If they are entangled, then we need ways of representing that entanglement. This is, admittedly, a challenge. Inventorying the explicit and visible is quite a different challenge from inventorying the tacit and hard to observe, as we will see in chapter 15.

There was also inconsistency over the sequencing of the two audits. Inventory audits, as we have seen, often preceded other kinds of audits. However, Buchanan and Gibb (2008, p. 158) reported on a case in which a knowledge audit conducted on a discovery review model identified strategic issues with a particular product and service innovation process and then pinpointed a subsequent need for an information audit using an inventory approach, and which would be focused on that process. Here we see another reversal of the normal use of an inventory audit as a precursor to another type of audit and the Henczel/Webb model of an information audit as a precursor to a knowledge audit.

Notwithstanding these attempts to give authoritative, seamless, and coherent accounts of knowledge audits in the literature, the KM field continued to present a confused picture of what knowledge audits actually meant and how they related to information audits. Anna Ujwary-Gil (2020, pp. 95–102) gives a comprehensive account of the varying interpretations.

Rather than consolidating around a common framework, meanings continued to proliferate. For example, subsidiary types of "knowledge audits" emerged in the cognitive psychology and educational fields independently of mainstream knowledge management in the 1990s. Both of them used the operating model of the inventory audit. Unlike mainstream KM, however, which focused on organizational knowledge audits, this parallel tradition focused on *personal knowledge audits*.

In the mid-1990s cognitive psychologist Gary Klein and colleagues developed a methodology for a *knowledge audit interview*, which was designed to identify elements of expertise held by deeply experienced people (Klein, 1995; Hutton & Militello, 1996). This methodology was later extended to team knowledge audits designed "to elicit aspects of team members' knowledge and skill regarding a specific task or set of tasks" (Crandall et al., 2006, p. 90).

At the same time, from about 1998 onward the term *subject knowledge audits* was regularly used in teacher training to describe a method for assessing the subject knowledge of trainee teachers against the required standards (e.g., Rowland et al., 1998). In the health-care field, the term *knowledge audit* was—and is still—sometimes used to assess the differences between the pre- and posttraining knowledge and skill levels of health-care staff (e.g., Wiener & Mulvaney, 2008).

A third outlier inventory audit type is the *cultural knowledge audit* model proposed by Caroline Kamau in 2009. Kamau was investigating the perceived influence of individuals in organizations and the role of *impression management*—the process of managing how one is perceived by colleagues. She developed a knowledge audit model founded on the ability to detect deficits in cultural knowledge—that is, when an individual detects that they are not giving the impressions they desire. The "audit" helps them identify the cultural knowledge they need to acquire in order to manage their impressions better. This model was extended to cross-cultural impression management in business (Kamau, 2009; Spong & Kamau, 2012).

We have classed this as an inventory audit type, although it is a highly unusual one, and is in some respects closer to the distant ancestor of knowledge audits, the communication audit. In fact, like the NHS case we mentioned earlier, it is founded upon a *negative* inventory—an inventory of *knowledge deficits* or *gaps*, followed by a process to mitigate the gaps and better manage the impressions. Although it is a very specialized sense of audit and appears to have been developed without reference to other knowledge audit models, it does contribute some insight into the potential for the inventory audit as an instrument not merely to identify resources that exist, but also to identify deficits or gaps that need to be made up.

Inventory audits have a long and complex history in both research and practice. They are very common in the information and records management literature but do not always appear consistently in the communication audit and knowledge audit literature. They are frequently used as a precursor to another type of audit, the discovery review audit or the assessment audit, but as we have seen, sometimes the sequence can be reversed, and an inventory audit can follow another type of audit, where the inventory is focused on areas of concern.

Sometimes, as in information management, inventory audits follow strict procedural guidelines and use consistent methods inherited from records management. In other cases, especially in KM, the audit methods can vary widely based on the target knowledge and the scope and objectives of the audit. While inventory audits are usually directed at organizations or groups, they can also be applied to individuals and teams (using different techniques), and they can be utilized to identify gaps or deficits, as well as resources in use.

Participative Goal-Setting Audits

Participative goal-setting audits are in some respects similar to discovery review audits. The audit model is initially open-ended and is geared toward discovery and learning. It concludes with some recommendations and actions based on what is learned from the audit. The crucial difference between the two is that in a participatory audit the recipients of the intended change are actively directing the audit, discovery process, and follow-through decisions, whereas in discovery review they follow an investigation path set by an auditor or audit team, and a management team then considers the recommendations for action.

The participative goal-setting audit model emerged very early in the history of knowledge audit references. Joseph Anderson's (1989) piece on innovation and productivity titled "Technology and Mindset: A Model for Generating New Product and Service

Ideas" describes a knowledge audit as a process to help executives assess the knowledge required to meet new opportunities in the market. The model he proposes for management teams is an iterative cycle between opportunity analysis and capability analysis. It clearly directs the formulation of a new business strategy and the acquisition of knowledge to meet that strategy (Anderson, 1989, p. 114).

We see similar ideas a few years later in the work of Karl-Erik Sveiby, focused on the monitoring and measurement of intangible assets. Although Sveiby did not use the term *knowledge audit* until 2001, his intangible assets monitor, first developed in 1996, looks at first glance like a simple knowledge assets inventory. His goal was precisely to enable the participative goal-setting of managers by making "the invisible visible . . . The purpose is to be practical and to 'open a few windows' so managers can start experimenting" (Sveiby, 2001; cf. Sveiby 1998).

In this sense, his intangible assets monitor was an inventory audit, which in turn supported a participative goal-setting audit in which various measures could be explored and experimented on, with the ultimate goal of improving the firm's performance.

Sveiby himself was responding to the challenge laid down in 1980 by the Japanese author Hiroyuki Itami (1987) on how best to help a firm's leadership to mobilize its "invisible" knowledge-based assets.

Sveiby came to believe that his methodology extended beyond enabling management control in the "tight" audit sense. In fact, he believed that using measurement for control opened up the risk of manipulation of the measures in order to appear to have achieved management objectives. By 2001 he was explicitly describing his measurement methodology not as a mechanism for control but as an enabler of organizational learning, a theme that we have already seen emerging in the communications research tradition:

> So entrenched are the traditional measuring paradigms that executives and researchers have not even started to explore the most interesting reason for measuring intangibles; the learning motive. Measuring can be used to uncover costs or to explore value creation opportunities otherwise hidden in the traditional accounts. What is the trend of cost of staff turnover? What is the value of the learning that takes place when staff interact with customers? What is the value creation opportunity lost in having inadequate processes? The learning motive promises the highest long-term benefits. First; the learning motive offers the best way around the manipulation issue. If the purpose is learning, not control or reward, the employees and managers can relax. Second, a learning purpose allows more creativity in the design of metrics, a more process-oriented bottom-up approach and less of top-down commands. (Sveiby & Armstrong, 2004; cf. Sveiby, 2010)

So here, although Sveiby did not like the connotations of the term *audit*, we have an example of an inventory audit, enabling participative goal setting and ultimately organizational learning. Without explicitly describing knowledge audits, Sveiby's intellectual development neatly portrays how the different audit types can be combined to build different layers of outcome: an accurate inventory, participative decision-making to improve organizational performance, and, finally, organizational learning based on analysis of the correlation of intangible asset measures and market outcomes (Sveiby & Armstrong, 2004).

There was a wider management studies backdrop to this shift toward greater owner-ship of the self-review, learning, and goal-setting process.

Up to the 1970s, corporate planning had been seen as the domain of "experts" such as internal corporate-planning departments, typically staffed by economists and business school graduates, and often informed by management consultants who per-formed analysis and advisory services. The economic downturn of the 1970s exposed the weakness of this functional specialization—it had separated the planners who drove strategic decision-making from a close apprehension and intimate knowledge of the organization's own inner workings and capabilities (Mintzberg, 1994; Stacey & Mowles, 2016, pp. 11–12).

In 1982, Richard Pascale and Anthony Athos published their popular book *The Art of Japanese Management*, pointing to the performance differences between Japanese companies that promoted dialogue and discussion as part of a more inclusive decision -making process, and American companies that took a hierarchical, functionally sepa-rate, and expertise-driven approach (Pascale and Athos 1982).

In the same period, organizational theorists were developing a body of theory that supported more participatory approaches. In chapter 6 we described an emerging body of theory, pioneered by Norbert Wiener and later enlarged upon by Karl Weick, around organizations as information-processing systems, where collective sensemaking mecha-nisms could differentiate organizations that were resilient and adaptive from organiza-tions that were not. A growing number of management thinkers started to promote the idea of sensemaking and decision-making through collective sensemaking and dialogue, as distinct from expert-driven recommendations driven by rational methods and tools.

The physicist David Bohm's work from the mid-1980s onwards on the practice of dialogue as a means to navigate through differences and reach a common understanding began to be incorporated into organizational theory (Bohm & Peat, 1987, chap. 6; Bohm, 1996; Isaacs, 1999, chap. 15; Osono, 2004). Dave Snowden (2000b), who pioneered par-ticipatory approaches in KM, called for a new approach to crafting organizational change interventions: "We need to shift from experts who analyze and interpret, to facilitators who through active discourse enable emergence of new understanding and perspective" (p. 63).

Participatory approaches are not without their difficulties. Max Boisot (1987, pp. 82–85) discussed the delicate trade-offs between the theory of knowledge codification and diffusion, and the technical challenge of how to extend organizational problem-solving activities to wider and more diverse audiences. Otto Scharmer (2009, chap. 17) traced the emotional challenges in navigating through the stages of a difficult conversation, which is what complex problem-solving requires, through the "trench warfare" of strong differences, to mutual understanding and appreciation, to co-creation of meaning.

INSEAD professors W. Chan Kim and Renée Mauborgne (2015) graphically describe the emotional and political challenges, as well as the rewards, of engaging in a participatory approach to strategic decision-making using a framework they call a *strategy canvas*. At a financial services group they worked with, there were differences in opinion on the current state of play, vested interests to be defended, and unquestioned assumptions about what was going on in different parts of the group. As a result, the corporate strategy was ill-defined and inconsistently understood, and there was no coherent mechanism for shaping and defining it.

> It was a painful experience. Both groups had heated debates about what constituted a competitive factor and what the factors were. Different factors were important, it seemed, in different regions. . . . Many people had pet ideas of which they were the sole champions. The [strategy canvas] pictures also highlighted contradictions. . . . Faced with direct evidence of the company's shortcomings, EFS' executives could not defend what they [themselves] had shown to be a weak, unoriginal, and poorly communicated strategy. Trying to draw the strategy canvases [together] had made a stronger case for change than any argument based on numbers and words could have done. This created a strong desire in top management to seriously rethink the company's current strategy. (pp. 87–89)

Case Study: The Asian Development Bank—Moving from Centralized KM Planning to Participatory Planning

In 2020 the Asian Development Bank (ADB) had almost fifteen years of structured KM initiatives under its belt, with diagnosis and planning driven by a centralized internal KM team. And yet the results of an external review of the bank had revealed that these efforts had failed to make much of a dent in the institution's operating culture, habits, and framing of business goals in relation to KM. So the team deliberately switched to a more participatory approach in the way that KM programs and plans were formulated. It was transformative.

The ADB's 2021–2025 Knowledge Management Action Plan (KMAP) was designed around an intensive consultation and negotiation process across the bank using a theory of change approach and deliberately bringing divergent opinions together. It established a wide network of "KM focals" across the departments who were responsible for implementation, and it began to support a series of local KM interventions under the broad framework provided by the plan.

The inclusiveness of the participatory approach means that the KMAP works at two important levels: it addresses ADB's strategic needs and goals while demonstrating quick, visible results of how KM can improve business processes and outcomes on the ground. KM is not a "separate" initiative. It is structurally integrated into bigger bank-wide reforms such as the Culture Change Initiative, Resident Mission Review, Organizational Review, and Digital Agenda. KM is not competing for attention with other change initiatives; it is supporting them. This has created wide support across the bank and reduced resistance. The process has helped to manage the emotional challenges of moving the bank from a focus on disbursements to a focus on development impact, in line with the corporate strategy 2030.

The switch to a participatory approach certainly brought with it a slower, more complex process and sometimes challenging engagements, but the team immediately began to report increased energy, ownership, and change (Roth & Carangal San Jose, 2021; ADB, 2021).

That participatory approaches can be painful to navigate is probably why they are often avoided. But avoidance creates insuperable barriers to real change. Chris Argyris cites the case of Royal Dutch Shell, which had a culture of maintaining a "counterfeit" consensus around a conceptual vision composed of motherhood business language ("achieving breakthrough performance," "encouraging ownership of business performance," "being tough on meeting performance objectives") while avoiding any real dialogue about tough business issues and the political blockers to change that needed to be addressed (Argyris, 2010, pp. 125–150). As one respondent said:

> Shell culture is brilliant at not actually ever having confrontation about anything. We arrive at consensus through a very complicated process. I believe very strongly that in the end, the old empire we ended up with was a dishonest culture. People were not saying what they really felt on a really massive scale. (Argyris, 2010, p. 131)

In such cultures, participatory approaches seem just too challenging and difficult for the participants to face up to, especially if there are deep-seated structural and cultural issues in place. Sometimes there is a culture of structural conflict avoidance in place that is so deep that the avoidance strategies are not even recognized as such.

Case Study: When a Culture of Control Produces Avoidance and Unresolved Conflict
Philippe Baumard described how Bank Indosuez sought to obtain structured finance expertise by acquiring a specialist team from the Drexel-Lambert Company in 1989. The working cultures of the two companies were very different, and the "Drexelites" isolated themselves in a specialist unit, falling back on the supposedly idiosyncratic tacitness of their knowledge as a way of avoiding the burden and conflicts involved in trying to support the institutionalization of that knowledge into the larger Indosuez group.

But the internalization of Drexel-Lambert's specialist knowledge had been Indosuez's motivation for the acquisition. The Drexelites, on the other hand, just wanted to do their stuff and not worry about the "how" or about teaching others "how." They knew they were special, and they demanded special treatment, and Indosuez, while making some attempts to assert stronger supervision and control, soon backed off because the unit was very profitable. In the midst of the initial tussles, some Drexelites had resigned, and others had threatened to resign.

So they got their special treatment and successfully resisted managerial oversight and control while organizational charts were adjusted to suggest a cosmetic form of control that did not actually exist.

The inability to work through that goal-conflict together resulted in relative autonomy for the surviving Drexelites, but this autonomy became difficult for the bank to manage later in the 1990s when the markets it was working in became extremely volatile (Baumard, 1999, chap. 7, pp. 220–221). Disaster ensued.

The bank's culture of control meant that serious attempts at participatory problem-solving within a recalcitrant culture would never be on the table, and as a consequence goal conflicts remained unaddressed.

Sometimes it takes a real crisis in performance, as well as not a little bravery, to engage in a participatory approach to solving problems that exist but are difficult to acknowledge. Here is an example.

Case Study: Getting beyond Us and Them

Some years ago I was asked to help design and facilitate a culture audit and change process for the country office of a global nonprofit. There had been a complete breakdown in trust and cooperation between the local operational staff and the leadership team, who were mostly expatriates on two- to four-year contracts. Virtually nothing could get done in the office. The country director felt that the local staff were entrenched in "old" ways of working that were inappropriate for the changing needs of clients and stakeholders. They resisted any attempt at improvement. Morale and trust were low on all sides.

The leadership team was fairly new, with no track record in that country, and they could not understand why they were so mistrusted, sometimes to the point of insubordination. Basic operational problems were left unaddressed—it was safer to avoid conflict than to try and force things through. It was clear that the local staff were just waiting the leadership team out until they left for their next posting. The director of the country office learned anecdotally that this had been the experience of previous management teams.

I was asked to help because of my previous work with the same organization in other countries and because of the techniques we used in knowledge auditing for representing and understanding organizational culture. The director of the country office felt that this was a cultural problem on the part of the local staff, so maybe a culture audit would help to identify root causes of the problem and potential levers for change. I suggested a dialogue-based approach because I felt that (a) there were clearly things that the leadership team were not seeing in the situation that a dialogue-based approach might reveal, and (b) there was a serious performance problem that would require a participatory approach to change, rather than a set of externally generated recommendations followed up by "change management." To his credit, the director agreed.

We settled on a three-day process. The theme of the three days was a question we felt everybody could subscribe to: "How can we work together more effectively and respectfully?" The first day was devoted to surfacing perceptions of how each group was seen from the other "side" of the chasm (self-expression). The second day was devoted to the appreciation of those perceptions of themselves by the other party (mutual awareness). The third day was devoted to an Open Space dialogue session on the focus of the three days, with an aim to mutually agree on concrete decisions that would help them move toward the goal of being able to work together more effectively and respectfully (dialogue).

Day 1

We spent a half day each with the local staff and the leadership team in separate office locations. Without mutual understanding they could not get to dialogue, but feelings were so strong and so negative that the preliminary awareness raising needed to happen with each side isolated from the other. At the beginning of each half-day session, we had a discussion with each group about appreciative inquiry—an approach to working through strong differences by making assumptions about the underlying good intentions of opposing parties and by deliberately framing problems in positive ways (Cooperrider et al., 2001).

Then we held an anecdote circle with each group where participants were invited to share both positive and negative experiences of working with the other "side"—whether the local staff or the leadership team. The stories, and the names shared, would be anonymous in order to avoid any finger-pointing, fear of sanctions, or defensive reactions. Local staff shared their experiences of working with management, and management shared their experiences of working with the local staff. Obviously, specific, identifiable incidents had to be shielded from view.

We used an *archetypes* method developed by Dave Snowden for creating self-representations of culture—one that we frequently use in knowledge auditing. In this case we were using it to create collective representations by one party of the "other" party (Snowden, 2000a, pp. 155–156, 2000b, pp. 58–59, 2005 Kurtz & Snowden, 2007; Milton & Lambe, 2020, pp. 203–204).

The written anecdotes of the experiences were tagged with adjectives describing the values, attitudes and behaviors exhibited by the characters in those stories. The anecdotes were removed and destroyed, and Post-it notes containing adjectives were then clustered into groups that made sense to the participants. Each cluster was then used as the basis for the creation of a fictional persona or archetype that either represented a management persona (for the local staff) or a local staff persona (for the management team). Some positive personas emerged, but each side produced largely negative personas of the other side. The personas were composed of drawings, expressive names, descriptions, and the original adjectives from which they had been composed.

Day 2

In the morning, the management team visited the office where the "gallery" of personas created by their local staff colleagues was set up. They came face-to-face with representations of how their local colleagues perceived them. At the same time, the local staff visited the other office, where they encountered the gallery of how the leadership team perceived them. Each side was effectively getting inside the heads of the other party in a "neutral" zone, without any possibility of jumping directly into a conflictual stance.

Each side was encouraged to make written responses and attach them to the personas they were responding to. In the spirit of appreciative inquiry, these notes were to be positively framed reflections or genuine inquiries, and participants were to avoid negative or dismissive or defensive comments. In the afternoon, each side returned to the gallery they had created and read through the comments that their counterparts had contributed.

This was a difficult and distressing experience, especially for the leadership team. However, it became apparent from the personas themselves that (a) not everything was bleak (some perceptions were positive), and (b) these perceptions had been built from interactions over the past decade, many of which the current management team could not be held responsible for. But it was harrowing. That night, the director looked exhausted and was doubtful that the dialogue the next day would go well.

Day 3

The third day was a full-day, off-site Open Space event, beginning with a reminder of the principles of appreciative inquiry and framed by the focus question of the entire three days. Open Space Technology is a technique for holding meetings that is based on the principles of dialogue, equality for all parties, making collective sense of common issues and challenges, establishing common ground, and framing collective action to which all parties will be committed (Owen, 1993).

Participation in Open Space events is voluntary, which means that people come because they care about the focus question of the event. The director had been doubtful that everybody would come on a voluntary basis, especially because this feature was explicit in our invitation. The office would be closed, and staff did not need to come if they did not want to. They could simply take the day off if they wished. There would be no attendance taking and no sanctions against nonattendees. On the day, over a hundred people showed up—in fact, all but one member of the staff, whose child was sick that day and who sent her apologies.

Another characteristic of an Open Space event is that apart from the focus question, the agenda is not set in advance. The agenda is set in an opening session by the participants themselves, who volunteer to host discussions on topics under the themes that matter most to them. Participants choose timetable slots for the agenda items, and the bulk of the day is spent in breakout discussions on those agenda items, with participants shifting between topics as their energy and interest moves them.

Nobody is obliged to remain in a conversation that they feel is unproductive, and this means that in practice, people who try to dominate others quickly lose their audience. The process itself tunes a participant into an appreciative, inquiring, dialogic mode of communication. People also formed spontaneous side discussions alongside the main agenda. At one point I spotted the director of the country office in deep, intense, obviously difficult, but respectful conversation with an outspoken and long-serving member of the local staff. He later admitted that it was the first "real" conversation he had engaged in with her and that he would never have imagined it possible.

The closing session of the day focused on what positive action points should take place as the next steps. The proposers of the action points would also take some ownership for them. Action points could not be framed as "XXX should . . ."

There was a remarkable contrast between the facial expressions we saw at the end of day two and at the end of day three. The first day had been disburdening. The second day was harrowing for everybody as they encountered, even at one remove, the hostility with which the other side perceived them, often with no basis in fact. By the end of day three, they were committed to moving beyond those perceptions to something more constructive for both sides.

The mood was still serious. There were still suspicions. People did leave in the middle of discussions and move elsewhere in the room. But the hostility and mutual avoidance that had permeated the office beforehand was gone, and the management and staff did reach a planned series of actions on which both would collaborate, to gradually move toward a more productive and respectful working environment. A year later, the office was still on track with that plan and still in regular dialogue. The underlying problems had not all disappeared, but there was a positive spirit of trying to overcome them together. And both sides agreed that working relationships had improved and so had the quality of work.

Was this a KM intervention, and could the methods used be considered knowledge audit methods? In the sense that the whole staff body used techniques to uncover and explore issues around how they worked together, and to build mutual knowledge that would help them work more effectively as an organization, yes. It is, in its general form, a very compressed form of participative goal-setting audit, though a highly unusual and baggage-laden one.

Geoff Parcell and Chris Collison (2009) go further and state that a participatory approach to creating a shared vision supported by shared objectives is more than just an assessment and sensemaking technique. It is also a collective capability-building and knowledge-building exercise. We will see further evidence for this in chapter 16 when we look at the characteristics of team knowledge, at how team knowledge is built and maintained, and at how team knowledge and capabilities amplify the power of personal knowledge.

Here is how Parcell and Collison (2009) describe a knowledge self-assessment and goal-setting exercise they facilitated for a global network of coaches and facilitators who were seeking to collaborate on building community competence to address the threats of HIV/AIDS:

> This [participatory] process is important because it ensures real alignment in the room of the shared vision of success—of the destination people have in mind. People can then decide on the actions they need to take to move towards it. The route they take toward the destination may be similar or different, and they may travel together or at a different pace. Ultimately, the "sharing your dream" technique gains real ownership of the self-assessment matrix so that the conversations focus on sharing strengths and experience and how to improve the level of competence, which, of course, is exactly where that focus should be. (p. 83)

By contrast, rational, expertise-driven "outsider" approaches to the design of change create what Parcell and Collison (2009) call a "victim" mindset in relation to change—a feeling that change is something that is done to you, and in which you have no real stake (p. 14).

In the victim mindset, change management becomes dominated by a process that assumes resistance as a given and implies a need for carrots and sticks: a process of persuasion, on the one hand, and of identifying and dismantling blockers, on the other. In this mindset, self-directed, productive change is unimaginable.

While the fear of engaging with highly charged opposing positions is a real one, avoidance just kicks the problem down the road, as we saw in the Indosuez example. When we avoid the difficult "trench warfare" that may emerge in the initial stages of participatory dialogue, we replace it with a "cold war" where the "victims" of change avoid its worst effects through avoidance, laying low, foot-dragging, or subterfuge and dissimulation. Where you have apparent consensus around the need for change but actual slow-walking of the "agreed" change, you have a strong signal of a need for participatory approaches and, probably, for difficult dialogue.

Participatory approaches are likely the only way to gain ownership for serious change, as we saw in the rather extreme example of the dysfunctional country office described above.

It may also be difficult to stay the course on participatory approaches, not merely to embark on them, as the case study below illustrates.

Case Study: Staying the Course

We recently worked with a dysfunctional department in a large multinational telecoms company. They knew they were dysfunctional. The management team freely acknowledged their department's issues and had invited the company's internal consulting team in to help. We were asked to assist with auditing the knowledge and information management aspects of the team's issues. We took a participatory approach to evidence gathering, where staff members themselves mapped out their own knowledge use, and identified and prioritized issues that needed to be resolved.

We gathered a lot of detailed evidence and analyzed it with the team to illustrate the key issues and themes, and these tallied well with the evidence gathered by the internal consulting team using focus groups and surveys. This evidence provided a single clear implication about how the governance of knowledge and information management needed to change.

But the management team felt threatened by this. It would involve much more disruption and work than they had anticipated, and they considered their plates to be too full already with change initiatives. The findings also implied the need for changes in the ways in which leadership interacted with staff. The recommendations threatened the current relative autonomy of the team leads.

So the leadership team responded with defensive quibbling about the validity of the sample sizes in the evidence-gathering exercise and complained about the complexity of the intervention. They kicked the project down the road to the next financial year. Ultimately, after a number of other blockages, the internal team members, frustrated, left the organization.

Our process would probably have worked better if it had been fully participatory—that is, if the leadership team had been fully engaged in the evidence-gathering and sensemaking process. But they had preferred the safer role of commissioning a study and reacting to the results. The incident and its response illustrate the perceived threats to entrenched structures and cultures that participatory approaches can bring.

By contrast, Donald Marchand and colleagues described a similar situation and approach in a specialist construction equipment company called Hilti in the 1990s. An earlier technology-led initiative to improve the information capabilities of the direct sales force by connecting them to a common customer database had failed to get adoption. Salespeople could not see the value of the extra work they had to do to record customer data, which was to be used by a central team. They cared about their main job, not supporting some central database management team somewhere else.

This time, Hilti took a participatory approach to solving the change problem, working with the sales force to map their work processes, their information use, and their pain points. They discovered opportunities for information sharing that solved a number of problems (but also complicated the original project, bringing in more departments). They designed a more complex but more holistic information-sharing "system" (beyond just technology) that addressed known needs and pain points. They located the customer knowledge-sharing project in the larger ecosystem of working relationships and knowledge flows across the company.

Significantly, this approach was possible because of the values of the founder and CEO Martin Hilti, who believed strongly in proactive information use by employees and in candid and open communications between managers and employees. The new system gained adoption because the leadership believed in working through participatory, learning-oriented problem-solving processes. Where change is fairly radical, participatory approaches may need strong leadership support (and stamina) to reach their full productive effects (Marchand et al., 2001, pp. 28–29).

* * *

Summary

In this chapter we traced the beginnings of knowledge-related audits, whether in the communication audit tradition, the information audit tradition, or the knowledge audit tradition.

1. Communication audits, information audits, and knowledge audits, when they first emerged, tended to be improvisations and took the form of discovery review audits.

2. Inventory audits soon followed but were most systematically practiced in information auditing, which looked to the well-developed tradition of records inventorying for precedent.

3. There is a tension in information auditing between *auditing information artifacts* or stocks (inherited from records management) and *auditing information flows* (a requirement of the management information systems context).

4. Knowledge auditing took inventorying practices from information auditing without fully appreciating the phenomenological and methodological differences implied by inventorying knowledge as distinct from information.

5. A number of methods for personal and team knowledge inventorying also emerged in cognitive psychology, education, and organizational studies.

6. Looking at precedents for inventory audits shows that they can either precede or follow a discovery review audit. They can also be used to inventory knowledge gaps as well as knowledge resources.

7. Participative goal-setting audits have been used as learning mechanisms for management teams to help them make strategic decisions and have also accompanied inventory audits.

8. Participatory approaches are powerful processes for gaining ownership of change, but they can also be difficult and challenging, especially if they affect entrenched power structures. They can be powerful processes for building the knowledge and capabilities of teams.

8 Authority Envy: Assessment Audits and Standards in Communication and Information Audits

... hunches and prejudices have been the guiding principles in giving information to employees ...
—Connaghan (1960, p. 1)

In this chapter we turn to assessment audits, which have their own distinct challenges in relation to information and knowledge use. We will cover communication audits and information audits here, before looking more deeply at knowledge audits in chapter 9.

Communication Audits: "Scientific" Assessment and Benchmarking

The early communication audits of the 1950s and 1960s had no clear precedents to work against and so were essentially exploratory exercises using a discovery review operating model. Inventory audits provided more systematic ways of surveying communications channels and media, and this encouraged the growth of benchmarking practices.

By the early 1970s, the demand for more "scientific" approaches was growing. There were several attempts to produce standardized communication audit instruments. This stemmed from a frustration in the field that despite almost twenty years of intensive communications research, there was a dearth of "reasonably scientific, empirical-data-based research efforts" (Redding, 1972; cited by Goldhaber, 1974, p. 269). This is what drove the initial development of assessment audits. We can learn a great deal about the productive (or unproductive) conduct of knowledge management (KM) assessments from this history.

In a 1976 review of the literature, Gerald Goldhaber (1976, pp. 9–11) identified seven major problems with the fragmented field of communication audits. His analysis is still relevant to knowledge auditing today. Table 8.1 summarizes these challenges and lays out how knowledge audits fare against them today.

In 1971, largely to meet these challenges, the International Communication Association (ICA), a US-based professional and scholarly association, decided to develop a

Table 8.1

The limitations of communication audit practices in the 1970s compared with contemporary knowledge audits

Goldhaber on limitations of communication audits	Contemporary relevance to knowledge audits
1. Reliance on single instruments—in such a complex field as organizational communications, multiple data-gathering instruments would give more reliable data than single perspective instruments relating to communication patterns and needs.	While our global survey of knowledge managers showed that knowledge auditors often use multiple methods, there is still an overly strong reliance on interviews and surveys. We do not yet systematically practise the multimethod approach that was developed in the multiple instrument organizational audits of the Hawthorne Studies or the University of Minnesota Triple Audit in the early twentieth century.
2. Nongeneralizability—studies were typically focused on single organizations and not conducted across multiple organizations to common standards, limiting the comparability of results.	Discovery review and participative goal-setting audits are by their nature customized to the needs of the driving organization. In principle, inventory audits should produce generalizable results, but in practice the lack of standard inventorying frameworks prevents it. Assessment audits against common standards could improve the ability to generalize audit findings.
3. Small unrepresentative samples—large conclusions were being drawn from small data samples.	The heavy reliance on surveys and interviews in knowledge auditing gives us unrepresentative data samples (for interviews) or data that are decontextualized from the work situations they are supposed to represent (for surveys).
4. Lack of standardization—a lack of agreement on common procedures and instruments hampered comparability of results across organizations.	The plurality of approaches, knowledge audit methods, and even the ambiguities in our language associated with knowledge audits means that we have no standard instruments and therefore no means to compare and generalize findings across, e.g., industries and regions or by organization type or size.
5. Focus on perceptions and not behaviors—understanding perceptions has limited value if we do not understand how perceptions influence behaviors.	This is exacerbated by our reliance on opinion-based methods such as surveys and interviews. We will gain greater insight into organizational knowledge behaviors if we are able to move to an "evidence-first, opinion-second" methodology portfolio using, e.g., observation, content analysis, mapping of behaviors and flows, standardized and objective inventorying techniques, and group sensemaking techniques to control for individual bias.

Table 8.1
(continued)

Goldhaber on limitations of communication audits	Contemporary relevance to knowledge audits
6. Snapshot approach—taking single time slices ignores the time dependence of communications; it would be better to measure communications on a regular basis in order to see the effects of communications programs.	Knowledge audits are frequently undertaken as ad hoc improvisations aimed at building the next set of KM intervention plans. Without standard approaches, each knowledge audit is unique, so results from one audit to the next within the same organization cannot be easily compared. Using standard instruments at repeated intervals would help to track progress and to learn about what is working and not working.
7. Predictive weakness—few audit instruments collect information about organizational performance, limiting the ability of researchers to identify causal links between communications and performance.	We have observed that KM assessment instruments focused on KM enablers or KM processes, when they are not framed by an understanding of the organization's environment and strategic goals, fail to connect to real strategic needs. There is an assumption that generic KM processes and enablers are good in and of themselves. With a lack of consistency of application over time, we are not collecting feedback on KM effectiveness that would produce a double-loop learning effect and help us adopt or adapt practices that are likely to have success.

Adapted from Goldhaber, 1976

standard audit instrument. The effort was led by Gerald Goldhaber and was explicitly designed to address the problems of reliability and robustness that he had identified.

The ICA at that time had recently changed its name from the National Society for the Study of Communication (NSSC) and was engaged in what might be loosely described as "empire building"—starting up multiple strands of activity that would some years later collapse under their own weight (ICA, 2021). In 1971, however, confidence was still high, and the ICA was in an expansionist frame. It attempted to address all of Goldhaber's key concerns.

In addition to using a multi-instrument approach (questionnaires, interviews, critical incident examples, network analysis, communication diaries), the ICA audit allowed for measurement over time and collected data on perceptions, attitudes, and behaviors. The measurement system was designed to aggregate data into a research database, which was made available to communications researchers. The idea was to support the analysis of patterns and trends across many organizations and organization types. Benchmarking had not yet become popular, but Goldhaber's successors in the communication audit tradition soon appropriated the notion (Hargie & Tourish, 2009, chap. 20).

The audit system was subjected to rigorous pilot testing and statistical validation, and ICA auditors were trained in the administration of the audit. It was a massive enterprise involving many communications experts and practitioners (Goldhaber, 1976, pp. 11–13).

The ICA communication audit offered at a minimum a discovery review audit model if it was administered solely as an audit framework without any control over the selection of auditors or access to the larger data set for comparison. With the provision of trained and certified auditors and the benefits of comparative data over multiple organizations, an assessment audit model became possible.

The promise of this model was that once there was sufficient participation, the large-scale aggregation of data would provide an even more useful assessment audit model focused on communications quality and standards. With sufficient data, the researchers should be able to empirically link communication factors to organizational performance and make empirically based recommendations from audit findings. Goldhaber himself likened the audit to the "tight" diagnostic, predictive, and prescriptive functions of a financial audit and a medical checkup:

> Just as accountants' and physicians' check-ups provide clients information necessary to retain the "health" needed for survival, so too does a "communication audit" provide an organization with advance information which may prevent major breakdowns that limit overall effectiveness. . . . Until recently surprisingly little effort has been expended by organizations in the preventative maintenance functions of communication audits. (Goldhaber & Krivonos, 1977, pp. 41–42)

As early as 1978, Goldhaber was able to predict job satisfaction rates based on the mapping of communication relationships, the reported amount of information received by employees, and employee age. Employees were more likely to be satisfied with information received from nearer sources in their networks than with more distant sources. Both insights have actionable implications for how communications should be managed (Wiio et al., 1980).

By 1979 the ambitious project had covered nineteen organizations and five thousand persons (Goldhaber & Rogers, 1979). However, the audit was complex and costly to implement (it would typically take three months to work through the different modules), and it failed to gain significant corporate support and take-up. After eight years of effort, its sole source of funding was still only the ICA and not audit revenues.

The ICA (2021) was in the midst of its own internal struggles on rationalizing the proliferation of projects and committees that members felt were burgeoning out of control. In 1979, just as the audit system was beginning to achieve wide recognition, the ICA withdrew its support. The entire system and database were put into the public domain and formally dissociated from the ICA name (Cissna et al., 2009, p. 11).

While the ICA instruments are still sometimes used, the lack of any central administration means that there is no way of maintaining the audit system and database and assuring its continued relevance. Understandably, its utility as a centralized benchmarking database has degraded over time (DeWine & James, 1988).

This audit still represents the most ambitious assessment audit model to date for information and knowledge use in organizations. Nothing else has surpassed it in sophistication, data aggregation, and promise of robustness from an external assessment perspective.

Almost at the same time as the ICA project, a group in Europe was developing a parallel communication audit instrument with a similar focus on standard approaches and centralized databases. In contrast to the extensive multi-instrument approach of the ICA audit, the European audit approach was based on a quickly administered, questionnaire-based single-instrument study (Wiio et al., 1980). The so-called Organizational Communication Development (OCD) Audit System was based on an earlier and even simpler audit instrument (the LTT audit) developed in Helsinki in the early 1970s by researchers Osmo Wiio and Martti Helsilä.

By 1977, 230 organizations in Finland had been audited, with a sample size of fifty-five hundred people (Goldhaber et al., 1979, p. 251). Although the LTT/OCD audit was a more lightweight instrument than the ICA communication audit, Wiio and his colleagues capitalized on three factors to extend the usefulness of their findings:

- They made it very easy to obtain wide participation and analyzed their findings in a database to identify "norms" by industry and organization type (Goldhaber et al., 1979, pp. 266).
- They conducted a series of "before and after" studies to demonstrate how communication audit measurements responded to interventions (Wiio et al., 1980, p. 89).
- They combined their data with the ICA audit data to make larger inferences about factors connecting communications practices with organizational performance (Wiio et al., 1980, pp. 86–95).

Wiio himself was cautious about the strength of the OCD audit system as a "strong" assessment audit, perhaps because of its simplicity, but he was sanguine about its value for benchmarking purposes, especially when combined with other auditing methods: "Data analysis cannot be primarily based on norm comparisons because of different organizational contingencies. This does not mean, however, that comparisons using norms are useless. When combined with other methods, norms are a valuable tool of interorganizational comparative analysis" (Goldhaber et al., 1979, p. 266).

The OCD audit is still taught and used as a communication audit framework. However, it is now used primarily as a stand-alone discovery review audit framework, and the ICA's ambitious data-sharing goals have not been pursued. On its own, the OCD audit framework can identify generic communication and information flow issues in a target organization, but it has been criticized for its lack of support for the development of action plans. For example, employees can give ratings and express preferences on information provision factors but cannot give detailed feedback on specific channels and specific content: "Although Wiio's OCD audit adequately assesses global informational needs and media preferences, the lack of specificity in allowing employees to match informational needs and content with specific media means less power and flexibility when reengineering corporate communication systems" (Kazoleas & Wright, 2000, p. 475).

This contrast between the two standardized audit instruments provides us with three key insights related to knowledge audits:

1. To be effective, assessment audits need extensive and detailed data gathered to a common framework to be used for comparison or benchmarking, or a reliable and robust standard against which an operation can be measured. Without either of those, the model will fall back into a simpler and looser discovery review audit model.

2. The specificity provided by inventory audits can be a useful complement to a discovery review audit framework to provide more actionable insights for the audit follow-through.

3. The audit instrument needs to be sufficiently versatile to meet organizational contingencies, and sufficiently lightweight if it is to be widely adopted. Without wide adoption, large-scale data cannot be collected.

To sum up, within the field of communication audits, assessment audits emerged in the 1970s on the back of the development of standardized auditing approaches, cross-industry participation, data aggregation and sharing, and rigorous statistical methods for identifying significant patterns and correlations. They were initially driven by benchmarking and then by analysis of correlations between organizational practices and organizational performance.

Assessment audits depend on having an external standard or benchmarking data sets to assess or evaluate against. Benchmarks provide informative comparisons to evaluate against, while standards are stronger assessment tools, leading in the direction of compliance and quality audits. We still have a long way to go in KM to see the adoption of reliable assessment-oriented instruments, but the examples of the ICA and OCD audits give us useful precedents to learn from.

Information Audits: Assessment, Compliance, and Authority Envy

Information audits are at least as confused as knowledge audits in their plurality of models and goals. Peter Griffiths (2010) cataloged eight distinct focus areas for information audits. I have tabulated them here against the analogues in our knowledge audit typology, together with the likely target phenomena in a knowledge audit context.

The table shows a predilection for assessment-oriented audits and value audits in information auditing.

In the field of information auditing, assessment audit models first emerged in the 1970s, but unlike communication audits, they were oriented less toward benchmarking and more toward compliance and quality evaluations. While communication auditors were asking, "What seems to be working well?" information auditors were asking, "What's the correct way to manage information?" (Ellis et al., 1993; Wilson, 2003).

This is the difference between *formative* and *summative* evaluations (Dozier & Hellweg, 1985). Formative evaluations are open-ended and geared toward the identification of improvements. Summative evaluations are more strictly measurement based and give a "reading" of how well you are doing against defined measures or standards. This recalls our distinction between improvement or maintenance audits.

Table 8.2
A typology of information audit types compared with knowledge audit types

Information audit focus areas	Audit model	Target phenomena
Information management practices in support of business effectiveness	Assessment audit	KM processes
Inventory of information assets and needs	Inventory audit	Knowledge stocks and knowledge gaps
Cost-value analysis of information resources	Value audit: cost-benefit	KM processes
Compliance, governance, and records management	Assessment: compliance audit	KM processes
Information security	Assessment: standards audit	KM capabilities; KM processes
Extraction and exploitation of strategic information for competitive intelligence	Value audit: capitalization of knowledge	KM capabilities; KM processes
Information flows and IT systems	Inventory audit	Knowledge flows; KM platforms and channels
Knowledge management	Any of the above	Any of the above

Based on Griffiths, 2010

In fact, assessment audits can be either formative (e.g., using external benchmarks to generate internal prescriptions) or summative (e.g., using external standards to identify areas of compliance or noncompliance).

Summative evaluations may look descriptive on the surface, as in financial and operational audits, but prescriptions are already implicit in the measurement criteria (this is how you should be working). They may still be improvement audits if their prescriptions represent an idealized state. The tight audit models we examined earlier (i.e., financial and operational audits) usually involve summative evaluations but are more clearly maintenance oriented.

In formative evaluation, the prescriptions are generated organically from the audit findings or from the insights indicated by the findings, either endogenously by comparison with organizational goals (as in a discovery review audit) or exogenously by comparison with other organizations (as in a benchmarking assessment audit).

The early information audits using the assessment audit model tended heavily toward summative evaluations. As with inventory audits, this difference was driven by the procedural approach to information management inherited from records management.

We saw earlier that the records management discipline developed a highly articulated and integrated set of records management procedures and methods throughout the 1950s and 1960s. We saw that the dominant narrative around records audits was shaped by the notions of efficiency and cost control in the management of records.

By the 1970s, records management had become proceduralized and largely standardized. Audits would begin with records audits on the inventory audit model and then continue with records management process audits on the assessment audit model (Leonard, 1971).

The methods and procedures promulgated in records management were highly visible, objectively verifiable, and eminently suitable for audit in the tight operational audit sense. They were highly amenable to summative evaluation.

It is true that an international standard for records management practices did not emerge until 2002 (International Organization for Standardization [ISO] 15489), based on an earlier Australian standard (AS 4390, 1996). However, by the 1970s records management practices were already highly stable, with a strong professional consensus behind them. Having an agreed-upon international standard certainly added authority and an assurance of completeness to a records management audit (Crockett & Foster, 2004), but even a strong professional consensus around a set of core practices can provide a de facto standard for a confident summative assessment audit.

Information management is much more diffuse, complex, and context sensitive than records management. However, many information managers inherited this sense of observable practice and "correct" methodology. Ellis et al. (1993) had already identified the ambiguity between the two types of audit, a compliance audit and an advisory audit. Ellis and his colleagues concluded at the time that information audits tended toward the advisory, although elements of compliance sometimes crept in. Quite astutely, they pointed out that this tension between formative and summative roles could lead to role conflict and confusion in the auditor as well as the auditees.

Through the 1990s and into the 2000s, the push toward compliance audits in information management gained strength as specific business information practices became more highly regulated by the state as well as by industry. Alongside the development of standards for records management, a family of standards governing information security started to gain traction in 1995 with the UK BS 7799 standard, a revised form of which was adopted by ISO in 2000 and then incorporated into the ISO 27000 family of standards in 2007. While this standard started as a best-practice guide (formative), it has become increasingly compliance oriented (summative).

Alongside information security standards, a string of other regulatory and legislative requirements has evolved. In highly regulated environments, such as pharmaceuticals, the nuclear industry, and the handling of industrial waste, the entire life cycle of information capture, dissemination, control, and management has come under increased regulatory control from governmental and transnational agencies, giving rise to the field of regulatory information management (Kerrigan et al., 2003).

In the US, the 2002 Sarbanes-Oxley Act and its successor the 2010 Dodd-Frank Wall Street Reform and Consumer Protection Act had significant implications for business information management and recordkeeping. Peter Griffiths (2012, p. 45) lists several other legislative contexts driving a compliance approach to information management, including freedom of information and data protection laws. The implementation of the European General Data Protection Regulation is the latest manifestation of this trend.

The compliance orientation of regulatory information management audits is simply an extension of a broader compliance regime governing the business actions of an organization. Information resources and records are being treated as reflections of activity, and the inference is that they need to be managed and reported in a fashion that makes the regulated actions amenable to external supervision and evaluation.

But the information management practices driven by regulation are externally driven. Of themselves they have no intrinsic value for the organization apart from their externally oriented verification function.

In fact, the information management practices consequent on the regulatory regime often impose a cost and a burden of friction on internal information use, and if not for their legislative origin, they would likely not be adopted for their intrinsic benefits.

We start to encounter problems when auditors want to transfer the perception of rigor and authoritativeness of these audits to different (nonregulated) contexts.

For example, the challenge of ensuring that information is being managed in a way that renders a company's industrial waste disposal practices visible to regulators is quite a different challenge from ensuring that information is being managed in a way to serve internal decision-makers and the organization's business objectives. Yet this important distinction is not always recognized when information auditors espouse a compliance assessment model for auditing internal information management practices.

The assumption that information audits *should* be compliance-oriented assessment audits has sometimes created a sense of anxiety. Where records management precedents did not serve, information managers cast around for "tight" audit models that would meet the perceived need to deliver authoritative and summative evaluations. For example, the origins of information audits are sometimes mistakenly associated with tight models of financial audit:

> The idea of the information audit is derived from financial audits in accounting, which, as Ellis et al. (1993: 134) note, are generally "compliance" audits, undertaken to ensure that the organization is adhering to proper fiscal and legal standards in its financial management. (Wilson, 2003, p. 270)

For others, the origin myth is not enough to establish sufficient authority. The *form* of the audit itself has to take on "tight" characteristics. For example, Graham Robertson (1997) described his relief when he found that he could use the tight assessment model of financial auditing if he thought about information as a corporate resource to be managed as an asset alongside other kinds of assets:

> In my view, any information audit process should include a mixture of professional techniques such as observation, enquiry, quantification, benchmarking, assessment, checking and evaluation. These are precisely the techniques applied by external and internal financial auditors when they set out to audit financial resources, although they might use slightly different terminology. (p. 31)

Once he had this frame, which shifted the focus from difficult-to-observe practices to assets that were capable of inventory and valuation, Robertson (1997) found it relatively easy to translate the financial audit model into an information audit model:

> As a starting point, I wrote out a very simple financial audit programme which I would expect to apply to any commercial organization. I then systematically converted financial processes and their corresponding audit checks into information terms. The creative part of the process took just 45 minutes and the results of this conversion have now been distilled down to seven broad levels. (p. 33)

Under the hood, however, the parallels invoked with tight audit models did not always hold up. Robertson's (1997, p. 33) information audit program had seven coverage areas modeled on the structure of a financial audit:

- Information processing
- Information control and security
- Information cost, price, and value
- Information presentation, usage, and circulation
- Information storage, maintenance, and destruction
- Information ownership, responsibility, and accountability
- Other general operating issues

While Robertson (1997) was able to scope the coverage of an information audit using the parallel of a financial audit, he was frustratingly vague about the standards to be used in evaluating performance in each area. He was more hopeful than specific:

> Audit tests which are relevant or critical to a particular organization will evolve within the relevant sections as they are required. Other levels, or sub levels, may emerge or expand later. The development process of such a programme should be evolutionary, and should be linked to existing internal and external financial audit practices where they exist. (p. 34)

In financial audits, the accounting standards used are underpinned by detailed rules stipulating how judgments are made and how such things as assets, valuations, and revenue are to be recognized. There is a hierarchy of principles, standards, and rules that make the financial audit actionable. No such hierarchy exists for information (or knowledge) management, and it is not clear that given its diversity of application such a hierarchy could exist.

Within records management, there are indeed standards for evaluating records processing, storage, maintenance, destruction, and so on, but within the broader field of information management, the contextual drivers are too diverse for such standard tests to exist. How exactly would we test that information circulation processes are optimized to support decision-making at different levels and in different places in an organization? What would a universally applicable verification test look like? While eminently reasonable in principle, the parallel Robertson was calling on simply has not emerged in practice.

Because of their very specific characteristics, both records and financial resources (as well as regulatory information) have to be managed in certain ways in order to retain these specific properties in the service of the organization. By contrast, *information resources* is a much more diffuse term covering a wider range of attributes. They are too diverse in form, importance, and function to be able to reliably infer such standard processes across all manifestations. In fact, in subsequent years Robertson seems to have retreated somewhat from a summative model and moved back toward a formative model of audit (Robertson & Henczel, 2015).

Just aligning the areas of an information audit's coverage with those of a financial audit does not give the assurance of standardized and optimized information practices. It simply simulates, at the surface level, a structured audit process common to other tight audit processes. The underpinning standards of behavior and rules implicit in financial or record-keeping regulations and standards are simply not present to carry it through.

The strength of a summative assessment audit lies in the ability to measure compliance against an accepted and highly observable standard of behavior. It does not lie simply in the fact of having a standardized audit process. I can examine art students in a highly standardized way. This does not mean that artistic creation is a highly standardized process nor does it mean that I can apply the same measures to different students with an assurance of consistency. Hence, while the financial audit provided Robertson with a useful framework for structuring the information audit process, this did not in itself provide a standard for measuring compliance. It works better as a metaphor than it does as a practical model.

We should not confuse standardization of audit *structure* with measurable standards for the *target phenomena* covered by the audit.

Now it is certainly useful to standardize the audit process and structure because this gives both auditors and organizations observations that are comparable across audits (P. Griffiths, 2012). However, providing comparability in itself does not in any way imply the accuracy of the phenomena being measured. Just conducting an audit in a standardized way does not in itself make it an assessment audit in the summative sense.

Robertson was not alone in this hankering after rigor. Throughout the 1990s both information auditors and communication auditors were casting around for tight models of audit to strengthen the authoritativeness of their approach. We can characterize this as a form of *authority envy* in a decade of increasing dependency on audits and measures of compliance (Power, 1997, pp. 1–4).

This review suggests that information auditing has a more complex and confusing history than communication audits. Our discussion suggests that this is because information audits have been subjected to different influences compared to the communication audit—that is, from two major external forces and two internal ones. These are summed up in table 8.2.

We can see that information audits are therefore often hybrids of different kinds:

- Inventory audits + value audits
- Inventory audits + assessment audits
- Inventory audits + discovery review audits

Today they remain most effective in the inventory + discovery review mode because despite the obvious hankering for the authority of an assessment audit there is neither (a) a single commonly accepted set of external standards to audit compliance against

Table 8.3
External and internal forces influencing information audits

External forces	Internal forces
• Heightened awareness of information as a corporate asset or resource in the 1970s accompanied by the need to justify the costs of information services	• Within the information management field, an attraction to the financial audit as an operating model, both for its perceived authority and for its mechanisms to assess the effective exploitation of corporate assets
• Increasing regulatory pressure affecting records and information management in the 1990s and 2000s, leading to greater visibility and perceived authority of compliance-oriented audits	• Ready-made compliance-oriented auditing methods deriving from records management

nor (b) a solid enough base of shared data, collected to common audit methods, to be able to assess on a benchmarking model (P. Griffiths, 2012).

Knowledge Audits: Assessment and Value Audits Using a Management Accounting Model

As we have seen, many knowledge audits are based on one of the less formal models of audit. The most sophisticated attempt at defining a tight model of knowledge audit comes from Pawan Handa (formerly of the Goodyear Tire and Rubber Company), Jean Pagani (an independent consultant), and Denise Bedford (formerly Goodyear Professor at Kent State University), in their 2019 book, *Knowledge Assets and Knowledge Audits*.

Their justification for a more formal model of audit is grounded in expectations of rigor from business managers and executives and "the increased role and value of knowledge capital in the knowledge economy. . . . Organizations can no longer afford to dismiss knowledge simply as an intangible asset beyond their capability to manage" (Handa et al., 2019, pp. xi–xiii).

According to Handa and his colleagues, a formal audit "is a structured inspection that has a process, a target, and expected outcomes"—outcomes that specifically relate to business performance. Three further characteristics of such an audit are: that it can be conducted by a neutral party, that there are accepted methods for reporting on audit findings, and that the audit will assist the organization in identifying "corrective action" (Handa et al., 2019, pp. xi–xii).

At first sight this reminds us of Graham Robertson's trust in a structured audit *process* (and the concomitant language) as the foundation of audit rigor, as distinct from a focus on the audit phenomena or the supporting audit methods. But this is where information and knowledge audits are vulnerable. The assimilation of a tight audit process gives the appearance of rigor, but rigor does not necessarily follow if the phenomena being studied are not susceptible to the application of the audit process *in depth* or if the supporting methods are incommensurate to the task.

Like Robertson, Handa et al. (2019, pp. 7–8) think that a financial audit methodology can be adapted to apply to knowledge audits. The approach goes further than Robertson in that the authors bring to bear approaches from management accounting, assignment of business value, and intellectual capital accounting. However, the language of tight models of audit appears to be overlaid (unheralded) upon a looser self-evaluation model.

The reference to "corrective action" is the first signal of inconsistency. The term *corrective action* implies a summative assessment against a known standard—that is, that deviation from the standard can be "corrected"—but this is not consistent with what Handa and his colleagues are actually advocating.

Their model of audit recognizes the contextual specificity of knowledge in relation to business needs, and it focuses on the identification of key business capabilities and the business critical knowledge that supports those capabilities "to ensure that they are functioning as expected" (Handa et al., 2019, p. xii). The manner in which those expectations are developed is a process of self-evaluation. The question of whether knowledge is adding business value "is a question only business managers can answer" (Handa et al., 2019, p. 6). In fact, their model of audit requires that the audit team have access to subject matter experts from within the organization who can help the auditor reach determinations on this issue. There is no external standard.

Moreover, Handa et al. (2019, p. 12) admit that many organizations do not have sufficient self-knowledge of their own organizational knowledge in order to undertake an audit; that is, they are not even able to define the expectations and assess deficiencies or improvement areas.

This is a rather startling admission and begs the question of how practical this audit approach might be. Is a knowledge audit process only for organizations that already have some knowledge management capabilities and self-awareness in place? What of those who do not, but who believe that a knowledge audit can be of help in charting their KM journey?

Does it really make sense to restrict the *knowledge audit* term to a tight model of audit founded on good self-knowledge and defined knowledge expectations (in place of standards), as distinct from the looser, less formal term *assessment* (Handa et al., 2019, p. 56)? As we have seen, in both research and practice, the term *audit* spans both loose and tight senses of audit. The Handa et al. (2019) attempt to constrain the meaning of *audit* seems artificial.

On examination, the simple initial exposition of an audit conducted by a neutral third party who reaches determinations using a standard methodology gives way to a rather more complex process of guided self-evaluation using open-ended probe questions for which there are no independent and straightforward means of verification.

But audit verification is a critical component of management accounting and the audit model that the Handa book is founded upon. The ISO 19011 standard for auditing management systems states that all audit evidence

> ... should be verifiable. It should in general be based on samples of the information available, since an audit is conducted during a finite period of time and with finite resources. An appropriate use of sampling should be applied, since this is closely related to the confidence that can be placed in the audit conclusions. (ISO, 2018a, p. 6).

The difficulty is that a great deal of knowledge use in organizations is not susceptible to direct observation and is often not documented in depth (these are the two principal verification methods). Moreover, in many instances the more critical and strategic that knowledge is, the more it tends to be less easily observable or concisely and comprehensively documented. Think about the experience-based tacit knowledge of key staff or the diffuse organizational capabilities woven out of a complex network of habits, routines, guiding documents, and implicit ways of working.

This is not to say that the methods and guiding questions that Handa and his colleagues propose are unreliable. Their approach to knowledge auditing is thorough and systematic and as rigorous as can be expected given the opaque and protean characteristics of how knowledge is used in organizations.

For example, they advocate multiauditor teams in which the auditors independently assess all of the evidence and then share their preliminary observations with each other. If this is a rather unwieldy and perhaps expensive process, it does provide greater assurance in relation to the reliability and trustworthiness of the audit findings (Handa et al., 2019, pp. 21–32).

However, the verification of knowledge and knowledge use is not by any standard the same as the verification of (a) financial transactions or (b) the performance of observable business transactions. We run into the same issues we encountered in our discussion of the limitations of the operational audit model in chapter 3.

The Handa et al. audit must be founded on an auditor reaching a sense of coherence and plausibility (falling back on their professional judgment) derived from the responses to a series of self-evaluation questions. We can use structured methods to reassure ourselves of the coherence and plausibility of our findings, but this is not the same as verification in the formal management accounting audit sense.

For illustration, let us look at how Handa and colleagues (2019) approach the evaluation of knowledge capabilities:

> What does it mean to say that a knowledge capability is effective? It means it does the "right thing." What is the right thing? This will vary for every organization and any point of time. (p. 43)

Or at how to collect and assess evidence relating to tacit knowledge:

> In the case of tacit knowledge and skills and competencies, the client is the source of information. In the case of attitudes and behaviors, some additional formalized information may be needed. It is important to leverage information that is independent, objective, and verifiable. This means leveraging assessment instruments from other fields to establish a baseline and to define expectations for investment and growth. (p. 52)

Unfortunately, we are not told what other sources would count as independent, objective, and verifiable while also respecting the contextual specificities and dependencies of the organization under study. Elsewhere we are reassured that there are some methods for verifying the existence of tacit knowledge (e.g., explicit representations or validation by other experts), but we are constantly brought back to the need for the organization to set its own expectations (not standards) based on its business context (Handa et al., 2019, pp. 54–55).

Handa and his colleagues have sought to integrate the four areas of business value, management accounting, knowledge management, and intellectual capital. In consequence, within their audit approach the ability to ascribe value to knowledge is a critical piece of their methodology. This is why their audit model aspires to be both an assessment audit as well as a value audit.

Each organization must define its own stock of knowledge assets, whether they relate to human capital, structural capital, or relational capital. Handa et al. (2019, chap. 5) propose illustrations and guiding questions for each category of "asset." From that definition comes a detailed discussion around the ascription of value to knowledge capital assets.

I am going to discuss the issues around ascribing value to knowledge in much greater depth in chapters 12–14. Here, I want simply to point out that self-evaluation remains the principal method of value determination in the approach advocated by Handa et al. (2019, p. 207), and they also acknowledge the difficulty of resolving differing perceptions of value.

There is one sense in which this approach pays off. The use of the management accounting and intellectual capital metaphors provides a model and a framework for discussing *knowledge investment strategies*. That is to say, the metaphor pays off in providing a language and concepts to think about an important and neglected piece of KM. Thinking from an accounting and capital standpoint is a natural lead-in to thinking about investment, and this is a productive line of inquiry for KM (Handa et al., 2019, chap. 11).

The book by Handa, Pagani, and Bedford is a brave, nuanced, and sophisticated attempt to drive improved rigor in knowledge auditing by assimilating the model of a tight management accounting audit. While this does stimulate the definition of some creative and useful audit concepts, focus areas, and criteria for establishing robust and plausible findings, I believe this audit model is much closer to a self-driven participative goal-setting audit than a "true" assessment or value audit.

Their book shows that the management accounting audit model can be somewhat helpful when consciously used as a loose metaphor to generate ideas for establishing robustness and reliability, rather than as a strict model against which to design an audit process or to underpin claims for audit authority. In the detail of verification and observability, the management accounting audit fails to convince.

We conclude that in KM, robustness flows not from the model of audit (as it does in management accounting) but from the quality of the participation and from the quality, comprehensiveness, and representativeness of the self-evaluations into which a business can be guided.

*   *   *

Summary

In this chapter we reviewed the precursors for assessment-based audits in communications, information management, and KM. Communication audits looked to standard assessment instruments as a means of gathering comparative and perhaps benchmarking data. Information audits aspired, unsuccessfully, to the supposed authoritativeness of "tight" prescriptive and compliance-oriented audits. A recent attempt to apply a tight model of audit to KM introduces strategies for rigor but does not convince as an assessment audit in the strict sense.

1. Assessment audits emerged within the field of communication audits in the 1970s as a means of making sense of disparate practices and as an attempt to create standardized ways of gathering and analyzing data about good practices in organizational communications.

2. To be effective, assessment audits need extensive and detailed data gathered under a common framework to be used for comparison or benchmarking analysis; or they need a reliable and robust standard against which an operation can be measured. Without those the model will fall back into a simpler and looser discovery review audit model.

3. The specificity provided by inventory audits can be a useful complement to a discovery review audit framework and can provide more actionable insights for the audit follow-through.

4. The audit instrument needs to be sufficiently versatile to meet organizational contingencies, and sufficiently lightweight, if it is to be widely adopted and hence able to aggregate data to common and comparable standards.

5. In information management there have been attempts to develop prescriptive standards-based assessment audit models initially influenced by records management (which is a tightly contained set of practices that easily admit of prescriptive standards) and by the influence of legislation and regulations on aspects of firm information management practices. Tight financial models of audit have been used as inspiration. However, such models have failed to account for the contextually driven variability of information management practices and needs.

6. Regulation-driven standards (and audits) for information management are externally driven and do not meet our requirement for formative assessments of what can be improved to enhance organizational effectiveness.

7. Handa, Pagani, and Bedford have recently argued for a tight assessment and value audit model based on the management accounting audit model and using concepts from the intellectual capital tradition. This has provided useful insights and approaches, but the claims for robustness fall down in the detail of how audit findings can be observed and verified. In KM, robustness does not flow from the model of audit (as it does in management accounting) but from the quality of the participation and the self-evaluations within the audit.

9 The Battle for Standards in Knowledge Management

"So this ISO KM standard, how's it going then?"

"It's pretty much what you'd expect. There's lots of people accusing each other of crass commercialism, being wrong, not recognizing each other's genius. Everyone really seems to hate each other in this group."

—Moore (2018)

Knowledge Audits: Fragmentation of Audit Types

Although heavily influenced by information management in many undocumented ways (for example, the migration of information management professionals into knowledge management), the KM tradition has followed a slightly different path from the information management tradition. In information management, information managers have tried to contain a plurality of models under the single label *information audit* and have made several unsuccessful attempts at developing an integrated approach. In KM, the audit models have partially stratified into three distinct activity areas, each with its own label:

- **Knowledge audits:** As we have seen, in the research literature the term *knowledge audit* has referred most often (but not exclusively) to inventory audits and discovery review audits of different kinds.

- **KM assessments:** The assessment audit model came to be referred to as *KM assessments*, often on a benchmarking model and focusing on the effectiveness of KM activities and processes with a series of determined but often frustrated forays into the development of KM standards. Some, such as David Skyrme (2007, p. 2), very clearly distinguish between practice-oriented "KM assessments" and asset-oriented "knowledge audits" (cf. also Lee et al., 2021, p. 72). Others, however, use the terms interchangeably (Hylton, 2004, p. 1). Handa et al. (2019, p. 56) argue for a distinction between tight (summative) audits on a management accounting model and looser, less formal "assessments", but this does not represent common usage in the literature or in practice.

• **Intellectual capital measurement:** The intellectual capital (IC) measurement movement largely oriented itself around a value audit model, with some side-glances into intellectual property valuation and exploitation. Handa et al. (2019) have attempted to integrate knowledge audits, KM assessments, and intellectual capital measurement into a single intellectual framework, but again this is not characteristic of the literature or of practice.

While the stratification between knowledge audits, KM assessments, and intellectual capital measurement has produced much less immediate confusion than in information management, such stratification is not necessarily a good thing. In information management the information audit so transparently encompasses many different types of potential activity that it has forced a much more explicit awareness within the profession of the variety of audit models contained in that term, and information management practitioners have therefore made efforts to map and make sense of those models.

The adoption of different labels for different types of audits in the KM sphere has meant that their respective practices have evolved in silos, each claiming ownership of its own definitions and methods and resulting in a much more fragmented view of the variety of audit models available. This has contributed to

• a greater fragmentation of knowledge audit practice,
• a lack of common language to describe what are closely related practices, and
• competition for primacy between different practice communities about the legitimacy of the labels and methods they use.

The resulting lack of clarity about the full range of knowledge-related audits is compounded by the fact that though these distinctions between knowledge audits, KM assessments, and intellectual capital measurement emerge pretty clearly in the literature, they are not widely understood distinctions among practitioners, as we saw in chapter 4 (table 4.1). And the labeling remains fluid in practice. KM assessments and value-oriented audits continue to be labeled *knowledge audits*, along with inventory and discovery review audits. It is never completely clear whether knowledge audits or KM assessments are considered to be the same thing or distinctly different things.

There is such a wide variety of meaning in the term *knowledge audit* as to make it virtually useless without some means of clarifying what is meant by it, what are the target phenomena, and what is its expected outcome.

In this chapter we will focus on the assessment audit model for knowledge auditing, specifically relating to standards, which will conclude this section of the book and our systematic examination of different models of audit in KM.

The next section of this book will move from our consideration of how audits are framed and described to how knowledge itself is framed and described. Chapters 10–11 will discuss the sometimes unanticipated effects of the metaphors we use to describe knowledge. Chapters 12–14 will explore the particular risks and ambiguities that arise from the notion that knowledge possesses intrinsic value and how this can easily distort the metaphors and language we choose to describe and measure knowledge. We will address the challenges posed by our choice of language to describe knowledge resources, knowledge assets, and intellectual capital, and we will discuss what this means for the conduct of value-based knowledge audits. Chapters 15–20 will return to the most significant challenge we face in conducting a foundational inventory-based audit of knowledge assets or resources—the need for a typology of knowledge resource types that is practical and easily reported and covers the full spectrum of forms in which knowledge appears and is used in organizations.

The Knowledge Management Pushback: KM Assessment, KM Standards, and Antiprescriptivism

So far we have seen that the communication audit tradition has been primarily formative in the way it approaches audit assessments and that the information audit tradition has attempted, with limited success, to be summative in nature. In many cases the failure to define clear standards for performance has meant that information auditing has tended to fall back into formative evaluations and, usually, on the discovery review model (Ellis et al., 1993).

The knowledge audit tradition inherits aspects of both audit traditions, and this contributes to the plurality of operating models and consequent confusion surrounding the knowledge audit.

Assessment audits have had a mixed history in the KM literature. The earliest-known explicit reference to knowledge audits comes from a 1981 article on the development of quality productivity measures in the public sector. Based on feedback about the impact of poor policy understanding upon the effectiveness of employees, one of the proposed measures was a "knowledge audit to evaluate policy communication effectiveness" (Adam et al., 1981, p. 55). The audit was designed to measure the congruence between the content of the policy and an employee's understanding of the content.

This was quite clearly based on an assessment audit model in which there was an external, objective measure not influenced by contextual goals or objectives. This kind of comprehension check audit is also, by the way, a typical activity you would find in a communication audit, which was occasionally used to check on the effectiveness of corporate messaging and information transfer (both internal and external), although in this case the authors seemed unaware of that connection. However, this was a rare usage in knowledge management, and it does not widely appear as a knowledge audit model elsewhere.

In general practice, knowledge audits over the past twenty years or so have been on the inventory audit and discovery review audit model, frequently but not always in combination. This is not to say that knowledge managers have lacked interest in assessment (whether formative or summative) and in the valuation of knowledge resources. But there has been resistance.

The 2019 book *Knowledge Assets and Knowledge Audits* by Pawan Handa, Jean Pagani, and Denise Bedford presents a sophisticated argument for applying the assessment audit and value audit models to KM, but as we have seen, on close examination it looks to be closer to a participative goal-setting audit than a true assessment/value audit, and it remains to be seen whether it provides a practical model for widespread adoption. It lacks application case studies (Handa et al., 2019).

While communication auditing has persistently wanted to become more scientific and information auditing has aspired to greater rigor and authority, knowledge managers have, on the contrary, often pushed back against the notion of assessment-based knowledge audits and particularly against summative assessments of knowledge management, and they have done so with surprising regularity and force.

Our global survey found that the three types of assessment audit (benchmarking, quality, and standards compliance) were the three least frequently encountered types of knowledge audit among knowledge managers experienced in knowledge audits. Of those, compliance audits were the least frequently encountered as figure 9.1 illustrates (Lambe, 2017).

The common hesitation of practitioners in relation to the possibilities for summative assessments of knowledge management emerge most clearly in the reactions to the development of standards for KM.

Several attempts have been made to develop KM standards, only some of them successful. All of them have been qualified to some degree upon presentation, in order to soften the implications of summative assessment. This tendency toward the promulgation of "soft" standards is expressive of the widespread hesitation about the efficacy of summative assessment in knowledge management.

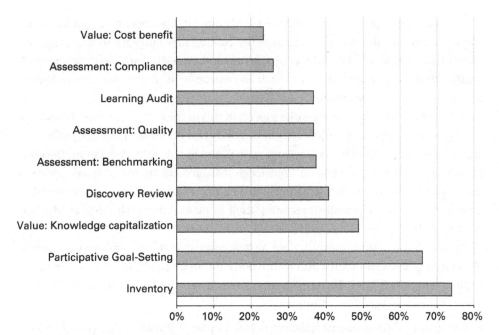

Figure 9.1
Frequency of audit types in a global survey of experienced knowledge auditors.
Source: Lambe, 2017.

The motivation for developing standards for KM is clear, and it is rooted in some of the challenges already identified by Goldhaber for communications practices in 1976—a lack of consistency in practice, improvisations driven by hunch and intuition without clear evidential foundations, and rampant ambiguity in language and in underlying concepts, all resulting in an inability to generalize and compare practices across organizations and industries. The motivation, then, is "to overcome the current unnecessary and avoidable lack of clarity in the discussion, debate and understanding of KM" (Farmer, 2002, p. 5).

To some degree at least, the inconsistency and ambiguity has been commercially influenced. And it has been commercially exploited. In the late 1990s and early 2000s, the field of KM practice was both popular and competitive. There was an evangelizing need to differentiate potentially lucrative commercial services in knowledge management by using distinctive methodology or language—colorfully described by Davenport and Prusak as "theories, fads, nostrums and silver bullets" (1998, p. xix; cf. Scarborough & Swan, 2001; Lambe, 2011a, p. 189).

In a highly competitive but ill-defined environment, common strategies for differentiation can include co-opting language (by coining new language or imposing new meanings on old words) to establish uniqueness and ownership and deprecating continuity with prior or competing art. In such an environment, ambiguities, uncertainties, and fine distinctions proliferate.

We have already seen some gentler aspects of this in the co-option of the knowledge audit into the information audit tradition by library and information science professionals (this was my pathway into knowledge audits), and in chapter 13 we will see the same phenomenon in the co-option of knowledge management by the technology-driven data management profession (cf. Lambe, 2011a, pp. 186–189). This is fairly typical of a novel field or of an older field recasting itself in new clothing (Firestone & McElroy, 2003, p. 332).

With each co-option, meanings are also appropriated to or from the background disciplines of the contestants, and distinctions and oppositions are drawn in relation to competing disciplines. The same terms can be given conflicting meanings. Here are some of the more egregious examples:

- KM is not primarily about technology (Davenport & Prusak, 1998, p. 123). KM is fundamentally driven by technology (Berry & Cook, 1976).

- KM is fundamentally about people (Wiig, 2004, p. 26). KM is about organizations and how they are structured for effectiveness, not just about people (Omotayo, 2015).

- KM is about managing knowledge as an asset (Mentzas et al., 2003). KM is not about managing knowledge as an asset but about managing talent and capabilities (Griffiths, 2018, comment, December 19).

- KM is not about information (Von Krogh et al., 2000, pp. 26–27). KM is about information and what people do with it (Wilson, 2002).

- Knowledge audits are not about KM practices and enablers but about knowledge resources (Skyrme, 2007, p. 2). Knowledge audits are about KM practices and enablers, not just knowledge resources (Frappaolo, 2006, pp. 118–120).

Perhaps because of the competitive drivers behind some of these distinctions and oppositions, there have been both rational and emotional layers to the resistance movement against KM standards.

To function as a standard, a document must resolve oppositions and ambiguities, and it must establish common vocabularies and meanings. A standard, to some degree, is a shared "code book" that enables different parties to work together, coordinate activities, and learn together, building a shared knowledge base (Bénézech et al., 2001, p. 1396).

However, where differentiations reflect politically or commercially vested stances, resistance to the establishment of a shared code book is inevitable and is not always rationally expressed—either because you believe your position will be weakened by a standard or because you depend upon a fragmented field to recruit people to your offering.

The earliest attempts at building standards for knowledge management occurred in the US, in Europe, and in Australia. Figure 9.2 shows a high level time line for KM standards activities in different countries and through the International Organization for Standardization (ISO). This time line shows intense activity in the period 2000–2005, resulting in a series of guides or, in the case of Australia, a nonprescriptive standard, followed by a hiatus until 2011–2018, when a new bout of efforts began, resulting in the publication, for the first time, of prescriptive standards.

In the US, standards development has been both contentious and fragmented. The suspicion and acrimonious behavior around the whole issue of standards development in the KM global community flow, at least in part, from early efforts to gain commercial advantages from the control of KM certification and standards in the US in the late 1990s—the so-called "certification wars."

Case Study: A Controversial KM Standards Effort

In July 2001 an outfit called the Global Knowledge Economics Council (GKEC) became a member of the American National Standards Institute (ANSI), the North American standards body, and immediately claimed it had begun a process to develop an ISO knowledge management standard (McElroy, 2001). ANSI is the US representative for ISO. GKEC, despite its rather grand-sounding name, was actually a two-person outfit operating out of a single-story office unit in Tucson, Arizona. Its founder was Edward C. Swanstrom, a tall, baby-faced man in his mid-forties, with ash-blond hair worn slightly long and with a couple of KM books to his name.

The GKEC was one of a network of nonprofit organizations operating as fronts for commercial certification services in knowledge management. This is a phenomenon particular to the US. Knowledge management certification is still the preserve today of supposedly professional associations or nonprofit "institutes" that license their commercial training and consulting offerings exclusively to private entities owned by the founders of the associations or nonprofits. It operates using apparently respectable fronts with self-dealing in the background.

In the US there is a small group of people behind all these bodies; they are almost all personally connected through early alliances followed by disputatious splits to set up competing outfits. The formula is to register under a grand-sounding name, to set up a volunteer advisory board comprising distinguished names (who, having lent their names, would be troubled no longer), and then to sell services to KM novices who are impressed by the appearance of institutional heft or who believe that their employers would be so impressed.

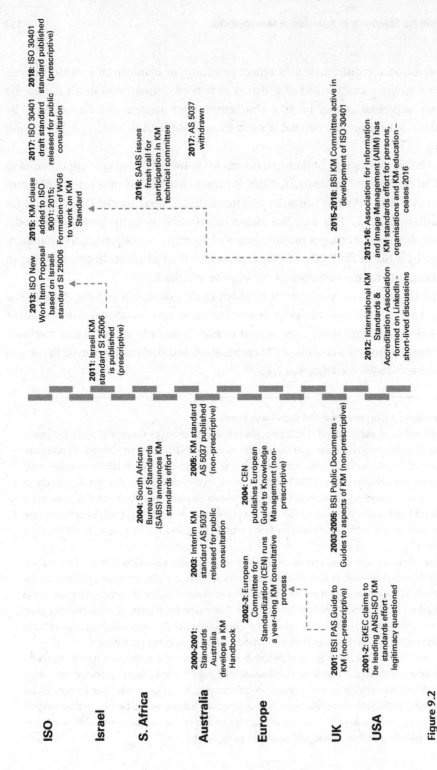

Figure 9.2

A time line of standards development for knowledge management.

The formula was also, in the heady early days of KM, to stalk the many online KM discussion forums, touting their competing offerings and decrying their competitors-cum-erstwhile partners. Here, from 2002 to 2006 a number of flame wars raged, resulting in a series of censorship actions by moderators and, in the most extreme case, the taking down of at least three Yahoo KM discussion forums following accusations of intellectual property theft against forum members (Lambe, 2005; Schenk, 2006).

Edward Swanstrom was one of the early players in this feeding frenzy, and he was especially opportunistic, spawning a large number of parallel *paper organizations*—a number disproportionate to the number of people who were actually drawing salaries.

He was creating, in effect, an internet-enabled appearance of an entire ecosystem, all tracing back to one ubiquitous man. These self-referential networks were commonplace. As we know, the internet facilitates this illusory propagation of presences. The goal is a virtual crowding out of the competition to occupy the cognitive space of the innocent consumer in the knowledge that at least some of them will fall for your offering.

For example, Jenny Odell (2018) recently investigated a bizarre and sprawling self-referential network of e-commerce businesses centered on one alumnus of a private Christian university in California and specializing in *drop-shipping*—when you carry no inventory but list items in online stores at vastly inflated prices and on receipt of an order (because not everybody compares prices), you buy the product from somebody else's online store and have it shipped to your customer, pocketing the difference. The greater the reach and presence of your network, the more likely it is that you will find people who will fall for your offer.

Swanstrom was a pioneer in opportunistic self-propagation. Immediately after the 9/11 attacks, he issued a press release promising an initiative to develop an antiterrorism KM task force to work with federal agencies, pointing to one of his vehicles, the Innovation Management Institute (Skyrme, 2001; Swanstrom, 2001a). A month later he announced the formation of a nonprofit organization called the Volunteer Organization of Certified Knowledge Managers to partner "with the Federal Emergency Management Agency (FEMA) in developing a National/ World Knowledge System for Civil Defense and Homeland Security," complete with a new website and impressive-sounding projects (Swanstrom, 2001b, 2001c).

Both initiatives were linked to upcoming "GKEC/ANSI KM Standards" meetings. The ANSI link was an integral part of the bolstering ecosystem, together with his vehemently defended certification program (Swanstrom, 2001a), and we can understand its allure. If you control the standard (or are seen to control it), you can reap rewards from the certification and training that follows. Swanstrom had already shown his willingness in 2001 to use standards as a cudgel with which to attack his certification competitors—in that case, through the affiliation of another of his creatures, the Knowledge Management Certification Board, with the National Organization for Competency Assurance (NOCA):

> The Knowledge Management Certification Board (KMCB) is a non-profit organization made up of knowledge practitioners from major KM firms worldwide. It is the only organization within the KM community that is a member of, and follows NOCA standards. Due to NOCA's strict guidelines, it is a waste of effort to have more than one certifying body in the same discipline. . . . Unless the organization is following NOCA or similar standards,

it is not a genuine certification program. Anything less than NOCA standards is extremely risky. (Scarpignato, 2001)

Swanstrom's claim to be leading an ISO KM standards development initiative did not go unchallenged. His erstwhile associates and then competitors in KM certification, the Knowledge Management Consortium International (KMCI), solicited from ANSI, and then published, ANSI's disavowal:

> ANSI has expressed its concerns to GKEC that this press release contains a number of statements that are either incorrect or reflect a misunderstanding of the ANSI and ISO standards development processes and systems, including:
>
> • The press release assumes that ANSI and ISO will proceed with this new activity. However, there will be a number of process and approval steps necessary before we know whether both ANSI and ISO will do so or not. . . .
> • GKEC would not be considered "the U.S. Knowledge Management (KM) and Knowledge Economics (KE) Standards representative to the International Standards Organization (ISO)." Each country has a specific organization that serves as the ISO member for that country, and ANSI is the dues-paying U.S. representative to ISO. Within the ISO committees, it is the ISO member organizations from the various countries (such as ANSI for the USA) that are considered the members. (McElroy, 2001)

Despite this, the standards-related meetings and the puffery apparently continued until late 2002, at which time Swanstrom (2002) was soliciting applications for membership in the "GKEC/ANSI main standards committee." The push for a KM standard in the US seems to have started losing steam shortly after that.

In early February 2004, a tall, baby-faced Tucson-based man in his mid-forties with ash-blond hair worn slightly long named Edward C. Swanstrom was arrested near a California middle school on suspicion of raping a thirteen-year-old girl. He was subsequently convicted and imprisoned for the offense. It turned out that he had been grooming the girl in an online chat room since July 2003 by pretending to be a seventeen-year-old boy. At the time of his arrest that February day in 2004, he was out on bail waiting to begin a ten-year jail sentence for molesting another thirteen-year-old girl in Tucson in 2003. Swanstrom had already changed his name to Andrew Skewis Andersen in September 2003 (Welborn, 2006; Inside Tucson Business, 2003).

With Swanstrom's disappearance from the scene, the GKEC and its multifarious web presences began to evaporate from 2004 onwards and with it the US push for a KM standard, not to be revived for another decade. But the bitter taste of blatantly commercial interests and predatory, manipulative behaviors would continue to taint reactions to the very notion of a KM standard. As Joseph Firestone and Mark McElroy put it in 2003:

> . . . when conflict behavior in standards development is too intense, the trust and objectivity necessary to synthesize and reduce the number of alternative formulations and produce consensus are bound to be casualties of conflict behavior. KM is a field in which conflict between certain organizations has grown intense. In the recent past, two well-known organizations in KM were contemplating legal action against one another, and one of these was heavily involved in the standards development process. (KMCI, 2003, pp. 3–4)

Across the Atlantic in the UK and in Europe, real institutions, as distinct from fake ones, were pursuing standards initiatives at the same time. In the UK the British Standards Institute (BSI) was keenly aware of the dichotomy it faced. On the one hand, the field of knowledge management, with its confusing and contradictory positions, was crying out for the guidance that a standard would provide. On the other hand, standards depend upon consensus, and it was not at all clear that consensus could be reached (Farmer, 2002; KMCI, 2003; Weber et al., 2002). The field, they felt, was not yet mature enough to produce a normative standard.

So the BSI stepped back and took a longer view. They felt that they could make a contribution through the provision of "a common framework of contextually based understanding, with the aim of facilitating the easy communication and co-operation of KM-aware bodies and persons" (Farmer, 2002, p. 5). This was an exercise in building common ground, which would nudge the field toward greater consistency and maturity and toward a situation in which a prescriptive standard might prove possible.

In 2001 the BSI issued a publicly available specification for knowledge management (defined as a prestandard document for which a high degree of consensus had not been achieved). It followed with a series of public documents (for which a moderate degree of consensus had been achieved) issued as "guides to good practice" in knowledge management between 2003 and 2005 (BSI 2001, 2003a, 2003b, 2003c, 2005a, 2005b, 2005c).

A similar position was taken by the European KM Forum in collaboration with the European Committee for Standardization (CEN), which shared some members with the BSI knowledge management committee (Weber et al., 2002). The CEN (2004) ran a yearlong consultative process between September 2002 and September 2003 to develop a *European Guide to Good Practice in Knowledge Management*, published in 2004 as a series of "common workshop agreement" documents.

Both the BSI and the CEN stopped short of producing full standards on the presumption that the field of knowledge management was not yet mature enough for a normative or prescriptive standard—maturity being measured primarily by the level of consensus in the field.

South Africa saw a short-lived effort to develop a standard in 2004, with no appreciable progress (Tobin & Snyman, 2004, p. 8).

Meanwhile, in Australia, Standards Australia International was also working on a KM standard. It had published a well-received guide to knowledge management in 2001 but, in contrast to the European agencies, had decided to go beyond this to aim for a full standard. Standards Australia set up a technical committee consisting of representatives from relevant industry, professional, and public bodies (Standards Australia, 2001; Hasan, 2004; Ferguson, 2006; Halbwirth & Olsson, 2007).

In 2003 it issued an interim standard for public comment (Standards Australia, 2003). It sparked debate well beyond Australia and was criticized on multiple grounds. The standard was said to be "too simplistic," "rigid," "too mechanistic," and "too linear"; it would "reduce KM to the lowest common denominator," it would "exclude legitimate approaches to KM," it would "be compromised by the commercial activities" of Business Excellence Australia (the commercial division of Standards Australia), and it had "too much jargon" (Halbwirth & Olsson, 2007, pp. 72–73; Hasan, 2004, pp. 110–111; Ferguson, 2006, p. 197).

Some of these remarks were clearly based on an immediate visceral response to *the idea of a KM standard* rather than a close reading of the text. For example, the interim standard had actually addressed the need to take a cyclical, iterative approach—to contextualize the framework presented in the standard to different situations and to adapt it to different needs—and it had stated quite clearly that "one size does not fit all" in knowledge management (Hasan, 2004, p. 107; Halbwirth & Olsson, 2007, p. 72). The document was also explicit in its intention to be a guide rather than a prescriptive standard, although the idea of a *nonprescriptive* standard was understandably novel to the KM practitioner audience.

But the emotional, visceral nature of the response can be seen in the words used to describe the reception of the interim standard: "Disparaging," "heated," "vociferous," "concerns of forced control, compliance and inflexibility," "blunt," and "contentious" (Hasan, 2004, pp. 110–111; Ferguson, 2006, pp. 197, 202). Even the basic definitions of knowledge and knowledge management were hotly disputed (Halbwirth & Olsson, 2007, p. 74).

By self-report of the committee, the standards development process itself was "challenging," "demanding," and "controversial," with many changes of direction, differences of opinion, and confusion. There was inconsistency of participation. Different people turned up at different meetings and pulled the standard in different directions. The process was "exhausting" (Hasan, 2004, p. 106; Hasan, 2014). Similar issues arose with the attempt by the Association of Image and Information Management (AIIM) to develop a KM standard ten years later (D. Bedford, personal communication, October 5, 2018).

In many respects it could then be considered a triumph that Standards Australia successfully brought out its standard in 2005, taking on board many of the earlier criticisms. It succeeded only by making front and center (including in its title) the point that this was in fact a "descriptive guide" rather than a prescriptive standard (Standards Australia, 2005; Sbarcea, 2007, 2010). But this raised the very legitimate question of how it was any different from the earlier guides produced in the UK and in the rest of Europe. Could it be considered a "real" standard without clear methods to measure conformity to the standard (Ferguson, 2006, pp. 203–204)?

The critiques, however bruising they felt, usefully revealed the rational basis for asserting the limitations of standards in knowledge management (as well as in other types of management systems in organizations). A good deal of the animus against KM standards (and certification) is driven by the taint of commercial interest in the framing of the standards. There is a fear that viable alternative approaches will be excluded from having any authoritative status either by premature convergence and compromise or through commercial interest. There were, for example, suspicions of commercially oriented bias in the "cash-strapped" standards institutions, leading to suspicions of a lack of objectivity in the standards themselves, and these must have been influenced in part by perceptions of the earlier standards development shenanigans in the US (Hasan, 2004, p. 111; Snowden, 2006a).

There were, however, two additional theory-driven strands to this response, going to the very heart of what a "standard" implies. The first relates to the characteristics of knowledge management as a field. The second relates to the nature of organizational life, which KM seeks to support.

Objection 1: Knowledge Management as a Field Is Too Complex

The first in-principle argument against KM standards is the challenge involved in bringing into a common picture the breadth and diversity of what is involved in KM but in a way that is sufficiently granular to consistently guide KM implementation. A standard is supposed to guide practice, after all.

As Stan Garfield (2015) remarked of KM certification, the "field of knowledge management spans over 100 KM specialties. It is too broad to be certified in as a whole." A similar argument could be made for KM standards. A single standard, the argument goes, cannot cover the entire field at any meaningful level of detail.

Furthermore, it is quite possible to hold opposing, but equally valid, views on a specific KM matter, often influenced by one's professional or disciplinary background (human resources, strategy, accounting, operations, information technology [IT], organization development, learning, research, library and information science). By "equally valid" we mean that there is often no real way to determine objectively, except by experimentation, which of two alternative perspectives should prevail in a given situation; moreover, unsuccessful approaches in one context can be shown to work in another context, without a clear understanding of what caused the difference in outcomes.

Finally, the argument goes, KM practice is still evolving and has not stabilized to the point where a consensus can be achieved. To produce a standard before theory and practice have stabilized is to risk "freezing" imperfect practice and "freezing out" innovation and future developments (Farmer, 2002, p. 6; Weber et al., 2002, p. 2; Firestone & McElroy, 2003, pp. 332–333; Snowden, 2006a).

These factors, taken together, present a problem because the standards development process is based on codifying a common position, which means building a consensus. This can produce poor outcomes where the field is both diverse and complex, as well as where it is not fully evolved:

- There was a fear that the pressure to converge can produce an artificial "committee" agreement but where substantive disagreement in the field still exists; that is, the standard may misrepresent the true diversity of practice or exclude valid practices (Hasan, 2004, p. 110; Snowden, 2012). As Eric Mullerbeck (2014) observed in an email to a KM forum, "The risk that such a standard would actually enshrine and promote bad practice in the name of uniformity [would] seem to exceed the likelihood that it would add impetus to good practice in KM." However, there is little evidence of any such rush to a false consensus in knowledge management—if anything, the opposite is the case. The rush to disagreement is more apparent.

- If the standards group is to achieve a real consensus, then there is pressure to abstract and generalize the language to the point where the standard has little practical application. As Dion Lindsay (2018) puts it, "Knowledge Management is a discipline where only the obvious finds common agreement, but where a lot of value lies in insights based on careful observation in situations which do not obtain universally." We raised a similar objection to the application of a prescriptive operational audit model to knowledge management in chapter 3. Any noncontroversial language describing knowledge management is too broad in scope to be measurable or actionable, as a prescriptive audit model requires. This can have a "decoupling" effect between measurement and actual practice, where you have apparent compliance with the standard, but because of the level of abstraction and ambiguity involved in the measurement description, it is not an accurate reflection of reality on the ground.

Of course, there are also counterarguments. Although there is indeed great breadth and complexity in knowledge management, it should at least be possible to frame the landscape in a way that is useful to the larger community (Griffiths, 2011). There is a vulnerability in our failure to register whatever consensus does exist and that is in the lack of any assurance for "innocent buyers" of KM products or services "that if they hire this individual or group that they are not buying a wo/man of straw" (Snowden, 2012).

1. It should be possible to frame KM in such a way to aid novices, or managers who do not want to get into the guts of KM theory, in ways of detecting insubstantial shysters and hucksters or in mitigating the ill effects of dogmatic enthusiasm for misleading and overly simplistic KM models (Handzic & Hasan, 2003, p. 534; Maier & Remus, 2003, p. 65; Snowden & Stanbridge, 2004, p. 142).

2. It does seem that in-principle resistance to the idea of the possibility for or value of consensus (KMCI, 2003) may be a self-fulfilling prophecy. As Arthur Shelley (2018) rather elegantly stated: "Our success depends on us collaborating around what we agree on instead of arguing endlessly about what we disagree about." The consensus-building work intrinsic to the codification of a standard may have some benefits in nudging a field toward consensus and limiting the space for divergence by creating common reference points (Terlaak, 2007, p. 973). KM as a discipline is having a hard time keeping up with the affordances that advances in technology provide to organizations. This creates a deep discontinuity between managerial practice and technical capabilities, and this is manifested in a perceived lack of both utility and stability in the KM discipline. Working on consensus building and standards "presents us with an opportunity to add stability" (Callioni et al., 2004, p. 59).

3. As to the point about generalizations and abstractions, what seems like an obvious motherhood truism to KM specialists may still have value to other stakeholders in organizations to whom this supposedly "common" sense is not immediately obvious or authoritative unless it has a standard to give it credibility (Carpenter & Rudge, 2003, p. 85; Lindsay, 2018). In fact, one of the reported practical benefits of the Australian KM standard was its use as a source to give legitimacy to communications with management, more than as an actual implementation guide: ". . . you have an authoritative organization putting out a guide and they go, 'Oh, yes in that case it's got credibility'" (Ferguson & Burford, 2009, p. 50; cf. Burford & Ferguson, 2011, p. 10).

4. And if a landscape-framing approach is taken, as distinct from a stipulated set of granular rules, and if the underlying model is sufficiently rich, generative, and hospitable to variations in practice, then there is in principle no reason why innovation, adaptation, and learning in practice should not continue to occur within the purlieu of a framing standard (Weber et al., 2002, p. 2). This was in fact a major argument behind the Australian KM standard: "The standard also aimed to be a guide or framework, which can be 'moulded' to suit the particular context of a specific organization. In this sense it is a living, fluid document" (Sbarcea, 2007; cf. Hasan, 2004, p. 110; cf. Ferguson & Burford, 2009, p. 51).

Objection 2: Organizational Life and Knowledge Use in Organizations Is Too Complex

The second in-principle argument against the appropriateness and applicability of standards in KM is that organizations are intrinsically complex adaptive systems, and complex behaviors militate against the predictability and regulation that standards assume (Burford & Ferguson, 2011, p. 3). While there are large elements of structure, predictability, and control in organizations, the phenomenon of knowledge use in organizations is held to be fundamentally complex. This means that it is locally constructed and adapted in response to local conditions and context and is not subject to universal, predictable rules (Stacey & Mowles, 2016; cf. Snowden & Stanbridge, 2004).

By their nature, in contrast, standards assume predictability, consistency, and stability (Wilson & Campbell, 2016, p. 830). So this argument states that the practice of KM is simply incommensurate with the application of standards. As Helen Hasan (2014) reported, "Taking complexity aspects into account is even more relevant now than 10 years ago and I agree that it is critical for KM. There is however a real hurdle to overcome in merging these ideas with the concept of a 'Standard.' It was fighting this battle that I think exhausted the committee in 2005."

Sally Burford and her colleagues took this thought even further. In a 2011 paper, they set up a contrast between mechanistic "top-down" and standards-driven prescriptions for how knowledge management *should* be done, compared to the complex, situated practice-led way in which knowledge management *actually* operates. This was presented as a "discordant" struggle between two opposing mental models of how organizations work. They cited examples in which mandated and resourced KM practices failed to succeed because they were not rooted in local contexts and needs: "Management intervention in communities of practice and rigidity in knowledge processes in Japanese organizations highlight the tension and dysfunction that can result when inappropriate interpretations and actions are invoked by adherence to traditional management theories when practice theories hold a dominant place" (Burford et al., 2011, p.11).

But again there are counterarguments. First, organizational life is not homogeneous. It incorporates systems, rules, and predictable environments as well as complex, emergent, and adaptive environments. As Snowden and Stanbridge (2004, p. 146) pointed out, organizations are inhabited by multiple parallel situation types, some of them structured and simple, some of them complex. Sensemaking for decision and action depends upon the ability to discern which ontologies are most pertinent to the issues (and contexts) at hand, whether complex or predictable (p. 146).

While standards-based approaches may be inappropriate to some KM contexts, this does not automatically rule them out for all contexts. There are clearly going to be valid scenarios for routinized knowledge use and systematic, repeatable knowledge-use processes that would be entirely amenable to standards-based approaches. Mandating lesson learning and transfer processes in major projects and capturing major decisions and rationales in a corporate memory system would be just two examples. Not all knowledge work is "make it up as you go along," nor should it be.

Second, it is a feature of complex adaptive systems that elements of those systems stabilize and gain wide social acceptance over time—practices become habituated, structured, and predictable and frequently become normative practice (Rouse, 2001; Gherardi, 2006, pp. 34–36). Normative practices may then acquire formal legitimacy and become prescribed. There is no reason to suppose that knowledge practices are any different in that respect. Knowledge management practices are neither wholly ordered (as a KM standard might assume) nor wholly emergent (as social complexity theorists might argue). It is not a straightforward either-or question.

> The arguments-in-principle against the possibility of a standard for knowledge management raise important questions about the constraints and challenges of developing a useful standard in knowledge management, but they do not succeed in entirely dismissing the possibility.
>
> They suggest that KM standards may work best as high-level framing and orientation devices for KM practice, and they are likely to work best for those aspects of organizational life that are stable, routinized and relatively predictable. They are less likely to be useful to structure or govern more complex, emergent and adaptive practices and contexts.
>
> A KM standard could easily be used inappropriately if these distinctions are not recognized, but it is not of itself completely without utility.

The Rise of the Prescriptive Standard in Knowledge Management

The publication of the Australian KM standard in 2005 as a nonprescriptive standard represented a temporary triumph for the antiprescriptivists, but it also represented a foot in the door for a more sustained and determined effort to develop a full prescriptive standard. And the desire for such a standard did not go away. Activities on the standards front were quiet for several years, but in 2011–2012 they started to move again (Milton & Lambe, 2020, pp. 300–303).

In the US, KM standards efforts had remained in abeyance after the Swanstrom-GKEC debacle in the early 2000s. It was not until 2012 that a group of largely US-based KM practitioners formed the grand-sounding International Knowledge Management Standards and Accreditation Association (IKMSAA) as a discussion group on LinkedIn. Its formation was more expressive of a resurgent desire for a consensus around standards than it was effective at getting anything done, and the group's ground rules display traces of the early bitterness of a decade previously: "1. No hawkers; 2. No arguments about 'the definition of knowledge'" (IKMSAA, 2018).

There is no evidence that this group was ever formally constituted as an association, and the standards-oriented discussions petered out after some initial controversy over the tactics that the group deployed to limit debate and restrict alternative views. The association was avowedly "consensus based," and the founding members were accused of being unreceptive to any positions that challenged a consensus (Loxton, 2012; D. Griffiths, 2012; Snowden, 2012).

The following year, 2013, the US-based Association for Information and Image Management (AIIM)—a real association this time—formed three KM standards committees, under the leadership of Denise Bedford, to develop standards for (a) KM in organizations, (b) KM for individuals, and (c) for KM education. This effort attracted wide interest, nominal participation from over one hundred practitioners worldwide, and some draft texts, but it was discontinued along with all of AIIM's other standards development work in 2016 following a financial review. AIIM relinquished its ANSI standards development affiliation in late 2017 (Bedford, personal communication, October 5, 2018; B. Fanning, personal communication, October 16, 2018).

The major progress, however, was to come from the ISO itself. In late 2011 the Standards Institution of Israel (Standards Institution of Israel, 2011; M. Levy, personal communications, October 10–11, 2018) issued a new standard for KM systems, after just over a year of work, prompted by a survey of customer demand for new standards to support organization effectiveness. This was an unabashedly prescriptive standard. The KM standard was well received in Israel, and the SII began to offer assessor and auditing services against the standard (Rozental, 2013). On the back of this success, in 2013 the SII proposed a new work item for the ISO to develop an ISO management systems standard for knowledge management, based on the Israeli standard (ISO, 2013).

Meanwhile, also in 2011, the technical committee responsible for the ISO 9001 quality management standard conducted a worldwide survey across 122 countries. They discovered a high demand to include a requirement for knowledge management in an update to the ISO 9001 standard—over forty-five hundred respondents (72 percent) requested it. In September 2015 a new requirement for knowledge management entered the standard for the first time:

> 7.1.6 Organizational Knowledge—The organization shall determine the knowledge necessary for the operation of its processes and to achieve conformity of products and services. This knowledge shall be maintained and be made available to the extent necessary. When addressing changing needs and trends, the organization shall consider its current knowledge and determine how to acquire or access any necessary additional knowledge and required updates. (Fry, 2015; Wilson & Campbell, 2016, pp. 831–832)

After consultation among ISO member countries, the proposal for work on a full knowledge management system standard was accepted, and in 2015 an international technical committee was formed and work commenced. It progressed remarkably quickly considering the history of contentiousness and disarray of much prior standards work. A draft standard for public consultation was released in late 2017 (Lindsay, 2018). It was at this point that the familiar manure hit the proverbial fan.

David Griffiths (2018), an early and prominent critic of both standards and certification in KM, wrote a blog post (since removed) critiquing the fundamental basis of the draft ISO standard. He raised three important objections:

- The draft standard expressed a retrograde view of knowledge management and failed to address emerging developments and future-oriented challenges in KM, such as artificial intelligence, robotics, learning and development, complexity, and strategy.
- The process for standards development lacked requisite diversity, was "incestuous," and was dominated by consultants who had a vested interest in "product placement" and protecting legacy services.
- Standards development is wholly inappropriate if the goal is to aid in the future proofing of organizations. KM is itself a complex phenomenon, and so is the challenge of adapting to the future. Standards of this nature are incompatible with this goal unless they serve simply to put in place loose constraints within which complexity-oriented approaches can be undertaken.

The blog post provoked very lively and sometimes heated discussions both on David Griffiths's site and in a number of other fora (Boyes, 2018). The perceptions of commercial bias by consultants seem to have been driven by the prominence of several well-known KM consultants on the BSI national KM standards committee. Moria Levy, the chair of the ISO technical committee for KM, clarified that the BSI committee was only one of fourteen participating national committees, and fewer than half of the active members in the development process were consultants (Griffiths, 2018, comment, December 20).

Her clarification went largely unnoticed in the broader debate, some of which revolved around personal attacks on a key member of the BSI committee for supposedly distorting the standards development process on the basis of commercial interest. The animus and suspicion arising from the US-based certification and standards wars of two decades earlier was casting a long shadow. As one commentator put it, partially but not entirely tongue in cheek:

> "So this ISO KM standard, how's it going then?"
>
> "It's pretty much what you'd expect. There's lots of people accusing each other of crass commercialism, being wrong, not recognizing each other's genius. Everyone really seems to hate each other in this group." (Moore, 2018)

The core antistandard arguments, both visceral and reasoned, were consistent with previous debates. They focused on commercial bias and on the supposed incompatibility of standards with an area as complex as knowledge use in organizations. However, the institutional nature of ISO as an organization and its highly structured (and bureaucratic) standards development process weakened the force of some of the criticism. Some of the suspected "consultants' product placement," for example, turned out instead to be a consequence of the requirement to use the standard ISO Management Systems Standard template, introduced in 2014 for all management systems standards. This template sets out a mandatory structure and set of elements to be covered (Wilson & Campbell, 2016, p. 831; Collison, 2018; Lambe, 2018).

Moreover, critics of the process seemed initially unaware of the system of national committees and national voting that lies behind the development and adoption of an ISO standard, and of the presence of ISO technical experts on the working committee to ensure due process is followed. ISO explicitly prohibits references to specific products and services in its standards. Independence from any given commercial offering is one of the fundamental guiding principles for any ISO standard (ISO, 2015, p. 118). This is not to say that bias is impossible, but there are strong institutional guards against it.

The questions about a lack of diversity in the development of the standard were reasonable for such a broad and diverse discipline, though the representation of one particular group was not as sharply skewed as the initial critiques had claimed.

In the debate that followed the release of the draft standard, the defenders of the standard pointed out that the public consultation period was precisely the point at which a larger representation of views should be gathered. And the visibility and emotional tenor of the debate helped in this—244 public comments were collected on the BSI's website alone, resulting in 270 recommendations for changes to ISO (Lindsay, 2018; Corney & McFarlane, 2018). To their credit, some of those most suspicious of the standard weighed in with substantive and wide-ranging comments, including David Griffiths, who worked with Stephen Bounds and Nancy White to develop a detailed set of recommendations for changes in the draft (Bounds et al., 2018).

The crisis passed and the revised standard was voted forward by ISO member countries and finally published in November 2018. Twenty years of struggle had finally produced a prescriptive standard. Arthur Shelley (2018), who had been involved in the development of the standard, acknowledged its continuing limitations in relation to the more intangible aspects of knowledge management but argued, as echoed in the earlier debate, that the perfect should not be the enemy of the good and that having an imperfect standard was better than having no standard at all:

> Organizations can perform better when people accelerate the flow of knowledge through sharing, conversations and stories. This is reinforced in the standard, but it does not take it as far as I would have liked to see. The challenge is the standard is a REQUIREMENTS document, so needs to be able to be measured or demonstrated to validate compliance. Many aspects of

knowledge are intangible and these are the elements that are hard to put into the standard, but in reality these intangible aspects are the elements that drive the value from the knowledge.

This is acknowledged in the standard and some of us wanted more on this, but we ended up with less than some of us wanted. This is the nature of documents versus knowledge. Knowledge will always be richer than information artefacts. Knowledge exists in people's heads as an intangible asset and is quite fluid. It can be well supported by tangible artefacts, tools and processes, but in the end it is unique [to] each person.

This does not mean a KM standard cannot be useful. It is in fact WHY a standard IS useful. It provides a basic common foundation for everyone to get the basics of what it is. Although it is simple, it is helpful to guide people outside the knowledge profession and also to assist those inside the knowledge profession from around who we are and what value we can (collectively) bring to decision-making and value creation.

Why Did the ISO 30401 Standard Succeed?

Succeed is a large word. At the time of writing, the ISO 30401 standard is largely unproven in practice. We will discuss what it is likely to be good for and not good for in the final section of this chapter. But gaining acceptance and reaching official status is a major victory, given the troubled history of standards in KM, and it is worth exploring how and why that happened because we may well find lessons there for how assessment audit instruments for KM might gain acceptance and utility in the future.

The "certification wars" of the later 1990s cast a long and bitter shadow on efforts in knowledge management to build consensus and common ground among KM practitioners. Without that common ground, the very notion of an assessment audit instrument was in constant contention.

The mechanisms of divisiveness are still with us today. The tale of two Edward Swanstroms, one the KM standards champion and the other a sexual predator, recapitulates this. It starkly illustrates a disturbing parallel between how you would groom "innocent buyers" by shaping a KM standards effort to serve blatantly commercial interests and how you would groom children for predatory ends. On the internet, as the saying goes, nobody knows if you are a dog. If you do happen to be a dog, you must prevent people from seeing you as a dog.

In both cases you must first establish trust by projecting a believable identity that disarms any suspicions the intended victims might have. In the KM list-serves, Swanstrom used the self-referential ecosystem of official-sounding entities and the constant name-dropping of real institutions' names. In the grooming of his child victim, he was first a lovelorn seventeen-year-old Arizona boy and then, when that pretense could no longer be maintained, a besotted older man who would travel cross-country to be with her and shower her with expensive gifts.

Next, the predator must separate the prey from the herd. In the KM list-serves, divisiveness and factionalism achieve the separation. You force an affiliation and position your prey against your competitors. In Swanstrom's grooming of the girl, he gave her a mobile phone that he told her to keep secret so that he could speak with her without her mother knowing.

> Any in-principle argument that consensus in KM is either impossible or without value plays into this "separation of the prey" strategy, whether intended or not.

Next, you must control the perceptions of the prey and dominate what they see and how they react. You do this in knowledge management by propagating official-sounding entities and websites and by talking up your official connections. In this way you simulate the necessary solidity. You further this by drowning out real discourse in online discussions by engaging in relentless tit-for-tat self-referential postings (Grey, 2004). In Swanstrom's grooming of the girl, he showered her with gifts and confused her with the intensity of his attentions.

But you depend for your success on your ability to keep your victims isolated. Swanstrom's Californian victim was fortunate enough to have school friends who were concerned about her liaison with a much older man. That fateful February day, they alerted their teacher that the man she had been seeing was parked in his van nearby, and the school authorities called the police.

> This is the larger lesson for standards development: The community has more defenses against deception than the individual has. Open scrutiny and discourse is better than closed-door discussions, and however bitter the disagreements might be or however opposed the interests, the ownership of a standard needs to be diffuse and not closed. It needs to be open to debate, and the community needs to be alert to how it is being deployed.

It is also important to be able to manage widely divergent views and the "tension and misunderstanding between proponents of different paradigms" (Handzic & Hasan, 2003, p. 550). As Firestone and McElroy pointed out in 2003:

> When few alternative formulations exist in an area of the domain of interest, the political negotiation that builds consensus is possible and perhaps not too difficult. But when many alternatives exist, negotiation is very time consuming and frequently cannot be successful without years of compromise and consolidation among contending points of view (and, incidentally, without any guarantee that such compromises produce knowledge claims that correspond to reality). The condition of a small number of alternatives does not exist in the various domain areas of KM and knowledge processing. (KMCI, 2003, p. 2)

If progress is to be made in a field as divergent in contributing disciplines, phenomena of interest, and operating paradigms as knowledge management, the discourse needs to be constrained in some way. Otherwise, it will not be able to build common ground within time periods that are acceptable to the interlocutors. The process will run into the ground, and the collaborators will drift away. This tension between openness and constraint is unavoidable in a field as divergent and fragmented as knowledge management. At some point discussion has to be curtailed and positions taken. In this situation, where dialogue is curtailed or constrained, the broad-based institutional underpinnings of the standards development process take on much greater significance for preserving trust. Otherwise, suspicion of bias toward special interests will never be far away.

The institutional basis for standards in knowledge management is the strongest guarantor of a standard's legitimacy. Part of the strength of a real institution is its ability to resist co-option to individual or special interests (often interpreted as bureaucracy).

- Real institutions have processes and rules that are impersonal and disinterested in their operations and have consistency through time.
- They have forms of governance with rules, procedures, and tests to detect and control for bias.
- They have salaried persons who come and go, limiting the potential for dependency on influential individuals or cabals with special interests.
- They have resource bases and income streams that support the above capabilities and limit their vulnerability to commercial bias.
- Their governance regimes, processes, and products are open to scrutiny and external examination.

While these characteristics can often produce frustrating red tape and bring limitations of their own, they also provide safeguards. This is also why would-be co-opters of standards to political or commercial ends seek to conceal their individual interests and try to simulate institutional characteristics.

Three key questions can test the strength of an institution against these criteria:

- Where does its money come from?
- Who makes decisions, and how are they made?
- What is the process for changing a standard or a decision?

The ISO process itself offers clues as to why this effort succeeded where others failed. For example, both the Australian KM standard and the AIIM standards effort had been grounded on KM frameworks developed through prior research undertaken by principals in the standards effort.

The initial Australian draft KM standard had been influenced by a specific model of KM developed through research conducted by Meliha Handzic (Hasan, 2004, p. 106; Handzic & Zhou, 2005). Similarly, an early draft of the AIIM standards documentation was founded on a KM maturity framework developed by Denise Bedford and colleagues (2014) through research at Kent State University.

In a field such as KM where a proliferation of frameworks exists, where any framework necessarily privileges one perspective over others (e.g., process orientation vs. maturity orientation vs. life cycle orientation vs. enablers orientation vs. system orientation), and where one makes one's mark in the discipline by gaining adherence to a particular framework, then such an approach seems—in retrospect—likely to generate as much argumentation as consensus. The proposition of one framework invites the counter-proposition of others.

By contrast, the ISO KM standard was highly constrained by the preexisting structure of the management systems standard template. The effect, while producing some limitations, was also to constrain the process by sidestepping affiliation with any underpinning framework and therefore sidestepping the attendant controversy over the merits of one framework over another.

The second constraint was the disciplined way in which the ISO technical committee discussions were managed. This was influenced by Committee Chair Moria Levy's experience in working on the Israeli KM standard. Areas for discussion were scheduled in advance so that members had notice of which areas would be discussed when, and endless revisiting of the same topic was strongly discouraged once it had been thoroughly discussed. Committee members were delegated tasks and given responsibility to move work areas forward. Work on the definitions section, which is where most contention would likely occur, was delayed until some of the other major sections were drafted and until trust had been built up among the committee members (M. Levy, personal communications, October 10–11, 2018).

The third and final factor was an enabler rather than a constraint. As Ron Young explains, the shift in ISO and BSI from a conception of standards as rules based to principles based suddenly created the conceptual space to consider a standard for KM that would accommodate the intangibility, context variability, and complexity of knowledge work in organizations (Young et al., 2018).

Principles represent generalized but fundamental guiding or framing axioms—they are more durable over time than rules, and they allow flexibility of interpretation and adaptation to different circumstances. Earlier worries in KM standards initiatives about overly rigid, linear, rules-and-recipe-based standards could be sidestepped.

And in fact, the special characteristics of knowledge work and of KM were embodied in the eight guiding principles underpinning the standard (ISO, 2018b, p. vi):

(a) **Nature of knowledge:** knowledge is intangible and complex; it is created by people.

(b) **Value:** knowledge is a key source of value for organizations to meet their objectives. The determinable value of knowledge is in its impact on organizational purpose, vision, objectives, policies, processes and performance. Knowledge management is a means of unlocking the potential value of knowledge.

(c) **Focus:** knowledge management serves the organizational objectives, strategies and needs.

(d) **Adaptive:** there is no one knowledge management solution that fits all organizations within all contexts. Organizations may develop their own approach to the scope of knowledge and knowledge management and how to implement these efforts, based on needs and context.

(e) **Shared understanding:** people create their own knowledge by their own understanding of the input they receive. For shared understanding, knowledge management should include interactions between people, using content, processes and technologies where appropriate.

(f) **Environment:** knowledge is not managed directly; knowledge management focuses on managing the working environment, thus nurturing the knowledge lifecycle.

(g) **Culture:** culture is critical to the effectiveness of knowledge management.

(h) **Iterative:** knowledge management should be phased, incorporating learning and feedback cycles.

Is ISO 30401 an Effective Knowledge Audit Instrument?

The question for us now is whether the ISO 30401 standard can function as an instrument for an assessment audit of knowledge management. The short answer is that, by itself, it cannot. There are several reasons for this.

The form of the standard, as a prescriptive standard, is somewhat misleading. Because it provides a list of requirements and because ISO prescriptive standards can be used as the basis for external audit and certification against the requirements, it has the formal appearance of a summative assessment audit instrument.

However, the standard by itself will, at best, only function as a summative assessment of whether some well-known basic hygiene factors for successful knowledge management are in place. It will not function as a comprehensive summative assessment for assurance of effective KM nor will it, by itself, function as a helpful formative assessment that can guide KM implementation in depth.

Because the standard is principles led rather than rules led, because it is intended to allow for a variety of KM practices and approaches, and because it lacks specificity and granularity, it is peculiarly dependent on auditor experience, interpretation, and judgment. This can lead to three audit-related issues:

1. **Ambiguity:** When the underlying principle is so vague or ambiguous that it provides no substantive guidance for action or for audit.

2. **Decoupling:** When the standard becomes vulnerable to the risk of decoupling between observed and measurable practice and the underlying behaviors and effects—that is, when documented practice may suggest compliance but we do not have accurate observation and measurement of the effectiveness of the practice or of whether the intent of the standard is actually met.

3. **Audit inconsistency:** When the same practices may give rise to different interpretations by different auditors.

Factors (1) and (2) necessarily lead to (3).

Issue 1: Ambiguity
Ambiguity means that the same principle can be interpreted in very different ways. Ambiguity is a widespread problem within any principles-led standard, and it is not just limited to "soft" management systems. It is also found in tight models of audit. Even in compliance audits that are principles led, guiding principles are not infrequently found to contain so much ambiguity that they require substantive fleshing out in the form of supporting rules and guidelines.

Over a decade ago, the Institute of Chartered Accountants in England and Wales (ICAEW) described how a single principle about the need to report on internal controls in section 404 of the Sarbanes-Oxley Act was so vague that it required a supporting auditing standard, which in turn spawned a set of rules and 57 FAQs, leading to a grand total of 225 pages on that principle alone—and the ambiguity was still not completely removed (ICAEW, 2006, p. 11).

In this case the principle's inability to control for auditing inconsistency resulted in the undermining of the principles-led approach and excessive rulemaking. It is true that principles can provide powerful, generative, and adaptive ways to guide conduct, but excessive ambiguity in principles can have the opposite effect and lead either to inconsistency or, to counteract this, excessive rule-making.

A test of the ambiguity and utility of a principle is whether it can be seen to lead directly to an expression of a requirement within the standard, whether it leads to only one interpretation, and whether it communicates enough guidance as to how that principle should be interpreted.

In ISO 30401, the first two guiding principles, the first on the complex and intangible nature of knowledge and the second on the potential of knowledge for unlocking organizational value, look more like broad philosophical statements than principles that would guide action. Unlike the other principles in the standard, it is hard to see any direct relationship between these principles and any specific requirements of the standard. Moreover, closer scrutiny reveals questions about how consistently these principles can be interpreted and applied in practice.

For example, knowledge emerges in different forms in organizations, some of them more tangible than others. A documented guideline, a schematic design, a response to a question, and exchange of advice by email are much more tangible and less complex than the slow acquisition of experience and capability in a midlevel engineer or the way in which a new team begins to operate cohesively and adaptively in a reflexive and responsive way. Annex A of the standard recognizes this variation but does not provide any means to address it.

Similarly, it is hard to argue with the statement that knowledge is a key source of organizational value and that it should be managed, but it is much harder to identify which knowledge, in which forms, is more important for the organization to manage. This simple statement belies the struggles of a generation of intellectual capital theorists and practitioners to get a handle on how intellectual capital can and should be measured and reported and managed. We will discuss the fraught issues with using the language of valuation in relation to knowledge in greater depth in chapters 12–14.

Issue 2: Decoupling

We first described the *decoupling effect* in chapter 3. Let me repeat the characteristics of a system where observation and measurement are systematically decoupled from what actually happens:

> The marks of a decoupled measurement system are (a) the use of general categories (or motherhood statements) in place of granular defined outcomes, (b) the use of ambiguous language that is capable of supporting multiple interpretations, and (c) an insistence on measurement and documentation of observed behaviors, regardless of how well they reflect the underlying activity of the system. This practice is deliberately maintained as a ritual that is unquestioned, in order to conceal the difficulties in measuring the effectiveness of complex human systems and to conceal the lack of clarity about how effectiveness is actually to be achieved. It is a masterpiece of misdirection. The result is to create an illusion of measurement while ensuring that the actual practice

of interpretation and audit is amenable to informal negotiations and is dependent on constant recourse to the skills of "specialist" (but opaque) expertise on the part of the auditors.

Decoupling is a well-known risk in the auditing of management systems (Terlaak, 2007, p. 981). It arises easily where there is a lack of consensus on specific best practices, where noncompliance is difficult to observe or detect, and where there is a perceived reward for compliance—for example, through the legitimacy benefits of certification (Terlaak, 2007, pp. 972–974). In relation to the environmental standard ISO 14001, Deepa Aravind and Petra Christmann (2011) found that "Recent evidence confirms that despite third-party auditing some firms obtain standard certification without continuously complying with standard requirements and incorporating the prescribed practices in their daily activities" (p. 74).

The point is that the inability of the standard to provide sufficient support for auditing rigor means that adoption of the standard may be purely symbolic and not "real" (Vílchez, 2017, p. 38).

Knowledge management is particularly sensitive to the decoupling effect because of the intangibility and poor observability of large portions of knowledge work compared to others: "The main challenge facing quality auditors and more importantly organizations themselves is to address the difficulty of accurately and systematically organizing and measuring deeply embedded tacit knowledge whether that be in organizational systems and processes or within the heads of employees" (Wilson & Campbell, 2016, p. 837).

In chapter 15 we will consider a case study showing how poor observability can lead a knowledge audit to fail to address a full spectrum of needs. Unless counteracted, observability tends to bias findings and actions toward explicit forms of knowledge.

Particular requirements within the ISO 30401 standard are especially vulnerable to the decoupling effect. For example, requirement 4.5 states: "The organization shall demonstrate that organizational culture has been addressed as a means to support the knowledge management system" (ISO, 2018b, p. 8). Annex C of the standard provides further guidance on how to demonstrate that culture has been addressed, falling short of strict requirements (ISO, 2018b, p. 19):

- defining a desired knowledge culture.
- running a gap analysis.
- creating a plan to address the gaps.
- acting upon this plan.
- revisiting and updating all previous steps at defined intervals.

This is a classic case of the decoupling of observable actions from the underlying intent of those actions.

It would be quite possible for an organization to demonstrate compliance with the requirement ("addressing" culture) without having had any real effect on the culture. It puts me in mind of an incident several years ago when I was called upon to brief a senior vice president of a telecom company on how to implement KM effectively. In my briefing I dwelled not only on good practices but also on known failure points. I was perplexed that the senior vice president seemed more interested in my descriptions of how to do KM badly than in how to do it well. So I asked him why. With surprising candor, he replied, "Actually, we don't really want to do KM 'properly' because it will rock too many boats internally—we just want *to look like* we are doing it, because it looks good to the shareholders."

Similarly, the ISO 30401 principle that people create their own knowledge through their own understanding of inputs that are shared with them leads, reasonably enough, to the requirement that there should be processes for interactions between people and people and people and content (ISO, 2018b, pp. 6–7). However, documented compliance as to the presence of such processes and interactions does not mean that you have verified that people are creating valid and useful understandings related to organizational needs—and indeed it is difficult to imagine how you would do this repeatedly, reliably, and reproducibly, as an auditor should. The contextual variabilities are too high (cf. Maximo et al., 2020).

Issue 3: Audit Inconsistency

When ambiguity and decoupling effects are combined, there is enhanced reliance on auditor interpretation and judgment. This will invariably lead to different auditor assessments of similar circumstances and nonreproducibility of audit findings.

Moreover, it places an unusual burden on (a) auditors' knowledge and experience of the variety of KM practices and outcomes and (b) auditors' knowledge of the contextual idiosyncrasies of an organization's stakeholders, business environment, and structural characteristics. It is not clear that external third-party auditors, such as those who would be engaged for summative certification audits, would possess such in-depth knowledge and experience (Milton & Lambe, 2020, pp. 306–307).

It has also been shown that overly vague standards frequently result in lower levels of auditor effort; that is to say, when a standard is vague, there is a lower payoff for an auditor to probe compliance with that requirement in depth (Willekens & Simunic, 2007; Knechel, 2013).

The notion of an experienced auditor's "professional judgment" is by no means fiction. Experienced auditors in any field are by nature generalists. They understand through exposure to many organizations the variety of ways in which actual practices may diverge from documented practices, they are swift in spotting discrepancies, and they are sharp in probing them. But without domain knowledge and detailed contextual knowledge of the target organization, these skills are blinkered.

Patricia Eng, coauthor of *The KM Cookbook* (Collison et al., 2019), is the only person I know of who is both a deeply experienced auditor (of nuclear power plants) and a deeply experienced KM practitioner, as well as trained and certified in ISO auditing methods. She is a rarity, and even she would be challenged in adequately sampling and probing the contextual particularities of any complex organization that she audits for its KM practices against the ISO 30401 standard. Eng points out that there are mechanisms to control for this variability:

> Auditors are subjective human beings—hence, what is acceptable to one auditor may not be acceptable to another. This is a valid concern and organizations have a means of recourse, should this happen. . . . if an organization believes that an auditor has gone beyond the ISO standard, or even if the audit findings seem unreasonable, the organization can discuss its views with the audit team leader during the audit. If . . . the matter is not resolved and the organization still believes that the auditor has gone too far, the finding may be appealed to the certifying body. There is no stigma attached to an appeal and some audit findings have been overturned in the past. (Collison et al., 2019, p. 48)

This is reassuring. However, what Meyer and Rowan (1977) referred to as the "ceremonial and ritualized" elements of the auditor's role and activities would tend, on the one hand, to apply friction to the likelihood of appeal, especially among less experienced KM teams within organizations. On the other hand, remembering Willekens and Simunic's (2007) findings on the small payoffs for extra effort, strongly framed challenges by assertive auditees can inhibit the ability of less assertive auditors to resist. In a field that is largely still populated by inexperienced KM auditors and auditees, the audit process is going to be fraught for some time to come with such tensions, and the quality of the audit process will not always triumph.

Ambiguous, decoupled requirements can easily lead to superficial, symbolic findings, particularly where the specific experience and knowledge of the pool of auditors is neither well defined nor well governed.

They may provide superficial validation that certain hygiene factors for KM have been met, but they are unlikely to consistently differentiate effective KM programs from ineffective ones on the basis of summative certification alone, and the vagueness of some requirements means that they are even less likely to provide formative assessments that will give specific recommendations to guide KM practice in detail.

In fact, Patricia Eng is explicit about this: "Just as restaurant critics do not tell the restaurateur or chef how to do things, the auditor does not tell the organization how to meet its objectives and goals—they simply assess the ability of the organization to do so" (Collison et al., 2019, p. 48).

Some KM practitioners are doubtful that the ISO 30401 standard will be widely used as a summative assessment instrument to certify a KM implementation (Milton, 2015a, 2015b; Lindsay, 2018). However, there is clear precedent in the use of the Israeli KM standard, the ISO 30401 precursor, for the provision of certification services by ISO certification agencies (Rozental, 2013). Certainly, Collison et al. (2019) envisage this type of use for the standard. So there are clear risks associated with the limitations of the standard and the present capabilities for its use in certification.

There are even some risks that widespread encouragement of the standard for certification might distort KM practices from productive to unproductive ends. This concern echoes the message of Dennis Tourish (2019), a longtime exponent of communication audits and a more recent critic of the distortions caused by an overly rigid audit culture in institutions of higher learning:

> The more layers of assessment that are added and the more bureaucratic the process becomes, the more game-playing ensues. . . . This can drive [academics] towards safe topics and short-termism, and a reluctance to engage in risky or multidisciplinary projects . . . (p. 77)

For example, while the ISO 30401 standard contains the principle that KM implementation should be phased and iterative, it also requires that all forms of knowledge flow and use be addressed, including knowledge sharing, knowledge representation, knowledge combination, and knowledge internalization.

But not all KM initiatives are equally dependent on all the knowledge processes. A rush to certification combined with the ease of decoupled measurement could, as the two case examples below illustrate, distract an organization from a properly scaled and useful piloting approach, which should by nature be limited in scope, and push it toward being able to demonstrate the processes, but not necessarily the effects, of the comprehensive system required by the standard *whether or not* all the elements of the comprehensive system were required at that stage in the organization's journey.

Case Study: A Cautionary Tale of Two KM Implementations

The received wisdom is that senior leadership support for KM, proper resourcing, and formal alignment with organizational objectives is a necessary requirement for successful, sustainable KM. The ISO 30401 standard articulates this wisdom. However, while this is generally valid, there are examples where the trappings of senior leadership support, as described in the standard, might well be present but where KM efforts are not sustainable or sustained in the long term. Conversely, there are examples where KM can flourish and be sustainable in the absence of underlying senior leadership support.

This means that while the requirement is a well-known hygiene factor for KM, it is neither a necessary nor a sufficient condition for KM success.

About a decade ago, I worked on a KM project in a government organization where all the requirements of the ISO 30401 standard would have been met. There had been a thorough audit of needs against stakeholder requirements and the business goals of the organization. Key knowledge domains had been identified and a number of phased projects instituted following a road map. All the key KM processes and enablers were addressed, and a clear measurement system was put in place. The KM team was expanded, and a KM competency development program was established with a network of KM champions across the organization. The CEO was vocal in his support for KM, and a KM policy was developed and communicated.

As time went on, any change initiative that had a knowledge dimension (and there were several) was directed to the KM team to take on and incorporated into the road map. Gradually, the momentum began to slow and eventually stalled. The addition of so many initiatives, initially seen as a mark of top management support, became a burden. KM became associated with change fatigue in the organization because it was associated with so many change initiatives. Departments started dragging their feet, and they relied on the KM department to perform basic actions for which the KM team itself was counting on departmental support. This was not overt resistance, but it appeared in small, chronic, and incremental ways that started to show up in lags against reaching implementation targets on the road map.

By the time the problem came to the attention of the senior leadership team at a biennial KM review, several programs were significantly behind, or lacking participation, and a number of projects were failing to show any progress at all. The KM leader was blamed, the team was restructured, and, eventually, disillusioned and burned-out, most of them left.

Now a very seasoned and experienced auditor might just have picked up this risk early on, but I think it is unlikely. Its effects were felt only marginally and incrementally, and the acceptance of what felt like "good" projects on the assumption of departmental support can only be understood as a major flaw in the implementation when looked at in retrospect. The standard does not have any means of determining when a KM program is overloaded. Had a certification process been available at any time in the earlier part of the year leading up to the disastrous KM review, it is likely that this organization would have been able to demonstrate full compliance with the requirements of the standard. Certification in this case would not have been an indicator of sustainability.

Shortly after this project, I worked with another government agency where the IT team had determined that the organization had several structural and performance issues that required a KM approach to resolve. However, the team members had not been able to convince their top management that this was appropriate or necessary. It was a heavily silo-based organization, and each divisional head felt that their needs were unique and special and that there was little merit in promoting a cross-organizational KM approach.

The IT team leader decided to work within his own span of influence (he had very good informal networks across the organization) and persuaded his counterparts in other divisions, over an eighteen-month period, to participate in a rolling knowledge audit exercise to identify major KM pain points they shared and to identify key knowledge domains that needed support. From this exercise he developed three small and very focused interventions, only one of them extending outside of his IT remit. While the needs analysis and design process were consistent with the

ISO requirements, the audit lacked the comprehensiveness across all knowledge processes and enablers required by the standard, as well as senior management support.

Overall, however, the initiatives showed major success in addressing common recognized pain points and won sufficient support for a repeat exercise three years later. That KM program is still ongoing at the time of writing, and while it has gained credibility and respectability, it is still struggling with the issue of getting and maintaining full-fledged top management understanding and support. It is not clear that this program, sustained over almost a decade, would meet all of the requirements for certification against the ISO 30401 standard. And yet it has clearly demonstrated sustainability and value over time.

How Might ISO 30401 Be Useful for Knowledge Auditing?

Notwithstanding the limitations of the ISO 30401 standard as an instrument for conducting a summative or formative assessment audit for KM, it is not without value (Milton & Lambe, 2020, pp. 303–304).

The ISO 30401 standard does capture a broad consensus on the basic hygiene factors for KM. For an organization that wants to do KM well and systematically and that wants to avoid common failure points, the standard may well function as a framing device to guide planning and implementation (Milton, 2015b; Milton & Lambe, 2020, pp. 303–304). This, of course, suggests that it would function better as an implementation guide rather than as an auditing instrument.

The limitations of the standard's use as a comprehensive and reliable assessment audit instrument come from its lack of specificity, the poor observability of some requirements, and some of its ambiguities. The standard by itself is especially limited if, as we have argued throughout this book, the power and utility of a knowledge audit is in its ability to direct improvement and change. In knowledge management, any useful assessment audit instrument must provide a valid and useful formative assessment.

Generalization is necessary in a KM standard in order to claim broad applicability. But, ironically, this limits its applicability in detail. As Ronald Maier and Ulrich Remus (2003) express it, useful guidance needs specificity, not generalized principles:

> It seems inappropriate to simply state a general model that describes the application of KM in organizations. Instead, it seems more useful to describe scenarios of potentially useful KM initiatives that can currently be found or are targeted by organizations and that apply a matching set of instruments and ICT. (p. 65)

This statement, and an earlier attempt to use the BSI guide to KM good practices, provides a clue to how the ISO 30401 standard might be used as one component within a set of audit instruments.

Case Study: From Framework to Audit Instrument

In 2003 Simon Carpenter and Sarah Rudge (2003) reported on an attempt to use the BSI (2001) guide to good practice in KM at the former British Energy Power and Energy Trading (BEPET), a subsidiary of what was then British Energy. They wanted to conduct a formative assessment, using a benchmarking approach, to identify useful improvements to KM practice for their organization.

While the BSI guide was thought to hold some authority as a precursor to a full standard, it was found to be too broad and generic. It did not provide the specificity that a benchmarking approach to improvement would require. So they supplemented the guide with data from the MAKE (Most Admired Knowledge Enterprise) awards.

They used the elements of the BSI document to identify areas of good KM practice and then mapped them against MAKE award criteria and results to identify firms with good practices in those areas. It was an ingenious way of enriching a generalized framing document with specific scenarios collected according to a common set of criteria. Combined, the BSI document and the MAKE awards data provided the basis for a self-assessment and a set of recommendations for potential good practices.

This reminds us of the primary intention of the communications assessment audit instruments developed by Goldhaber and Wiio in the 1970s. A standard instrument for auditing and measurement becomes a collecting device for examples of effective practice and then comparison across organizations.

There is no reason why the ISO 30401 standard should not function as a similar framing instrument for an audit—not alone, but in combination with other instruments and sources of evidence—and as the basis for a benchmarking assessment audit rather than just a compliance-oriented assessment audit.

Chris Collison, Paul Corney, and Patricia Eng provide such a pathway in *The KM Cookbook*. They lay out what Maier and Remus (2003) described as "scenarios of potentially useful KM initiatives," and this is why *The KM Cookbook* is such a useful companion resource to the ISO 30401 standard. They use the metaphor of a restaurant, a kitchen, and a cookbook to frame illustrative examples of effective KM practices drawn from organizations around the world, and these examples are organized around what they call the "KM Chef's Canvas," a framework of guiding questions following the general structure of the ISO 30401 standard's requirements (Collison et al., 2019, p. 55).

It is clear that a variety of audit methods could be used to respond to those guiding questions. The illustrative examples from a wide variety of organizations connect the good practices to their practising organizations' goals and objectives. This downplays the idea of the standard as a decontextualized and prescriptive list of standardized practices. Variety and context sensitivity are preserved.

This idea of the standard as a guiding and framing instrument is supported by a reflective and pragmatic piece written by David Skyrme at the height of the KM "certification wars" in 2002. Skyrme (2002) listed a number of expected benefits for standards, which I reproduce in table 9.1 along with some of my own observations on how the ISO 30401 standard can perhaps provide value for knowledge auditing, when used in combination with other approaches and instruments.

It is unlikely that ISO 30401 will serve on its own as an effective assessment audit instrument for KM. Its coverage of a range of KM processes and KM enablers could help to frame an assessment of those elements of KM implementation, but it lacks the specificity to do this in depth. It needs supporting audit instruments to perform this function.

Although the ISO 30401 standard may not be a particularly effective audit instrument on its own, in combination with other instruments it might be. And other knowledge audit approaches might help organizations to implement KM according to ISO 30401 requirements.

For example, section 4.3 states that "the organization shall identify, evaluate and prioritize the knowledge domains which have the greatest value to the organization and its interested parties, and to which the knowledge management system should be applied" (ISO, 2018b, p. 5). The standard does not specify how this should be done, but this is the purpose that an inventory audit typically serves.

Similarly, while a range of KM processes and enablers is specified, the standard does not give examples of what good practice looks like or how to identify effective practices that already exist within the organization. Discovery review audits can uncover such practices, as can some forms of assessment audit instruments. For good practices in other organizations, the case study interview approach used by Collison et al. (2019) in *The KM Cookbook* can also help. So a knowledge audit, more broadly framed, could also serve as a preparatory step to implementing ISO 30401 requirements.

*　　*　　*

Summary

In this chapter we traced the troubled history of developing assessment-based audits for knowledge management.

1. In KM there has been a long and contentious history of resistance to the notion of prescriptive standards, with arguments and counterarguments on both sides.

Table 9.1
Potential benefits of the ISO 30401 standard

Benefit	Observation	ISO 30401 implication
Compatibility and interchangeability	Components and practices can be combined without error.	The consistency of approach in the ISO management systems standards, especially with the 2015 addition of a KM clause in ISO 9001, should help organizations take an organization-centric rather than a function-based approach to KM (cf. Boyes, 2018).
Common understanding and consistent vocabulary	Knowledge management practitioners and top management teams will use key KM terms with greater consistency and less ambiguity.	While some ambiguity exists in parts of the standard, the standard provides a comprehensive and reasonably consensus-based frame of reference for KM.
Transferability of learning between contexts	Having a common frame of reference for KM systems and implementations will allow KM practitioners and organizations to compare practices more easily and learn from each other.	This is consistent with using the standard as a supporting frame for a benchmarking assessment audit and for using assessment against the standard as a common evidence- and scenario-gathering device.
Competitiveness and comparability between suppliers	KM has suffered from a tendency in commercial software and service providers to use distinctions in language, fine conceptual distinctions, and fancy rhetorical footwork to befuddle and confuse buyers and to justify one product or service over another. Partial or incomplete approaches to KM cannot be distinguished from more comprehensive approaches.	The standard, in providing a common frame of reference and a comprehensive suite of hygiene factors for KM, gives service and product providers a common platform against which they can define their offerings in a consistent and easily comparable way.
Quality and safety	Implementers want to have greater assurance of the likely quality of implementation and reduce the risk of poor implementation.	The standard does not bring absolute assurance of quality, and a superficial use of the standard could increase implementation risks, as described above, but where there is a balanced and pragmatic use of the standard alongside other instruments, quality and risk should be better managed.
Enhancing levels of competence among professionals	Having a common frame of reference also provides a profession-wide approach to describing competencies and skills areas for KM practitioners, identifying gaps, and providing development opportunities.	The standard does describe a comprehensive range of activities that KM professionals and top management will need to be engaged in, and requires that competencies be developed to match needs.

Based on Skyrme 2002.

2. The arguments in principle against the possibility of a standard for KM raise important questions about the constraints and challenges of developing a useful standard in KM, but they do not succeed in entirely dismissing the possibility.

3. The history of standards development suggests that KM standards are likely to work as high-level framing and orientation devices for KM practice, and they are likely to work best for those aspects of organizational life that are stable, routinized, and relatively predictable. They are less likely to be useful to structure or govern more complex, emergent, and adaptive practices and contexts.

4. A KM standard could easily be used inappropriately if these distinctions are not recognized, but it is not in itself completely without utility.

5. The institutional basis of a KM standard and a format and structure independent of commercial providers or schools of thought are critical for its credibility, adoption, and productive use.

6. Although the ISO 30401 standard for KM systems is presented as a prescriptive standard with requirements that can in principle be audited against, three factors weaken its potential use as the main instrument for an assessment-driven knowledge audit:

   - It contains substantive ambiguities that make it difficult to measure all requirements evenly.

   - The standard tends to conceal the fact that some aspects of knowledge use are less easily observable, and this may lead to a decoupling effect in which what is measured is not an accurate and complete description of what actually happens.

   - The presence of ambiguity and decoupling creates a dependency on individual auditor judgment and experience that will almost certainly lead to audit inconsistencies and a tendency to retreat to the easily observed.

7. The ISO 30401 standard formalizes a number of well-known basic hygiene factors for effective KM implementation but does not successfully capture all the necessary and sufficient conditions for successful KM implementation.

8. The ISO 30401 standard may be useful as a framing instrument alongside other audit approaches (such as inventory audits and discovery review audits), against which to collect data according to a common framework across multiple organizations to enhance the possibility for productive comparison of practices, for cross-organizational learning, and for competency development within the profession.

9. Other knowledge audit approaches, such as inventory audits and discovery review audits, might be used to help organizations implement KM according to ISO 30401 requirements.

IV Speaking Clearly about Knowledge

10 Risky Metaphors

No, Hump, these things are too difficult to explain to people and too abstract to interest them.
—Heinlein (1967, p. 340)

In part I of this book, we established the historical context of knowledge auditing and connected it to earlier forms in communication audits and information audits. That rich history gives us a better understanding of the diversity of auditing approaches and methods available today.

In part II, we disentangled the multiple possible senses of *audit* and provided a framework for linking audit type to audit purpose. This should help us think more clearly about how to scope and plan audits, as well as to set expectations for how they should be conducted and the authority of their findings.

In part III we investigated these different audit types as they played out in the evolution of communication audits, information audits, and knowledge audits. We saw how their source disciplines, and the contexts that generated them, influenced the methods they used and the unspoken assumptions they relied upon. We saw how problematic the assessment audit model has been in relation to information auditing and knowledge auditing, and laid out some principles for thinking about knowledge management (KM) assessments clearly and systematically.

In this final part, we turn to the inventory audit, that most foundational form of knowledge audit, and we attempt to first complexify, then clarify, the way that "knowledge" can be understood, described, and cataloged in organizations. Because in an audit we rely on reports from the ground, the language we use about knowledge can help or hinder the KM planning and implementation endeavor.

Useful Ambiguity and Treacherous Ambiguity

The vocabulary of knowledge management, and by extension knowledge audits, is rife with ambiguity and imprecision of language (Ward, 2010). Not all ambiguity is bad. In "portmanteau" or "umbrella" terms that bring together otherwise disparate concepts and practices for productive purposes, ambiguity can be useful. We could view this as a strategic use of ambiguity.

Knowledge management is an example of a usefully ambiguous umbrella term. It has multiple understandings depending on the disciplines that use it, but the use of a single umbrella term forces those disparate disciplines into dialogue with each other in useful and interesting ways. People who are forced to share an umbrella concept can then start to learn across disciplinary boundaries as they expose their assumptions, principles, and methods (Raub & Rüling, 2001; Alavi & Leidner, 2001).

However, ambiguity can also have bad effects. Some of the key language of knowledge audits is prone to ambiguity that is both slippery and treacherous:

- *Slippery* because a series of connected statements explaining KM practice can start off with a term meaning one thing and end with the same term meaning something else entirely.

- *Treacherous* because when meanings shift like this, the rationales behind those activities can also be undermined by the unacknowledged shift in meaning.

Slippery language obscures the point at which a rationale for an activity or process ceases to become relevant. The instability of meaning thereby introduces irrationality into the management process itself and undermines it. Worse, the irrationality is concealed from view. Worse still, our lack of care for establishing a precision of language in knowledge management leads us into poor practices.

We will see examples in this chapter of how slippery language can have an impact on the way we use the term *audit*. In the same audit exercise, we can start with an inference of a "strong" compliance and standards-based audit based on measurable data, and we can end by using methods that belong to a looser evaluative type of audit and that carry much less authority or allow wider latitude in interpretation. The point at which we have moved from the strong sense to the weak sense of the term *audit* is not clear, and with that concealment, the point at which we should start to treat our findings with greater caution is concealed.

In knowledge audits and in knowledge management more generally, we have no safeguards built into our use of language, or into our reasoning processes, to avoid this.

In fact, as our opening quote from the science fiction writer Robert Heinlein suggests, in most cases the recipients and audiences of knowledge audits are largely incurious about the underlying rationality of the exercise, except insofar as it affects their participation and any benefits they might acquire from it. More worrying, when knowledge managers want to bolster the credibility of their methodology and approach, they have a strong motive to conceal or ignore these slippages of meaning.

In the next few chapters, I want to show that the phenomenon of slippery and treacherous language can also happen with a foundational concept within the practice and discussion of knowledge audits, the concept of *knowledge asset*. I will suggest that some of the terms associated with knowledge audits, such as knowledge as *capital* or *resource*, contain *addressable ambiguity*—meaning that the negative effects of the ambiguity can be mitigated by qualifying the term more precisely—but that the use of the term *knowledge asset* cannot be mitigated in this way. I will claim that the term *knowledge asset* suffers from unaddressable and treacherous ambiguity.

The Benefits and Dangers of Working with Metaphors for Knowledge

How should we think and speak about knowledge in organizations? What labels should we use? Is knowledge an asset or a resource? Is it capital? Is it a capability or a strategic competence? Is it a state of mind or a condition? Is it a process? Is it a thing to be husbanded or a flow to be facilitated?

The literature of knowledge management would suggest, rather confusingly, that it is all of these things (Alavi & Leidner, 2001). The intellectual capital expert Daniel Andriessen (2006), in a textual analysis of the most widely cited knowledge management and intellectual capital textbooks, once counted twenty-two different and sometimes competing metaphors for describing knowledge, and his list could have been expanded by including strategy-oriented metaphors such as capability or competence.

He later speculated on how interesting KM would be if we characterized knowledge as "love", with its implications of nurturing human relations, instead of as "stuff", which entails a mechanistic, less human-oriented approach (Andriessen, 2008). Our choice of language is of course determined in part by the orientation we want to take or the argument we want to make. At the same time, the language we choose can impose limitations on how we think about knowledge and how we think about managing it.

Several of these candidate labels (asset, resource, capital) reflect an orientation focused on the *value of knowledge* to the enterprise. Other "knowledge as stuff" metaphors (knowledge artifacts, products, objects) reflect a managerial orientation focused on *control*.

"Value" metaphors are closely linked to "stuff" metaphors. "Assets" are productive resources that are owned and controlled and accounted for, but they are only productive economically if they are managed as artifacts through their life cycle. Both "value" and "stuff" metaphors appear very attractive to KM thinkers and practitioners. "Value" metaphors help us to make a case for the importance of KM, and "stuff" metaphors communicate the possibility of imposing mechanisms of acquisition, growth, and control.

We can see these motivations playing out in the literature and in practice. When Andriessen analyzed his bucket of seventy-one different verbs used to describe how knowledge is managed, he found that "knowledge as stuff" metaphors made up two-thirds of the quota. A third of those verbs carried some inference of value (knowledge as resources, assets, or capital) (Andriessen, 2008).

In a global survey my firm conducted on knowledge-auditing practices, we found that taking an inventory of knowledge stocks and capitalizing the value of knowledge was the second most common type of knowledge audit conducted (the most common type was to take a knowledge inventory in order to review internal knowledge practices; Lambe, 2017). "Stuff" and "value" matter to knowledge managers.

Other types of metaphor, though less common, also have their uses, and so they survive as secondary themes. "Flow" metaphors (connections, transfer, mobilization) reflect a managerial orientation focused on people and process. The labels around competence and capability reflect a strategic orientation to knowledge as an enabler of organizational goals. Each type of label creates opportunities for thinking about managing knowledge, but it also imposes constraints.

When faced with fluid, abstract concepts such as knowledge, we choose our labels to serve our goals. They help us by giving us hooks to work with, which Lakoff and Johnson, in their seminal work on metaphor, call entailments.

When faced with fluid or fuzzy phenomena, a metaphor entails or implies attributes that we can work with. Using the metaphor of "knowledge flow" entails thoughts and actions associated with identifying sources and enabling mobility, directionality, and connections between places and people. The metaphors we choose help us to interpret our situation and in turn help us to structure what we do (Lakoff & Johnson, 1980, pp. 5–9). This is how we help ourselves to pin down an idea and take a course of action.

But the labels we choose also come with baggage. While our metaphors highlight aspects we can work with, they achieve this by hiding other, sometimes conflicting, characteristics of the phenomena. This baggage can become a problem when we forget we are thinking metaphorically and think we are thinking literally. We can mistake the map for the territory (Merali, 2000, p. 16; Bronk, 2009, pp. 23–24).

As Andriessen (2008, p. 9) points out, using a "stuff" metaphor for knowledge enables a managerial approach to knowledge management, especially in codification, storage, and trading systems, but it conceals the human and especially the emotional dimension of knowledge use. We can easily become mechanistic and neglectful of human factors in KM planning and the design of KM processes.

The "stuff" metaphor is not completely incompatible with a "flow" metaphor, but it privileges codification and storage over movement. If we are not aware of these limitations, we can end up with knowledge bases that nobody uses, and in trying to get people to use our "warehouses," we may actually be distracting people from productive work.

And metaphors in KM can be confusing and misleading—confusing, for example, if we are speaking at cross-purposes with a colleague who works with a different metaphor for knowledge, and misleading if we assume that our metaphor implies things that do not actually apply to our situation: "they can fool us when we take them as literal" (Andriessen, 2008, p. 7).

This implies the following:

1. We need reminders that we are thinking metaphorically and not literally.
2. We need a portfolio of metaphors that we can consciously adapt and deploy according to need, not an ideology of metaphors that oversimplifies the complex landscapes we work with.
3. We need to be cautious about metaphors that mislead us.

So if we are engaged in a systematic review and evaluation of knowledge in organizations, we had better be sure of the labels and metaphors we use, of where they help and where they hinder, of when to use them, and of when to jettison them. Some labels are more problematic than others because of the baggage they bring along with them. *Knowledge asset* is one of them, as we will see.

In this section of the book I want to

- show how we can be misled by the language we use,
- review the principal metaphors we use in knowledge audits to describe knowledge, especially in inventory and value audits, and
- identify their limitations and the risks they expose us to.

By the end of this section of the book, we should have a clearer understanding of how to work with these metaphors without getting confused, or misleading ourselves or others.

*   *   *

Summary

In this chapter I have distinguished between useful ambiguity and dangerous ambiguity and suggested some ways of discriminating between them. Here is a summary of the main points:

1. The idea of inventorying knowledge leads to the prevalent use of metaphors of knowledge as *stuff* or as *stocks*.
2. The metaphors we use bring entailments. These can be productive or counterproductive.
3. The idea that we should be able to demonstrate the value of knowledge (and by extension KM) is very attractive. This fixation on value leads to the widespread association of the metaphors "asset", "capital", and "resource" with knowledge.
4. We suffer from imprecision of language and lack of conceptual clarity in how we talk about knowledge with sponsors, stakeholders, collaborators, and fellow practitioners. This has led to our advocacy of vague, misleading, and sometimes just plain confused ideas and practices.

11 The Syllepsis Trap: When Choice of Language Becomes Problematic

What man! I trow ye rave: wold ye both eat your cake and have your cake?
—Heywood (1906, p. 96)

The notion that knowledge has intrinsic value is a fundamental one in knowledge management (KM). As we saw, it is a basic principle in the ISO (International Organization for Standardization) 30401 standard. It underlies several of the key metaphors we use to describe knowledge.

When metaphors and labels have entailments, they become problematic if they lead us on unproductive paths or if they conceal poor logic and sloppy thinking and then lead to action plans that are inappropriate to the real environment we must deal with. They do this when our choice of language leads us to suppose we have an argument or a basis for action that is not well founded in fact.

We are especially prone to this when we choose metaphors or labels that contain intrinsic ambiguities—that is, they imply multiple, incompatible meanings. The language of knowledge audits is especially susceptible to this. To take just two examples:

1. We choose the term *audit* in *knowledge audit* because *audit* implies rigor, close scrutiny of evidence, and authoritative conclusions. But it is not so clear, when we look at the practice of knowledge audits, that all knowledge audit methodologies can legitimately claim the authority of their "strong" analogues, financial or operational audits. There is a wide range of sometimes incompatible meanings implicit in the term *audit*, including a simple inventory, an impressionistic but thorough examination, a discovery and evaluation exercise, or a rigorous and systematic check against external standards.

2. We choose the term *asset* to describe knowledge in use within the organization because *asset* implies something that has value and that can and should be inventoried, governed, and managed. But it is not at all clear that all forms of knowledge in

organizations are susceptible to the same degree of control as tangible or financial assets, nor are they susceptible to a homogeneous set of valuation and management techniques. What then does *asset* mean?

When we don't understand the boundaries of meaning in the labels we use, we can characterize the things we work with wrongly. We ascribe the properties of one thing (an economic asset) to another (knowledge we depend on), and we take actions that are not appropriate to the second, simply because they apply to the former. Then we sit and wonder why our management approaches are not effective.

There are two underlying mechanisms at work here: (1) a lack of clarity about the language we are using, and (2) a lack of clarity about how the world really works. One leads to the other: a lack of clarity about the language we use about knowledge audits and knowledge management, leads to magical thinking about what we can do to improve the way our organizations work.

To understand how this works out in practice, we need to take a brief digression into word play—specifically, the rhetorical device of syllepsis.

The classic form of syllepsis is when two completely different meanings of a word are implied in the same sentence, usually a literal or "strong" meaning, and a figurative or "weak" meaning. For example, "He drove her to London and to drink." The literal sense of *drive* involves vehicular transport, while the second, figurative sense implies a form of emotional abuse. Both imply directionality and intent, but that is about all the two senses have in common.

Here is another example: "She was only a whiskey maker but he loved her still." Are we looking at a noun or an adverb here for the word "still"? Many instances of syllepsis produce a jarring effect, as in the examples above, because we can detect a discontinuity between the apparent syntactic coherence of the sentence form and the semantic "split" in meaning. For this reason, syllepsis is often used as a kind of punning word-play for comic or literary effect (Tissol, 1997, p. 18). It is the instrument of poets and dramatists, where the syllepsis is artfully displayed, and also of pundits and politicians, where it is often concealed. But it can also just indicate poor language skills (Bernstein, 1965, p. 401).

Syllepsis can be subtle, and in this form is most frequently encountered as *double entendre*. Consider the subtitle of the physicist Richard Feynman's (1992) autobiographical memoir *Surely You're Joking, Mr. Feynman! Adventures of a Curious Character*. "Curious" here looks deliberately whimsical: it can either mean strange or it can mean inquisitive, and we immediately learn something interesting about how Feynman sees himself. He is both. The syllepsis is not so jarring, because the syntax conceals the dual reference that we can see clearly in the London/drink example, but we appreciate it. It is still detectable.

Syllepsis can be used to embed intrinsic contradictions within superficially innocent sentences. Shakespeare deployed syllepsis frequently to set up dramatic (and tragic) tension. It is used by his villains to convey innuendo or by the suspicious to see evil where there is none. In *Othello*, Desdemona seeks to understand Othello's aggressive behavior, asking, "Alas, what ignorant sin have I committed?" She intends a loose, figurative meaning for *commit*, but in Othello's seething mind, he fastens on to the strong sense of the word *commit*, summoning up the literal commission of adultery, already seeded in his mind by Iago. He responds by calling her a whore (Keller, 2009, p. 71).

In most literary examples, the intended meanings behind the syllepsis are clear. But there are examples of contradictory meanings held in syllepsis in which the "true" intent is not so clear. In fact, it is deliberately concealed.

In his discussion of Stéphane Mallarmé's 1897 essay "Mimique," the French philosopher Jacques Derrida (1981) points to the "double, contradictory, undecidable" value given to the word *hymen* in Mallarmé's essay. Does it imply the sacred union of marriage, or does it imply the lustful breach of physical sex? The question is unresolved and unresolvable and "thus plays a double scene upon a double stage. It operates in two absolutely different places at once, even if these are separated only by a veil, which is both traversed and not traversed" (pp. 220–221). Derrida suggests that this deliberate indeterminacy pushes the syllepsis out of the fully explicit into the unconscious, one of the few places, apart from fantasy, where we know how to tolerate contradictions.

So in the literary context, syllepsis sets up a deliberate blurring of the boundaries between the literal and the metaphorical senses of the words, to create a kind of slippage of meaning between the two senses. The Latin poet Ovid's great work, *Metamorphoses*, which describes the transformations between nature, the human, and the divine (humans being transformed into animals and plants, gods taking human form), makes systematic and pervasive use of syllepsis to achieve the effect of permeable boundaries between the concrete and the abstract and between the planes of the mundane and the sacred (Tissol, 1997, pp. 19–20).

In summary, syllepsis can go from being jarring (He drove her to London and to drink), to subtle (a curious character), to absolutely unconscious and almost undetectable (We're going to conduct a knowledge audit).

In this latter case, it takes effort to see that the blurring of boundaries is there. But the language of knowledge audits is full of syllepsis. In this book we identify multiple possible meanings of what an "audit" can mean, some of them very loose, figurative, and open-ended and some of them very tight, literal, and constrained. And yet the plurality of meanings contained within the syllepsis passes almost completely unremarked in the literature of knowledge management. It is, however, heavily exploited in our flaunting of the language of audit for authoritative effect. It is the elephant in the room nobody notices or wants to talk about.

Why Are We Vulnerable to Syllepsis in Knowledge Management?

The phenomena that KM deals with, and the ways that knowledge gets used, influenced, and controlled in organizations, are both fluid and abstract. This alone invites the use of metaphor to get a handle on these phenomena, in order to shape our understanding and inform action. As we have seen, metaphors invite entailments, attributes that get shifted from one thing to another just by virtue of choosing certain words over others. They provide flexibility and fluidity of meaning.

Unconscious syllepsis is more worrying than simple entailment, however, because syllepsis does not transfer useful attributes, but incompatible attributes. And incompatible meanings that go undetected, imply ineffective actions.

Why are we vulnerable to this? The answer to this question goes to the broader observation that KM is both complex and difficult. The discourses of knowledge management, the languages we trade with each other in research and in practice, and the range of metaphors we live by are confused and confusing. We have a strong motivation to simplify, and where life is especially complex, we have a strong motivation toward wishful thinking.

Ovid used syllepsis to blur the boundaries between the human and divine; we use it to blur the boundaries between the measurable and quantifiable (the formal language of audit and assets) and the intangible, complex, and elusive (the complex and diffuse way in which knowledge is experienced). We see this in the tendency toward decoupling effects in KM standards. The difference is that Ovid used syllepsis as a deliberate rhetorical device for literary ends. We use it unconsciously as a compulsive imprecision of language combined with wishful thinking. Then, (here is the dangerous part) we use the syllepsis to direct managerial actions toward inconsistent phenomena.

As Derrida suggested in his discussion of Mallarmé, our inability (or refusal) to disambiguate contradictory meanings tends to push the syllepsis into unconsciousness (or taken for grantedness). We fling around the precision vocabularies of *audit*, *asset*, and *capital* as if they are uncontestable truths, milking the certainties that come with the strong meanings of those terms, but ignoring our incapacity to work as concretely and precisely with knowledge as that language would suggest. If we were poets, that would be fine. If we are trying to design management and measurement systems, it is not.

Cargo Cult Vocabularies: Wishful Thinking in Our Choice of Words

Consider the cargo cult. In 1974 the physicist Richard Feynman (1992) gave the commencement address at the California Institute of Technology on pseudoscience and how to detect it. He titled his talk "Cargo Cult Science":

> In the South Seas there is a Cargo Cult of people. During the war they saw airplanes land with lots of good materials, and they want the same thing to happen now. So they've arranged to make things like runways, to put fires along the sides of the runways, to make a wooden hut for a man to sit in, with two wooden pieces on his head like headphones and bars of bamboo sticking out like antennas—he's the controller—and they wait for the airplanes to land. They're doing everything right. The form is perfect. It looks exactly the way it looked before. But it doesn't work. No airplanes land. So I call these things Cargo Cult Science, because they follow all the apparent precepts and forms of scientific investigation, but they're missing something essential, because the planes don't land. (p. 340)

Feynman has somewhat simplified the nature of cargo cults, but he has the essence of how their formal features resemble pseudoscience. Similarity of form is thought to invite similarity of effect, in the same way that we believe we can transfer the authority of a financial audit to an information audit by taking on its form. If I produce the form of citations and data tables, get myself into respectable-looking publications, and persuade people to cite me, then it will be "science."

How do you tell whether it is real or pseudoscience? Not from the appearances, Feynman says. You tell from whether the science works or not. Do the results always end up the same way no matter who conducts the experiment? Can you reliably predict how to get a certain result? Do the data from independent sources bear you out? Do the planes actually land on the runways bringing the desired cargo? Does the knowledge audit give you the same reliable, repeatable insights, no matter who conducts it?

Now cargo cults were never meant to be scientific. They are expressive of a deeply held cultural aspiration. *Cargo* in Melanesian culture refers to the formal exchange of gifts and useful goods. This exchange maintains social relations within and between families, between islands, and—importantly—between the physical world and the spirit world of gods and ancestors. Many cargo cults started in the early 1940s as a kind of nativist rejection of Western culture and religion, which were seen as disruptive to traditional knowledge, culture, and social hierarchies. They became millenarian when the desired return to reempowerment and social harmony was slow to emerge. They took on the physical trappings of imitation airstrips after a brief period during World War II when US troops established landing strips and bases during the Pacific campaign and brought employment, goods, and prosperity, only to disappear again afterward.

These airstrips became symbolic of the desire for a new order in which rich "cargo" would come from another world and reestablish their culture and identity in a new prosperity. And so they are reproduced, to invite back to the world the prosperity and social harmony they represent (Lindstrom, 1990). One of the most famous of cargo cults, the John Frum movement, is still active today on the island of Tanna in Vanuatu, where adherents hold annual parades every February with carved wooden rifles and US flags (Mercer, 2007).

Like syllepsis, cargo cults harbor contradictions. Cargo cults appear on the surface to be worshipping the trappings of Western civilization, but underneath they are expressing a reappropriation of those trappings into the frame of traditional culture *against* the incursions of Western culture (Lindstrom, 1990). In fact, cargo cults do not express a flawed understanding of causal relations in the world or bad science (in Feynman's terms) so much as they express wishful thinking about how their world could be.

I want to hold on to that thought: *cargo cults represent a form of wishful thinking by imitating the desired state of affairs*. We in our turn have fallen prey to a kind of willful confusion of meaning based on wishful thinking about how we would like the world to be, and this distracts us from seeing how the world actually is. Syllepsis relates to how we manipulate ambiguities in what terms mean, and cargo cultism relates to a belief that by mimicking a desired state of affairs, we can claim its benefits.

> Bring the two together and we assume that where a term has both strong and weak meanings, we can claim the attributes of the strong meaning simply by using the term, whether or not our practice is consistent with the strong meaning.

The construction of imitation airstrips is an example of what the great anthropologist J. G. Frazer called *homeopathic magic*, where similarity of form invites the attributes of the desired object. In Indonesia, Batak women who wish to become pregnant sleep with wooden objects carved into the shape of an infant. In witchcraft there is the idea that we can harm an enemy by sticking a pin into a doll that resembles them in some way.

In homeopathic magic, as in verbal syllepsis, we see the idea of permeable boundaries between a desired reality and a simulacrum of the reality, so that attributes can leak from one to the other (Frazer, 1922, chap. 3). Or, more physically, we see the desire to "get hold of something by means of its likeness" (Taussig, 1993, p. 21).

We know that the operations of homeopathic magic can be verbal as well as physical. The use of punning wordplay (of which syllepsis is one form) in curses or charms goes back to ancient times (Frank, 1972; Stark, 2009, p. 191). This is where syllepsis meets the wishful thinking of cargo cult behaviors. We do not have to make physical simulacra of our desired states; we can acquire the trappings of what we desire by using the correct language. We can get hold of something by means of its associated words. Let us call it an audit, and maybe the rigor will somehow follow, irrespective of anything else we do.

We might think ourselves superior to the "unscientific" thinking of cargo cults, but if we look closely, we can see cargo cult syllepsis all around us, from the custom of some Christian denominations of naming children after the saints whose protection—and attributes—they implicitly invoke, to the language of political spin that reveals the operations of wishful thinking in the choice of words used.

Here is a particularly egregious example from Singapore. In December 2011 heavy rains combined with high tides resulted in flash floods affecting the heart of the upscale shopping district, Orchard Road. There had been instances of unusual flooding since mid-2010, but Singapore's fabled infrastructure was supposedly designed to cope with such vagaries of the weather. The agency responsible for drainage systems, the Public Utilities Board (PUB), had attributed the floods to debris blocking the drains, not to the capacity of the system.

But by December 2011, images of half-submerged cars and flooded shopping malls did not sit well in the public eye. At this point the PUB denied they were floods and described them as "ponding" in their press releases, earning widespread mockery and a ministerial rebuke. Belatedly, a study was commenced to increase the capacity of the drainage systems (Hong, 2012).

Here was an attempt to reshape the public perception and to avoid self-questioning by substituting a word that meant a breaking of bounds (*flooding*) with one that indicated boundaries (*ponding*)—a clear use of language as a wishful-thinking device to assert control where control had demonstrably failed. If it was "ponding", then we had never lost control, and if it caused problems, then it was somebody else's fault. In the Orchard Road case, the PUB blamed the inadequate drainage and flood prevention facilities of the affected shopping malls.

Despite a 2012 "call a spade a spade" rebuke from the Singapore Minister for the Environment, *ponding* is still the term commonly used today in the official media for flash floods. Fortunately, the Singapore government does not rely solely on the homeopathic magic of words. It has recognized that climate change has had an impact on rainfall patterns, and though delayed by the previous state of wishful thinking, it is now working on an improved drainage infrastructure across the island. But in the public discourse, the cargo cult language of ponding expresses the wish for an alternate reality more than it expresses the reality on the ground. Flash floods are still occurring.

Why is this example important? Because it shows that our choice of language can betray a wishful thinking that delays or subverts effective action, if the language does not match the reality, but contradicts it. By extension, the syllepsis intrinsic to the term *audit* can lead to frequent examples of cargo cult thinking and distract us from effective action. If we think rigor comes from the label, we may not push for rigor in the practice. Or we may infer that rigor exists where it does not.

We saw in chapter 6 that Peter Checkland called out exactly this kind of syllepsis in the use of the term *system* by systems thinkers in relation to management information systems. Did they mean *system* as a bounded and measurable entity or figuratively as a complex (but not measurable) thing with loosely connected parts? He recounted his experience in trying to apply a systems engineering approach to the management of the Anglo-French Concorde project in the 1970s, only to discover after considerable work that it was not a "system" in the tight sense at all but a very loosely connected set of projects. As a consequence of this illusion, the management system he devised was wholly unrelated to the real-world environment in which the aircraft was being designed and built (Checkland, 1999).

Daniel Andriessen (2004) warned against jumping to conclusions based on uncritical uses of metaphors for knowledge without due reasoning or discernment of what the metaphor actually entails. Once we have syllepsis covering contradictory meanings, the reasoning the language supports becomes faulty and misleading and inevitably leads to flawed practice.

Syllepsis and the Rhetoric of Knowledge Audits

If we look at the language of knowledge audits and their elder cousins, information audits and communication audits, there are many examples of the attempt to appropriate the most authoritative senses of the term *audit* for an audit methodology that is not as strong as the model being invoked. I have described this as a symptom of "authority envy". By this I mean that knowledge-related audit practices, lacking in history or strong theoretical underpinnings, have frequently sought to claim authority for their approaches by borrowing language and methodology from other disciplines that have an accepted authority associated with them. Here are some of those examples.

In their chapter on auditing the effectiveness of communications in professional practice, Owen Hargie and Dennis Tourish (2000, chap. 7) start by framing the chapter solely in terms of "strong" audits conducted against established standards—that is, financial audits, medical audits, clinical audits, and organizational audits. However, the remainder of their chapter explores methods of auditing that are not standards or compliance based but are rather exploratory "ground-up" inquiries trying to identify useful improvements to practice. They include the critical incident technique, constitutive ethnography, and the Delphi technique. These are rich and useful discovery techniques, but they are not consistent with a hearkening to the authority of the "strong" standards-based audit.

We saw that in an attempt to strengthen the credibility of the information audit in the 1990s, Graham Robertson sought to appropriate the rigor of the financial audit to the information audit by adopting the structure of the financial audit. By considering information as a resource similar to a financial resource, he was able to adopt the terminology of financial processes and their audit checks, and was able to produce an information audit process model that mirrored the financial audit model (Robertson, 1997).

But his account failed to provide specificity as to the standards to be used in evaluating information management performance. Taking a model from the accounting space is one thing. Applying it is another. The contexts of information use in general are both more diffuse and harder to observe than finance and accounting practices. It is difficult to imagine that specific standards for performance can translate easily from the finance and accounting space to the information management space. The attempt to do so, however, speaks volumes. By imitating the form of a financial audit, there is a sense that we can "get hold of" the authority implicit in that audit type.

Ann Hylton (2004), one of the more vocal exponents of knowledge audits in the early 2000s, echoed Graham Robertson's authority envy—in her case by emphasizing the "scientific" nature of knowledge auditing:

> A knowledge audit, like any other audit, is a scientific investigation and examination tool. Therefore a K-Audit must conform to or comply with fundamental rules and standards of scientific investigation, with respect to its system, process, methodology and approach. The K-Audit must be formulated, designed and conducted so as to provide a thorough systematic and objective investigative enquiry into the true nature of the organization's knowledge assets and the management of these assets. It must examine, analyse, assess, verify, validate, review, and report. If a knowledge audit methodology is not comprehensive and robust, in adherence to fundamentals of auditing, it cannot properly qualify as an audit, and can at best be counted as a partial or incomplete knowledge audit. (p. 1)

This paragraph is full of strong, authority-laden words. Unfortunately, Hylton seems to have made the same mistake as Graham Robertson in assuming that the simple application of a *systematic* audit methodology conducted by an *objective* outsider would automatically endow its findings with the same authority as a financial audit conducted according to set external standards, or a scientific investigation of physical phenomena in a lab. Hylton never spells out exactly *how* the methodology is scientific or what the "fundamental rules" are, and her proprietary knowledge audit methodology is now no longer available for examination.

Vehemence is a poor substitute for evidence or for clear documentation of methods, or for replicable results.

Some people eschew the term *audit* altogether, preferring the terms *assessment, evaluation,* or *review* instead. Syllepsis is at work here too. For example, in organizations that are subject to regulatory or compliance control, participants' experience and understanding of *audit* is of a summative assessment backed up by sanctions. They are not familiar with looser, more open, inventorying- and discovery-oriented audit approaches, and so the use of the term *audit* provokes anxiety. Desdemona asks what she has done, Othello hears adultery. I tell you I am going to conduct a knowledge audit, and you think I am going to cite you for poor practices.

Not all syllepsis is problematic. Following Richard Feynman, cargo cultism or pseudoscience only becomes problematic when it posits unreliable conclusions—for example, when you expect planes to land on your airstrips carrying economic goods and they do not. Or when you depend on homeopathic remedies for cancer that do not work instead of seeking effective treatment. Or when you think it is not your problem once you have defined flooding as ponding. Or when you demand greater authority for your conclusions than they deserve because you use the language of a strong audit but not the substance and data. Or when you believe you can quantify the present value of any knowledge resource and dispose of it as you wish because you have labeled it an "asset".

Syllepsis of the cargo cult variety is a bad thing when it is concealed or unconscious. It can lead too easily, and in an undetectable way, to inappropriate courses of action and conclusions that cannot be validated. But if the distinctions in meaning are made explicit and if the syllepsis is visible, then a term can still be useful as a portmanteau term, a term that transparently contains many possible meanings.

I believe the term *knowledge audit* does function as a portmanteau term and that it does comprehend better than any alternative the full range of possible activities you might want to perform in an investigation of how knowledge is used in an enterprise. *It is ambiguous but it contains addressable ambiguity.*

If we dig into, and discriminate between, the various meanings of the term *audit*, as we do in this book, we see that the term is perfectly capable of comprehending in a concise and economic way the various senses of inventory, exploration, assessment, and check. Alternatives such as *assessment* or *evaluation* or *study* carry less inclusive and more limited connotations and so they imply a narrower range of possible approaches to consider.

So when discussing knowledge audits in general, the syllepsis in the term allows us to express more economically the range of possibilities open to us—as long as, when discussing specific initiatives, we are explicit about the types of audit being deployed. It is possible to strip away the rhetoric of knowledge audits and to be specific about the

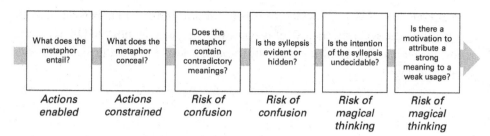

Figure 11.1
Criteria for identifying the risks associated with syllepsis.

practices we are engaged in. If we do so, the syllepsis embedded in the term *audit* is not harmful or misleading. Cargo cultism does not necessarily ensue from the use of the term, although it is clearly a temptation.

Another way of saying this is that while the term harbors multiple possible meanings, it contains so much ambiguity that it forcefully invites disambiguation. And as we explain in this book, it can be disambiguated. Using Derrida's language, the potential contradictions are not intrinsically "undecidable." We can look at the form of a specific knowledge audit, assign it to a specific audit type or set of audit types—for example, using the framework presented in this book—and then infer the degree of authority that flows from it. We just need to have clarity and discipline in how we frame and communicate our investigations and how we set expectations about what we can legitimately claim about the authority of our findings.

Figure 11.1 illustrates a chain of reasoning to help us decide when syllepsis is dangerous or safe.

Let us apply this set of criteria to the term *knowledge audit*:

1. In the use of *knowledge audit*, the entailment is primarily one of review and evaluation.

2. The metaphor conceals the fact that a great deal of knowledge use in organizations is not easily observable.

3. There are multiple conflicting meanings in the usage of the term *audit*, some of them implying high authoritativeness and some of them implying low authoritativeness.

4. These differences are not always explicit when knowledge audits are described and discussed. This leads to a high potential for confusion in what is meant by the term *knowledge audit*.

5. The syllepsis is not, however, undecidable. The term *audit* itself is used with such wide application and contains so much ambiguity that it forcefully invites clarification and specification.

6. So although there is a motivation to bolster the authority of a knowledge audit by concealing the syllepsis, the risk of magical thinking can be mitigated by revealing how the term *audit* is being used, usually through a description of the methodologies being deployed.

*   *   *

Summary

In this chapter I have described a particular form of ambiguity in the language of knowledge audits in which the same term can have contradictory meanings within the same communication. Here is a summary of the main points:

1. Many of the metaphors we use in knowledge auditing (e.g., *audit, asset, resource*) are ambiguous—they carry conflicting and inconsistent meanings.

2. They are also frequently used in both literal and figurative senses in the same communications without signaling the transition between the two senses. The term for this is *syllepsis*, meaning an unclear slippage of meaning and implication.

3. Syllepsis in our language use (and avoiding the correction of syllepsis) often springs from wishful thinking about what we would like to achieve or see happen. When the confusion in meaning leads to inappropriate practices, we call this cargo cult thinking or magical thinking, where practices follow desires and not real-world properties.

12 The Language of Value: Assets and Capital

The inseparability from the human mind and body makes human capital saleable only in a slave economy. . . . The absence of market prices for human capital is one of the greatest obstacles to empirical tests of this segment of economic theory.
—Machlup (1984, p. 423)

Some of the labels and metaphors we use in knowledge management (KM) and specifically in knowledge audits are more problematic than others. We will look at the most popular metaphors around knowledge as stuff and knowledge as having value—that is, the metaphors of asset, capital, and resource. We will examine asset and capital metaphors in this chapter and resource metaphors in the next.

The source disciplines for the labels that ascribe value to knowledge (asset, resource, and capital) are in economics and accounting. It is important to recognize this, because these disciplines determine what a "strong" sense of each of these terms might mean, and it helps us to discriminate the normal entailments that the metaphor provides, and to assess any risk of harmful syllepsis.

Knowledge as Asset or Capital: The Background

If we are interested in ascribing and measuring the value of knowledge, we need a vocabulary to aid us. Here, a number of different concepts from economics get tangled up—the concepts, frequently confused, of what is meant by a *resource* and an *asset* and how they both connect to the idea of *capital*.

Economics is famous for its precision of language. But in the information and KM literature, these basic economic concepts (resource, asset, and capital) are often used interchangeably as if they are synonyms, when they are not. While there are overlaps in meaning and they can sometimes be used to denote the same things, they also have quite distinct connotations, and these differences turn out to be important when they are applied to information and knowledge. The meaning of the word *resource* is not the same as *asset*, and neither is exactly the same as *capital*. And the figurative uses of these terms can directly contradict the literal senses. This is a marker of syllepsis.

The economist Alison Dean and the intellectual property expert Martin Kretschmer are more scathing: they call this imprecise use of language "conceptual negligence" (Dean and Kretschmer, 2007, p. 574). They are referring to the general use of the term *intellectual capital*, but their remarks apply to all three of our metaphors for knowledge-as-a-valuable-thing:

> Does this conceptual negligence matter? We believe so. To . . . define ideas as intellectual capital—that is, a specific form of capital—that definition must conform with the commonly held understanding of capital *while retaining the additional interpretative power that results from defining ideas as capital*. In other words, not only must ideas "fit" a widely understood concept of capital, but we must gain further understanding of the nature, function, role of knowledge, or ideas as a result of defining them as capital. (p.454)

Here's the crux of the matter. The appropriation of an existing concept to new uses needs to add explanatory power, not reduce it. Superficial resemblance or rhetorical affinities do not suffice. We need to establish that the appropriation of the economic concepts of "resource", "asset" and "capital" can pass this test.

In fact, our uncritical appropriation of these concepts often creates more explanatory problems than solutions.

We'll start by looking at the terms "asset" and "capital" and then look separately at the term "resource".

The notions of "asset" and "capital" are closely intertwined and share similar properties (though they mean slightly different things). Their roots lie in both economics and accounting. The same goes for the narrower notions of *knowledge assets*, *intangible assets*, and *intellectual capital*.

The modern resurgence of knowledge management in the 1990s coincided with the growth of the modern intellectual capital movement and with an increased interest in accounting for intangible assets. The dynamics of all three schools of thought were very closely related at that time.

The need to be able to account for the value of intangibles became particularly pressing with the growth of technology-assisted "knowledge-based" businesses in the 1990s. Was there a robust method for quantifying the value of firms that had very little in the way of tangible assets but had a great deal (it seemed) in future economic potential? The value of intangible assets, it was argued, could be ascertained in the aggregate by subtracting the value of tangible assets and cash from the market price paid for a firm.

The challenge was in how to disaggregate the value of different components and types of intangible assets—that is, to account for them at a more granular level.

Similarly, the intellectual capital movement and the knowledge management movement were very closely connected in the 1990s, though they subsequently disengaged and have since followed separate pathways. In fact, Tom Stewart's 1998 book *Intellectual Capital* treated KM and intellectual capital management as if they were very much the same thing.

The term *intellectual capital* in particular is often used as a portmanteau word to include a variety of intangible forms of capital, and is frequently used interchangeably with *intangible assets* (e.g., Brooking, 1996; Edvinsson & Malone, 1997; Sveiby, 1998; Stewart, 1998; Sullivan, 2000; Lev, 2001; Andriessen, 2004; Sherman, 2012). The history of the development of the theory of intellectual capital is closely aligned with the increased attention to the importance and value of intangibles to organizations in the 1980s and 1990s, and it was largely driven by the challenge of valuing intangibles at more granular levels beyond an aggregate transacted lump sum.

However, the idea of knowledge as an asset or as capital has much older roots. As with "knowledge management", there is a mistaken impression that the concept of intellectual capital is a very recent one. Patrick Sullivan traces the history of the intellectual capital movement only as far back as the 1980s, with the work of Hiroyuki Itami and Karl-Erik Sveiby on the role of intangible assets in contributing to company performance (Sullivan, 2000, p. 13; Itami, 1987; Sveiby & Risling, 1986; Sveiby & Lloyd, 1987).

Debra Amidon, who introduced the concept at a Purdue University conference in April 1987, was unaware of any references to intellectual capital prior to that event (Amidon, personal communication, August 27, 2010; Amidon & Dimancescu, 1988).

Yet there are many earlier references to intellectual capital. William Hudson (1993, p. 15) found a reference to intellectual capital in a 1969 letter of J. K. Galbraith (cf. also Roos & Pike, 2007). Zbiegniew Domaniewski, a Polish émigré to the US, published a treatise on intellectual capital in 1950 under the pseudonym of Johannes Alasco (1950; cf. Hodges, 2000, p. 44).

Sociologist Robert Faris (1947) described the cultural and social knowledge that is passed down between generations as a form of intellectual capital. The economist John Kendrick (1961) traced the use of the concept to the early nineteenth-century German economists Adam Heinrich Müller and Friedrich List in exactly the sense we mean it today—that is, "the technical knowledge or know-how of men as expressed in their activities, forms of organization, and tangible capital goods . . . the result of investments in the discovery and spread of productive knowledge" (p. 105). Serenko and Bontis (2013a) trace the roots of the term back to the British economist Nassau William Senior

(1836). William Roscher (1878, pp. 176, 191) traced references to intellectual capital back to several German political economists in the first half of the nineteenth century.

What is most likely is that the concept of intellectual capital has been part of normal parlance as well as economic thought for at least a hundred years and probably more. It even appears as a casual aside in a January 1914 letter to the editor of *The North American Review* discussing the policies of President Woodrow Wilson (Perkins, 1914, p. 157).

However, as Serenko and Bontis (2013b) observe, common parlance does not build a body of theory, which only emerges from extended discussion across a scholarly discipline, evidenced by citations of other scholars' work across publications. In this sense a coherent body of theory did not begin to emerge until the 1980s, and it was the drive to account for the value and the managerial possibilities of intellectual capital in the 1990s that shaped how that body of theory became structured.

So what changed in the 1980s and 1990s was not the discovery of a new form of capital, but a final bending to the increasing pressure to move beyond simply *recognizing* the existence of intangibles and of different forms of intellectual capital, to being able to *measure and manage them at a fine level of detail*—and, following that, to be able to assign value to intangible assets and to understand how to grow the value of intellectual capital.

John Kendrick (1961) had argued that intellectual capital was inextricably intertwined with tangible capital and that "it would require major statistical surgery to try to value intangible separately from tangible capital" (p. 105).

By the late 1980s, that hesitation no longer held weight, as it became obvious that the management challenges of intangibles were becoming ever more complex. At the same time, the performance advantages of being able to measure and manage intangibles with greater precision became more and more apparent. Serious attempts at "statistical surgery" had become necessary. There was to be an attempt to separate the conjoined twins.

The bad news is that although the literature on the valuation of intangibles has burgeoned in the intervening decades, these efforts at measuring and reporting value have not proven successful in terms of adoption by companies (Roos & Pike, 2007; Pike & Roos, 2011; Serenko & Bontis, 2013a; Schaper, 2016). There is no shortage of frameworks and measurement models, but there is a dearth of application, which in its turn implies a dearth of utility. As we will see in chapter 18, intellectual capital measurement methods are more successful at description and communication at a strategic level than they are at measurement and accounting at an operational level.

This historical review helps us discern the central motivation for associating the terms *capital* or *asset* with knowledge. As soon as we use the term *asset* or *capital*, however loosely we mean it, there is no escaping the implication that we should be able to assign value. This is why the metaphors of knowledge as assets and capital seem so compelling in the field, but it is also why we need to be especially careful of syllepsis and cargo cultism. There is a strong motivation to ascribe strong meanings to weak senses. The test of cargo cultism is whether we can in fact ascribe value or whether we are simply going through the motions of ascribing value.

Slippage of Meaning: From Literal Asset to Figurative Asset

At the beginning of this chapter, I said that the term *knowledge asset* was especially susceptible to slippage of meaning and reference. As Scarborough and Swan (2001, p. 5) observed quite early on in their analysis of KM as a management fashion, the slippage between "soft" and "hard" meanings of *asset* was sometimes used deliberately to give greater substance to KM and to bolster its association with the intellectual capital movement.

More often, it would appear, this slippage just appears to be a consistent blind spot, where inconsistency of treatment is the norm. Let me give some examples from the literature.

Patricia Eng and Paul Corney (2017) give a compelling example of the motivation for treating organizational knowledge as an asset:

> My wireless keyboard stopped working so I ordered a new one. It cost less than $20. Today someone from Premises comes to my office and puts a sticker on the keyboard with a barcode. He says, "It's okay now it's shown in our inventory of assets" and goes away. That same day the company's first US Patent notification arrives complete with a certificate. It cost about $30k to acquire, not to mention the time spent developing the idea. It's not shown as an asset of the organization yet its revenue potential is huge and it needs to be maintained. (p. 75)

So far, so good. The example makes an eloquent case for the need to treat important knowledge with the same seriousness as the organization treats its tangible assets. Yet the same paragraph that discusses the importance of managing patents as assets then moves seamlessly to a discussion of an inventory of critical knowledge held by subject matter experts, as if the knowledge held by experts is of the same asset class as a patent.

Organizations do not own the personal knowledge of the people they employ. They may have reasonable expectations over how their employees' knowledge and expertise should be deployed in their service, but this knowledge is not an asset in the same sense as a patent, or a piece of equipment, or a building.

The ISO (International Organization for Standardization) 30401 standard falls prey to the same problem: "Knowledge is an intangible organizational asset that needs to be managed like any other asset" (ISO, 2018b, p. v). In the detail the standard does distinguish between knowledge that is owned by organizations and knowledge that is owned by humans (ISO, 2018b, p. 4), but in the aggregate the document assumes that it can all be managed "like any other asset."

The *European Guide to Good Practice in Knowledge Management* does the same thing, starting with a narrow definition assigning the term *knowledge asset* to an organization's structural capital, and then broadening it to personal knowledge without any signaling that it is doing so:

> Knowledge assets are those, which remain with the company when the employees walk out through the door—such as manuals, customer databases, process descriptions, patents etc. (CEN [European Committee for Standardization], 2004, pt. 1, p. 16)

That is fine. Then the slippage occurs:

> Knowledge is the combination of data and information, to which is added expert opinion, skills and experience, to result in a valuable asset, which can be used to aid decision making. Knowledge may be explicit and/or tacit, individual and/or collective. (CEN, 2004, pt. 1, p. 6)

Repeatedly, through the remainder of the *Guide* the term *asset* slips beyond the narrow (and defensible) definition at the outset into the less defensible realm of personal knowledge. Here is an example given in part 2 of the *Guide*:

> During these sessions a number of areas of competence were investigated with the knowledge, skills and attitude elements of each competence investigate [*sic*] and then similar analysis undertaken by the general manger [*sic*] in sessions with her staff. Next the key knowledge assets were determined, and not surprisingly much of the knowledge differentiating the company from its competitors was in the heads of three of the staff. This gave the company vulnerability in a marketplace where poaching good staff by competitors is commonplace. (CEN, 2004, pt. 2, p. 39)

This slippage of denotation, with lip service being given to the narrow sense of asset but with constant assimilation of the broader (metaphorical) sense, is not only pervasive, but we also appear to be oblivious to it. What should be striking (setting out a clear definition in one breath and contravening it in another) is consistently unnoticed.

Here is the problem with this: if it turns out that the properties of knowledge are fundamentally different from "any other" types of assets, then the expectation that it can be managed "like any other asset" is a false one. This calls into question our whole assumption that the same managerial practices can extend across the "real" assets that we own and the "metaphorical" assets that we do not own. Crudely put, if KM acknowledged the distinction between organizationally owned and nonowned knowledge instead of concealing it, then we might be clearer about practices aimed at managing what we own, and influencing the deployment of the things we do not own.

So if this is a real issue and not simply an argument about semantics, it has important implications. Is it then a real issue?

Let us go back to definitions. The *Oxford Dictionary of Economics* defines assets as "Possessions of value, both real and financial. Real assets include land, buildings, or machinery owned. Financial assets include cash and securities, and credit extended to customers. The assets side of a company's balance-sheet includes both real and financial assets" (Black et al., 2012).

The term *asset* has a few connotations that the term *resource* does not have:

- *Asset* implies *ownership*, which brings the possibility of *excludability*—that is, the capability to exclude people from gaining access to the asset.

- The concepts of ownership and known value also imply *power of disposition*—assets can be controlled, disposed of at will, and traded or converted into capital or other forms of asset.

- *Asset* implies a *known (or ascertainable) value* that can be established through transactions in the market and that can be accounted for.

Excludability and the power of disposition are central to whether or not assets can be recognized as such for accounting purposes. In 2016 the International Financial Reporting Standards (IFRS) were discussing the definition of an asset as "a present economic resource controlled by the entity as a result of past events. An economic resource is a right that has the potential to produce economic benefits" (IFRS, 2016). This appears to treat an asset as a rather special type of economic resource. But there is marked uncertainty over how the present value of the asset should be quantified.

This imprecision reflected a debate that held for well over a decade regarding whether to change this definition to state with greater precision the most essential characteristics of an asset. An alternate definition proposed in 2007 strengthened the similarities between *asset* and *resource*, and it reinforced the notion of current value and control, while deprecating the uncertainty of how to value the expected future benefits of assets:

A24.The definition of an asset requires that the entity has rights or other privileged access to the economic resource. The assets that are useful for financial reporting purposes are those that are relevant to users' decisions about the entity. Therefore, the relevant economic resources are those of the entity. An entity establishes its ability to benefit from particular economic resources by having access to those resources. Access is what links economic resources with the entity. A25.Access that gives an entity no advantage beyond the common advantages of others because it is available to all does not result in an asset. Access by others must also be denied or limited. Having a public road outside an entity's property might seem like an asset of that entity. However, as long as there are no restrictions as to who can drive on that road (i.e., who can access the road), access to it is not an asset of the entity (although the proximity of the road might add value to the entity's property). (International Accounting Standards Board, 2007, p. 15)

The principles behind this proposal were only adopted within the IFRS in January 2020, with the new definition defining asset as "The amount of a present economic resource controlled by the entity as a result of past events. Economic resource is a right that has the potential to produce economic benefits" (IFRS, 2019).

That it took well over a decade to discuss this change points to the *difficulty* of resolving meanings between the terms *asset* and *resource*. As we will see shortly, this difficulty is founded on the difficulty of establishing a market price for all types of economic resources combined with the necessity of being able to do so for economic resources that are considered assets.

But most importantly for us, the persistent theme is that the recognition of an asset for accounting purposes requires the enterprise to have effective legal control over the asset (Lev, 2001, p. 36).

In common usage, some resources can be assets (e.g., plant or equipment), but not all resources are assets (e.g., oxygen is a natural resource consumed in an internal combustion engine that you own, and that also consumes gasoline, a commodity resource). There is overlap in the meanings, but they are not commensurate. Some assets clearly fit the definition of resources, while others do not. For example, money is not considered a productive resource according to one common definition of resources because it does not produce anything in and of itself—it is simply a mechanism by which productive resources are mobilized (McConnell et al., 2015, p. 12). And while assets can clearly be used as productive resources, they do not have to be used as such to qualify as assets. They can be exchanged for other assets or productive resources as well.

As if this were not confusing enough, the term *asset* can also be used very loosely, sometimes contrary to its primary meaning. Consider the phrase "Our most important assets are our people." Clearly, we do not own our employees, although we do possess partial excludability rights by virtue of employment contracts. It is hard to assign a value to our employees (and manage that value) as we do other forms of asset, although we can put some form of price on them through salaries and employment costs. We do not (unless we are soccer clubs or slavers) trade our people or convert them to other forms of asset. The prices we do put on our employees do not thereby establish a directly convertible price for the value of our organizational knowledge. And when we look at nontangible things such as the skills, influence networks, and experience of our employees, those rights of excludability, ownership, and trade become even more tenuous (Stacey, 2000, p. 23).

What is clear is this: the use of the term *asset* in a literal sense implies two critical features that distinguish assets from other kinds of useful resource:

- Assets are wholly owned, and as such the owning organization or person has complete power of disposition over them.
- Assets are tradable in the market, and it is possible to *establish a* reliable commercial value for them.

As such, assets can be bought and sold, they can be converted to other things, they are disposed and controlled at the will of the owner, and they can be discarded or destroyed.

To return to the chain of argument suggested by Eng and Corney, while both attributes may be true of an intangible asset such as a patent (although the valuation of intangible assets is more uncertain than tangible ones), they are not at all true of the tacit knowledge, cumulative skills, experience, and expertise of a subject matter expert.

Nor are these attributes true of the collective positive economic effects of an extraordinarily talented and effective team. Individual and team capabilities can contribute to the total valuation of a firm's intangibles, but they are not susceptible to the same powers of tradability and disposition, and the abilities and effectiveness of an individual or a team are very sensitive to context in a way that real assets are not. An ascribed value to the knowledge embodied in a person or a team in one set of conditions can dissipate very quickly with small changes in the working conditions and context. And conversely, poorly functioning teams can increase the performance of their collective knowledge through small changes that make a big difference.

Case Study: Enabling Team Knowledge

I was once appointed manager of a commercial training company. I had a lot of managerial experience but was relatively inexperienced as a trainer. The company had about thirty trainers and had been struggling with low morale. My predecessor had warned me that there was a long-standing culture of resentment toward the holding company and that there were two or three rather vocal, very experienced trainers who could be relied on to articulate this resentment in meetings and in the staff room. The culture was also resistant to the idea of quality management. Each trainer was "king" or "queen" in their own training room, and it was a closed-door training culture—there were no peer observation or learning practices. This isolationism was self-reinforcing. The less you saw of other people's practice, the less you could be sure that yours was beyond reproach and the more resistant you would be to being observed (or "audited"). I was viewed with great suspicion, both as their new manager and as a relatively inexperienced trainer.

I made three small changes: (a) In my first week, I refused to confirm the contract for a very experienced trainer at the end of his probationary period. His client feedback was not great, and he was a consistently negative presence in the training center. (b) I appointed in his place a fresh graduate with an entry qualification who was full of enthusiasm and eager to learn. (c) I promoted one of the trainers, an extremely gifted and thoughtful trainer and a quiet, always helpful presence in the staff room, to become my deputy, as director of studies. With my encouragement he instituted a regular trainer observation process, followed up by "excellent practice" sharing sessions in the staff room, which highlighted the good things he was seeing in the training rooms; and he got the trainers to demonstrate the techniques they used. Trainers started inviting each other into their training rooms for informal feedback and suggestions.

Within a couple of months, the working culture was transformed and so was the feedback we were getting from clients, resulting in lots of repeat business. As we became known for the excellence of our trainers, the quality of trainers seeking employment with us improved. The company was not without its challenges and occasional conflicts, but we achieved a sense of solidarity and mutual respect that is still unparalleled in my working career. Twenty-five years later, many of us are still in touch.

I had made just three small changes—replacing an experienced trainer with an inexperienced one in a staff of thirty, promoting a respected colleague, and instituting a simple review and learning process. Quantitatively speaking, the collective knowledge of the company had been reduced with the loss of an experienced trainer and replacement by an inexperienced one. However, the collective performance was transformed through a change in configuration and team-based learning practices.

Knowledge embedded in people is engaged through contracts of employment. It is not owned. This engagement is supported by the disposition of real assets and services, but it is neither wholly owned nor disposable beyond the terms of that contract and the general provisions of labor law. Two decades ago, management consultant and finance specialist Ken Standfield (2002) pointed out the risks associated with operating under a mental model of ownership and control when it comes to knowledge:

> In the knowledge-based economy, organizations do not own employees or their knowledge or their relationships. . . . As organizations become more knowledge-based (and less production-line based), the means of production (knowledge and relationships) will frequently reside in employees and not in physical systems. In these cases, employee knowledge is not owned by the organization, neither is the means of production. In short, in the KBE, the notion of ownership is an obsolete management concept that is a residual from the manufacturing age. Yet conventional (current) management systems are built on the concepts of ownership and control. . . . Due to the now mission-critical nature of intangibles, it can be concluded that conventional systems (1) measure the wrong things, (2) make the wrong conclusions, and (3) force erroneous decisions on organizations. In short, conventional management systems now actually destroy organizational sustainability. (pp. 37–40)

Contracts of employment do not generally give you powers of ownership or complete powers of disposition (again, unless you are a soccer club or a slave owner). The knowledge embodied in teams is a complex product of the interactions between the members of the team and the context and resources provide by the host organization. It is not at all clear where ownership begins or ends, or even that ownership is an appropriate concept to use.

ISO 30401 articulates and preserves that ambiguity by defining knowledge as a "human or organizational asset enabling effective decisions and action in context," but it does not clarify how the ambiguity is to be addressed (ISO, 2018b, p. 4).

To be clear, some forms of knowledge *are* owned and disposable and can be considered organizational assets—for example: documented knowledge, proprietary routines, stable and teachable ways of working, knowledge resources that are protected by confidentiality and intellectual property law. But not all forms of organizational knowledge can be considered assets in this sense, most especially the knowledge that is embedded in people's capabilities and competencies. Aside from questions of intellectual property ownership, it does not seem to be particularly useful to try to divide up knowledge by ownership, as Pawan Handa and his colleagues have attempted (cf. Handa et al., 2019, chap. 6).

The first sin lies in using the same language to describe all forms. It is often not clear when *knowledge asset* is being used to describe a literal asset (owned and controlled), or a figurative asset (something important that we feel should be managed like an asset but is not actually owned and controlled in the same way), or some combination of the two. This slippage results in the universal application of a philosophy of management based on concepts of ownership and control, that is appropriate only to the subclass of literal knowledge assets.

The slippage in meaning we see in the Eng and Corney story, from literal to figurative senses, without any signaling, happens time and again in the literature and in some of the most authoritative writers on knowledge assets: David Teece, Ron Young, and Max Boisot.

David Teece David Teece and Abdulrahman Al-Aali see knowledge assets as a subset of intangible assets. As such they are fundamental to the capabilities of a firm, and they are owned by the firm, even if they are grounded in individuals' experience and expertise.

However, despite this careful attention to a high-level view of firm capabilities (which can be "owned" in a loose sense), Teece and Al-Aali (2011) fall prey to the same slippage between meanings as Eng and Corney: "Examples include process know-how, customer relationships, *and the knowledge possessed by groups of especially-skilled employees*" (p. 507; my italics).

Teece and Al-Aali are sophisticated thinkers. They are sensitive to the ambiguities over both ownership and valuation in this homogeneous clustering of heterogeneous types of knowledge. They qualify their position: "firm-specific assets are idiosyncratic in nature, and are difficult to trade because their property rights are likely to have fuzzy boundaries and their value is context dependent" (2011, p. 507).

The use of "fuzzy boundaries" for property rights is a very peculiar signal of syllep-sistic embarrassment. We must assume it is invoked to conceal the problematic nature of the syllepsis at work here. It is analogous to Singapore's use of *ponding* to describe flooding. The ability to assert and defend boundaries is fundamental to the ability to assert and defend ownership rights. *Fuzzy ownership boundaries* is an oxymoron.

If we take this idea apart, we have to assume that what it means is that ownership can-not be asserted consistently across the class of knowledge types. It would be more accurate then to state that ownership of the class of things making up "knowledge of the firm" is fuzzy, disputable, or shared. But that would prevent the consistent use of the term *knowl-edge asset* and its implications of clear ownership for the entire class. This is an example of confused thinking—"It is an asset, but not all forms of it have clear ownership rights."

Ron Young   Our second example comes from the work of Ron Young and associates in the early 2000s to develop what became a detailed and fairly influential methodology for knowledge asset management. This was part of two European Commission–funded industrial research projects. Consistent with the resource-based view of the firm, knowl-edge assets are held to be "the critical strategic resources of the firm" (Mentzas et al., 2003, p. 19). Knowledge assets have dynamic and generative attributes and have the properties of both *things* (stocks) and *processes* (flows). Their key characteristic is that they create, store, and/or disseminate knowledge objects (Mentzas et al., 2003, p. 23). For example:

- A person is a knowledge asset that can create new ideas, learnings, proposals, and white papers (knowledge objects).
- A community of interest is a knowledge asset that can create new ideas and best prac-tices (knowledge objects).
- A process is a knowledge asset that can create and/or store and disseminate best prac-tices, company standards, and research and development material (knowledge objects).
- A vision is a knowledge asset that can create a new mission statement, strategic plan, and goals (knowledge objects)

Although Young and his colleagues focus on the capabilities of people as the assets in question, it does seem more than vaguely dehumanizing to define people as knowl-edge assets. The "asset" metaphor seems to be strangely limiting and rather mechanistic when we consider the complex ways in which people work with, absorb, articulate, and apply knowledge and when we consider the physical, emotional, social, and goal-driven lives within which knowledge is acquired, processed, and applied.

Young and his colleagues are conscious of the dilemma around ownership raised by the use of the asset metaphor. They differentiate between knowledge embedded in people (human knowledge assets), knowledge expressed as organizational capabilities (structural knowledge assets), and knowledge about the market together with relationship capital (market knowledge assets):

> People are the "owners" of human knowledge assets; they "rent" their knowledge assets to the company. Human assets grow when the working environment fosters and facilitates knowledge creation and sharing; when more people know in depth what knowledge is actually useful to the organization and when the company uses more of what people know. As human assets grow the results are a higher concentration of skills in what is important for the company, increased innovation and participation, and an increase in people working in areas that are critical for the business. (Mentzas et al., 2003, p. 27; cf. Powell, 2020, p. 47)

There is a circularity in defining people as knowledge assets and then as owners of themselves. But at face value, this is a fair representation of the symbiosis that exists between knowledge in people and knowledge in organizations, and it reflects a better way of expressing distribution of ownership than the "fuzzy boundaries" of David Teece. However, it only superficially addresses it.

In this account, *knowledge assets* are distinguished from *knowledge objects*, which are the items of knowledge produced, exchanged, and stored by these different types of assets (Mentzas et al., 2003, p. 24). Knowledge assets are the higher-order processing capabilities lodged in the different elements that make up the enterprise.

That would imply that the knowledge itself is distinguishable from the assets and that the assets are the platforms or channels processing it. If this distinction can be maintained, then an asset management approach to knowledge might be defensible.

However, the distinction is not maintained, and with Young and his colleagues, the knowledge asset metaphor repeatedly slips between "asset as capability" and "asset as knowledge object"—and the slippage is persistent and unmarked. This is another classic case of syllepsis. Take this example: "Knowledge analysts are people able to capture knowledge assets, organize them into a form anyone can use, and periodically update and edit those knowledge assets" (Mentzas et al., 2003, p. 33). In practice, a knowledge asset is taken to mean *both* the knowledge-processing capability and the knowledge being processed. Linguistic contortions and inconsistencies are signals of the syllepsis.

With this syllepsis in mind, on closer examination the analogy of "renting" human knowledge assets seems both inaccurate and strange. While it just seems a bit of a stretch to say we rent people's knowledge-processing capability, it seems distinctly odd to say that employment contracts are about renting people's knowledge. Except in certain special cases (e.g., consulting a lawyer), what we are mostly renting is people's time, devoted to certain kinds of tasks and activities and in which certain delimited areas of their larger stocks of knowledge and skills and capabilities are expected to be applied.

In fact, people's total stocks of knowledge and capabilities far exceed the stock that is expected to be applied at work. Even then, the notion of ownership of that stock, invoked by the notion of *asset* itself, neglects the question of where that knowledge came from—from society, from education, from personal networks, from personal investigation and experimentation, or from previous employers (cf. Arrow, 1962, p. 168; Machlup, 1980, pp. 178–179). In classic economic theory, thinking of knowledge as a public good makes much more sense than the use of a commodity or property-based metaphor (Machlup, 1984, pp. 159–160).

Let me give an example from Robert Graves's (1957) account of life in the trenches of World War I:

> The single memorable event was one of purely technical interest: a new method that an officer named Owen and myself discovered for silencing machine-guns firing at night. We gave each sentry a piece of string about a yard long, with a cartridge tied at each end. When the machine gun began traversing, sentries farthest from the line of fire would stretch their string towards it and peg them down with cartridge points; so we got a pretty accurate line on the machine-gun. When we had about thirty or more of these lines taken on a single machine-gun, we fixed rifles as carefully as possible along them and waited; as soon as it started again we opened five rounds rapid. This gave a close concentration of fire, and no element of nervousness could disturb the aim, the rifles being secured between sandbags. Divisional headquarters asked us for a report of the method. (p. 170)

People (and teams) in organizations create this kind of *method knowledge* constantly (Brown & Duguid, 1998, p. 91). Certainly, in cases where the knowledge is useful, an organization should put management processes around it, propagate it, and perhaps protect it. We can understand why it should be written up and sent to divisional headquarters.

But who owns it, and where did it come from? Graves and his fellow officers were, by and large, fresh out of public school. They would have been taught geometry, and this was a simple triangulation technique using the materials at hand applied to a serious problem. The same method or similar ones could have been invented dozens of times by people with similar backgrounds in similar situations, out of the public stock of knowledge available to them all. It would not stand the legal test in terms of intellectual property protection: they used knowledge in the public domain that could have been developed independently, and had no special characteristics that would prevent it from being invented independently elsewhere.

So it seems to make a rather larger and overly simple claim than reality would support to say that people's knowledge and/or their knowledge-processing capabilities are owned by themselves and "rented" to their employer.

Moreover, as the Graves example illustrates, work in organizations is not simply additive. I do not take a "piece" of my knowledge and apply it or contribute it to an organizational capability. Knowledge work is compound, complex, and emergent. An organizational capability emerges out of the interactions between persons and teams and organizational infrastructure and problems—*as well as* out of interactions with proprietary organizational knowledge. While the "knowledge-rental" gambit *appears* to address the ownership entailment that is raised by using the term *knowledge asset*, it does so through a rather strange analogy that does not in any way reflect the complexity of the way knowledge is articulated in organizations, or how it is acquired in the first place.

The inner syllepsis remains—to what extent is the knowledge in people that is engaged in the firm really subject to the powers of disposition of the "renters"? Can property rights be so cleanly divided and defined when the organization invests in the enabling environment for human-owned knowledge? David Teece did not think so, which is why he had recourse to "fuzzy boundaries."

Furthermore, having asserted the ownership of the individual, where does the transition in ownership occur between knowledge originated by an individual or a team, that then modifies the structural or market knowledge assets of the firm? Or the reflexive case in which the knowledge of the firm modifies the knowledge of the individual?

This set of conundrums comes directly from the entailment of the asset metaphor. Ron Young's classification of knowledge asset types and the knowledge asset metaphor itself do not adequately represent the complex interactions that go into making up a firm's capabilities, and they inevitably raise the specter of ownership and control without providing the means to address it.

Max Boisot   Our third case is Max Boisot, who wrote what is still the most theoretically robust analysis of the pathways by which knowledge assets can be created, transacted, and diffused in organizations and the ways in which knowledge can be made to realize economic value.

In his theoretical exposition of knowledge assets in organizations and in the I-Space (information space) framework for classifying their characteristics and potential, Boisot (1998) largely sidesteps the question of ownership and disposability altogether. His usage of the term *knowledge asset* takes as its point of departure an accountancy-based definition: "Knowledge assets are stocks of knowledge from which services are expected to flow for a period of time that may be hard to specify in advance" (p. 3).

The ownership entailment is silent, but Boisot's focus is the firm, and by and large he appears to focus primarily on descriptions of knowledge assets as the undisputed property of the firm.

In line with the resource-based theory of the firm, knowledge assets, according to Boisot, are transacted and combined in the environment of the firm and expressed in the form of technologies, competences, and capabilities. Organizational culture can also be considered a knowledge asset, insofar as it provides the habits and norms that enable (or disable) the processing of knowledge to produce technologies, competences, and capabilities. Personal knowledge of individuals is very rarely confused with this sense of "knowledge asset". So far, so good.

Yet even Boisot (1998) occasionally slips, as in this passage: "Knowledge assets are embedded in things, documents, and in people's heads, and these in turn are configured to produce organizations, technologies, and products" (p. 164).

It is clear that knowledge in people is not capable of "configuration" in the same sense as knowledge in things and documents, and the question of contestable ownership arises again to queer his otherwise fairly consistent use of the term *knowledge asset* to refer to the firm's knowledge.

Moreover, once Boisot started to apply the I-Space framework for mapping knowledge assets in real-world situations, it became apparent that his workshop participants were mapping knowledge held by people and groups and not just owned and controlled by the firm itself (Boisot, 1998, p. 246; Ihrig & MacMillan, 2013, p. 136).

The slippage was of course inevitable, because the knowledge of the firm cannot in practice be surgically separated from the knowledge of the people who make up the firm. The use of the term *asset* then begs the same basic questions over ownership and control.

Boisot's avoidance of the ownership question is not unusual. In the broader discipline of asset management (i.e., tangible asset management), ownership of assets is rarely explicit—it is simply taken for granted. Even the ISO 55000 standard for asset management treats ownership as implicit and does not include the attributes of ownership or powers of disposition explicitly in its definition of *asset*: "An asset is an item, thing or entity that has potential or actual value to an organization. The value will vary between different organizations and their stakeholders, and can be tangible or intangible, financial or non-financial" (ISO, 2014, p. 2).

There are a few obvious reasons why this particular ISO standard remains silent on the question of ownership in relation to physical assets:

- The management of physical assets is frequently outsourced, and so the asset managers who are following the ISO standard may not be the owners.
- The standard is intended to provide a consistent management regime for a physical asset across different owners, as any given (physical) asset passes from one owner to another during its life span.

- Assets are often managed to produce value for stakeholders other than the owners (e.g., renters).

Nevertheless, the concept of ownership is implicit elsewhere in the standard (e.g., "An organization may choose to manage *its* assets as a group, rather than individually"), and power of disposition is implicit in the existence of the standard itself. Asset management implies some degree of power of disposition, whether by direct ownership or responsibility delegated by an owner.

The taken for grantedness of ownership, while unproblematic for physical asset management, supported as it is by the laws of the land, does create problems when that silence is extended to the idea of knowledge to be treated as an asset. As a result, the ISO 55000 standard attempts to cover both physical and intangible assets in its purview, with some consequent dislocations. Silence on the matter leads to a couple of erroneous assumptions:

1. The erroneous assumption that standards and processes appropriate to physical asset life cycle management are applicable to knowledge life cycle management, including, without distinction, explicitly owned knowledge and knowledge embedded in individuals and teams.

   In fact, when we look at the ISO 55000 standard, the framework does provide useful ways of viewing the management of intangible assets in a very general way, but as Boisot (1998, p. 3) himself pointed out, in practice, knowledge behaves quite differently from physical assets, and it is absurd to think that the same basic life cycle management regime could be applied across both types. It may be useful to use an asset life cycle metaphor for thinking about how to manage knowledge through its life cycle (cf. Handa et al., 2019, chap. 7), but the comparison falls down when we get down to the detail.

   For example, a facility that is sold by one owner and bought by another will legitimately inherit the same asset management history and regime as its precedent owner. There is no such continuity with a person who moves to new employment nor should there be—they may be moving to a completely different role and engaging different forms of knowledge.

   Moreover, physical assets, being tangible, may be directly managed. Knowledge in people, if it is managed at all, is imperfectly perceived, ill-bounded, and indirectly managed and influenced, because it is not subject to the same mechanisms of observation and control.

2. The erroneous assumption that knowledge embedded in individuals and teams can be configured, combined, and deployed to produce services with the same freedoms as physical assets.

Boisot's work acknowledges with great sophistication the complexity of generating services from tacit knowledge assets, but aside from brief references in his discussion of culture, he does not adequately address the issue of the disposition powers or the influencing powers of the firm over the holders of that knowledge. The use of the asset metaphor conceals this blind spot.

The entailment of the "asset" metaphor raises the specter of knowledge ownership. Once raised, addressing and resolving the question of knowledge ownership becomes a central challenge in knowledge management. Avoidance of the question simply produces confusion. For example, we know that perceptions of ownership have a direct influence on openness to knowledge sharing. If there is a clear perception that the organization owns the knowledge in question, people tend to be more open to sharing. If there is a prevailing belief that the individual owns the knowledge, people are less open to sharing (Saetang, 2011). Contested or unclear ownership will produce inconsistent attitudes toward sharing.

Once ownership is raised as a question, further questions of ethics and natural justice arise over how the products of knowledge work should be acknowledged, rewarded, and exploited (Koulikov, 2011; Rechberg & Syed, 2013). And what of knowledge that is an emergent, compound product of the interactions of individuals, teams, organizational structures, and society? Questions of ownership complicate and tend toward the artificial decomposition of what could otherwise be a phenomenological account of the knowledge that exists.

These are all questions that lie at the core of a firm's ability to successfully engage the more complex and people-based forms of knowledge so that the host organization can form them into the capabilities and knowledge services that they compete on.

Whether it be using the term *asset* to imply universal ownership and managerial control where it is actually patchy and ill-bounded or using the term *asset* while remaining silent on questions of ownership, both these strategies, of implication and silence, have unhelpful consequences when applied to knowledge work:

- For most KM contexts and audiences, it will not be clear whether we are speaking about literal assets, where formal asset management processes can and should be engaged, or figurative assets, where processes analogous to asset management (but with indeterminate degrees of similarity) should be engaged.

- It is, however, very clear that not all the core processes of physical asset management are appropriate to knowledge embedded in people and groups.

- Implications of ownership and control are communicated whether or not they are asserted and whether or not they are accurate.

This ambiguity leads to poor practices:

- It raises questions of ownership and ethics that are inappropriate to, and can interfere with, the complex ways that knowledge works in organizations.

- It favors KM processes that focus on what *can* be controlled, neglecting areas of knowledge use where ownership and control are ambiguous, if not entirely inappropriate, concepts, or it can lead to attempts to impose processes that are inappropriate to how people really work with knowledge (Standfield, 2002, pp. 37–40).

- It deflects attention from the ways of managing and influencing knowledge use that do respect the creative, collaborative, and emergent dispositions of knowledge in the enterprise.

- It leads toward KM practices that "disembody" knowledge from the people and contexts in which knowledge is created, is applied, and has value (Snowden, 2002, p. 101).

This argument is not made lightly. The use of the asset metaphor is widespread in knowledge management. Before I engaged in the analysis for this book, I used it frequently myself for its persuasive appeal. Let us remind ourselves why the term *knowledge asset* is so attractive:

- First, there is a clear need to manage knowledge as something that is important to the enterprise (like an asset or resource).

- Second, the metaphor communicates a sense of physicality and manipulability to knowledge, which is reassuring in the face of so much evidence of complexity and fluidity and ambiguity surrounding knowledge. It promises to give us something concrete and specific to do. Ron Young's slippage between asset as capability to asset as a *product* of the capability can be explained as a felt need to move from a theoretical description of knowledge assets to a practical definition of knowledge processes (Mentzas et al., 2003, p. 30).

- Finally, there are established processes, good practices, and even an ISO standard for asset management, and this lends authority to a knowledge asset management approach, even though in many cases (and in some of the most challenging and important cases of knowledge application facing us) we do not have the necessary ownership and disposal rights to actually use them.

> Here is the danger. When we explicitly adopt the appearance of asset management processes, we are subjecting ourselves to the requirements and entailments of the language whether or not they are appropriate to the phenomena we are working with.

Sometimes (as with properly owned and bounded explicit knowledge resources) these entailments are appropriate. Sometimes (as with knowledge embedded in people or created in interactions between people) they are not. There is, moreover, an opaque transition zone where corporately owned knowledge merges with unowned (publicly derived) knowledge in people and where it is dynamically transformed and applied. Knowledge here is wholly mysterious and unaccounted for in the "asset management" view.

Analyzing the Syllepsis

In using the asset metaphor, it is not clear in our discourse, in our operating models, and in our practice, when we mean the thing we own, the thing we do not own, or something in flux between the two. This is undecidable syllepsis. When it forms the frame for managerial thinking and the design of systems and processes, this is the basis for magical thinking writ large. This is cargo cult thinking. If I call it an asset, I can treat it like it is an asset, and I am thereby delivering value from it. Creating an inventory of expertise is taken to be the same as managing expertise.

Let us show this in a formal analysis of the syllepsis involved in the term *knowledge asset*, with the help of figure 12.1.

1. In the use of *knowledge asset*, the entailment is one of ownership and power of disposition and that a tradable value can be established.

2. The metaphor conceals the fact that many important forms of knowledge to be managed and influenced in the firm do not have the same ownership and disposition rights as physical assets, and those types of knowledge also have uncertain valuation potential.

3. There are two contradictory meanings in the usage of the term *knowledge asset*, one of them implying full ownership and power of disposition, together with tradability, and the other remaining silent on ownership and power of disposition, and on tradability, because they cannot be established.

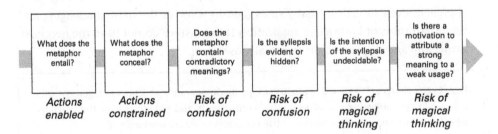

Figure 12.1
Criteria for identifying the risks associated with syllepsis.

4. These differences are not visible when "knowledge assets" are described and discussed. This leads to a high potential for confusion as to what is meant by the term *knowledge asset* when it is used to describe organizational knowledge in general.

5. The syllepsis is intrinsically undecidable, as both ownership and nonownership, and both valuation and nonvaluation are implicit but not signaled or credibly addressed in most usages of the term.

6. There is a motivation to bolster the authority of KM processes by appealing to the concreteness of asset management as a discipline and to the authoritativeness of preexisting standards for asset management. It also reflects the desire to ascribe clear value to knowledge in the organization. This syllepsis creates a susceptibility to magical thinking in which the management actions will not reflect the reality of all the forms of knowledge at play. Knowledge in experts cannot be managed in the same way or with the same assumptions as knowledge in patents. The syllepsis also both raises and suppresses the importance of the question of knowledge ownership, which creates apparently irresolvable tensions for KM to address.

We have to conclude then that the use of the term *knowledge asset* satisfies our criteria for both slippery and treacherous syllepsis.

It is useful to note that the term *capital* is not susceptible to the same problems when used in relation to an organization's knowledge. First, there is a developed typology of intellectual capital types, and the term *capital* itself is already an abstract concept (unlike asset) and must be qualified whenever it is used (e.g., structural capital, relationship capital, customer capital, and human capital). It must communicate its special, knowledge-associated properties in order to be used. This makes the ambiguity of the root term *capital* addressable through clear labeling.

Second, the use of the term *capital* is, like *intangible assets*, a term that ascribes a high-level aggregate value. While, like *asset*, the term *capital* implies both ownership and control by the organization, intellectual capital mapping rarely leads directly to granular examinations of specific knowledge in application, so it does not present us with the challenge of concealed, contested ownership between the organization and the individual or the group.

Agnė Ramanauskaitė and Kristina Rudžionienė (2013) reviewed the literature on intellectual capital valuation and discovered over sixty different valuation methods but significant gaps in the area that had received the greatest initial interest in the intellectual capital movement, the translation of intellectual capital into clear statements of financial value. In practice these methods are largely qualitative valuation methods.

The metaphor of intellectual capital, like that of intangible assets, is simply not an attractive vehicle for describing the specifics of the working knowledge in use in the same way as the knowledge asset metaphor. It does not expose us to the same magical thinking temptations. This is why issues of contested or ambiguous ownership do not arise with those metaphors in the same way. However, the metaphor carries some benefits; for example, it provides a framework for thinking about knowledge investment strategies or knowledge capitalization strategies, both of which are useful for determining how an organization could improve the management of its knowledge (cf. Handa et al., 2019, chap. 11).

Discussions of "knowledge assets", on the other hand, appear persistently to range between high-level views of strategic capabilities (compound or bundled knowledge) and very granular views of specific components of knowledge, both personal and institutional, calling for granular managerial processes.

This feature accounts for the initial attractiveness of the metaphor, as compared with intellectual capital and intangible assets. It implies a promise as to its ability to help managers manage. As it turns out, this is an unreliable promise. As we saw with Boisot's experience of knowledge asset mapping, the irresolvable confrontation between organizational ownership and personal ownership is inevitable with the use of the term *knowledge asset*, and this is why the syllepsis is treacherous and why the term *knowledge asset* is best avoided.

Not everyone will agree with this analysis. There is a great and widespread affection for the term *asset* in relation to knowledge management. It carries a promise of control and value determination, even if it does not easily live up to that promise. For example, Pawan Handa, Jean Pagani, and Denise Bedford's (2019) book *Knowledge Assets and Knowledge Audits* adheres firmly to the *asset* terminology while also acknowledging, in a very clear-sighted way, issues around contested and divided ownership (pp. 107–117). This is a nuanced approach that somewhat (but not wholly) mitigates the negative effects of the syllepsis I have outlined.

Handa et al. are highly motivated to retain the *asset* terminology because they want to bring together the ascribed rigor of a management accounting audit with the intellectual capital tradition. The syllepsis is partly mitigated by an overt acknowledgment of shared ownership of knowledge (between individuals, teams, and organization) and by assimilating the term *knowledge asset* into the term *knowledge capital* and treating the two concepts as virtually synonymous. I do not believe they are synonymous, and I believe the term *asset* brings more problems than benefits.

More to the point, I believe we have a much safer term we can use instead, as we shall see in the next chapter.

*   *   *

Summary

In this chapter I have analyzed the entailments and risks associated with the commonly used metaphors for knowledge as an "asset" or as a form of "capital". Here is a summary of the main points:

1. The metaphor of knowledge as an asset is an example of the kind of syllepsis that can lead to magical thinking. It leads to the notions of ownership and control being applied indiscriminately and inappropriately to all forms of organizational knowledge.
2. This affects the quality of practice. The metaphor can negatively influence people's willingness to share, and it produces a mechanistic approach to KM that does not fully represent the complexity and variety of knowledge use in organizations.
3. The negative effects of this syllepsis can be partly mitigated by overt discussion of contested and shared ownership.
4. The metaphor of knowledge as a form of capital is so general that it requires qualification. This is an example of a form of syllepsis that can be, and often is, managed through further qualification and definition. It does not necessarily lead to magical thinking but has little practical use in the "hard" ascription of value to knowledge.

13 The Language of Value: Resources

Lay not up for yourselves treasures upon earth, where moth and rust doth corrupt, and where thieves break through and steal: but lay up for yourselves treasures in heaven, where neither moth nor rust doth corrupt, and where thieves do not break through nor steal: for where your treasure is, there will your heart be also.
—Matthew 6:19–21

If knowledge as *asset* is a risky and misleading metaphor to use, what about knowledge as *resource*?

Knowledge as Resource: The Background

The notion of knowledge as a resource has a more complex history than that of knowledge as capital or asset, and although the term *resource* also has a value implication, the association with determination of value is much less clear with *resource* than with *asset* and *capital*.

The genealogy of this idea lies principally in economics, leading into the theory of business strategy (cf. Powell, 2020, chap. 3), but there is also a separate tradition in information management. Although a less well-known tradition in management theory, the information management heritage has had an outsize influence in knowledge management (KM) because of the way that traditions of information auditing have influenced the thinking on knowledge audits.

The *Oxford Dictionary of Economics* defines a resource as

Any factor endowments that can contribute to economic activity. This includes natural resources, including those located on land and in or under the sea; human resources, including labor of various skills and qualifications; and capital goods or man-made means of production. Economics can be defined as the study of how resources are, or should be, allocated. (Black et al., 2012)

Modern economics has at its core the idea that economic resources are deliberately deployed toward their most productive uses, and while the best-known exponent of this view is the relatively modern resource-based view of the firm, the basic idea can be traced back as far as Adam Smith (Stigler, 1976).

Adam Smith (1975) uses the term *resource* in three main ways. His first sense of *resource* is as a recourse in a situation of need—that is, something to fall back on. For example, when two or three manufacturing trades require essentially the same skills and one or more of those trades is weakening while the other is strengthening, workers might find the stronger trade a "resource" to turn to (pp. 151–152). Resources therefore provide options and flexibility.

Smith's second sense of *resource* is as something that can be consumed to address an economic or political purpose—for example, a drawdown on the domestic money supply to finance a foreign war (p. 441).

Smith's third sense is the productive capability that underpins consumable resources such as money—in this case, the productive capacity of a nation or "the annual produce of the land and labour of the country" (p. 444). This third sense implies a capacity that has versatility of deployment and not simply something that is consumed.

In the first sense, a variety of resources provide a variety of options; in the second sense, resources can be consumed; and in the third sense, resources can be deployed in different ways for productive ends. All three senses are important to the way that an understanding of the idea of knowledge as a resource evolved, but the one that is most pertinent is the last one: something that provides a capacity and that can be deployed with versatility in different ways. Interestingly for us, the term *resource* is agnostic as to ownership, so we anticipate that it will avoid at least one major problem raised by the use of the *asset* metaphor.

Early in the twentieth century, the German economist Joseph Schumpeter (1934) proposed that economic change and development are driven by innovation and that innovation is grounded in the behavior of suppliers who develop new products and services from novel combinations of productive resources. It follows that the command of resources is not primarily associated with ownership (as with assets) but simply implies an ability to shape and combine with versatility the ways in which resources are compounded and deployed (pp. 65–66).

This idea was taken up and developed more extensively by Edith Penrose in her 1959 classic, *The Theory of the Growth of the Firm*: "Thus, a firm is more than an administrative unit; it is also a collection of productive resources the disposal of which between different uses and over time is determined by administrative decision."

Penrose distinguishes between physical resources (some of which would qualify as tangible assets of a firm, others as resources acquired from the marketplace, and others as natural resources) and human resources comprising skilled and unskilled labor. She points out, foreshadowing the intellectual capital and knowledge management movement of the 1990s, that the loss of people at the height of their abilities is "akin to a capital loss."

Her most interesting distinction, however, is between the resources themselves and the actual services those resources deliver in performing the productive work of the firm. *Resources are characterized by their potentiality, and the scope of this potentiality may not be wholly determinable at any given point of time.*

In other words, resources do not have an absolute value independent of the contexts in which they are used and the services they render. The valuation of resources depends heavily on attention to the contexts and outcomes of use, and it is more reliable in retrospect than in prospect. There is intrinsic uncertainty in the valuation of resources because of this context dependency. Assets can be bounded, measured, and valued, but for resources this is "almost impossible to discover in practice":

> The services yielded by resources are a function of the way in which they are used—exactly the same resource when used for different purposes or in different ways and in combination with different types or amounts of other resources provides a different service or set of services. The important distinction between resources and services is not in their relative durability; rather it lies in the fact that resources consist of a bundle of potential services and can, for the most part, be defined independently of their use, while services cannot be so defined, the very word "service" implying a function, an activity. As we shall see, it is largely in this distinction that we find the source of the uniqueness of each individual firm. (Penrose, 1959, pp. 24–25)

Today those of us working in the KM space could easily transpose *resource* with *knowledge resource* and still find the explanation completely expressive of the way that knowledge is used to produce value in organizations. However, Penrose's insight remained relatively unexploited for the next twenty years.

It found a new lease on life in a series of attempts to redefine the nature of strategic management following the collapse in confidence in long-range strategic planning in the economic turmoil of the 1970s. We described some aspects of this in our discussion of the rise of participatory approaches to strategic planning in chapter 7.

As Henry Mintzberg (1994) describes it, strategic planning at that time had become divorced from a deep understanding of a firm's own operations and capabilities. It relied too much on making predictive extrapolations from industry trends, using functionally distinct corporate planning departments filled with "experts" who were informed by the theories taught in business schools, and often supported by management consultants (Stacey & Mowles, 2016, pp. 11–12).

When the sharp economic discontinuities of the 1973–1975 recession challenged this practice, attention turned toward gaining a greater understanding of the internal strengths and weaknesses of the firm, and toward an understanding of strategy as a deliberate means of leveraging one's strengths in relation to the environment, and to competitors.

In 1982, economists Richard Nelson and Sidney Winter published *An Evolutionary Theory of Economic Change*, arguing that firms and their competitiveness are best understood in terms of their unique resource bases. Distinctive bundles and deployments of resources give competitive and strategic advantage.

In 1984 Birger Wernerfelt published his seminal paper "A Resource-Based View of the Firm" in the *Strategic Management Journal*, taking up Edith Penrose's challenge by attempting to build a robust method for hardening strategic options out of the variable potentialities of a firm's resources.

He did this by analyzing the attractiveness of different kinds of resources, both tangible and intangible, using Michael Porter's Five Forces model as a framework to examine resource characteristics. For example, the attractiveness of a resource might depend on whether the resource is wholly owned or comes from elsewhere, whether it requires an experience curve to develop and thereby creates a barrier to entry for competitors, whether it is easily substitutable, whether it can be used to reinforce or amplify another resource, and whether the same resource can be used to deliver multiple products or services.

While acknowledging the lack of research around the practical implementation of the resource-based approach, Wernerfelt draws a clear line leading from an understanding of a firm's resources to its capabilities and hence to its strategic options in a competitive market. Wernerfelt (1984) admitted at the time that his work was preliminary, describing the issue as a "huge can of worms":

> Apart from the obvious need to look at growth strategies for other types of resources, much more research needs to be done on the implementability of the strategies suggested. Nothing is known, for example, about the practical difficulties involved in identifying resources (products are easy to identify), nor about to what extent one in practice can combine capabilities across operating divisions, or about how one can set up a structure and systems which can help a firm execute these strategies. (p. 180)

Wernerfelt's paper was quite theoretical, and it lay relatively unnoticed for a few more years. Then the idea of a capability as a strategic resource was catapulted into the limelight by C. K. Prahalad and Gary Hamel's *Harvard Business Review* article in 1990, "The Core Competence of the Corporation," and this sparked a flurry of interest both in the resource-based view of the firm and in the knowledge-based view of the firm

(Prahalad & Hamel, 1990; Wernerfelt, 1995; Foss, 1997; Teece et al., 1997; Teece, 1998; Bharadwaj, 2000).

The resource-based view of the firm also had a strong influence on the development of a body of theory around the notion of intellectual capital (Roos & Pike, 2007). As we saw in our discussion of knowledge assets, it provided a theoretical background for several strands of thought around the notions of knowledge assets expressed in the work of David Teece, Max Boisot, and Ron Young.

It was Dorothy Leonard, in 1992, who explicitly wove together the various vocabularies of firm resources, core capabilities, core competences, intangible assets, and strategic knowledge with their connections to KM and to the different forms of intellectual capital. "I adopt a knowledge-based view of the firm and define a core capability as the knowledge set that distinguishes and provides a competitive advantage" (Leonard-Barton, 1992, p. 113). She identified four dimensions by which a core capability could be characterized:

• The knowledge and skills embodied in employees
• The knowledge embedded in technical systems
• The knowledge processes controlled in managerial systems
• The values and norms associated with people, processes, and systems

In the same year, Bruce Kogut and Udo Zander (1997) first published their landmark paper "Knowledge of the Firm, Combinative Capabilities, and the Replication of Technology":

> ... organizations are social communities in which individual and social expertise is transformed into economically useful products and services by the application of a set of higher-order organizing principles. Firms exist because they provide a social community of voluntaristic action structured by organizing principles that are not reducible to individuals. (p. 307)

One of these higher-order organizing principles is what Kogut and Zander (1997) called *combinative capabilities*, "the intersection of the capability of the firm to exploit its knowledge and the unexplored potential of the technology" (p. 317).

David Teece described this as *dynamic capabilities*, "the firm's ability to integrate, build and then renew their resource [knowledge] base, keeping it aligned with what's needed to serve customers and meet or beat the competition" (Teece & Al-Aali, 2011, p. 509; cf. Teece et al., 1997).

Notice the shift in focus through this evolving view of organizational resources: from the sense of resource as having both potentiality and an indeterminable economic value, to reconfigurable bundles of resources that deliver services that have strategic value, and can be defined as core capabilities enabling specific competitive advantages.

With the transition from a consideration of knowledge as a resource to knowledge as a strategic competence or capability, we have shifted from a simple value perspective to a more complex strategic perspective. We have also crossed the line between Penrose's distinction between a resource (or a bundle of resources) and a service (or a bundle of services).

Although Prahalad and Hamel (1990) sometimes refer to a core competence as a resource, their detailed description below of what a core competence entails is much more clearly about the services delivered by specific combinations of resources, not about the base resources themselves:

> Core competencies are the collective learning in the organization, especially how to coordinate diverse production skills and integrate multiple streams of technologies. Consider Sony's capacity to miniaturize or Philips's optical-media expertise. The theoretical knowledge to put a radio on a chip does not in itself assure a company the skill to produce a miniature radio no bigger than a business card. To bring off this feat, Casio must harmonize know-how in miniaturization, microprocessor design, material science, and ultrathin precision casing—the same skills it applies in its miniature card calculators, pocket TVs, and digital watches. If core competence is about harmonizing streams of technology, it is also about the organization of work and the delivery of value. (p. 81)

In other words, the focus on underlying resources is somewhat eclipsed. Suffice it to say for now that a view of knowledge as a resource or raw material started as a consideration around economic value and transitioned into a consideration of strategic impact. Along the way were numerous but failed attempts to quantify and assess the economic value of knowledge as a resource. It turns out that the value of resources is highly dependent on the contexts in which they are used and also dependent on the specific ways in which the resources are combined.

In fact, sometimes, in some conditions, knowledge as a resource can have a negative value, manifesting as a *core rigidity*—that is, a deeply embedded knowledge set that actively inhibits our ability to innovate or respond to competitive needs: "the very same values, norms and attitudes that support a core capability and thus enable development can also constrain it" (Leonard-Barton, 1992, pp. 118–119).

How these potentialities play out at the resource level is still deeply mysterious because there are too many unknown factors at play. Uncertainty factors include

- lack of insight into the knowledge resources available,
- existing motivations to recombine,
- the ways in which decisions about combination get made,
- potentiality for combination and complementarity,
- contextual factors creating opportunities, and
- constraining rigidities.

There is also a deep causal ambiguity at work between a given array of resource availability and the practical ability to deploy this array to productive use. We do not always understand the mechanisms by which a set of resources actually produces value. This gives rise to what Lippman and Rumelt (1982) described as *uncertain imitability*—that is, uncertainty about a firm's ability "to fully control the nature of their production function."

The major implication of uncertain imitability is that while, like an asset, an economic resource can be said to be owned, it does not carry the same entailment as a complete power of disposition and control.

This is why the value aspects of knowledge-as-resource are still elusive. And this is why, I think, it appeared much more tractable to look at capabilities (resources delivering services) at the strategic level, rather than at resources at the value (accounting) level. The trade-off, however, is that measurement remains a challenge (Barney et al., 2011, p. 1311). This plays out in the nontradability features of knowledge-as-resource. "The essence of resources/competences as well as dynamic capabilities is that they cannot generally be bought; they must be built" (Teece & Al-Aali, 2011, p. 509).

This is the first major distinction between a consideration of knowledge as an economic resource compared to knowledge as an asset. Both metaphors stem from a consideration of value, but the resource metaphor deriving from economics actively resists value determination, while the asset metaphor actively encourages the thought that value can be determined. And the resource metaphor does not imply the same powers of disposition and control as the asset metaphor.

Slippage of Meaning: From Economic Resource to Commodity Resource

There is a second, less widely known pathway influencing the consideration of knowledge as a resource, and that is through the information resource management (IRM) movement of the 1980s. IRM's source disciplines were data management and information management, and although not rooted in the accounting discipline, IRM took a decidedly accountancy-oriented approach to the valuation of information (and by extension knowledge) as a resource within the enterprise. The strategic view is largely absent.

The IRM school is also a key channel of influence for KM because many of the information management practices it developed (including information auditing methods) flowed directly into KM with little modification, carrying with them hidden and unacknowledged assumptions.

Retrospectively, some have assumed that IRM also had its roots in the resource-based view of the firm (e.g., Alavi & Leidner, 2001). However, none of the early pioneers of IRM, nor their chroniclers, showed any knowledge of Penrose and her successors in that tradition (McDonough, 1963; Horton, 1974, 1979; Cronin, 1985; Marchand &

Horton, 1986; Burk & Horton, 1988; Trauth, 1989; Savić, 1992; Toavs, 2004). Moreover, the IRM movement took an entirely different approach toward how information and knowledge was to be valued. I believe IRM was a wholly independent and quite self-contained tradition.

By and large, proponents of the IRM movement seem not to have considered too deeply the meaning of the term *resource*. In many cases, *resource* is used interchangeably with *asset* as if they mean the same thing (e.g., Edelman, 1981; Horton & Marchand, 1982; Webb, 2003; Wilson, 2003).

There was an early call to treat information as a commodity resource—that is, a resource that could be priced and transacted in the market, influenced perhaps by the dominance of corporate information services (Snyder, 1976, p. 305). In the main, however, the term was used largely unreflectively as a rhetorical device, loaded with hidden ambiguities, to gather support for greater organizational investment in the management of data and information. The message was that information, like an asset or a resource, was important.

The enthusiastic adoption of an ambiguous term together with a lack of reflection on what it actually implied is characteristic of a political stance. It is also a warning sign for possible syllepsis. And ambiguity of meaning was entrenched in the usage. In a 1991 study of the IRM literature, British researchers Jonathan Eaton and David Bawden (1991) isolated two distinct senses of the term *resource* in use: "First, the phrase indicates an intention to treat information as a resource 'like any other,' and manage it appropriately. Second, it may simply indicate a clear awareness of the importance of information to the organization" (p. 164).

In the former sense, the meaning implies something much more like a commodity resource or tangible asset than Penrose's economic resource. In the second sense, we have a rather uninteresting truism—something you can assent to without necessarily discerning any clear follow-up action. It mirrors exactly the syllepsis we saw earlier between the literal and figurative senses of the term *knowledge asset*.

Eaton and Bawden (1991) did not use the idea of syllepsis, but they were aware of it. They warned against confusing the obvious but uninformative truth of the second meaning ("Information is important and useful") with the actionable specifics of the first meaning ("It can be costed and managed like any other commodity or asset"). Appropriating the managerial implications of the strong meaning to the weak meaning can be misleading and harmful:

> In speaking of information as a resource, we must be careful to state in which sense the term is meant. We must not use the term [to] indicate the importance of information, and then find ourselves led to adopt an inappropriate, and potentially harmful, resource management

model which cannot allow for the singular properties of information. The analogy, useful as it is, should not be pushed too far. (Eaton & Bawden, 1991, pp. 164–165)

IRM was indeed politically driven. There was a strong motivation to conceal the syllepsis and to treat information (and knowledge) as a resource that could be valued and costed. The first stimulus for this political motivation came from the rise of data processing in the 1960s and 1970s.

In the 1940s the activities of programming and data management, previously tightly coupled in single-system applications, became separated. With this move the same software code could now operate on distinct data sets in much more flexible ways. As the potential for this new approach became better appreciated and as computing became more pervasive in large organizations, the data-processing community became more and more frustrated with the scatter and duplication of data enclaves in separate systems around the enterprise.

For programs to be able to exploit these different data enclaves, standardization and coordination would be required. The management information systems community in particular began to see the potential for radically new architectures that could exploit for managerial purposes the latent knowledge residing in these different data resources and locked away in various transactional systems (Vazsonyi, 1975; Berry & Cook, 1976; Edelman, 1981; Trauth, 1989).

The implication was that data were now to be considered a resource, in two senses: at the literal level as "an available means to programmers to meet requirements" (Vazsonyi, 1975, p. 47) and at the figurative level "as a valuable resource of the enterprise on a par with personnel, money, material, and facilities, [where] the need has surfaced to manage this resource actively and effectively from a global or enterprise point of view" (Berry & Cook, 1976, p. 1).

In order to address this need, the data-processing and management information systems community needed

1. increased budgets and manpower so they could implement these new architectures (Vazsonyi, 1975, p. 51), and

2. greater power in the enterprise so they could impose governance across scattered systems and databases (Berry & Cook, 1976; Trauth, 1989).

To win both investment and power, advocates of "data/information as a corporate resource" needed a value proposition, and they used a two-pronged argument.

The first prong was to appeal to the strategic importance of managerial decision-making and to recast data processing from its image as a back-office technical discipline to a new image as the prerequisite for managers to be able to make effective strategic decisions. In a landmark report for the US Department of Defense in 1976, Berry and Cook directly assimilated the importance of data as a resource to the idea of corporate knowledge as a resource, which in turn (they claimed) would lead to better strategic decisions. They claimed that management of data as a corporate resource was a foundational element in the ability to manage knowledge as a corporate resource.

This same, basically political, position would ultimately lead to the infamous data-information-knowledge-wisdom (DIKW) hierarchy—infamous because it is based on flimsy reasoning and easily encourages poorly founded practices (Lambe, 2011a; Williams, 2014).

The goal in the 1970s, however, which was ultimately successful, was to make a political claim for a focus on the management of data as a strategic corporate resource:

> An enterprise which seeks to manage its data as a resource is really seeking to formally organize its knowledge acquisition and preservation process. Managing data as a resource is really just a means to accomplish this end. Thus, the concept of knowledge as a corporate resource is a rather straightforward, though nontrivial extension of the current approach of treating data [as] a resource. Knowledge is the most important resource of any enterprise. It is one of the key factors which make the enterprise unique. (Berry & Cook, 1976, p. 5)

The second prong of their argument was to appeal to the benefits of adopting this approach which would allegedly outweigh the considerable costs involved in making the necessary transformation. When making such large claims, it is important to be able to extrapolate your cause to other causes, and this is what data resource management did, by broadening its appeal beyond data and taking into its portfolio both information and knowledge (as dependent upon data).

In the 1980s this movement merged with the IRM movement and followed IRM in its adoption of a cost-benefit approach to information resource management. The benefits, it was argued, would outweigh the costs. This was to drive subsequent methods for valuation of information (and by implication) knowledge resources.

Now we have slipped from the broad sense of information and knowledge as a strategic economic resource to the sense of a commodity resource that is akin to an asset—something that can be costed, bought, sold, and transacted.

Notice that once you are in a cost-benefit conversation you are now in an operational cost-accounting mode of thinking in which resources are commodities to be acquired and managed in relation to their costs. This is quite different from thinking about an economic resource as a strategically important source of value (present and future) for the enterprise at large, loaded with potentiality but of indeterminable value at any given point of time.

The work of a management information systems professor from the Wharton Business School, Adrian McDonough, was instrumental in this period. He originated IRM's cost-benefit approach. In 1963 McDonough published a book called *Information Economics and Management Systems* to address the precise question of how to value information as a resource in the management of enterprises.

In fact, McDonough's approach was more of a cost accounting approach than a pure economics approach, and it had little in common with the mainstream information economics springing from the work of Friedrich Hayek and Kenneth Arrow. In contrast to mainstream economists, McDonough did not look at the economic impact of information asymmetries and information flows in a market. Rather, he attempted to develop a system of valuing information based on its application to organizational problems.

Hence, despite its title, McDonough's work was almost completely ignored by economists and mainly had an impact on the valuation approaches adopted by IRM theorists and practitioners. This is why the IRM school is so different in focus from the knowledge-based view of the firm, though they both nominally start from the same notion of information or knowledge as a resource.

McDonough rather neatly avoided the problem of the indeterminacy of information and knowledge potential by defining the value of information as being determined at the point *it is used to solve a problem*; that is, he focused on the point of demand rather than the point of supply.

For McDonough, an organization can be understood as a collection of problems to be solved. Data are without value until they meet a problem and are evaluated to be a solution to that problem, at which point they become an information resource whose value is equivalent to the value of having that problem solved. Taking a broader view, knowledge refers to the overall stock of what is available to be known in the organization and can be applied to problems. *Information economics*, as he defined it, was essentially a management information systems exercise aimed at ensuring that knowledge and information can flow to points of need (problems to solve).

The value of the knowledge stock is thus taken to be equivalent to the value of the problems to be solved at any given time (we might call this the "payoff"). McDonough (1963) addressed the follow-up question of how to quantify that by developing a taxonomy of organizational functions, each of which represents a cluster of predictable problems to be solved and each of which, he suggested, can be amenable to valuation.

Others followed the practice of mapping information and information flows to key functional activities (Brien & Stafford, 1968). The approach was to be a crucial influence in the development of practical methods for IRM, particularly as developed by Forest Horton in the 1980s, including the central idea of inventorying knowledge stocks, and matching them to knowledge demands, represented by key functional areas (Horton, 1979; Burk & Horton, 1988). Inventories were coterminous with valuation if they were aligned with functions that had determinate value.

Now, the underlying idea of functional areas representing *demand points* for knowledge and information is a useful one and is still useful in knowledge auditing today, as we shall see later. The problem arises in trying to use this as a mechanism for a comprehensive and convincing assessment of information and knowledge value.

Like McDonough, economists Jacob Marschak and Fritz Machlup were also interested in the valuation of knowledge needs met, as well as in ways of measuring knowledge demand. However, they maintained that this could only give clues for the valuation of *knowledge processes or services* (Marschak, 1968) or *knowledge flows* (Machlup, 1980)—not for the valuation of the underlying knowledge stocks or knowledge as a resource.

According to Machlup, and in line with the mainstream idea of an economic resource, the valuation of knowledge or information as a "stock" was not possible: ". . . stocks of knowledge are neither measurable nor comparable, whereas flows of knowledge can be quantified and appraised by the measuring rod of money applied either to what is being paid for the knowledge by those who buy it . . . or to what is being given up for it to be made available."

Yet even this "measuring rod of money" is imperfect, as "large components in the flow of knowledge require neither payment nor sacrifices," and this brings us back to the "knowledge as a public good" argument (Machlup, 1980, p. 178). In other words, the transactive approach (a price ascribed to information meeting a specific point of need) does not fully capture the value potential that resides in the system.

McDonough's cost accounting approach confuses what can be observed (information as it is applied to a problem) with the unobservable and unquantifiable (potential uses of a piece of information and external factors influencing the availability, cost, and applicability of information).

By relying only on observable transactions at single points in time, this method leads to an incomplete picture of value: ". . . it is not possible to explain fully the value of information in terms of exchange values" (Repo, 1989, p. 83). As we saw from the discussion of Edith Penrose and the valuation challenges surrounding the notion of an economic resource, economic resources do not have an absolute value independent of the contexts in which they are used. The same resource can have vastly different values from one instance to another, depending on changes in conditions.

This implies that any valuation of resources will depend heavily on attention to the contexts and outcomes of use over time, and will always be more reliable in retrospect than in prospect. There is intrinsic uncertainty in the valuation of resources because of this context dependency and because of the fluidity with which resources can be combined and applied. In fact, Penrose thought it was almost impossible to value the full suite of resources employed by a firm, and that is why she mainly focused, for practical reasons, on the subclass of tangible fixed assets.

At first sight, McDonough's approach appears to respect this idea of "valuation in retrospect." However, the prospective value of an economic resource is much more interesting than the retrospective transacted value of particular applications of information. It is precisely the potentiality of information and knowledge (along with its uncertainty) that is of greatest value in an enterprise, however indeterminate.

There is a superficial attractiveness to being able to develop an accounting system that sets up transacted values for information and knowledge derived from the assessed values of problems solved or functions served. But there are several unintended negative consequences to this approach.

First, the knowledge and information management processes are directed toward predictable, known operational functions and processes; they focus on delivering administrative value as distinct from strategic value.

This is the main difference between a cost accounting approach and the resource-based view of the firm. The resource-based view leads to an appreciation of core capabilities and the strategic options they deliver, and the cost accounting approach does not. Strategic options and innovation capacity all but disappear from view in the cost-benefit approach:

> Only those aspects of information which fit neatly into the resource framework—formalized, accountable, controllable, predictable, categorized, static, consistent, uniform, dehumanized—will be regarded as "information resources," and hence important. What then of the informal, anomalous, multifaceted, interdisciplinary, idiosyncratic, individualistic aspects of information transfer—those which are most closely associated with creativity and innovation at both individual and corporate level? In reading too much into the word "resource," and overly concentrating on promoting an analogy with tangible resources, there lies the danger of negating the real value of information. (Eaton & Bawden, 1991, p. 165)

Second, in the cost-benefit approach the costs of delivering information and knowledge services are much easier to quantify than the value of the benefits. The causal ambiguity surrounding the effects of knowledge and information means that it is difficult to separate the effects of these intangibles from other possible confounding factors, such as environmental factors, motivations, chance opportunities, goodwill, and culture.

Third, there is the problem that observability directs attention. The cost-benefit approach has an unintended effect of focusing managerial attention more on costs

than on benefits. The presence of information and knowledge that is not demonstrably currently in use becomes difficult to justify—a consequence being that knowledge
latency is removed from the inventories in the name of efficiency in the same way that
other assets and commodity resources are removed from physical inventory if there is
no immediate use (King & Kraemer, 1988, p. 11).

We have seen some classic examples of this in cases of organizational forgetting,
not least in the destructive delayering of knowledge capabilities in the business process
reengineering movement of the 1990s (Guimaraes & Bond, 1996). It is most famously
exemplified in NASA "forgetting" how to build rockets powerful enough to travel into
deep space (DeLong, 2004; Teitel, 2011).

And yet knowledge latency seems to be a specific feature of organizational resilience,
innovation, and creativity over the longer term. The cost-benefit approach to knowledge and information as a *commodity resource* delivering present transacted value has
consequences that are in direct conflict with the notion of *economic resources* as delivering
a strategic capability, and that can be recombined in novel ways to generate new services.

The IRM movement, and the information auditing practices that followed from it,
were largely seduced by the valuation promise of the cost-benefit approach, although
the leading proponent of IRM, Forest Horton (1979), struggled with the shortcomings
of valuing information wholly through its results, and was aware of the gap between
potential value and realized value: "Thus information that is relevant may reside in
a situation where human decisions and actions cause negative or neutral outcomes,
despite the potential value of the information. Results, in short, cannot be used fully to
infer information value" (pp. 12–14).

But the cost-benefit approach was influential in information auditing, and very
likely accounts for the conservative, rather defensive approach to information management as an administrative support discipline that dominated in the 1970s and 1980s.
The notion of information management as a strategic discipline suffered as a result. To
some extent we have inherited this weakness, when our organizations consider KM to be
an administrative support discipline to be costed in the same way.

This explains why the earliest references to the information audit in the 1970s combined an inventory audit model with a cost-benefit analysis of information resources
and processes (Riley, 1976; Quinn, 1979). The approach was bolstered by the library
and information science backgrounds of those early practitioners. In many cases their
information resources were in the form of books, articles, and data sets procured for
corporate libraries, and they were under increasing pressure to justify their budgets
and operations. The field of IRM was emerging in the same period and provided a convenient theoretical rationale for this approach, not to mention the precedents in the
cost-benefit analyses of records managers in the 1960s and 1970s.

Even when the focus shifted from information as resource to an information systems approach, the cost-benefit mindset remained in place. Henderson (1980) took an information systems approach rather than an information resources approach to information audits, but again produced a cost-benefit analysis of alternative ways of achieving the desired objectives through the information system. Burk and Horton (1988, pp. 75–114) took a more holistic approach, delineating a tripartite understanding of information resources as information products, information services, and information systems. They presented a model to analyze all three but again took a mostly defensive cost-benefit analysis approach.

The focus then throughout the 1970s and 1980s was on justifying the costs of information resources and services.

Willard (1993) transformed this rather defensive approach by advocating the development and exploitation of information resources to enhance their value, anticipating the *value capitalization* approach that would emerge in knowledge management shortly thereafter. Here we begin to see a key distinction between *valuation* (against costs of provision) and *value creation* with a more strategic orientation. This is not a dominant theme in the information audit literature, but it is an important one that shows how some forms of knowledge audit were to evolve.

Knowledge managers and knowledge auditors are generally more skeptical about the cost-benefit approach and its potential payoff for knowledge auditing. They seem more oriented toward the economic resource view with its strategic vision, and this is consistent with the idea of knowledge as an economic resource with potential value, as compared to a commodity resource with transactive value.

In our 2017 global survey of knowledge managers on knowledge audit approaches, cost-benefit approaches were significantly less likely to be adopted in knowledge audits than value audits that attempted to establish the strategic value of knowledge to the organization. The cost-benefit assessment was the least common audit type to be adopted, at 23 percent of respondents, while the more generative "creating value from knowledge" audit model was the third most common, at 49 percent of respondents (Lambe, 2017).

Summing Up: Safe and Unsafe Metaphors—Asset, Capital, or Resource?

Where does this leave us? We can see that *resource*, like *asset*, has both a literal and a figurative sense, and when they are confused, we can run into problems.

But unlike *asset*, and similar to the notions of *capital* and *audit*, there are multiple obvious ambiguities within the general concept of resources. We can mean an economic resource with unquantifiable but acknowledged strategic value or a commodity resource that can be priced, acquired, and consumed. Commodity resources do not have the same excludability properties as assets, but they also do not have the same inimitability or value uncertainty as economic resources. *Resource* is a portmanteau term that points to several possible meanings and invites disambiguation. It does not lead one to simple but conflicting conclusions, which was our main quarrel with the term *asset*.

And we have not considered natural resources, which again do not behave in the same way as commodity resources or economic resources. In fact, the metaphor of natural resources might come closest to helping us to characterize the *public good* characteristics of knowledge as it is acquired and used by individuals, groups, and organizations.

In sum, like the terms *audit* and *capital*—and unlike *asset*—there is sufficient ambiguity within the term *resource* as to visibly require disambiguation and qualification. The term is slippery but not completely treacherous. It is addressable.

Not everybody would agree with me. Nancy Dixon (2018) is not a fan of the resource metaphor. She thinks it is a metaphor that comes with dehumanizing entailments:

> ... the metaphor of "labor as a resource" results in organizations viewing jobs as a cost that, like the cost of raw materials and tools, should be kept down. With this mindset, cheap labor is viewed as a good thing, much like cheap oil. If human beings are viewed as a resource to organizations they can be treated in the same way as supplies and tools, that is, obtain labor at the least cost and replace or eliminate workers when profit is threatened, with no need to consider the mental health consequences of lay-offs. The metaphor also leads organizations to make no distinction between meaningful work and dehumanizing labor, no need to think about job design to make work more interesting.

She has a point. The notion of resource, especially the idea of the commodity resource, does imply exploitation and does exclude entailments of human engagement. However, her quarrel is principally with the notions of people and labor as a resource. Knowledge as a resource has more flexible connotations for both people and organizations. As we will see in the next chapter, it can be compatible with ideas of influence and engagement (and stewardship) and not simply with exploitation. And its signaling of potential/future value creation is a positive entailment. When all is said and done, I believe the metaphor is flexible enough and rich enough that its syllepsis and its negative entailments can be overcome. Here is our formal analysis of the syllepsis following the structure in figure 13.1:

1. In the use of *knowledge resource*, the entailment is one of value. It does not entail ownership and control to the same degree that *asset* does.

2. The metaphor conceals the ambiguity between different types of resources, with very different implications for how knowledge is valued and managed.

3. There are two contradictory meanings in the usage of the term *knowledge resource*, one of them implying indeterminate but strategic value (economic resource) or

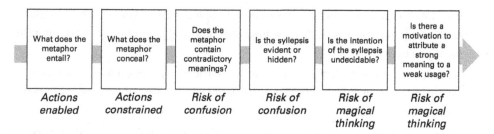

Figure 13.1
Criteria for identifying the risks associated with syllepsis.

determinable (operational) value (commodity resource). Aside from the valuation perspective, it could also be possible to think of knowledge as akin to a natural resource that needs to be stewarded.

4. These differences are not always explicit when knowledge resources are described and discussed. This leads to a high potential for confusion as to what is meant by the term *knowledge resource* when used for knowledge in general.

5. The syllepsis is not undecidable because the ambiguities in the term lead to very distinct and different lines of argument, so it calls for disambiguation.

6. There is a motivation to bolster the importance of knowledge management by appealing to the economic notion of knowledge as a resource. There is a temptation to slip into the sense of information and knowledge as a commodity resource because this would appear to make the value of knowledge easier to measure. The ambiguities are sufficiently visible, however, that as long as we use clear definitions and qualifications, the risk of magical thinking in management practice can be mitigated.

*   *   *

Summary

In this chapter I have analyzed the entailments and risks associated with the commonly used metaphor for knowledge or information as a "resource". Here is a summary of the main points:

1. The metaphor of knowledge and information as a resource also contains syllepsis. It can be used figuratively or literally.

2. When it is used in the sense of a commodity resource, it can produce similar negative effects as the use of the term *asset*. It can focus attention on the most observable, measurable features of knowledge and information in use, distracting us from

investing in the most interesting and useful applications of knowledge. It produces misleading and counterproductive measures, and suggests inappropriate management practices.

3. When the resource metaphor is used in the sense of an economic resource akin to intangible assets, it succeeds in expressing several of the special properties of knowledge and information without exerting a distorting effect on practice.

4. Because of its syllepsis, the term *resource* needs careful qualification when used in association with knowledge and information. However, its ambiguity is addressable.

14 Ascribing Value to Knowledge and the Implications for Influence and Control

Bias thrives wherever there is the possibility of interpreting information in different ways. . . . people tend to reach self-serving conclusions whenever ambiguity surrounds a piece of evidence.
—Bazerman et al. (2002, p. 4)

The notions of value, valuation, and value creation are dangerous motivators. Metaphors associated with value are bandied about with little clarity in both the information management and the knowledge management (KM) literature. It is only mildly reassuring that other management fields suffer from the same disease.

In fact, the notion of *value* itself, as used in management generally, even before we get to metaphors such as *asset*, *capital*, or *resource*, turns out to be just as slippery and ambiguous as its metaphors as soon as we try to pin it down. Andrew Swan (2003), in a systematic review of the concept of value in supply chain management, noted that some definitions of value are simply circular or tautological, or they are incomplete and inconsistent: "In fact, value management as a subject area in much of the purchasing literature can be characterized as, at best, suffering from a jumble of value definitions; or at worst, as liberally using an undefined 'buzz phrase'" (p. 5; cf. Jacques, 2000, p. 209).

Different definitions of value are adopted to serve different purposes and perceptions, resulting in different stakeholders pulling the organization in directions they deem most appropriate. "Value" serves as a rhetorical rallying banner more often than as a concrete organizing concept. The differing perceptions of value can produce dislocation effects when they enter end-to-end management processes. In one place in the system, it means one thing; in another place, another. How do we align and measure consistent value flow across the entire system (Swan, 2003, pp. 10–11)?

So much for the notion of value in general. We should expect more, however, from terms such as *asset* and *capital*, rooted as they are in economics and accounting. We understand why they are attractive metaphors to use for knowledge. Hyperbolic or metaphorical references to knowledge and information stocks as "assets" seem to be driven by the idea that they are important ingredients of business success and require a strong attention to effective management processes. These are legitimate intentions.

However, the use of the term *assets* also implies—falsely—that the objects of the metaphor partake of the other attributes of assets—ownership, power of disposition, excludability, tradability—and this is not true for many forms of knowledge stock. We conclude with Pike and Roos (2011) that *resources* is the least troubling term to use for describing stocks of knowledge (p. 269). The term *asset* has positive risks.

The point is that in auditing, any imprecisions of language and ambiguity, combined with strong motivators in one direction over another, invariably lead different auditors to reach different conclusions on the same evidence base. Ambiguity induces both inconsistency of interpretation and a tendency to bias in drawing conclusions, as the quote from the beginning of this chapter (from a study of bias in accounting audits) points out.

Table 14.1 summarizes what we have learned about the benefits and limitations of the different value-associated metaphors for knowledge, information, and data. It shows the degree to which each metaphor helps to explicate aspects of knowledge, information, and data (*darker shaded cells*). These shaded cells show where the metaphor can have some utility. But the table also highlights key differences and inconsistencies in areas where the metaphor can lead to unhelpful conclusions and inappropriate management actions (*lighter shaded cells*). The attributes at issue are as follows:

- *Owned*—can the item be owned? Information and knowledge cannot be uniformly owned in the same way as assets, capital, or most forms of resource. Some forms can; others cannot. A great deal of data can be owned, though this can be contestable if it contains or is derived from personal or confidential data or information.

- *Controlled*—can we have wide-ranging power of disposition over the item? This is most true of tangible assets, commodity resources, and capital. It is not uniformly true of information and knowledge but can be true of some data.

- *Management mode*—can the item be managed directly, or does it have to be managed through intermediate means? This has implications for measurement as well. Here, knowledge has similarities with intangible assets and economic resources. It is mostly managed indirectly (ISO [International Organization for Standardization], 2018b, p. vi). Information occupies a middle ground—some of it (e.g., information in processes, workflows, and systems) is susceptible to direct management techniques, and some of it is not (e.g., information flows between people).

Table 14.1

Comparative analysis of the properties of assets, resources, knowledge, information, and data

	Tangible asset	Intangible asset	Economic resource	Commodity resource	Natural resource	Capital	Data	Information	Knowledge
Owned	Yes	Yes	Yes	Yes	No, unless converted to commodity resource →	Yes	Contestable	Not uniformly	Not uniformly
Controlled – (power of disposition)	Yes	With difficulty	Uncertain	Yes	Not uniformly	Yes	Yes	Not uniformly	Not uniformly
Management mode	Direct	Indirect, uncertain	Indirect, uncertain	Direct	Direct	Direct	Direct	Direct and indirect	Indirect, uncertain
Is consumed in use	Yes, as depreciation	No, in fact can grow in use	No, in fact can grow in use	Yes	Yes	Sometimes, but can also grow in use	No, in fact can grow in use	No, in fact can grow in use	No, in fact can grow in use
Tradable - can be priced	Yes	With uncertainty	With high uncertainty	Yes	Yes	Yes	Yes	Not uniformly	Not uniformly
Value orientation	Present	Present + future	Present + future	Present	Present + future	Present + future	Present + future	Present + future	Present + future
Excludable	Yes	Yes	Yes	Yes	No	Yes	With difficulty	With difficulty	With difficulty
Imitable	Yes	With difficulty	With difficulty	Yes	Yes	Yes	Yes	With effort	With difficulty
Output scales with abundance	Yes	Only in the right con-figuration	Only in the right con-figuration	Yes	Yes	Yes	Possible (with good analytics)	No (cost of noise and attention)	No (cost of noise and attention)
Potentiality	Measurable	Uncertain	Uncertain	Measurable	Measurable	Measurable	Uncertain	Uncertain	Uncertain
Acquisition to exploitation	Immediate	Slow	Slow	Immediate	Immediate	Immediate	Immediate	Immediate	Slow and uncertain

- *Is consumed in use*—is the item consumed in use or does it self-propagate? The peculiar properties of data, information and knowledge come to the fore here, as compared with assets and commodity resources or natural resources. They can actually grow in use, as can economic resources and intangible assets. Tangible assets are not strictly consumed in use, but depreciation over time is an analogue to consumption.
- *Tradable*—can the item be priced? There are no reliable mechanisms for the pricing of information (in general) and knowledge, and this feature is common to intangible assets and economic resources. Only some well-defined forms of information can be traded, and in those cases the transacted value is not taken to be a direct analogue of "real" value. Tradability is a distinctive property of tangible assets, commodity resources, and capital—and sometimes also data.
- *Value orientation*—when we attempt valuation, what is our time horizon? Intangible assets, economic resources, natural resources, capital, data, information, and knowledge all have some form of future orientation when their value is assessed (Machlup, 1984, p. 409; Probst et al., 1998, p. 241). Tangible assets and commodity resources tend to be valued at the point where a transaction is effected.
- *Excludable*—can competitors be reliably prevented from exploiting the same item? With the exception of natural resources, data, information, and knowledge, all the other metaphors imply some powers of excludability. Natural resources are supposed to be public goods until they have been improved or processed in some way (Machlup, 1984, p. 419), and excludability is contrary to the character of a public good, although it is frequently challenged in practice. Data, information, and knowledge are notoriously leaky, and excludability actions are imperfect, even if (with intellectual property) they are bolstered through the assertion of ownership rights.
- *Imitable*—can the item be reproduced and replaced easily (e.g., by a competitor)? Again, information and knowledge are closest to intangible assets and economic resources in the degree of difficulty they pose for reproducibility. Intangible assets, economic resources, and information or knowledge have *uncertain imitability* (meaning that they cannot easily be reconstructed from scratch), even for their owners.
- *Output scales with abundance*—does the value output produced by the item grow in proportion to the amount of the item you have? If you have more assets, commodity resources, natural resources, or capital, you can do more things. Information and knowledge present the greatest contrast here. Knowledge abundance can often be counterproductive since productive use also involves the capacity to filter, process, and combine. More knowledge and information does not automatically create greater capability. This is also why economic resources, like intangible assets, do not

necessarily create more value as they become more abundant. They need to be in productive configurations to do so.

- *Potentiality*—can the future value of the item be reliably measured? Again, data, information, and knowledge are closest to intangible assets and economic resources in the degree of uncertainty they pose. They are held to have high potential value, but there is also uncertainty about the ability to produce that value or predict that value.

- *Acquisition to exploitation*—how long does it take to reap value from the item once it has been acquired? Of all our items, knowledge has the most uncertain time line, though we know that it tends to be slow. Intangible assets and economic resources are well known for the learning curves that they impose on their owners before they can be made productive (Arrow, 1962). All our other items can be put to work to produce value pretty much as soon as they are acquired.

The table shows that there are numerous overlaps and numerous differences. However, the table also shows that tangible assets and commodity resources behave completely differently from the way that knowledge behaves, and they are only tangentially similar to information. Data come closest to the properties of tangible assets, commodity resources, and capital. The shaded cells in the table suggest, quite forcefully, that the most productive alignments are between intangible assets, economic resources, information, and knowledge.

It is not helpful to describe information and knowledge as akin to assets or commodity resources

(a) without careful specification of the specific forms of information or knowledge we are referring to, and

(b) without assurance that the properties of these metaphors will indeed illuminate our understanding and practice in our intended usage, as opposed to confusing them.

There are some well-bounded circumstances in which the language of assets and capital is less problematic. Figure 14.1 represents what we have learned about the challenge posed by assessing the value of knowledge. It discriminates between the *span of control*, where the language of assets and to some extent of capital is legitimate, and the *span of influence*, where the language of resources seems more appropriate.

Some knowledge sits within the sphere of control—typically, the more explicit or implicit, explicable forms of knowledge. The span of influence extends to forms of knowledge (public knowledge, tacit knowledge) that cannot sensibly be considered subject to the same forms of control as assets or capital, whether for ethical or pragmatic reasons.

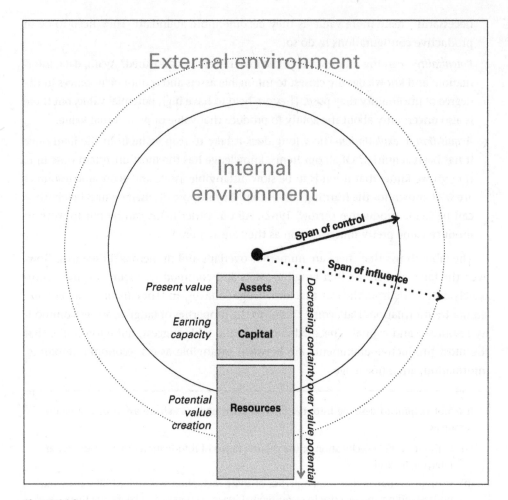

Figure 14.1
Assets, capital, resources: from span of control to span of influence.

The language we use matters. The assumptions we can make about appropriate management practices will change as we move beyond the bounds of the span of control and into the span of influence. This should also guide us on how we approach the task of assigning value to knowledge and knowledge practices, and the certainty with which we can do so.

This has a direct impact on how we approach the change imperative in knowledge management. Influencing knowledge use is different from controlling knowledge use. The notion of influencing produces a different mindset from that of control: it requires strategies for mutual understanding, common-ground building, and engagement. Understanding the boundary conditions between control and influence is critical to developing KM interventions that are appropriate to the phenomena and activities they seek to guide.

In chapter 6 we read about Douglas MacGregor's work on Theory X and Theory Y and saw the importance of being able to perceive clearly the boundary conditions where a shift occurs between the span of control and the span of influence, and the behavioral and managerial changes that need to take place when that transition takes place.

The same requirement holds for how we use the metaphors of value to describe knowledge and information. On no account should we use these metaphors indiscriminately across all knowledge forms and all knowledge environments. This has significant implications for how we go about inventorying knowledge stocks in the organization and for how we go about implementing KM processes and knowledge governance based on our knowledge audit insights.

*　　　*　　　*

Summary

In this chapter I have attempted to bring greater precision to the most common governing metaphors we use to describe knowledge in organizations, on the supposition that clarity and precision of language and thought can guide clarity and precision of action. Here is a summary of the main points:

1. The metaphor of knowledge as an asset is more harmful than helpful in knowledge auditing.

2. The metaphors of knowledge as capital or as a resource are acceptable as long as they are properly qualified. "Capital" tends to refer to high-level aggregated bundles of knowledge, while "resource" can refer to specific knowledge items at an operational level.

3. Restricting the use of the *asset* metaphor and preferring the *resource* metaphor introduces a practical and useful understanding for knowledge managers of the boundary conditions for the transition between knowledge control and knowledge influence.

15 The Inventory Audit: Auditing Knowledge Stocks

An unbridled lucidity can destroy our understanding of complex matters.
—Polanyi (1966, p. 18)

Having sought to disambiguate some of the more confusing metaphors we use to describe knowledge, my task in the remainder of this section of the book is to stir up the waters again by looking at how we identify knowledge in organizations.

I believe we work to overly simplistic models of how knowledge is deployed and used in organizations, and this compromises the effectiveness of how we can audit and inventory knowledge. So in the spirit of the quote from Polanyi above, I want to break apart these simplistic views, and in doing so explore a range of competing ways in which we might understand and describe knowledge. By the end of the following chapters, when the sediment has settled, we should have a clearer but less simplistic way of seeing, a way that is more suited to our purpose in a knowledge audit.

The inventory audit of knowledge stocks was the most frequently recognized type of knowledge audit in our 2017 survey covering 150 knowledge management (KM) professionals. It was recognized by 80 percent of respondents. It is almost always combined with another form of audit, the most frequent being a participative goal-setting audit, a discovery review audit, or a value audit. So the inventory audit functions as the preparatory, evidence-gathering stage for these other audit types (Lambe, 2017).

It follows that if we are going to compile useful inventories of knowledge stocks, we need a reliable and robust way of describing a set of knowledge types that we can easily differentiate and identify. This set of knowledge types is what we call a knowledge typology.

What We Need from a Typology of Knowledge

There are two unhelpful dualisms in how knowledge stocks are categorized in the general KM literature and in common practice. The first is the *individual knowledge versus collective knowledge* distinction, and the second is the *tacit knowledge versus explicit knowledge* distinction (Hislop, 2013, pp. 21–23). They are unhelpful because they are too crude to adequately describe the variety that exists in the organizational knowledge landscape. Chapters 16 and 17 will examine each of these dualisms in turn, but first I want to clarify what a good typology of knowledge should provide.

Any good typology divides the landscape into a sufficiently diverse set of types to support sensemaking and action in relation to a given purpose. Binary typologies imply a very simple landscape, and this is manifestly not true in relation to knowledge management (Nissen & Jennex, 2005).

Moreover, every typology should have a clear purpose, and we measure its adequacy against its ability to inform the desired outcomes of that purpose. A typology is a representation of a landscape to serve an interpretive or sensemaking purpose. Without a purpose, a typology is just an intellectual fiction, bearing little utility in practice. Let us look at an example of an unhelpful binary typology.

Case Study: When Typologies Fail

Endometrial cancer is a cancer of the lining of the uterus. It is among the top four cancers in women in the US and in 2013 was estimated to account for over eight thousand deaths. Until recently, the cancer has been placed into one of two categories by specialists on the basis of a physical examination of thin slices of the tumors under a microscope. Type I tumors are considered likely to have a favorable outcome after surgery and radiation, while Type II tumors are more aggressive, have poor outcomes, and require chemotherapy.

However, the two types are difficult to distinguish, and there is disagreement among pathologists about how tumors should be classified. Disagreement about classification means inconsistency of classification and disagreement about the course of treatment. In short, the typology is not very helpful. It does not appear to match the complexity of the phenomena it is attempting to describe, and it does not provide robust recommendations for useful interventions.

In 2013 the Cancer Genome Atlas Research Network published a study of 373 endometrial tumors based on genome analysis, and they distinguished four distinct types of endometrial cancer, including variants that had structural and mechanical similarities with some types of colorectal and breast cancer, for which good therapeutic options had already been developed.

The findings, based on a new way of analyzing the tumors at the molecular level, provided much more fine-grained, reliable, and consistent methods for distinguishing endometrial cancer types, and this had immediate therapeutic implications, including the possibility of adapting prior therapies for the related cancer types.

This is what we should expect from an effective typology: greater differentiation of types based on real-world observable features, enabling practical, useful actions (Cancer Genome Atlas Research Network, 2013; Kolata, 2013).

So what is our purpose here, the purpose against which we need to evaluate the quality of our typologies of knowledge? We want to know what knowledge the organization has and what knowledge it needs to do its work. We want to be able to conduct an inventory audit of knowledge stocks in order to inform a discovery review, participative goal-setting, or assessment audit. Or perhaps even a value audit.

In simpler terms, we want to gain an understanding of how the organization depends upon (and produces) knowledge in relation to its core activities, so that we can design improvements to the way it uses, exploits, and produces knowledge. Extending the medical metaphor, we want to be able to design "therapeutic" interventions.

Case Study: Auditing Knowledge with Binary Typologies

Let us look at a case study of a knowledge audit based on a binary typology (tacit and explicit knowledge types or individual and corporate knowledge types) to see what happens when the typology is too simple. In 2001 a group of researchers at the Robert Gordon University in Aberdeen conducted a knowledge audit for the tax department of a large oil and gas company comprising twenty employees. They used an assessment survey followed up by interviews on knowledge processes, and they worked with the employees to develop knowledge maps of the tacit and explicit knowledge needed and used in their work (Burnett et al., 2004).

These knowledge maps had two problems. The first was that there was no common standard for reporting collective dependencies on knowledge, and in consequence, the individual knowledge maps were so disparate the audit team was not able to compile a common department-level knowledge map (Burnett et al., 2004, p. 33).

The second problem was in the maps themselves. In the examples reported by the team, we can discern fifteen distinct explicit knowledge types, while tacit knowledge (or "people") was a single category without any further differentiation (Burnett et al., 2004, pp. 32–33). Because explicit knowledge is more observable than tacit knowledge, when we rely on unguided self-reporting, it is easier to assign detailed labels to subtypes of explicit knowledge. For tacit knowledge, without an agreed-upon way of differentiating subtypes, a single large bucket has to do the job.

When the work has a heavy dependency on tacit knowledge, the consequences for intervention planning based on an audit's findings are profound. There is a strong bias toward overarticulation of explicit knowledge and low definition of tacit knowledge, which may not be consistent with the nature of the work. High levels of detail for explicit knowledge sources and vague references to tacit knowledge mean that recommendations will focus on explicit knowledge and have higher specificity for those resources, while interventions focused on tacit knowledge will be frustratingly vague. And indeed, the recommendations from this audit follow that pattern. While tacit knowledge was covered in the recommendations, the details were vague, and the level of detail in any follow-up would necessarily be biased toward the detail that was available to describe the explicit knowledge resources.

As a case in point, one of the recommendations in that study was for a taxonomy to improve access to, and the availability of, current knowledge. Where tacit knowledge is an important resource, then any taxonomy must describe areas of tacit knowledge. When knowledge maps privilege explicit knowledge, so will the taxonomy, leaving great uncertainty about the capacity of the taxonomy to support access to tacit knowledge resources.

What does this case study tell us? First, that gathering data at the wrong level of granularity can pose problems. As Tom Stewart (2001) pointed out two decades ago, the first task of the knowledge manager is to determine the right unit of analysis, and in organizations that means being able to answer the question "what does the group need to know?" (p. 119; cf. Kogut & Zander, 1997, p. 312).

A typology that examines either the individual or the organization as a whole impedes the ability to gather data at the right level of detail—the group that does the work. The knowledge of the individual ("knowledge in people") is a distraction from what the group does and so is the pressure to describe knowledge at a higher organizational level. If that seems a controversial assertion, we will defend it later.

Second, the case tells us that the crude differentiation between tacit and explicit knowledge privileges the more observable portion of the duality (in this case explicit knowledge), resulting in an imbalance in how the follow-up attention and action is directed. The dualism biases knowledge management toward the explicit.

How then should we gather data about the knowledge in use within organizations? As with cancers, physical observation of the full spectrum of knowledge use is neither easy nor necessarily reliable. A great deal of knowledge use in organizations happens within people's heads and in transient interactions between people. There is a lot of noise in all this activity. The salient and most important knowledge use is often not the most easily or directly observable. We can only observe the full spread of knowledge use by looking at proxy signals of knowledge use. It follows that a good typology should help us find and describe good proxies for knowledge use.

By far the most authoritative witnesses to knowledge uses and needs are the people who use knowledge in their daily activities. While external consultants are frequently used to conduct knowledge audits, when it comes to inventorying knowledge resources, external facilitators are merely that: facilitators. They do not carry intimate knowledge of how the organization does its work. The staff who do the work do carry that knowledge, so we need to find a way of enabling self-reporting of knowledge use. This is also more sustainable in the long run for the ongoing maintenance of these knowledge inventories.

However, individual reports may be prone to bias, or to poor self-insight, and they may only represent partial views of the work. We need to find a way of using collective reports, oriented around the knowledge that work groups need and use. Our typology should therefore be accessible to the people who work with knowledge and who understand how it feeds their performance. It should not be too abstract or artificial. If the typology is not accessible to them, if it does not enable a naturalistic description of the way they work, and if it is not capable of being discussed and agreed upon in a group format, then our respondents will not be able to report their knowledge uses and dependencies reliably, consistently, and sustainably. This implies an approach to inventory audits based on collective knowledge-mapping exercises and not individual interviews where responses need to be somehow integrated by analysts with secondhand knowledge.

In summary, to be useful in an inventory audit a typology of knowledge must demonstrate the following five characteristics:

- *Observable*   The knowledge types need to be capable of being described and documented in consistent ways by different respondents. This condition goes to our desire for a broadly reliable and reproducible way of inventorying knowledge.

- *Naturalistic*   The knowledge types need to represent distinctions that make functional sense to people in the enterprise. Respondents can readily identify knowledge resources as contributing factors in work and describe them in ways that will be consistently understood by their peers. This also goes to reliability and reproducibility.

- *Actionable*   Following from our belief that a knowledge audit presupposes a theory of change, the knowledge types need to be relatively easily associated with actions to manage them, so that identification of knowledge resources can lead to decisions about how to conserve, grow, and manage them.

- *Comprehensive*   The knowledge types need to cover the full range of knowledge resource types in common use within the enterprise.

- *Granular*   A knowledge typology also needs to support inventorying knowledge resources at the right level of granularity—that is, knowledge as it is used in the context of work. Many of the typologies of knowledge we will discuss describe knowledge as it is used by individuals abstracted from specific tasks within their work group—that is, *personal knowledge*. Some of them describe higher-level typologies dealing with the way that organizations work with knowledge, often at a strategic level—that is, *organizational* or *strategic knowledge*. For an organizational knowledge inventory, we need reports that are contextualized to work.

As Joseph Horvath (2000) puts it, "Philosophers may define knowledge in *structural* terms (i.e., in terms of its relation to other concepts) but, in business settings, it makes more sense to define knowledge in *functional* terms (i.e., in terms of its use)" (p. 35).

Business functions are organized in the service of organizational objectives and are natural aggregators for the information and knowledge resources required to meet those objectives (Orna, 2004, p. 71; Henczel, 2001, p. 64). Business-function-oriented audits capture knowledge in use at probably the most stable level of detail for naturalistic and reproducible discrimination of knowledge types, and they support action planning.

By business functions I do not mean organizational structure; I mean the more stable, underlying business functions that organization structures attempt to organize and connect. Organization structures may change relatively often, but business functions remain fairly stable over time. And business-function-oriented audits have the most authoritative witnesses we can hope to find as to knowledge use: the people who perform those business functions on a daily basis.

As we will see later in this section of the book, organizational or strategic knowledge is too broad based for our purposes in an inventory audit, and knowledge associated with individuals, while extremely fine-grained, can be difficult to associate with follow-up actions. Business functions persist as individuals come and go, and they reflect the detailed components of activity that depend upon, and produce, consistent supplies of knowledge resources. Function-oriented audits also have the advantage of being more easily connected to business performance measures and the bottom line when it comes to intervention planning (Hasanali et al., 2003, p. 15).

Many typologies of knowledge exist in the KM literature, all developed for different purposes, but few meet our five conditions for auditability, and few can be used to identify and describe knowledge that is used at the functional level. That is not to deny their usefulness for other purposes.

In the remaining chapters, we will look in detail at the way typologies of knowledge have been constructed in the past, and why many of them fail our criteria for auditability. We will propose a typology that does meet these criteria, and we will close with a case study using this typology, that shows how a more differentiated typology, collected at the work-group level, redresses the bias toward explicit knowledge that we saw in the oil company example above.

*   *   *

Summary

In this chapter we returned to the importance of the inventory audit as a foundational audit activity for other forms of knowledge audit. I laid out the importance of having a clear typology of knowledge types and the risks of using an inappropriate typology. Here is a summary of the main points:

1. A useful typology needs to describe observable forms of knowledge or observable proxies for knowledge use.
2. In order to get reliable witness reports, the typology needs to describe knowledge in naturalistic ways.
3. The typology of knowledge types should be actionable—that is, lead to inferences about how the knowledge types can be managed.
4. The typology should be comprehensive and cover the full range of knowledge use in organizations.
5. The typology should be sufficiently granular to reflect the types of knowledge work at a functional or operational level in the organization.

16 Unhelpful Dualisms: The Personal-Collective Dualism

> There is a broad expanse of uncharted territory between the real knowledge work that occurs in an organization and the formal organizational structure and espoused practices.
> —Linger et al. (2005, p. 76)

The distinction between personal/individual knowledge and collective or organizational knowledge is a very common one. It implies that an understanding of the knowledge that individuals possess will lead to an understanding of the knowledge that an organization possesses, expressed as organizational capabilities, although, as we have already seen, the mechanisms by which personal knowledge contributes to or is transformed into organizational knowledge are held to be deeply mysterious. Superficially, the implication makes sense. The organization is supposed to harness and leverage the knowledge deployed by individuals.

There has been some debate about whether organizational or collective knowledge is the sum of all individual knowledge, or whether collective knowledge has additional properties that cannot be reduced to the sum of individual contributions (Nelson & Winter, 1982, pp. 104–105; Simon, 1991; Spender, 1996b; Leonard & Sensiper, 1998, p. 122; Chua, 2002; Hardin, 2009, chap. 6; Crane, 2016, pp. 64–68).

However, my view is that organization capabilities do not behave like aggregates of individual knowledges: "Individual interactions are not simply additive, but can take on complex forms and lead to surprising aggregate and emergent outcomes that are hard to predict based on knowledge of the constituent parts" (Barney & Felin, 2013, p. 141).

And as we saw, the consideration of organizational knowledge as an "asset" brings problematic considerations of whether all forms of organizational knowledge can be truly alienated from individuals to the extent that they can be monetized independently of them (Mentzas et al., 2003, p. 137).

The Missing Middle: The Problem with the Personal-Collective Dualism

The dualism between individual knowledge and organizational knowledge is distracting. Personal knowledge and organizational knowledge are only two ends of a complex knowledge integration system (Simon, 1991; Grant, 2002), and neither end makes sense without considering the *"missing middle"*—the spaces where knowledge is constructed, deployed, and consumed in the enactment of work practices within work groups and teams and that are themselves organized around business functions. As Henry Linger et al. (2005) stated:

> The concentration on formal organizational programs aimed at the individual workers ignored the real nature of work practices that reside in a space between the organization and the individual. . . . Until the full extent of . . . work practices is articulated, they will remain hidden from the organizational landscape, unappreciated and undervalued. . . . There is a broad expanse of uncharted territory between the real knowledge work that occurs in an organization and the formal organizational structure and espoused practices. (pp. 72–76)

Now, a review of strategic organizational knowledge is all well and good, but it expresses high-level capabilities that resist detailed breakdown, and it tends to focus on future work directions. Such a review it is likely to be much better at reflecting needs, gaps, and goals than it is at inventorying current resources and knowledge in action.

A review of the knowledge held by individuals, particularly key individuals, is all well and good, but the knowledge of everyone in your organization certainly represents a surplus over the knowledge that is actually deployed in key and critical activities. Nor does all the knowledge available in people exactly correspond to what is needed for those activities. There are typically both surpluses and gaps.

In the "missing middle", we have the invisible but crucial knowledge that emerges from people working together to address common tasks and challenges from day to day. Inventorying both strategic and personal knowledge is interesting and has its benefits for specific purposes, but for the purposes of an organizational knowledge audit, it is the knowledge consumed and produced in key operational activities that tells us most of what we need to know.

A more important point is that significant differences exist between the knowledge behaviors of

- individuals,
- teams and work groups, and
- organizations.

These differences are governed by the relative complexity of knowledge integration or knowledge articulation activities at these different levels of scale.

Knowledge integration refers to the ability to bring different forms and parts of knowledge to bear on a problem or an activity. This involves a delicate trade-off between (Grant, 1996; 2002, p. 138)

(a) supporting specialized knowledge creation and use (i.e., splitting knowledge up among different people) and

(b) efficiency in knowledge deployment in support of complex tasks (i.e., bringing together different forms of specialized knowledge held by different people).

Elsewhere, this is described as knowledge resource orchestration or resource mobilization, "according to which mobilized resources are integrated into a robust system to support better alignment, coordination and direction for specific use" (Asiaei et al., 2021, p. 1948).

Knowledge articulation is the work we do in groups and organizations that allows us to articulate our knowledge and coordinate our actions effectively without having to discuss and agree on every step in detail (Lambe, 2007, p. 54). "Articulation work names the continuous efforts required in order to bring together the discontinuous elements—of organizations, of professional practices, of technologies—into working configurations" (Suchman, 1996, p. 407).

At the level of the individual, most knowledge integration is done internally within the brain and body, with some external calls on the knowledge of team members or key network contacts. In consequence, a great deal of personal knowledge integration is not easily observed or described. But it can be extremely adaptive and responsive to changes in context.

In teams and in organizations, knowledge integration and knowledge articulation represent activities that need to take place for this scattered knowledge to become actioned effectively. These integration and articulation activities are different for teams and organizations because of the different levels of complexity involved (Kogut & Zander, 1997, p. 312–314).

This is why the dualism between personal and collective knowledge (and as we will see later, the dualism between tacit and explicit knowledge) is misleading. For knowledge managers to be able to design helpful interventions, it is not enough to talk about the knowledge itself. We also need to know the kinds of activities and processes that facilitate knowledge creation, sharing, and use at each of the three levels of individual, group, and organization, and how they differ across levels of complexity. In particular, we need to understand what it takes to facilitate knowledge integration and articulation for teams, as well as the higher-order needs of organizations (Halbwirth & Olsson, 2007, p. 69).

The Special Characteristics of Team Knowledge

Teams and work groups—if they are effective—often have highly developed metacognitive strategies and routines to support interpersonal knowledge integration and articulation (Klein, 1998, pp. 233–257). *Metacognitive strategies* refers to the various ways we become aware of, manage, and organize our own thinking.

In simple terms, this means that members of teams have to develop competencies in how to build and integrate different personal knowledges across the team, if they are going to ensure that the team is coordinated, directed, and kept aligned. Many of these are informal but habituated routines, and many of them are emergent and constructed on the fly, as they are needed. It is a mark of a high-performing team when these metacognitive strategies and routines become largely automatic. The work group's ability to respond to changes in its situation depends on the degree of sophistication of these metacognitive strategies.

From an auditor's point of view, team knowledge has an advantage over personal knowledge. Because this knowledge articulation work depends almost entirely on interactions and the sharing of knowledge artifacts, a team's knowledge use is significantly more observable than individual knowledge use in isolation. Except in highly individualized work contexts, it is also more directly connected to the way that work is done.

Consider the example below from a workshop I conducted with two of my colleagues and a client a few years ago. The italicized portions highlight the metacognitive work done by myself, by my colleagues, and by our client

(a) to ensure that we are able to integrate the various insights, observations, and learnings as the workshop progresses; and

(b) to ensure that we are able to articulate our collective knowledge and capabilities in pursuit of common, agreed-upon goals.

Case Study: Team Knowledge in Action

I and two of my colleagues are facilitating a knowledge-mapping workshop with sixteen departments, *about twice the normal size we would normally take on* in one session. It is a global pharmaceutical company with very smart, highly educated, and very vocal participants. *We have already discussed* how we will tackle this large and challenging group.

My colleague Edgar *notices* that one group of participants is getting drawn into very abstract discussions (they are in research and development) and they are not getting their knowledge maps documented, *so he sits with them* to guide them through the mapping process. I *notice* that he is out of circulation, *so I widen my monitoring activity* to include the groups he is no longer covering.

My colleague Jules *notices* that one of the groups is being dominated by a strong, negative character, who "doesn't see the point" of why he should map the knowledge his group uses and produces. After trying to engage him, Jules *lets me know* there may be a problem with this group. Looking at the guy, *I can see* he is demotivated and unhappy.

My client *has already let me know* that a few strong personalities in the group need to be convinced of the importance of this activity, and *she plans to enlist* her director's support to "lean on" them during the tea break. *Reflecting on the big picture, I know that* the negativity is not universal because *I can see that* most groups are working away well, and Edgar *has told me* that at least one group leader has said the technique is extremely useful and that she wants to take it back and apply it in her own office. However, *I can foresee that pockets of discontent could easily spread* if they are not addressed.

During the tea break (while the "dissenter" is being leaned on), *I tell my colleagues that I want to change the sequence of planned activities* and do a "pain points" diagnostics exercise immediately after the break, before recommencing work on the knowledge maps. We usually use this exercise to consolidate a sense of the most important issues arising from the knowledge-mapping activity. However, it is also a good way of identifying common issues quickly.

They prepare the materials, and after *we acknowledge to the group the feedback* we have been receiving, *we run the activity*. The room is a hum of energy and discussion. The activity surfaces many shared pain points around poor knowledge sharing and poor access to knowledge when it has to move between departments, and this shared realization, combined with the influence of the senior director on the naysayers, *refocuses* the group. Several participants say they feel relieved at being able to articulate their pain points and at realizing they are not alone in experiencing them.

We *had originally intended* for the pain points exercise to help the groups integrate and apply the insights from their knowledge maps once they had been completed. *We were able to reconfigure the activity* to show the value of investing effort in the knowledge mapping when we ran into resistance.

After the workshop we *conduct a lessons-learned activity* with the client and *discuss* whether *we should change the plan* for future workshops to position the pain points exercise before the knowledge-mapping activity. Our client *disagrees*, saying that these participants are strong-minded individuals who will always need convincing, and who would not have sufficient context to apply the insights from the pain points exercise until they had performed at least some knowledge-mapping activity. *We decide* to leave the pain points exercise as a midway point within the knowledge-mapping activity to help participants understand how the maps can contribute. However, in future exercises we now have a different mode of running the activity within our *repertoire*.

For myself and my colleagues, this metacognitive work is highly routinized, largely informal, and almost automatic, borne of long experience in facilitating workshops together.

> We have a repertoire of skills, practices, routines, and cognitive actions in common that are specific to the team: checking, monitoring, noticing, anticipating, and knowing when to alert colleagues and discuss issues.

It is in this sense that we can speak of team or work-group knowledge that exceeds the sum of individual stocks of personal knowledge. Any new team member would have to acquire this knowledge from the team as a whole, quite likely modifying the team's collective knowledge in the process.

With the client, we do not have this shared repertoire, so we have to schedule regular check-ins to ensure we maintain a common picture and can adapt our strategies in an agreed-upon way to adapt to unfolding circumstances.

The highlighted cues in the story above illustrate the types of metacognitive work being done at the team level:

- Managing and maintaining common goals and checking expectations
- Noticing and compensating for mutual gaps in awareness, information, and competency
- Informing others of cues they may have missed and maintaining a common situational picture
- Running and comparing mental simulations on the different ways that events might play out
- Adapting planned activities and routines in the confidence that others will step in automatically to provide support
- Checking for the big picture to avoid being led astray by strong but nonrepresentative signals
- Reflecting on events and forming collective views on future action
- Developing new routines to be added to the portfolio for when they are needed

Now, of course, personal knowledge, skills, experience, and judgment are all being engaged here. What the team's metacognitive work enables, is the scaling up of our individual brains, eyes, ears, and abilities, to act harmoniously and in concert on solving common problems, with minimal coordination costs, mistakes, or misunderstandings. The capability of the team exceeds the capability of any individual within the team, and it exceeds the capability of a bunch of individuals who do not have those metacognitive strategies and routines.

This can sometimes have profound consequences. When Captain Chesley Sullenberger landed his Airbus A320 on the Hudson River in New York that cold wintry day in January 2009, improbably saving all 155 passengers and crew, he had been flying with the same crew on a tiring back-to-back flight schedule for four days. They had known each other only slightly before that.

The transcripts of the cockpit recordings and the calmness and efficiency of the entire crew in the crisis reveal the immense value of a highly tuned team. Take this example from Sullenberger's (2009) account:

> As I listened to the [cockpit] recording, I saw clearly that Jeff [Skiles, co-pilot] was doing exactly the right things at exactly the right moments. He knew intuitively that because of our short time remaining before landing and our proximity to the surface, he needed to shift his priorities. Without me asking, he began to call out to me the altitude above the surface and the airspeed. . . . Jeff and I had found ourselves in a crucible, a cacophony of automated warnings, synthetic voices, repetitive chimes, radio calls, traffic alerts and ground proximity warnings. Through it all we had to maintain control of the airplane, analyze the situation, take step-by-step action, and make critical decisions without being distracted or panicking. It sounded as if our world was ending, and yet our crew coordination was beautiful. (pp. 380–381)

Drilling together or working together on shared routines has a "tuning in" effect that exceeds the group's capability to perform just the steps in the routines together. It creates a synchronizing effect even in very chaotic and unpredictable situations. These teams can become surprisingly adaptive and resilient.

Here is an example from Robert Graves's (1957) account of officer experiences on the western front in World War I, in which the importance of good drill discipline is being discussed in the officers' mess:

> Suppose a section of men with rifles get isolated from the rest of the company, without an N.C.O. in charge, and meet a machine-gun. Under the stress of danger, this section will have that all-one-body feeling of drill, and obey an imaginary word of command. There may be no communication between its members, but there will be a drill movement, with two men naturally opening fire on the machine-gun while the remainder work round, part on the left flank and part on the right; and the final rush will be simultaneous . . . this war, which is unlikely to open out, and must almost certainly end with the collapse, by "attrition," of one side or the other, will be won by parade-ground tactics—by the simple drill tactics of small units fighting in limited spaces, and in noise and confusion so great that leadership is quite impossible. (pp. 166–167)

Lest you think that this special "all-one-body" capability is just a simple product of highly proficient individuals working together according to common trained standards, the point is *not* that the drills have predicted the precise scenario the troops (or flight crews) find themselves in. They have not. The shared routines, and the mutual knowledge and expectations built up through the drills, give teams the capability and techniques to adapt and coordinate, almost by instinct, when faced with nightmarish situations in which plans and normal operating structures fail.

In fact, there are many examples of air crashes in which the crew is—quite naturally—overwhelmed by the speed with which events are unfolding, by the confusing signals of the instruments, and by poor team coordination and communications. Where teams lack metacognitive strategies for knowledge integration and articulation, they perform less effectively (Bassellier et al., 2003). Knowledge management (KM) can support team metacognition by addressing how team metacognition works and by providing the processes and tools to build shared metacognition and mutual familiarity.

What we see of the team mind in the "miracle on the Hudson" is backed up by research on the effects of fatigue on the performance of flight crews, especially when faced with unusual or challenging circumstances. Team metacognition builds over time, and it not only powerfully compensates for the negative effects of fatigue but actually enhances the team's performance beyond expectations, to a degree that the theory of the "sum of individual knowledge" cannot explain.

Research funded by NASA found, rather counterintuitively, that a fresh crew in which the members are new to each other is often outperformed by a *fatigued* crew that has built team metacognition into the way its members work together (Klein, 1998, p. 219; cf. Helmreich & Foushee, 2010, p. 13). The fact that Sullenberger's crew had been working together intensively for several days mattered a great deal.

In fact, errors are more likely to occur with freshly composed crews (Hackman, 2002; Helmreich & Foushee, 2010, p. 14). This finding led to recommendations to airlines to plan the scheduling of flight crews specifically to maximize crews' mutual familiarity and to avoid frequent crew reassignments that disrupt this mutual familiarity (Hackman, 2002, p. 50).

Familiarity in this sense does not just mean casual mutual knowledge. Team metacognition incorporates the shared routines, patterns of communication, and mutual expectations that a team builds up as a shared basis for coordinated action, whether through routine interactions, deliberate rehearsal, or a period of coworking.

In April 1980 a US military mission to rescue fifty-two American hostages being held by the regime in Iran had to be aborted because of poor weather, several helicopter malfunctions, and a lack of situational awareness among the task force on the ground. The inquiry into the mission found that one of the critical failure points was the fact that the rescue task force comprised an entirely new organization assembled purely for the purposes of that mission. The failure to run full rehearsals for the mission had exacerbated this weakness. The gaps in mutual familiarity led to a critical breakdown in the task force's capability and ability to adapt. The mission fell apart, leading to the deaths of eight American servicemen, an extension of the hostage crisis by nine months, and the catastrophic performance of President Jimmy Carter at the ballot box in his reelection bid later that year (Holloway, 1980, pp. 59–60).

Shared knowledge artifacts also matter. In the less dramatic case of our workshop, we were supported by knowledge artifacts—workshop plans, preworkshop briefings, workshop materials, support materials for the activities, profiles of the participants, postworkshop review, and so on. Sullenberger and his colleagues were backed up by training, instruments, and protocols. Some of our team's lessons and decisions were documented and built into planning templates if we deemed them worthy of reuse. The Sullenberger crew's experience was reviewed by the National Transportation Safety Board to decide what changes needed to be implemented and which knowledge artifacts and training needed to change.

This is consistent with the way that innovation professor Achim Hecker described the collective knowledge resources of functional groups. Without discussing the meta-cognitive aspects, Hecker (2012) points out that the collective knowledge base of functional teams has three essential elements:

- A shared repertoire
- Knowledge of who knows what
- Shared artifacts

> In this sense, the knowledge work of the team has more scaffolding and is more visible than the knowledge work of individuals working alone. It is relatively easy to audit compared to personal knowledge.

However, though the presence of team-based knowledge can be identified (with a suitable typology) in an inventory audit, we need to do more than register its presence. We also need to know *how it plays out in behaviors*. This is why we find it useful to conduct a culture audit, specifically based on narrative techniques, alongside an inventory audit. The following case study illustrates why.

Case Study: The *Grafton* and the *Invercauld*—the Power of Team Knowledge

There is another important factor involved in the ability to activate collective knowledge. This is a recognition of, and commitment to, the welfare of the whole group. Practically speaking, this means the ability to form and sustain shared goals, to work collaboratively toward those goals, and to maintain common ground, as well as develop a measure of care for each other (Hackman, 2002, p. 50).

We might call this mutual solicitude, and an important ingredient of this solicitude is mutual trust (cf. Krackhardt, 1992; Wilson, 1996, pp. 138–139). When trust breaks down, team knowledge is also fractured, pushing people back on their individual knowledge resources, so that team performance also suffers. In those circumstances it is extremely difficult to rebuild both trust and team performance without strong participatory interventions—as our chapter 7 case study about the standoff between the local staff and expatriate leadership team in a global nonprofit illustrates.

In 1864, by sheer coincidence, two ships were wrecked on different parts of the same remote island in the Southern Pacific Ocean. The differing fates of their crews can be taken as a fascinating natural experiment in the workings of collective knowledge.

The *Grafton*, with a crew of five, was shipwrecked on January 2, 1864, at the southern end of Auckland Island, several hundred kilometers south of New Zealand. The *Invercauld* was wrecked in May 1864 on the north end of the island, with a crew of twenty-five.

At the time of their wrecks, both ships had a sick crewmate on board. The *Grafton*'s crew got their fellow to shore and nursed him to health. The *Invercauld*'s crew abandoned their crewmate when they abandoned the ship. From the start, the crew of the *Grafton* were marked by their common purpose, their willingness to go out on a limb for the benefit of the whole crew, and the willingness of team members to defer to the knowledge and skills of the others, regardless of status.

By contrast, the crew of the *Invercauld*, five times larger and nominally greater in aggregate knowledge and thinking capacity, were marked by a spirit of every man for himself, by internal divisions, by violence, by mutual neglect, and by a rigid adherence to status and hierarchy.

By far the most resourceful member of the *Invercauld*'s crew in relation to maintaining adequate access to food was Robert Holding, a gamekeeper's son. This was a useful skill set on a remote island. But as he was a mere seaman, neither his peers nor the ship's officers, being socially conscious, heeded his advice on survival strategies (although they were happy to eat the food he caught).

The crew split up, abandoned their fellows, fought with each other, stole food from one another, and ate from one of the corpses. For lack of discipline and common purpose, all but three perished. The captain, his first mate, and Robert Holding were rescued by a passing ship in May 1865, a year after their ordeal had started. They had as little solidarity on the rescue ship as they did on the island, Holding being relegated to the seamen's quarters.

On the south side of the island, where the food stocks were actually more precarious, the *Grafton*'s crew had delayed the abandonment of their ship until the last moment so they could salvage as many supplies and tools as possible. They did not have anybody with the same foraging and trapping experience as the *Invercauld*'s Robert Holding, but they worked much more effectively together than the crew marooned on the other side of the island.

They built a cabin and a forge, and they experimented with cooking and eating local plants to maintain a balanced diet and avoid scurvy. They established a routine of study, prayer, work, and entertainment. They even caught and raised pets. Living in such straitened circumstances was not without its stresses and strains, but they were solicitous of each other's strengths and weaknesses. One of the crew destroyed his pack of playing cards because losing at cards put their captain, Thomas Musgrave, in such a foul mood.

Fourteen months after their wreck and living in constant hunger, they resolved to adapt their ship's rescued but fragile dinghy for the perilous ocean voyage to reach New Zealand. Realizing it could not carry all five crew members, three of them set sail in mid-July 1865, eighteen months after their shipwreck, reaching Stewart Island, south of New Zealand, a week later. They traveled on to Invercargill in New Zealand immediately, and the gaunt but indefatigable Captain Musgrave set about raising funds for a rescue expedition for his stranded colleagues. A month later he was back at Auckland Island to rescue them. All five of the *Grafton*'s crew survived, and it was not until October of that year that they learned that another shipwrecked crew had been just twenty miles north of them for most of their time there (Druett, 2007).

The Special Characteristics of Organizational Knowledge

The collective knowledge activated by teams is marked by its attention to mutual knowledge and mutual goals, and its high adaptive capability. By contrast, the collective knowledge activated by organizations is marked by routinization and the scale of its impact.

Let us look at an example of this kind of collective knowledge in action. Here is former Delta Force commander Pete Blaber's (2008) account of the pre-positioning of men and supplies on an island in the Persian Gulf, preparatory to the US invasion of Afghanistan in 2001:

> As soon as the sun went down and visibility dropped to zero, giant cargo planes, flying without lights, came screeching out of the night sky in perfectly synched intervals of ten minutes. As the wheels touched down, the roaring turbocharged engines changed pitch and braked the behemoth flying machines with physics-defying precision. Each cargo plane would then turn off the main runway without a second to spare before another plane, waiting empty at the opposite end of the runway, would release its brakes, accelerate to full power, and go roaring past in the opposite direction to take off and make room for the next plane to land a few minutes later. With Hollywood special effects-like orderliness, this cycle went on all night long. Once the giant planes were in their parking spot, they'd drop their tail ramps and regurgitate their cargo to the ravenous tongues of tandem two-ton forklifts driven by young men who deftly handled the machines like they were Porsches. The entire choreography was done impervious to the naked eye. . . . One wrong turn or second of inattentiveness by any of the actors involved, and a hundred things could kill any of them in a hundred really ugly ways. A small city grew like a weed in front of our mission-focused eyes. (p. 149)

Blaber's description paints a striking picture of large-scale collective capabilities that cannot be explained solely in terms of aggregations of personal knowledge. No single person knows all there is to know about setting up a forwarding base for a large-scale invasion half the world away, even though a multiplicity of deeply specialized knowledge sets are clearly at play.

Blaber's "choreography" is handled through the systematic division of knowledge and of cognitive labor, the provision at functional level of mutual knowledge (i.e., who knows what and who is equipped to handle which tasks), and the shared routines and procedures that are precoordinated and embedded in drills, training, simulations, procedures, and plans. There is a sense in which

> knowledge can be "stored" in team or organizational routines, without even having been explicitly described (e.g. as successful sports teams show us). As long as such people and teams remain accessible, one can say that their knowledge is "memorized" by the organization and available for (re)use. (CEN [European Committee for Standardization], 2004, pt. 1, p. 10)

Nobody knows everything. In fact, in relation to the scale of the enterprise, individuals know remarkably little of the knowledge that is being engaged (Hardin, 2009, p. 122).

Teams know more, collectively, than their members do, by virtue of their overlapping but not entirely duplicated repertoires, their knowledge of each other, and their knowledge of how to work together effectively. But they have only the vaguest sense of the larger picture within which they operate.

Everybody has deep knowledge relating to their own small-scale routines and tasks and a light knowledge of how their knowledge, skills, and responsibilities intersect with their immediate coordination partners (Hecker, 2012; Sloman & Fernbach, 2017).

Now there could be an impression from Blaber's description of the airfield growing like a city that organizational knowledge is simply composed of tightly coordinated functional knowledge. But functional or team-level knowledge is not the same as organizational knowledge.

Take the shared knowledge artifacts upon which teams depend to support their work. Many functional groups will store and organize their knowledge artifacts in arrangements that are convenient and transparent to the group, often around the needs of frequent task completion. But these arrangements appear idiosyncratic and opaque to people outside that work group (Lambe, 2007, pp. 146–148, 222–223).

> In fact, optimization for functional working often compromises the ability of the enterprise to get an organization-level view of its knowledge artifacts.

This is the source of the much bemoaned *silo working* we complain about in knowledge management—specialized arrangements that serve a useful function for their work groups but that, in the absence of organizational infrastructure to lift them into visibility, inhibit wider organizational uses of knowledge artifacts (Nichani, 2012).

In fact, the fragmentation and scatter of organizational knowledge is often seen as a major challenge in even being able to plan and conduct knowledge audits, because the scope of the audit is not always clear (Lambe, 2017). In one knowledge audit project we were involved in, our lack of visibility into the organizational structure and functions, caused by the devolved and uncoordinated nature of its operations, meant that approximately twice as much work had to be done to cover the ground compared to original estimates.

In practical terms this means that an organization-level view often has poor visibility into functional-level knowledge resources, even when the focus is on explicit knowledge. Paradoxically, organizations can *do a lot more* than teams or individuals but they *know less*. We will return to this thought later.

Blaber's example from the invasion of Afghanistan shows us that organizational knowledge can be striking in its power and capabilities, far exceeding the knowledge capabilities of individuals or even of teams (cf. Hardin, 2009, pp. 125–126). But organizational knowledge has its limits as well. It is far less flexible than team and functional knowledge, and that in turn is less flexible than personal knowledge in how it can be disposed.

A large number of organizational capabilities are delivered on automatic, and unreflectingly (Nelson & Winter, 1982, pp. 124–125). This is a product of our limited cognitive capabilities. Alfred North Whitehead (1911) stated this succinctly:

> Civilization advances by extending the number of important operations which we can perform without thinking about them. Operations of thought are like cavalry charges in a battle—they are strictly limited in number, they require fresh horses, and must only be made at decisive moments. (p. 61)

So organization-level knowledge has quite different characteristics from team or personal knowledge. They can even be in tension with each other, or in conflict.

In another account, Blaber (2008) describes the key battle of Shahi Khot in March 2002, an almost abortive attempt to wipe out an al-Qaeda enclave hidden in a mountainous valley near the Afghan border with Pakistan. The heavily routinized mission-planning process, and the dogmatic mission planners' dependence on helicopters, contrived to set in motion a plan that both individuals and teams could see was set up for failure, given the weather and topography, but that they were powerless to prevent (p. 259).

The large-scale capabilities delivered by precoordinated organizational knowledge come at a cost: an inability to change a complex plan once it has been set in motion. This has been a persistent theme in military history since at least the First World War. Barbara Tuchman (1962, p. 235) relates how the German Kaiser, upon learning of Britain's intent to enter the war, almost immediately changed his mind on the wisdom of the "go" decision to commence hostilities. However, in the space of minutes since his initial assent, the wheels had already been set in motion, and the decision—and the machinery of invasion—could not be recalled. There can be strong tensions and discontinuities between team knowledge and organizational knowledge.

The mechanisms for the integration and articulation of personal and work-group knowledge into organizational performance are sluggish and sclerotic. They are more standardized and formalized. They cannot rely on the informal, responsive, and flexible "coordination by mutual adjustment" that springs from the mutual familiarity of the team (Thompson, 1967, p. 56; Weick & Sutcliffe, 2001, p. 31). That is why the urgent need to combine agility with scale of impact is the holy grail of modern multinational management (Gerstner, 2002, p. 214).

Robert Grant (2002, pp. 138–139) identified four principal knowledge integration mechanisms that organizations use in support of their goals (and that Ralph Stacey asserted were mechanisms for storing and accessing organizational knowledge; cf. Stacey, 2000, p. 25):

- *Rules and directives*—impersonal mechanisms of varying degrees of formality and strength including standards, policies, procedures, plans, schedules, and other instruments for coordinating large-scale knowledge-based activity.

- *Sequencing*—process definitions that direct how individuals' contributions are inserted into a sequence of activities and tasks. These can function independently of the individuals' knowledge of the whole process.

- *Routines*—simple sequences that are learned and can be performed in different combinations without significant direction or thought.

- *Group problem-solving and decision-making*—typically meetings, designed to bring individual knowledge(s) to bear on an unusual problem and find consensus on a solution. This mechanism is typically deployed in situations for which the other knowledge integration mechanisms are not sufficient. In fact, a proliferation of meetings is a symptom that the other mechanisms are deficient.

These share some similarities with team-based knowledge integration and articulation mechanisms. Both use routines and group problem-solving and decision-making mechanisms, but they work at significantly different levels of formalization.

At the organizational level, relatively few routines are shared across the organization, and they are generalized, not specialized, compared to the work group's repertoire of routines, shared context, and mutual knowledge.

Also at the organization level, the coordination costs of group problem-solving and decision-making activities are much higher when the different parties lack high levels of mutual familiarity and trust. High coordination costs manifest themselves in lots of seemingly unproductive meetings.

In an effective work group, there are considerable economies of effort in this kind of coordination because we can take a shared context for granted, especially where there is a commitment to shared goals, and a mutual solicitude. Things get settled much more easily. Communications can be very compact: "By compactness I mean that a phrase, word or gesture is packed with meaning—meaning that would generally not be extractable by a layperson, without extra information or explanation. Mutual knowledge of various kinds allows for this compactness" (Johannesen, 2008, pp. 199–200).

At the organizational level, shared context (and certainly mutual solicitude) is much thinner, so there is a lot of context-setting, explaining, and context-maintenance work, as well as commitment-maintenance work, in the absence of which there is regular opportunity for misunderstanding, conflict, misalignment, and error.

Within KM we recognize this in the different ways we manage sharing and learning processes. For example, in the transfer of lessons, Nancy Dixon (2000) distinguishes between *serial transfer* (transfer of lessons within a team from one situation to the next), *near transfer* (transfer of lessons between teams sharing very similar contexts), and *far transfer* (transfer of lessons with marked differences in context), each requiring quite distinct support processes.

Over and above their attempts to maintain consistent capabilities in mobilizing knowledge in support of their goals, organizations also go to the trouble of formalizing and protecting some forms of codified knowledge as organizational assets, whether in the form of intellectual property, trade secrets, or proprietary processes and routines. While individuals and teams also create knowledge artifacts, they are typically creating them not as assets but as aids to thinking or memory for individuals, or as coordination devices for teams (Baber & McMaster, 2016, pp. 39–56, 64).

Table 16.1 summarizes the main differences between individual, team/functional, and organizational knowledge. The major differences center around the goal orientation, how the knowledge is applied, the responsiveness of the actors to change, the observability of how knowledge is being used, the complexity of the knowledge work, and the influence of culture on the use of knowledge.

Organizational knowledge as a set of capabilities and resources is therefore managerially and phenomenologically distinct from the functional knowledge leveraged by teams and workgroups, and this is again quite distinct from personal or individual knowledge.

Does it make sense to speak of "team knowledge" and "organizational knowledge" as if they are "things"? I believe it does. There are those who argue against the "reification" of collective knowledge as if it exists independently of individual knowledge, following Herbert Simon's (1991) declaration that only individual humans can "know" (p. 125; Grant, 1996, p. 113). I think this is overly restrictive. As Paul Cilliers (2000) put it, human knowledge is constituted socially and cannot subsist outside of social relations:

> Knowledge comes to be in a dynamic network of interactions, a network that does not have distinctive borders. On the other hand, this perspective would also deny that knowledge is something purely subjective, mainly because one cannot conceive of the subject as something prior to the "network of knowledge," but rather as something constituted within that network. (pp. 8–9; cf. Sloman & Fernbach, 2017)

Of course, groups and organizations are not single-brained creatures as humans are; they have many brains that have to be aligned. But on the converse side, humans with their single brains do not possess their knowledge entirely independently of others. Knowledge is a shared resource and is possessed and acted upon both within and

Table 16.1

Differences between individual, work-group, and organizational knowledge

	Knowledge of individuals	Knowledge of teams and work groups	Knowledge of organizations
Goal orientation	Typically focused on task completion.	Focused on outcomes of the integration of multiple tasks. Requires coordination and goal-setting activities and regular check-ins to repair differences in perception about goals and how to achieve them.	Focused on high-level organizational goals and typically communicated in broadcast mode, with poor feedback loops and repair mechanisms for divergent understandings of goals compared to those of the work group.
Application of knowledge	Application of knowledge is largely habituated.	Application of knowledge is routinized in high-performing teams. The team develops both formal and informal metacognitive strategies and routines for building and maintaining common ground, maintaining member situation awareness, goal setting and tracking, and compensating for performance, knowledge, and understanding gaps in members (Klein, 1998, pp. 233–257).	Emergent, loosely supervised, and loosely controlled application of individual and team knowledge.
Responsiveness to change	Emergent, highly responsive to context.	Highly responsive in teams with good metacognitive strategies and routines. Poor metacognitive strategies and routines can produce mistakes and poor responsiveness to changing contexts.	Relatively unresponsive. Improvements in responsiveness carry high coordination costs and may be impeded by culture and politics.
Observability of knowledge work	Hard to observe, high effort required to describe in any detail.	More easily observed than individual knowledge, knowledge activities are made visible through interactions and trading of knowledge artifacts.	Observed and described at high levels of abstraction or, if in detail, in limited ways for the purpose of legal protection through contracts, intellectual property, trade secrets, and privacy or confidentiality regulations.
Complexity of knowledge work	Primary focus is on direct knowledge application in support of personal and joint tasks; secondary focus is on formal and informal knowledge integration and articulation.	Primary focus is on informal knowledge integration and articulation in support of joint tasks; secondary focus is on formal knowledge integration and articulation; tertiary focus is on ensuring availability of requisite knowledge.	Primary focus is on formal knowledge integration mechanisms (e.g., policies, procedures, routines); secondary focus is on informal knowledge integration activities. Support for knowledge articulation is typically weak.
Influences	Influenced primarily by team or work-group culture.	Influenced primarily by team or work-group culture.	Influenced by the emergent organization-wide effects of competing subcultures.
Role of knowledge artifacts	Mainly as memory and sensemaking aids, often informal.	Used to maintain situation awareness and collaborative sensemaking, both informal and formal.	Formal, focused on reporting, organizing action, analysis, and record keeping.

between human beings, at differing levels of scale. As long as we realize we are using a "thing"-based label metaphorically and not literally, and recognize that it does not completely express the dynamism of knowledge work, then the benefits of doing so (the entailments of the metaphor that knowledge can be managed, accumulated, built upon, and deployed) outweigh the limitations.

In this sense, the stable, enduring factors that persist as individuals come and go, and that give teams and organizations the capability to extend, apply, and gain knowledge in pursuit of common goals can legitimately be called forms of knowledge. As Gary Klein (1998, p. 257) points out, while the parallels between human minds and team minds should not be taken too literally, they share features in common (e.g., limited working memory, storage of information, limited attention spans, parallel processing of information), and the workings of each can illuminate the workings of the other (cf. Hardin, 2009, p. 121).

A Middle-Out Method for Auditing Knowledge Stocks

What then are the implications for knowledge auditing if we break down the dualism between personal knowledge and organizational knowledge into a tripartite distinction, looking at personal, team, and organizational knowledge?

From an auditing point of view, we can see that functional (work group) knowledge provides an important window into how knowledge is produced and used in the organization. Figure 16.1 shows schematically how functional knowledge mediates

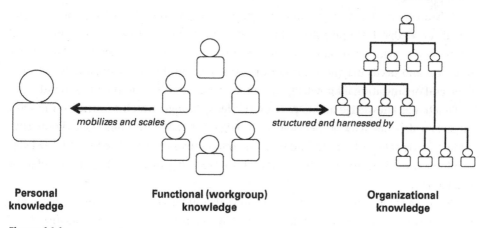

| Personal knowledge | Functional (workgroup) knowledge | Organizational knowledge |

Figure 16.1
The role of functional (work group) knowledge in mediating personal knowledge to the organization.

personal knowledge to the organization and can support what we call a *middle-out method* for knowledge auditing.

First, functional knowledge, enacted within work groups and teams, renders the aspects of personal knowledge that are of interest to the organization's objectives and goals both observable and actionable.

Second, to understand organizational knowledge, it is necessary to understand the particulars of functional knowledge, because this is what the organization has to harness and utilize and coordinate to meet its goals. Starting an analysis with an examination of organizational knowledge is an abstract and theoretical exercise at best, until there is a prior understanding of what tasks are actually performed and how.

This is why the dualism between personal and collective knowledge is too simplistic. The "missing middle" prevents us from understanding how personal knowledge is mediated and rendered actionable to the organization.

On the other hand, to understand the functional knowledge in an organization it is neither necessary to understand all the particulars of personal knowledge nor practical to do so. Personal knowledge typically exceeds that which is required for the performance of organizational tasks.

A good characterization of functional knowledge will indicate which particulars of personal knowledge need to be investigated and described in greater depth. This is why the focus of an inventory audit should be organized primarily around functional knowledge in what Linger et al. (2005, p. 72) call a "middle-out" approach. This is consistent with Nonaka and Takeuchi's (1995, chap. 5) advocacy of *middle-up-down* knowledge creation processes.

This does not mean we should disregard either personal knowledge or organizational knowledge. It simply means that an inventory audit organized around functional knowledge provides a practical avenue to understanding which personal knowledge resources and needs may need further investigation, on the one hand, and which strategic and organizational knowledge resources need attention, on the other hand.

Functional knowledge audits provide the lens through which to identify the most important dependencies on personal knowledge. For example, a functional knowledge audit that revealed a high dependency on certain areas of specialized tacit knowledge would provide the warrant to investigate those areas in greater depth with the relevant individuals.

When we come to reviewing strategic knowledge audits later on, we will see that strategic knowledge needs and capabilities are typically mapped against strategic organizational goals. Strategic knowledge needs do not necessarily match existing functional knowledge resources, especially where new strategies are being pursued and new capabilities need to be built.

When conducting a strategic knowledge audit, the functional knowledge audit can perform a valuable preparatory function. It enables us to compare what we have at the functional level against what we need at the strategic level. We can look at how functional knowledge (and behind that, in targeted areas, personal knowledge) supports those strategic goals and what must be done to improve that support—that is, where we have the strategic knowledge resources we need, and where we do not.

So although it has not been especially common to think of knowledge as primarily a team-level phenomenon, there are good arguments for doing so. And it turns out that there are some good precedents for inventorying knowledge resources at the function and task level.

Both Karl Wiig and Dave Snowden have used ethnographic techniques to analyze knowledge needs and uses at the task and function level. Wiig followed a traditional ethnographic approach of using skilled interviewers, while Snowden advocated self-ethnography, a facilitated method for self-reporting knowledge use (Wiig, 1995, chap. 8, 10; Spradley, 1979; Crane, 2016, p. xix). Self-ethnography is an example of the participatory approaches we described in chapter 7, where evidence collection and interpretation are driven by the participants themselves.

Wiig focused on the task and the task environment, while Snowden focused on major decision points and decision clusters, assuming that key decisions represent the critical points in tasks where knowledge is most closely engaged and revealed. Both Wiig and Snowden used this analysis to map information and knowledge resources and flows associated with tasks and decisions.

In the information audit domain, Elizabeth Orna (2004) took an implicitly functional approach. While she did not orient her questions toward the particulars of performed tasks, she worked systematically through different functional departments and got them to collectively map their knowledge and information needs, uses, and flows in a workshop format. This approach was also advocated by Dave Snowden and by Max Boisot (1998, p. 231).

Workshop formats using group-mapping techniques are especially good at surfacing shared representations of collective, team-based knowledge, and are superior (for this purpose) to interviews, which are optimized for exploring aspects of personal knowledge. These workshops are classic examples of participatory approaches. Collective self-representations in workshops mitigate against the subjectivity of individual perspectives: "We are thus initially dealing with a collection of individual perspectives and representations that are subjective in nature and that confront each other. Gains in objectivity are achieved gradually through iterated discussions and further investigations" (Boisot, 1998, p. 231). And in consequence, key tasks and decision points quite naturally emerge as the main organizing elements in the resulting maps (Orna, 2004, pp. 69–71).

The functional and task-oriented approach is one my company Straits Knowledge has used for the past twenty years, adapting features from Boisot's, Orna's, and Snowden's approaches. We facilitate workshops with knowledgeable and experienced representatives of work groups to help them self-report a shared understanding of their critical tasks and activities and the knowledge uses associated with those. The approach is deliberately participatory. In this way we mitigate the risk of bias from partial views, poor self-knowledge, and perspectives dominated by the individual's knowledge rather than the team's knowledge.

Case Study: Collectives "See" More than Individuals

Be My Eyes is a Danish tech start-up launched in 2015, with a free iOS application that connects sighted volunteers worldwide with people who are blind or have low vision. An Android version followed in 2017. The idea is ingenious. If you are blind and in a situation in which you need to figure out what a package label says, the nature of the object you are handling, or a direction sign, you open the app and put out a call for help. Public transport and shopping can be particularly challenging situations to navigate for people who are blind or have low vision. When preparing food, you may need help to identify which food cans or packages you need.

Typically within a minute, one of the 1.5 million volunteers signed up with the service will connect with you via video call, you will point your smartphone at the thing you need help with, and the volunteer will act as your "eyes" to describe to you what they see. As of October 2018, over 100,000 people who are blind or low sighted were using the app. There is also a business version that helps companies meet the needs of customers who are blind or low-sighted (Be My Eyes, 2018).

Other start-ups, such as Aira, are more commercially oriented, using wearable smart glasses and streaming video to connect clients who are not sighted with paid, sighted hourly contractors to help them perform tasks. Aira's plan is to use artificial intelligence to build learning algorithms around repetitive tasks so that it will eventually be able to recognize certain tasks and provide automated assistance (Lee, 2017).

Both examples provide particularly vivid illustrations of a fact that we know implicitly but do not always acknowledge in the way we investigate knowledge use in organizations. Individuals on their own see less and know less than collectives working together. We are all partially sighted to some degree, constrained by our work contexts and by the daily events that direct our attention and interest. Knowledge maps built by individuals are invariably poorer, and commonly contain significant gaps and inconsistencies, compared to maps built by groups working together.

---

*   *   *

Summary

In this chapter we broke apart the simplistic distinction between personal and organizational knowledge. Here is a summary of the main points:

1. Personal knowledge, team knowledge, and organizational knowledge are phenomenologically and managerially different from each other and are not simply composites or reducible elements of each other.

2. In an inventory audit, it is necessary to observe and understand the metacognitive strategies for integrating knowledge use within and across teams.

3. A knowledge resources inventory needs to document knowledge uses at the functional or team level in a middle-out method for knowledge auditing that can be extended downward to personal knowledge where necessary and mapped upward to strategic needs at the organizational level.

4. Functionally oriented knowledge audits can help to mediate an understanding of how personal knowledge contributes to strategic organizational capabilities.

17 Unhelpful Dualisms: The Tacit-Explicit Dualism

All this intellectualist legend must be rejected, not merely because it tells psychological myths but because the myths are not of the right type to account for the facts which they are invented to explain.

—Ryle (1946, p. 8)

Now we need to turn our hand to the other problematic dualism in describing knowledge types, that between *tacit* and *explicit knowledge*. This dualism has a complicated history and is not without its passionate advocates and accompanying politics. So it needs to be picked apart quite carefully.

Nonaka's Sleight of Hand: The Tacit-Explicit Dualism

The tacit-explicit distinction was of course popularized by Nonaka in his famous 1991 *Harvard Business Review* article "The Knowledge-Creating Company," followed up by his collaboration with Hirotaka Takeuchi in the1995 book of the same title. Nonaka claimed he drew the distinction from the philosopher Michael Polanyi (1966), but there are several problems with the way that Nonaka appropriated (and distorted) Polanyi's concept of tacit knowledge. Here is the book version of Nonaka's distinction:

> As for the epistemological dimension, we draw on Michael Polanyi's (1966) distinction between *tacit knowledge* and *explicit knowledge*. Tacit knowledge is personal, context-specific, and therefore hard to formalize and communicate. Explicit or "codified" knowledge, on the other hand, refers to knowledge that is transmittable in formal, systematic language. (Nonaka & Takeuchi, 1995, p. 60)

This is not an accurate characterization of Polanyi. For Polanyi, tacit knowledge was not "hard" to formalize and communicate—it was *impossible* to formalize and communicate successfully. The act of formalizing and communicating, according to Polanyi, actually destroys tacit knowledge as tacit knowledge. As Polanyi (1966) put it: "An unbridled lucidity can destroy our understanding of complex matters" (p. 18).

Polanyi uses the example of the piano player who, by striving to become conscious of the movements of his fingers, becomes temporarily paralyzed. His knowledge sits in his body, not in his head. I have another example: a very competitive friend of mine, a psychologist by profession, was trying to figure out how to beat his regular tennis partner. One day he commented, "That's a great serve you have there—show me how do you do that." His buddy's serve collapsed for the rest of the game, as my astute friend had calculated.

Consciousness and explicitness is the enemy of tacitness. As the sociologist of science Harry Collins (1993) said, "we are not very good at doing certain things when we think about them" (p. 109).

The essence of tacit knowledge is that it is open and indeterminate—meaning it can have multiple diverse outcomes. Tacit knowledge is directed outward at its productive outcomes and *not* inward at its own performance or upon its own construction as propositional knowledge (Nelson & Winter, 1982, p. 76 n2). It is fundamentally un-self-aware, or as Karl Wiig (1993, p. 134) put it, fully "automatic."

Now Polanyi did not disagree that tacit and explicit knowledge can interact. He was clear that they work in concert with each other. It is simply that they operate in fundamentally different ways. He acknowledged that knowledge from analysis and explication (such as the engineer's understanding of the workings of a car) can be richer and more powerful than just tacit knowledge in the same area of practice (how to drive a car). He agreed that particulars of tacit knowledge that had been observed and reflected on to construct explicit knowledge could be reinteriorized through practice into a newly tacit form, but he held that this would constitute novel tacit knowledge. The original tacit knowledge would be overwritten. We cannot roll ourselves back to prior states of tacit knowledge.

Most damaging for the Nonaka doctrine, Polanyi (1966) stated very clearly that the tacit and explicit forms of knowledge were not interchangeable. Tacit knowledge cannot be exchanged for explicit knowledge (p. 20). A more accurate representation of the relationship between the two types would be this formulation (Tsoukas, 2005, p. 158):

(a) that explicit knowledge can be constructed

(a) by attending to the particulars of a practice

(c) that is produced out of tacit knowledge.

This was inconvenient for Nonaka because the central premise of his work, and the central premise of his SECI model (socialization, externalization, combination, internalization) rested on "conversions" through this cycle of stages, from knowledge in a purely tacit form to explicit form. He knew he was stretching Polanyi's distinction, and he glossed it over with the claim that he was being more "practical" than the philosopher.

But philosophers' distinctions are hard-won—they matter. And they are hard to dismiss. To bolster his case, Nonaka borrowed from cognitive psychologist John Anderson's work on artificial reasoning systems, positing the ability to reduce tacit knowledge to explicable rules—without, however, acknowledging Anderson's cautions about the uncertainties surrounding what was just a theoretical construct and unproven in practice (cf. Anderson, 1976, pp. 80–81).

Nonaka had an entirely respectable goal; that of figuring out how to render tacit knowledge explicable and transferable, and how to use explicit knowledge to gain tacit knowledge. However, he skated over a critical distinction as if it did not exist and produced an overly simplistic and dualistic explicit-tacit-explicit conversion paradigm that simply does not hold up to detailed scrutiny in practice, and has in recent years come under increasing criticism (Tsoukas, 2005, p. 158; Gourlay, 2006).

Nonaka's anchor story for the conversion, or "capture," of tacit knowledge was about how the Matsushita Electric Company observed a master baker at work in order to convert his knowledge into the specifications of a new bread-making machine. It follows Nonaka's cycle beautifully, from socialization of the master baker's tacit skill (observation) to externalization (identifying the "twist" in the kneading process), combination (with the other machine-related knowledge), and internalization (into the machine-maker's tacit knowledge base).

But this is conceptually misleading. Internalization into one's tacit knowledge base from explicitized forms of somebody else's expert knowledge does not necessarily make you an expert. As Harry Collins (1997) points out, "lack of self-consciousness is not a condition of expertise for inexpert actions may be un-self consciously performed" (p. 153). A novice who has internalized the explicit rules and works on habit, but is an inexpert performer, is still a novice.

The use of the anchor story was powerful from a communications perspective, but it erroneously implied continuous movement of the same knowledge from one stage of the SECI cycle to the next. It also tended to gloss over and homogenize the variety of forms of tacit knowledge. Consider the following:

- The nurse in a neonatal intensive care unit who is worried in an indeterminate way about how a premature baby "looks" and therefore checks in more frequently

- The fire chief who makes a split-second decision, based on intuition, to call her crew out of a burning building moments before it collapses

- The expert chicken sexer who can determine the gender of a day-old chick before sexual characteristics have emerged
- The restaurant chef who organizes and orchestrates her kitchen to manage the flow of different meal orders
- The restaurant waiter who maintains a situational awareness and memory of orders and sequences of dishes as he navigates the restaurant space with economy while managing interruptions
- The project engineer in an oil rig construction company who is planning the refurbishment of a dry dock, an event that takes place every couple of decades
- The negotiator who knows exactly when to make an offer or a concession in a negotiation, to get maximum benefit
- The lawyer who is uncomfortable about the way a proposed contract is framed and decides to do more due diligence research to try to pin down his intuition that something is wrong
- The leader whom employees consistently trust and follow in a crisis
- The colleague who can defuse a tense situation in a meeting and move it toward resolution with a few well-chosen words

These different people rely on a wide variety of forms and "bundles" of tacit knowledge, including embodied skills, experiential knowledge, technical knowledge, perceptual skills, social skills, and cognitive skills. If we wished to replicate, transfer, or build the forms of knowledge these people display, we would need to use a very wide variety of methods. Some of them could be assisted by creating explicit knowledge aids. Many of them could not. The "conversion" metaphor is too crude, and the simplistic distinction, between explicit and tacit, results in a homogenized view of "tacit" knowledge that does not respect its complexity.

As a high-level sensemaking framework for thinking about how to support knowledge transfer in organizations, Nonaka's SECI model has some utility (Lis, 2014). But as a framework for auditing and managing knowledge types in organizations, it is next to useless. We already saw its effects in knowledge mapping in the oil company case study in chapter 15—it biases interpretation and action toward the more observable knowledge forms—that is, explicit knowledge resources.

Another complication, not reflected in this dualism, is that most of the knowledge used in organizations simply does not exist in either fully explicit or fully tacit states. As Botha et al. (2008) point out, "A practical view of knowledge is that tacit and explicit knowledge are not absolute opposites, but that they form a spectrum" (p. 13).

In other words, in any knowledge-driven performance there are differing degrees of tacitness and explicitness at play, and in knowledge management (KM) we need to know how those different combinations play out (Kogut & Zander, 1993; Leonard & Sensiper, 1998, p. 113). Explicit knowledge resources require some level of tacit knowledge to be actioned. Any tacit knowledge has the capacity to be described and explicated to a degree, giving rise to a variety of knowledge forms. And the literature of knowledge management, as we shall see shortly, is replete with nondualistic typologies of knowledge with intermediate forms between tacit and explicit. However, the field of knowledge management practice has tended to lock on to the simplistic dualism between tacit and explicit with concomitant negative effects, as we saw in our oil and gas company case study in chapter 15.

To be fair to Nonaka, he did try to differentiate between different ways that tacit knowledge manifests. He divided tacit knowledge into cognitive elements (mental models such as schemata, beliefs, and paradigms) and technical elements (concrete know-how, crafts, and skills; Nonaka & Takeuchi, 1995, p. 60).

Notice, however, that both subdivisions favor his thesis of tacit knowledge explicability. They also recall a much older knowledge typology (of which Nonaka was aware) first proposed by the Oxford philosopher and military intelligence officer Gilbert Ryle in 1946—the distinction between *know-that* (which became labeled declarative knowledge in the cognitive psychology literature and can serve as a proxy for the term *explicit knowledge*) and *know-how* (which became labeled procedural knowledge and often serves as a proxy for the term *tacit knowledge*; Ryle, 1946). Again, Nonaka does not acknowledge Ryle's caveat, like Polanyi's, that *know-how* cannot be defined in terms of *know-that* (Ryle, 1946, p. 5). One is not convertible to the other.

Factual, explicit know-that does not of itself produce tacit know-how, and know-how can exist without prior know-that. "A silly pupil may know by heart a great number of logicians' formulae without being good at arguing. The sharp pupil may argue well who has never heard of formal logic." Ryle (1946) continues in what would surely have been a sharp jab at Nonaka if Ryle had lived long enough to read him—or for that matter, in an even sharper jab at the cognitive psychologists who later adopted his declarative and procedural knowledge distinction and tried to make the one reducible to the other:

> There is a not unfashionable shuffle which tries to circumvent these considerations by saying that the intelligent reasoner who has not been taught logic knows the logicians' formulae "implicitly" but not "explicitly"; or that the ordinary virtuous person has "implicit" but not "explicit" knowledge of the rules of right conduct; the skilful but untheoretical chess-player "implicitly" acknowledges a lot of strategic and tactical maxims, though he never formulates

them and might not recognize them if they were imparted to him by some Clausewitz of the game. This shuffle assumes that knowledge-how must be reducible to knowledge-that, while conceding that no operations of acknowledging-that need be actually found occurring. It fails to explain how, even if such acknowledgements did occur, their maker might still be a fool in his performance.

All this intellectualist legend must be rejected, not merely because it tells psychological myths but because the myths are not of the right type to account for the facts which they are invented to explain. However many strata of knowledge that are postulated, the same crux always recurs that a fool might have all that knowledge without knowing how to perform, and a sensible or cunning person might know how to perform who had not been introduced to those postulated facts; that is, there still remains the same gulf, as wide as ever, between having the postulated knowledge of those facts and knowing how to use or apply it; between acknowledging principles in thought and intelligently applying them in action. (pp. 7–8)

Know-how is manifested in action; know-that is manifested in words. Propositional thinking and speaking is an *adjunct* of action, not a *conversion* of the knowledge-in-action: "the tacit co-operates with the explicit, the personal with the formal" (Polanyi, 1958, p. 87).

The different knowledge types engage different human capabilities, and working effectively with the different knowledge types requires a faculty of agility, an ability to switch between tacit and explicit modes of working while solving real-world problems (Baumard, 1999, p. 227). This is a more complex operation than any dualistic model can handle. For example, even the know-how and know-that distinction ignores perceptual skills, which certainly are constitutive of knowledge but fall in neither category (G. Klein, personal communication, September 1, 2021).

Nonaka's sleight of hand (or what Ryle described as a "fashionable shuffle") fails to hold up, as do several of his other conceptual borrowings (Crane, 2016, p. 70–73). Haridimos Tsoukas (2005) gets to the nub of the fallacy of tacit-explicit conversion when he says that

> . . . every practice establishes a set of what MacIntyre calls "internal goods"; namely, goods that cannot be achieved in any other way but by *participating* in the practice itself. For example, the particular analytical skills and strategic imagination that are associated with playing chess, the kind of satisfaction derived from caring for patients, or the thrill that comes from exploring new avenues of scientific research cannot be achieved in any other way than by respectively *playing* chess, *nursing* patients, and *researching* in a particular field. (p. 81)

The consequence of Nonaka's fundamental misprision is profound, not less so because of its influence on subsequent KM practice. As Dave Snowden (2006a) has frequently said, "To my mind in the hands of consultants and IT vendors it has become the model that launched a thousand failed knowledge management initiatives" (cf. Grant & Qureshi, 2006).

Bad typologies produce poor and inconsistent results. And typologies can be bad, not simply by containing the wrong categories but also by inadequately reflecting the complexity of the phenomena they are attempting to describe.

The superficially convincing case studies that Nonaka presented in that original *Harvard Business Review* article, and in the subsequent book with Takeuchi, do not stand up to the scrutiny of a manager who needs to understand what was going on in detail in the so-called "conversion" processes between tacit and explicit knowledge in order to be able to repeat the process elsewhere.

As Stephen Gourlay (2006) has convincingly shown, the evidence for Nonaka's claims evaporates under scrutiny. There are multiple possible pathways other than *knowledge conversion* for the successful outcomes in Nonaka's case studies, and these possible pathways were not accounted for. The supposed knowledge conversions are reduced, in Ryle's (1949) somewhat acidic phrase, to "occult episodes" incapable of further analysis (p. 25). The typology just does not convince in practice. It does not represent or explain phenomena in a way that supports understanding or the design of helpful interventions.

We did not have logical coherence as one of our criteria for the utility of a typology in an audit. If we had, Nonaka's distinction would have failed at the first test. But Nonaka's binary distinction between tacit and explicit with two (explicable) subdivisions for tacit knowledge also fails our tests of observability and naturalism, as the examples from Polanyi, Ryle, and Tsoukas illustrate. On observability, the dualism biases toward the explicit, and on naturalism, it does not adequately and transparently describe how humans work with knowledge in practice. And a binary typology just does not seem to do justice to the complexity and variety of knowledge use in organizations. It is insufficiently granular and comprehensive.

An Intermediate Knowledge Type: Implicit Knowledge

Worries about the binary nature of the tacit-explicit distinction have led to several attempts to interpose an intermediate form of knowledge. Horvath (2000) proposed a tripartite division into explicit, embodied (tacit), and embedded knowledge. Although he does not attribute any sources for this typology, its elements very likely originated with the British sociologist of science Harry Collins (1993) and/or the organizational theorist Frank Blackler (1995). We will get to Collins's and Blackler's typologies in a while, but for the moment let us focus on the idea of "embedded" knowledge.

Embedded knowledge is elsewhere described as structural knowledge or implicit knowledge (Wiig, 1993; Leonard & Sensiper, 1998; Nickols, 2000; Botha et al., 2008;

Davies, 2015). As distinct from explicit knowledge that resides wholly outside of people, and tacit knowledge that sits inside people, we might think of it as the knowledge that floats "between" people in the conduct of work. It refers to knowledge that is embedded in products, services, and processes, that is socially and collectively held, and that is very likely not fully explicit (Brown & Duguid, 1998, p. 91; Dixon, 2000, p. 12; Gamble & Blackwell, 2001, p. 2). It can also be said to correspond to the notion of *structural capital* in typologies of intellectual capital (Edvinsson & Malone, 1997, p. 11).

Embedded, implicit, or structural knowledge, because it reflects the knowledge "between" people, clearly operates at both the functional level as well as at the organizational level. As such, in principle it should have considerable importance and utility for function-oriented knowledge auditing.

Of the three labels, *implicit knowledge* probably has the greatest currency as an intermediate form of knowledge between explicit and tacit. While it is sometimes identified with tacit knowledge (Ryle, 1946; Spender, 1996a; Grant, 2007; Crane, 2016, p. 129–130), in many cases it means knowledge that is not yet articulated but is theoretically capable of being so (Nickols, 2000; Leonard et al., 2015).

This sense of knowledge that is capable of being made explicit has a long lineage of use. We can trace it from Saint Augustine's concept of a human's "implicit knowledge" of God, which is engaged by human memory (*memoria*), intelligence (*intelligentia*), and will (*voluntas*) and becomes articulated (made explicit) through the word (*verbum*; Taylor, 1989, p. 139). We can see the same thinking in the work of the philosopher, cognitive scientist, and prominent skeptic Daniel Dennett (1983).

In this tradition, implicit knowledge has a sense of latency and openness to multiple possibilities, in contrast to explicit knowledge, which has already been constrained by its form. An explicit artifact such as a manual or standard operating procedure is optimized for the purpose it was created for, and it takes work to adapt it to novel uses. While implicit knowledge does not have the unconsciousness of practice of Polanyi's tacit knowledge, it partakes of some of the openness and indeterminacy of tacit knowledge (Dennett, 1983). Prior to explication, it has the potential to emerge in multiple forms and have diverse outputs and outcomes.

Where we use the term *implicit knowledge* in this book, we follow the Augustinian tradition of signifying embedded and not necessarily conscious knowledge that is capable of becoming articulated and made explicit in various forms. For clarity's sake we do *not* take it as a synonym for tacit knowledge that cannot be explicated. Others do so, and in so doing they play into the simplistic post-Nonaka notion that tacit/implicit knowledge can be captured and efficiently transferred through codification (cf. Lee et al., 2021, chap. 4). In our case we are using the term as a typological device to break down the binary dualism of tacit-explicit and to help us identify intermediate forms between extreme tacitness and extreme explicitness. We are starting to think in terms of a continuum of knowledge types.

This interposition of an intermediate form between tacit and explicit is a necessary starting point that will help us identify a more differentiated and useful typology of knowledge forms. In the following chapters, we will use the disruptions to the two unhelpful dualisms we identified (personal-team-organizational knowledge; explicit-implicit-tacit knowledge) to frame a more meaningful and useful spectrum of knowledge types for knowledge-auditing purposes.

*   *   *

Summary

In this chapter we broke apart the second simplistic distinction between tacit and explicit knowledge. Here is a summary of the main points:

1. We need to understand the tacit-explicit knowledge distinction as representing a continuum, not a dualism. Knowledge types express different degrees of tacitness and explicitness.

2. The notion of implicit knowledge forms a useful bridging category between the two extremes of tacit and explicit knowledge and can be used to develop a more differentiated typology of knowledge forms.

3. The tacit-explicit distinction represents a misleading conceptual distinction and does not satisfy our tests of observability and being naturalistic.

18 Typologies of Personal Knowledge

Go make thyself like a nymph o' the sea: be subject
To no sight but thine and mine, invisible
To every eyeball else. Go take this shape
And hither come in't: go, hence with diligence!
—Shakespeare, *The Tempest*, Act 1, Scene 2

Even if the best place to start in an inventory audit is with functional, work-group, or team knowledge, we still need to have a means of "seeing" the knowledge that persons hold. That is the ground upon which team knowledge operates. In this chapter we will review a number of typologies of personal knowledge and assess them (a) for their utility in an audit and (b) to see if they can give us a more modulated view of different forms of tacit knowledge.

Know-What, Know-Why, Know-How

Writing in the late 1990s, Michael Zack took a different, more nuanced path from Nonaka's tacit-explicit dualism. Starting with the ideas of procedural and declarative knowledge rooted in Gilbert Ryle's work, he elaborated several other types of knowledge and described a more fully fleshed typology (Zack, 1999a, 1999b, 2001):

- *Declarative knowledge*—"knowledge-about"—knowledge that can be explicated.

- *Procedural knowledge*—"know-how"—knowledge of how something occurs or is performed. Zack's formulation implies that it can be explicitly represented, unlike usages where it is used to refer to tacit knowledge.

- *Causal knowledge*—"know-why"—knowledge about how things work and how to achieve goals and desired outcomes.

- *Conditional knowledge*—"know-when"—knowledge about the conditions in which to apply certain actions and decisions.
- *Relational knowledge*—"know-with"—an understanding of the relationships and interactions between concepts, ideas, and elements in a system.

With slight variations, this expanded typology of knowledge crops up in multiple places (Wiig, 1993; Quinn et al., 1996; Vasconcelos et al., 2000; Botha et al., 2008).

Zack (2001) believed this typology primarily worked at a functional level and could be used to solve knowledge problems in the organization. I am not so sure. These types, while framed in a way easily related to the context of work, describe the knowledge held by individuals, which is then put at the disposition of groups without accounting for how groups process that knowledge.

As Alexander and Judy (1988) pointed out, declarative, procedural, and conditional knowledge at the least (and very likely the others as well) are not strictly separate in naturalistic settings in the real world. They come together and interact in performance. They represent conceptual distinctions, not naturalistic ones.

In the real world, from the judgments of a skilled negotiator, to the operation of complex machinery, to the nuanced decisions of an experienced entrepreneur or the intuitions of a seasoned investigator, the know-how, know-what, know-when, and know-why are inextricably tangled in the everyday performance of work, to the point that it is hard to abstract them as operational knowledge types for analyzing work in general. And if they are not separable, then they fail our tests of observability and describing naturalistic distinctions.

Where this kind of typology may have some utility is in identifying and systematically accounting for the types of knowledge that are at play in the expertise of highly skilled individuals as they engage in specific situations and contexts.

In fact, Kate Pugh uses this kind of typology to support the elicitation and transfer of the different layers of knowledge required to solve specific business problems. She uses it as a framework to draw out the different elements of how a "knower" solves a given problem in her facilitated "Knowledge Jam" sessions. Pugh's (2011, pp. 206–208) framework includes

- declarative knowledge—a description of existing processes/products/strategies relevant to the problem;
- procedural knowledge—processes, methods, and heuristics in use;
- conditional knowledge—considerations for triggering some approaches over others;
- social knowledge—who is engaged in addressing the issue, and how; and
- systemic knowledge—larger system-wide considerations in addressing the issue, including learning and feedback loops.

Some of the techniques of cognitive task analysis, a field that seeks to understand how knowledge and expertise are applied in performance, are designed precisely to probe these areas of personal knowledge, particularly in the context of critical incidents (Crandall et al., 2006, pp. 69–90). When framed by the narrative structure of a critical incident that an expert has participated in, the deployment of know-what, know-why, know-when, and know-with can then be probed in detail.

So the typology may work for probing personal knowledge in depth but probably will not work for inventorying functional or team knowledge. Indeed, incident-based, anecdotal, or narrative-based knowledge can be a very helpful prop as an integrating mechanism or as a contextual framing device within which we can identify the finer structural elements of personal knowledge, tacit or otherwise (Wiig, 1993, p. 156; Tsoukas, 2005, pp. 80–88). These finer structural elements can include the ability to (Crandall et al., 2006, p. 89)

- connect past and future and run mental simulations on different possibilities;
- look at the specifics of a situation and relate them to the big picture;
- notice anomalies, unusual elements, or the strange absence of cues you would normally expect to see;
- apply learned "tricks of the trade" and heuristics;
- spot opportunities and leverage points and exploit them; and
- monitor and modify one's own thinking and cognition processes.

All of these elements of personal knowledge depend on having access to a repertoire of past experiences (incidents) that can be described as stories or anecdotes, and that can be probed for the knowledge deployed in that repertoire.

However, incident-based, anecdotal, or narrative-based knowledge is largely personal, and not strictly functional in the sense we need for an inventory of knowledge stocks. Certainly, a team or a group can possess "shared stories" of significant shared experiences, but these tend to be fewer in number than the narrative personal knowledge of experienced individuals, and as shared experience stories they are less revealing of knowledge than they are expressive of shared identity. It is not strictly knowledge of a functional group in an organization; it is essentially personal in nature. The best way to get at these finer points of personal knowledge is still through individual interviews.

So while this kind of investigation may provide insights that usefully roll up into a functional or work-group level (e.g., if a given function relies on having people with certain types of experience relating to certain types of incidents), it is not sufficiently comprehensive to cover the knowledge needs of a business function and does not have the functional typicality we need for it to serve as a guiding framework for a function-oriented knowledge inventory audit.

Breaking Down Tacit Knowledge

We spoke earlier about the benefits of describing knowledge as a continuum rather than as a binary dualism. The sociologist Harry Collins (2010) recognizes that the phenomenon of *tacit knowledge* manifests itself in many different ways, including within a social context. He deserves to be more widely read by knowledge managers. He speaks about "weak, medium and strong" tacit knowledge (p. 85).

Weak tacit knowledge is what he calls *relational tacit knowledge*, which is an almost exact parallel to our simple notion of implicit knowledge and is not to be confused with Zack's relational knowledge, which is about conceptual relationships. It refers to the nonexplicit *common knowledge* of the group.

Collins's version of relational tacit knowledge could in principle be made explicit but happens not to be, simply because of the way that we organize ourselves socially. Reasons for this knowledge remaining implicit can include reserving full details from people whom we do not trust, lacking the time or energy to explain it or show it (e.g., for ostensive knowledge that needs to be demonstrated), or not being aware that somebody needs the knowledge or assuming they have it already. Additionally, it can be knowledge that we have not yet fully reflected upon and analyzed for its explicit components.

Collins points out that our world is full of this kind of relational tacit knowledge. We swim in it. While any individual part of this knowledge is capable of being made explicit, the practicalities of life in society mean that it just does not make sense for much of the relational tacit knowledge we work with to be made explicit.

Except where there are specific reasons to make our implicit knowledge explicit (e.g., for reasons of standardization, coordination, or continuity), we work much more effectively and efficiently when we keep relational tacit knowledge in the implicit domain. Simply put, it is more economical (Collins, 2010, chap. 4).

Medium tacit knowledge is labeled *somatic tacit knowledge* by Collins. This is elsewhere described by Horvath (2000) as embodied knowledge, and it is closest to Ryle's "know-how" and Polanyi's examples of tacit knowledge (e.g., riding a bicycle or playing a piano). There is physical skill involved, and there is a case for saying that the knowledge exists "in the body" more than it exists conceptually in the brain.

And yet there is an element of explicability to this knowledge. It can be acquired socially, it can be demonstrated and guided, rules can be extracted and taught, and in training programs, it can be modeled and taught. We can analyze and model somatic knowledge, and we can design machines to do similar things (although not necessarily in the same way as humans).

To be clear, these explicit elements are not converted forms of somatic knowledge, but they are vehicles for acquiring and refining it. When we acquire somatic tacit knowledge, through repeated practice, we gradually become unconscious of the rules and drills through which the knowledge was originally taught. Somatic knowledge has a degree of explicability to it, but cannot be reduced to explicit knowledge (Collins, 2010, chap. 5).

Strong tacit knowledge is what Collins (2010, chap. 6) calls *collective tacit knowledge*. This refers to the collective *knowledge world* that provides the tools and frameworks to interpret and apply other forms of knowledge, especially explicit knowledge. We inhabit many different knowledge worlds at different levels of scale.

So Collins invites us to consider the collective knowledge deficits that would have to be considered if we were to attempt to transfer Nonaka's famous bread-making machine (supposedly encoding a master bread maker's tacit knowledge expertise) to the Amazon jungle. Assumptions about diet, the availability of ingredients, the desirability of bread, the ability to manipulate and power and maintain technology would all come into play. Taken for granted in one context, they provide an invisible, constant, socially maintained lens for interpreting and acting upon the world. In another context, the lens is different and the knowledge fails.

Collective tacit knowledge also turns up as a *knowledge stickiness* factor affecting the ease or difficulty of knowledge transfer between engineers working in different cultures or different kinds of engineers working in different modalities. For example, Hsiao et al. (2006) looked at how the different "knowledge worlds" of field engineers and equipment engineers in the same semiconductor fabrication company prevented the successful use of a common knowledge resource without some form of "translation." Their working assumptions and practices were too different.

Hsiao's student Lei Yijie produced a revealing case study examining why an apparently straightforward technology and knowledge transfer exercise between two aircraft maintenance, repair, and overhaul companies in Germany and China failed spectacularly in the early 2000s. Adoption of the German enterprise resource-planning system by the Chinese ran into insuperable problems around the different working, thinking, and problem-solving cultures, and it also ran into contextual problems around key differences in their respective supply and logistics environments. The supposedly complete explicitization of process and function that had worked so effectively in the German context turned out to have buried assumptions and dependencies that simply did not transfer (Lei, 2005).

These problems can occur across time as well. NASA famously "lost" its knowledge of how to build the Saturn V rocket, the most powerful rocket ever built. A rocket of such power was necessary to escape the pull of Earth's gravity and get the Apollo space missions to the moon in the 1960s.

When NASA started to revisit the need for deep space missions in the early 2000s, this time aiming for Mars, it found that it lacked the capability to reconstruct the Saturn technology. It was not for want of explicit knowledge resources. Though the records are not complete, there are lots of records. The contractors had documented their designs and blueprints in some detail. What was missing was the knowledge of the individuals who had coordinated the project and knew how all the pieces fit together, the hidden assumptions and thinking processes behind the designs, the design options considered and rejected, and the many experiments that went nowhere.

Simply put, the knowledge worlds of engineers educated in the 1940s have very little in common with the knowledge worlds of engineers educated in the 1980s and 1990s. Even where decisions and designs were documented and made explicit, at a distance of fifty years engineers were running into major knowledge world differences, making it impossible to reconstruct the knowledge embedded within them (DeLong, 2004; Jennex, 2006; Teitel, 2011).

Collective tacit knowledge persists over time. Like culture (which acts as a carrier for collective tacit knowledge), it survives the comings and goings of individual members. As Leonard and Sensiper (1998) put it, "Even if some individuals leave the organization, a shared 'net of expectations' created through organizational routines and accepted standards remains. Moreover, these expectations are conveyed through artifacts as well as through behavior" (p. 122).

Collins's collective tacit knowledge is a crucial blind spot in our normal understanding of tacit knowledge. Although we can certainly become aware of it, analyze it, draw attention to aspects of it, and articulate insights about it, it is the hardest of all three types to explicate and transfer, depending at least to some degree *upon active participation in the collective social world* to or from which we are attempting to transfer knowledge. Words alone will not do it.

We have to become inculturated, at least to some degree, into the *other* knowledge world in order to become aware (a) of our own collective knowledge assumptions and dependencies and (b) to begin seeing and understanding the knowledge assumptions and dependencies of the strange environment we are trying to interpret.

What is more, this area of tacit knowledge is more complicated to deal with because we often do not realize we need it until we run into problems in interpreting other forms of knowledge, particularly explicit forms of knowledge that otherwise should be relatively straightforward to use. We suddenly realize we do not have the mental "operating system" that "runs" this form of explicit knowledge. Our own collective tacit knowledge is largely unconscious, so we do not feel the need to explicate it to people from other knowledge worlds, and vice versa.

In that sense, collective tacit knowledge is a necessary substrate of other forms of knowledge, a substrate that helps us interpret and deploy those forms, not necessarily a parallel knowledge type, alongside them. Most importantly, it is clear that it makes no sense to try to explicate our collective tacit knowledge until we encounter a shortfall or a specific problem requiring some recalibration. Knowing that it exists and that it causes certain kinds of knowledge transfer problems and affordances, is sufficient for our purposes (Collins, 2010, chap. 6).

Frank Blackler (1995) extended and modified Collins's typology, describing five knowledge types neatly covering the full span between tacit, implicit, and explicit:

- *Embrained*—knowledge dependent on cognitive abilities and equivalent to Ryle's "knowledge-that." This is implicit knowledge in the sense that it is capable of being explicated.
- *Embodied*—equivalent to Collins's somatic knowledge and Ryle's "knowledge-how." This is more tacit than implicit, although aspects of it can be articulated.
- *Encultured*—equivalent to Collins's collective tacit knowledge, it describes the means by which social groups achieve and maintain shared understandings and is roughly equivalent to our earlier discussion of Klein's "team mind".
- *Embedded*—implicit knowledge embedded in organizational routines that is capable of explication if observed and described.
- *Encoded*—explicit knowledge in artifacts such as documents.

Blackler's knowledge types spectrum, from tacit through implicit to explicit, and Collins's foray into the complexities of tacit knowledge are richly rewarding. In principle, aspects of them can be applied across personal, work-group, and organizational levels. They help us see aspects of tacit and implicit knowledge that we have not seen before and so provide a much finer-grained picture of knowledge type that will help us on our way.

However, as a working typology for auditing purposes they fall short. Although they can describe functional or team knowledge, they would probably fail the naturalistic test—it does not seem "natural" to describe functional activities in terms of the relational, somatic, embedded, encultured, or collective tacit knowledge required to perform them.

And as with Zack's typology, these knowledge types seem to operate in combination with each other, interacting one upon the other, and so they do not provide a particularly useful set of distinctions for observation and self-reporting within a corporate setting. They provide useful conceptual distinctions, not the naturalistic distinctions that we need in an audit.

While the Collins-Blackler typologies alert us to distinctions that clearly matter and while they will inform the typology we eventually adopt, in and of themselves they do not satisfy all our needs. Their greatest value lies in breaking up the middle ground between very explicit and very tacit, and they show us how different forms of knowledge can occupy that ground with greater and lesser degrees of tacitness and explicitness and greater or lesser degrees of potential for explication and transfer.

They also demonstrate the importance for knowledge auditors of being able to trace the social and relational aspects of tacit knowledge.

*   *   *

Summary

In this chapter we looked at a number of typologies for describing personal knowledge and evaluated them for their usefulness in auditing knowledge in organizations. Here is a summary of the main points:

1. Most typologies of personal knowledge represent conceptual distinctions and do not satisfy our observable and naturalistic tests. However, they can be useful for probing and inventorying individual knowledge in depth, especially when placed in a narrative context to explore challenging incidents.

2. Collins's and Blackler's typologies break down our understanding of tacit knowledge in useful ways and clearly demonstrate how some types of tacit knowledge are socially constructed and held. They point to the importance of maintaining social relationships for acquiring and maintaining tacit knowledge.

19 Typologies of Organizational Knowledge

When all is said and done, it really is the commander's *coup d'oeil*, his ability to see things simply, to identify the whole business of war completely with himself, that is the essence of good generalship. Only if the mind works in this comprehensive fashion can it achieve the freedom it needs to dominate events and not be dominated by them.

—von Clausewitz (1976, p. 578)

If typologies of personal knowledge give us a sense of the base resources of an organization, then typologies of organizational knowledge should give us a strategic sense of organizational capability and need.

There are several different ways of getting at an inventory of organizational knowledge. The method recommended in this book is to

(a) start mapping at the work-group/function level;

(b) drill down to investigate areas of personal knowledge in detail where they clearly have an impact on business performance; and

(c) aggregate up to the organizational level—in particular, looking at collections or bundles of knowledge resources that have a broad impact on key capabilities.

We call this the middle-out method of knowledge auditing, which is illustrated in chapter 16 (figure 16.1).

Other practitioners start at the organizational level, by looking at key organizational capabilities and inferring from those what knowledge resources are present or are needed to deliver those capabilities sustainably. This approach is often associated with the intellectual capital literature but sometimes uses the terminology of *strategic knowledge* instead. As with everything else in knowledge auditing, there is a great variety in approaches to how we can characterize strategic knowledge.

Intellectual Capital Typologies

The intellectual capital literature has a well-known typology structure for characterizing organizational knowledge (e.g., human capital, structural capital, relational capital). It has also developed quite sophisticated indicators and measures for these broad knowledge types, geared toward reporting and managing the intangible (knowledge-related) assets of an enterprise.

However, the domain is also problematic because although the phrase *intellectual capital* is widely used in the knowledge management (KM) literature to refer to organizational knowledge resources, and although the two disciplines were once closely linked, they have drifted apart over time, and what happens in one domain does not necessarily translate easily to the other.

As we saw in chapter 12, the concept of intellectual capital has been around for at least a hundred years, but the burgeoning of the intellectual capital literature in the early 1990s became closely intertwined with the rapid growth of interest in knowledge management. In principle, therefore, a typology for intellectual capital should work well for KM. However, this close relationship was not destined to last.

The forerunner of the modern intellectual capital movement was Hiroyuki Itami, whose 1980 book in Japanese, *Mobilizing Invisible Assets*, was translated into English in 1987. Itami (1987) believed that information stocks and flows lay at the heart of a firm's *invisible assets*, which he interpreted as a firm's competitive differentiators—or, as we might say today, strategic capabilities (p. 18).

Just four years later, Tom Stewart (1991) kicked off his famous series of *Fortune Magazine* articles on intellectual capital with a decidedly KM-centric description of intellectual capital:

> BRAINPOWER has always been an essential asset. It is, after all, why Homo sapiens rules the roost. But it has never before been so important for business. Every company depends increasingly on knowledge—patents, processes, management skills, technologies, information about customers and suppliers, and old-fashioned experience. Added together, this knowledge is intellectual capital. (p.44)

Stewart's (1998) bestseller *Intellectual Capital* continued to weave intellectual capital and KM themes together as if they were conjoined twins. Even today, writers and practitioners in KM and intellectual capital still use the term *knowledge assets* and *intellectual capital* interchangeably or use *intellectual capital* as a collective term for organizational knowledge assets (Handzic & Zhou, 2005, p. 109).

However, over the past twenty-five years the main intellectual capital (IC) movement has evolved into a specialized discipline focused on value measurement and value accounting. It has developed journals, conferences, and publications that sit largely apart from their KM counterparts. The conjoined twins have been separated, and if they do meet sometimes for major festivals, they live in different neighborhoods and are not intimate.

The seeds of this separation and the IC orientation toward measurement came early. Karl Erik Sveiby's first book in English spoke of "knowhow capital" management and at the same time pioneered the concept of measuring, accounting for, and investing in this "new" form of capital (Sveiby & Lloyd, 1987).

Leif Edvinsson's famous Skandia Navigator, developed in the 1980s, popularized a systematic approach for measuring and reporting intellectual capital (Edvinsson & Malone, 1997). At the same time, the accounting profession was becoming interested in the challenge of accounting for the value of intangibles in an organization (Lev, 2001).

This progressive specialization effectively spun off intellectual capital from KM. Donald Hislop (2013) ventures to call intellectual capital "an almost forgotten footnote" in the literature of knowledge management (p. 20). This is hyperbole—as we have seen, *intellectual capital* is still being used (loosely) as a synonym for value-creating corporate knowledge assets. The association is still there in common parlance, if not in research and professional practice.

Arguably, the last major attempt to cover KM and intellectual capital in the same systematic, broad sweep was the massive and rich compendium *The Strategic Management of Intellectual Capital and Organizational Knowledge*, edited by Chun Wei Choo and Nick Bontis in 2002. For now we shall exclude the recent attempt by Handa et al. (2019) which has issues of its own. But even in 2002, the cracks were starting to show: intellectual capital was relegated to a separate section and used a vocabulary distinct from the KM chapters (Choo & Bontis, 2002).

By 2013 the KM-IC disciplinary separation was all but complete. The separation is concealed by the rhetorical use of the term *intellectual capital* within KM circles. Here is a fairly typical example from a recent KM article (Alias et al., 2016, p. 507): "Knowledge is increasingly being recognized as a vital organizational resource and intellectual capital in organizations. The tacit and explicit knowledge of employees is crucial to any organizations." As we can see from this example and the many other others like it, KM references to intellectual capital are virtually content-free and do not engage with the deeper IC literatures and methodologies.

The in-depth literatures of KM and IC are increasingly drifting apart in terms of cross citations. Alexander Serenko and Nick Bontis track the bibliometrics of both domains and until 2008 measured KM and IC literatures together as if they constituted a single field (Serenko & Bontis, 2009; Serenko et al., 2010). More recently, they have been analyzing them separately (Serenko & Bontis, 2013a, 2013b).

James Guthrie and colleagues (2012) argued that IC accounting had evolved into a distinct field in its own right and in their retrospective of the previous decade made minimal reference to the KM literature. Intellectual capital papers tend to cite authors within their own subdiscipline more than they cite authors from other disciplines, including knowledge management (Hsu & Sabherwal, 2011, p. 637; Serenko & Bontis, 2013a, p. 489).

Federica Ricceri's (2008) book *Intellectual Capital and Knowledge Management: Strategic Management of Knowledge Resources* is an unusual outlier in attempting to treat IC and KM as coterminous.

Another notable outlier is the 2014 knowledge-auditing module within the KM program taught at Kent State University, which first applied Daniel Andriessen's intellectual capital typology to an organization's strategic capabilities and then categorized the IC types into observable knowledge asset types, following through into KM implications. We will revisit this example later simply because it is an interesting illustration of a rare but strong attempt to maintain a bridge between the two disciplines (Bedford, 2014).

Some authors try to resolve the discontinuity in other ways. In a study of over five hundred companies in Taiwan, I-Chieh Hsu and Rajiv Sabherwal concluded that intellectual capital *produces* KM capabilities, and KM in turn helps to turn intellectual capital into innovation. The two are thought to have reciprocal effects. In this view, KM *serves* intellectual capital—the two disciplines are related but distinct (Hsu & Sabherwal, 2011; cf. Liyanage & Jones, 2002, p. 184). In this formulation they can be functionally separated, but they are not estranged.

Why is this important to us? First, intellectual capital and knowledge management have a shared history, and both aspire to describe and extract value from organizational knowledge. They are entangled with each other, even if they now largely ignore each other, aside from nodding at each other across the street. We have already discussed how closely the notions of "knowledge assets", "intangible assets", and intellectual capital are intertwined.

More importantly for our current chapter, the intellectual capital literature has a well-known and widely accepted typology to describe types of organizational knowledge. We do need to examine whether this typology can help to create actionable inventories of knowledge resources in an organization.

The most famous, and common, typology is that proposed by Leif Edvinsson (Edvinsson & Malone, 1997, p. 34–37):

- *Human capital*—the knowledge, skills, and experience of employees, the rate at which they evolve, and how they are shared. We can see linkages here to our discussion of personal and collective knowledge types.

- *Structural capital*—the infrastructure, both soft and hard, including routines and processes, that makes the capabilities of the human capital productive. Edvinsson broke structural capital down further into organizational, innovation, and process capital. We can see connections here with our discussions of implicit and embedded knowledge.
- *Customer capital*—relationships with customers. We can see how this would emerge in a value accounting context, speaking as it does to the traditional accounting concept of *goodwill*. In Edvinsson's original Skandia Navigator model, customer relationships were originally part of structural capital but were later called out separately because of their importance. Reflecting on our prior discussions, we can anticipate that it might be difficult to disentangle the relationship capital of an organization from the knowledge-bearing relationships nurtured by individual staff.

While these general IC types turn up in many intellectual capital models, there is great diversity in how the typology is detailed, broken down, and turned into indicators and metrics. Daniel Andriessen (2004, p. 61) surveyed ten different competing classifications.

Nick Bontis (2001, p. 57) complained about the lack of a standard nomenclature in the field and about the confusions in meaning between different IC types being propagated by different writers. Six years later, in a ten-year retrospective on the field, Göran Roos and Stephen Pike (2007) suggested that the lack of common definitions around capital types had led to confusion and poor take-up in the business community:

> . . . the devotion of numerous paragraphs or even entire sections to a discussion of taxonomy ten years after the two most popular systems were first published seems absurd. Commentators have argued that diversity of view leads to greater flexibility in thinking about new concepts or considerations but the cost is that this lack of consensus inhibits the acceptance of intellectual capital in the business community. (pp. 10–11)

Here are just a few of the fine discriminations:

- Some models substitute the broader *relational capital* for customer capital (Roos et al., 2001; Liyanage & Jones, 2002; Ricceri, 2008).
- Some separate out *market capital* and *innovation capital* from structural capital (Brooking, 1996; Bounfour & Edvinsson, 2012).
- Some include intellectual property (Brooking, 1996; Sullivan, 2000).
- Some elevate technology and processes (Mouritsen et al., 2001a; Andriessen, 2004).
- Some include competitive capital (Rothberg & Erickson, 2002).
- Some make a link to social capital (Nahapiet & Ghoshal, 1998; Bounfour & Edvinsson, 2012).

Simply put, despite the effort put into classification, differentiation, and measurement, there is no still generally accepted detailed typology of IC types (Roos & Pike, 2007, p. 11).

Daniel Andriessen (2004, p. 65) deprecated calls to standardize the typology, pointing out (as we did in chapter 15) that a typology should be evaluated by the purpose it is intended to serve. The reason for what he calls a "confusion of tongues" is that there is a profusion of purposes. Those purposes may not be consistent with ours.

The purpose of a knowledge inventory audit is primarily to register the availability of resources as inputs to work or as work products. When IC typologies are geared toward defining indicators that isolate the business effects and value of intangible assets—as many are—then they are probably not suitable for representing manageable resources in context, or the interventions needed to manage them. This suggests that an IC typology may not be fit for purpose for a knowledge audit, at least on its own. Anna Ujwary-Gil (2020) has made an interesting case for including intellectual capital within a "meta-model" based on network theory, and incorporating other typologies from the resource-based view of the firm and the knowledge-based view of the firm. While analytically interesting, this may be too complex for a pragmatic, distributed, and naturalistic approach to inventory audits, where the goal is to inform operational as well as strategic KM interventions.

Danish researchers Jan Mouritsen and colleagues (2001b), who were concerned with building IC statements that could inform a KM strategy, put their finger on the nub of the problem for many IC typologies—in particular, for the original tripartite model of human capital, structural capital, and customer/relational capital:

> However, the three categories are not only related, they are also integral to each other. People work through technology; customers get services from people, information technology circulates both customers and employees. . . . Therefore the three kinds of resources are complements. They are part of a network of things and people that co-produce the effects of the whole network. (p. 362)

While it may be useful to disentangle them for accounting and strategic management purposes, in the operational context they are inextricably entwined (cf. Murray, 2018). Moreover, different combinations or entanglements of intellectual capital elements can result in the same capability outcomes (Ujwary-Gil, 2020, p. 59). In fact, Shantha Liyanage and Alan Jones (2002, chap. 6) implicitly acknowledged this when they proposed a three-stage process to create intellectual capital from knowledge resources. They posited that "knowledge capital" had to be deconstructed and decomposed into the IC typology to become intellectual capital.

As far as Liyanage and Jones (2002) are concerned, the IC framework seems to be a mechanism for (a) accounting for IC and (b) helping leadership address the enabling aspects of the most important strategic capabilities represented in the "knowledge capital" pool. The "deconstruction" of knowledge assets and then reorientation around the IC typology seems rather forced and overly complicated, at least for the purposes of an inventory audit. It is not very useful as a means of discovering what exists.

The distinctions made by IC typologies are helpful in some contexts. The whole effort of IC research in that first vibrant decade was brought to bear on identifying clear, objective measures of knowledge investments and outputs in an enterprise.

The problem is that it does not lead easily from observation and description to action; that is, it does not elicit managerial prescriptions for action at the operational level—it fails the *actionable* test. The typology abstracts from, and distracts from, the operational contexts that we seek to influence in KM: "the three-way model neither describes nor prescribes the development of intellectual resources well since it tends to draw the indicators away from the context they represent" (Mouritsen et al., 2001b, pp. 360).

Where does a skill in using a technology system belong? Structural capital or human capital? Where does deep experience in working with a particular customer group belong? Human capital or relational capital?

Let us see how this works in an audit model that was organized around an IC typology. Annie Brooking (1996) designed an intellectual capital audit geared around four types of intangible assets. Here is an illustrative selection of some of her many indicators, which is fairly typical of audits of this type:

Market assets: Possession of and management processes for brands, investment in brand protection, synergy between the company and its brands, scope and scale of brand; customer knowledge, repeat business and repeat business potential, contact patterns and contact frequency with customers, customers who evangelize, cost of customer acquisition and loss; sales pipeline, ratio of sales staff to pipeline, distribution mechanism, cost, effectiveness and appropriacy; partnerships and alliances, processes for tracking and identifying collaboration opportunities, failure and success rate of partnerships

Human-centered assets: Education levels of staff, investment in and recognition of vocational qualifications, work-related tacit, explicit, and implicit knowledge, work-related competencies and skills, knowledge capture and dissemination processes, measures against knowledge loss, processes for assessing competencies and attitudes, organizational learning processes, corporate libraries, participation of senior management in training

Intellectual property assets: Patents, copyrights, designs, trademarks, service marks, trade secrets, know-how (quantity, investment, processes and policies, return on investment)

Infrastructure assets: Management philosophy and alignment with corporate goals, corporate culture and alignment with corporate goals, presence of heroes, collaboration practices, motivations and rewards, corporate dress codes, style of working environment, IT systems, their management and currency, users and reports, quantity and use of databases and their management, web access and use, remote working, relationships with financial institutions and investors

The first thing to note about this is that the indicators comprise a confusion of categories. Some of them are quantifiable (number of patents, investment levels), and some of them are highly abstract and subjective (management philosophy and its alignment with corporate goals). Some of them are highly context sensitive and have no independently observable objective value (dress codes, style of working environment). I have a fair idea of how much I can sell a patent for. What is a dress code worth? How is work-related tacit knowledge a corporately owned asset?

Some of the indicators have clearly traceable links with corporate performance (sales pipeline), and some of them do not (participation of management in training). Some of the indicators rely on nonempirical value judgments and are highly vulnerable to reporting bias (alignment of culture with corporate goals). There are great disparities in the likely degree of impact on performance or even assurance of impact on performance. There is potential for category confusion, particularly in relation to knowledge resources and their management (know-how is in Intellectual Property; work-related knowledge and its management is in Human-Centered Assets; and collaboration practices, motivations, and rewards are in Infrastructure Assets).

Ambiguity abounds. What exactly does it mean that a given dress code exists? How does one give a standardized response as to its meaning and significance? What does it mean that senior management participate in the same training programs as staff? Why should I invest in the latest technology if I am a midtier competitor that succeeds by constraining my operational cost and risk—that is, if I succeed by following the market rather than leading it?

> These features make it clear that the IC indicators and their supporting audit instrument are better optimized to build a narrative for self-sensemaking (and communicating with the market) than they are to identify real knowledge resources, their relative contributions to the enterprise, and how they can be better configured.

This is why, for example, Brooking asserts that before an audit the organization needs to set a goal for what each idealized intangible asset area should look like. While framed

(I think misleadingly) as an audit, what we actually have is a process for influencing internal mechanisms toward corporate goals (and explaining to the market what you are doing to achieve corporate goals) more than a process for assessing the resources available to the enterprise.

And we run into the same problems of ambiguity that we found with endometrial cancer in chapter 15. The broad categories of the typology seem to make sense. Once they are translated into detailed indicators, the typology's ability to support consistent reporting, diagnosis, and prescription breaks down. Different respondents will locate similar knowledge resources in different places, and related knowledge resources will be scattered across the classification, disabling coherent sensemaking and intervention design.

Thus far, it seems pretty clear that the high-level typologies designed for IC reporting are not particularly helpful for framing a knowledge inventory audit. Many of the indicators are more pertinent to strategic self-assessments, and could perhaps be useful in strategic-level value audits or discovery review audits (cf. Lee et al., 2021, p. 71).

This is fairly typical of IC audits, and I think it is a function of (a) using a strategy-oriented typology to try to derive operational-level insights and (b) confusing the value of existing resources with the value to be delivered by meeting strategic goals. This is why it is so important to be clear about the type of audit we are conducting.

Some parts of the IC typology can support a very narrowly focused inventory audit with concomitant intervention plans. When working with Dow Chemical in the 1990s, Gordon Petrash and his colleagues made Dow a poster child for both the intellectual capital movement and KM. They demonstrated the power of inventorying intellectual capital and using that inventory to manage their intellectual capital and create value for the company. They did this through strategic focus on the most observable, tangible form of intellectual capital, the intellectual property assets in Dow's patent portfolio (Skyrme, 1998, pp. 99–106; Bontis, 2001, pp. 56–57; Oriel, 2003).

When you have laser-sharp focus and a single class of resources to inventory, assess, and make decisions about, then you can get clear wins. There are no mixed categories or ambiguities of assignment and valuation in the Dow case.

What the case does *not* demonstrate is the capacity of a broader IC typology to frame a broad-based inventory of knowledge resources supporting managerial intervention. In fact, the broader IC typology was only a framing device for the Dow Chemical story. The broader typology beyond patents never figured substantively in the broader value-creation story for Dow. To date, Dow Chemical still does not put out a broader IC statement in its annual reports. They had a clearly identifiable asset class, they exploited it, and they got results. This did not persuade them into the larger managerial challenge of taking on the more diffuse aspects of intellectual capital.

Denise Bedford, when she was Goodyear Professor at Kent State University, made the most interesting attempt I have seen to align the intellectual capital approach with a functional-level view of knowledge resources in the enterprise. She took a blended, five-step approach, illustrated by my interpretation in figure 19.1.

1. In the Kent State model, you start by identifying the strategic capabilities of the organization. The seeds of these are often found in mission and strategy statements. They are the handful of things that the organization needs to do well in order to compete in their field. An example from a pharmaceutical company is given in figure 19.1.

2. Each strategic capability will break down into several subcapabilities, which broadly outline the classes of action that need to be undertaken at the operational level to deliver the respective strategic capability. In the example in figure 19.1, we have identified one class of operational activities that would support the strategic capability.

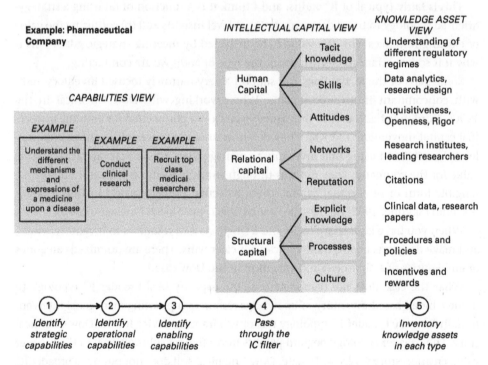

Figure 19.1
From capabilities to intellectual capital to knowledge inventory. Adapted from Bedford, 2014.

3. Once you have the strategic and operational capabilities, you can identify the set of general enabling activities that underpin the others. This will typically be things like financial management, human resource management, technology and infrastructure management, quality and risk management, and so on.

4. Each operational *and* enabling capability is then passed through the IC typology as a filter, which Bedford adapted from Daniel Andriessen (2005).

5. This provides a set of knowledge asset types, against each of which you can identify the specific knowledge resources that underpin the operational and enabling capabilities. You have yourself a knowledge map, which flows from a capabilities view of the enterprise, viewed through an IC lens.

This is an ingenious framework. In general terms it shows a completely clear and systematic flow-through from a strategic view of organizational capabilities into the supporting functions; it ends with a generally satisfactory inventory of knowledge asset types. Most of these types meet our criteria for auditability: observable, naturalistic, actionable, and, at face value, comprehensive. There are some minor anomalies, ambiguities, and artificial separations:

• Culture is hard to measure and observe as an asset, and the typology does not easily capture or represent the interactions between individual attitudes and culture.

• The observable evidence for processes is the documentation surrounding them, but that does not necessarily reflect the actual processes, which are in their performance entangled with the skills, experience, contextual adjustments, and know-how of people.

• Not all the subtypes seem to lead easily to function-level knowledge resources— culture and reputation look like organization-level resources, while attitudes are person-level resources (if they can be considered resources at all).

These are minor issues compared with the Brooking audit model. The main issue for us, however, is the question of whether or not the IC typology plays any substantive role in the analysis.

Let us look at the same framework again *without* the interposition of the major IC types (figure 19.2).

It seems perfectly possible to pass directly from the capabilities view to the knowledge inventory view via a typology of operational knowledge types without any loss of clarity in identifying the knowledge resources required to deliver the respective capabilities. In fact, excluding the intellectual capital layer allows us to exclude indicators that do not seem to work as knowledge types at the operational level, and that are only

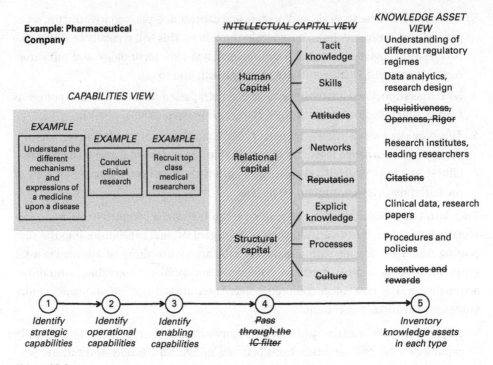

Figure 19.2
From capabilities to knowledge inventory, bypassing intellectual capital.

there on the coattails of their intellectual capital hosts (culture, reputation, attitudes). Those indicators seem more appropriate to an audit of KM enablers than to an inventory of knowledge resources at the functional level.

> In sum, the intellectual capital lens seems to add no value, and in fact adds some confusion, in the task of framing and directing a knowledge inventory audit at the operational level. We can achieve a cleaner set of knowledge resource types without the need to force fit them into intellectual capital "buckets."

I can see where the Kent State approach does add value. The intellectual capital layer adds value, not for the framing of the inventory collection exercise (working from left to right) but in reporting upward the role that knowledge resources play in an IC statement (working from right to left)—if the organization has an intellectual capital measurement and reporting system (which relatively few do). This was exactly the "upward reporting" approach proposed by Liyanage and Jones (2002).

The categories that intellectual capital provides bring knowledge closer to the market than they do to operational management (Yakhlef & Salzer-Mörling, 2000, p. 34). In the absence of the desire to communicate to the market, if we remove the IC layer, we have a much cleaner approach that works from strategic capabilities, through to operational and enabling capabilities, and down to the inventorying of knowledge resources. Our next question must then be: How would this streamlined approach work? In particular, does it meet our auditability criterion of comprehensiveness?

Strategic Knowledge Typologies

Bedford's is not the only approach to categorizing strategic knowledge at the organizational level. We saw in chapter 18 how Michael Zack provided an expanded typology of personal knowledge that went beyond the tacit-explicit dualism. However, Zack's (1999a) primary interest was in auditing strategic knowledge, and for this he depended upon a much simpler typology—namely, one "oriented towards strategy that reflects the competitive uniqueness of each organization" (p.132):

- *Core knowledge*—the minimum scope and level of knowledge required for a firm simply to "play the game"
- *Advanced knowledge*—the knowledge that helps a firm to be competitively viable
- *Innovative knowledge*—the knowledge that helps a firm to innovate and significantly differentiate itself from its competitors

This is again too high level to satisfy our requirements for a functional-level knowledge inventory typology. It describes attributes of knowledge rather than identifying discrete types. If anywhere, it belongs to the realm of strategic knowledge analysis, not inventory. Even in that context, there is a degree of subjective interpretation required that goes beyond our requirements for observability and naturalistic description.

How does one distinguish between core knowledge and advanced knowledge? What are the observable intrinsic characteristics of a given knowledge resource that put it in one category rather than the other? Who is qualified to make that distinction? Can the distinction be made repeatedly and consistently by different individuals? How do we describe the different forms of knowledge within each category in such a way as to be comparable with other people's descriptions?

With so much ambiguity, there is a good chance that we will encounter the problems associated with the crude microscope-based methods for distinguishing forms of endometrial cancer. Different specialists will disagree, and the criteria for doing so may not be transparent.

When he developed a knowledge audit methodology focused on strategic capabilities, Amrit Tiwana (2002) adapted an eight-stage *knowledge growth* model originally developed by Roger Bohn. The maturity scale ranges from ignorance, through measurement and control, and finally to complete knowledge of the process, its environment, and its parameters. Bohn developed his framework for the field of process and technology management. Tiwana attempted to incorporate tacit knowledge and to apply it to a general organizational knowledge landscape (far broader than Bohn's original intent).

This provided a more granular and slightly better-described series of stages of knowledge maturity than Zack's, but Tiwana's adaptation has some very strange effects in relation to tacit knowledge. For example, level 0 is pure ignorance, and the next stage refers to "pure art," where the knowledge is completely tacit. Only then do we see gradual systematization of the knowledge. The model is strongly oriented toward privileging explicated knowledge and knowledge embedded in systems, as you would expect in process management but not in more subtle domains (Tiwana, 2002, chap. 8; cf. Bohn, 1994).

Tiwana combined that model with a way of looking at strategic capabilities developed by Richard Hall and Pierpaolo Andriani (1998). They decomposed strategic capabilities into a typology consisting of

- intellectual property-related capabilities,
- competitive position-related capabilities,
- functional capabilities, and
- cultural capabilities.

This works very much like Liyanage and Jones's method of figuring out how intellectual capital is managed, with an additional "Bohn" frame imposed to assess the maturity of each capability type. It gives a very high-level view and provides little insight into how to get at a detailed account of operational knowledge resources. It may be useful for facilitating high-level discussions among managers on how to understand and analyze strategic capabilities (and indeed, Hall and Andriani intended it to be used in assessing potential strategic business partners).

Stephanie Barnes and Nick Milton (2015) use strategy maps to work outward from strategic objectives to derive what they call *strategic knowledge areas*. They define a strategic knowledge area as "a knowledge topic that is of primary importance to the business, representing knowledge and know-how that supports delivery of the strategy" (p. 68).

Examples for a development bank could include expertise in poverty reduction, enhancing the productivity and competitiveness of national economies, strengthening institutions, and economic management (Barnes & Milton, 2015, p. 74). In a tax agency, the ability to detect tax fraud would qualify as a strategic knowledge area (Milton & Lambe, 2020, p. 116).

In this sense, strategic knowledge areas are high-level capabilities of an organization. Because they are broad topic labels, they do not in themselves satisfy our criteria for auditability. They are not granular enough to identify specific knowledge resources that are susceptible to management action. They need to be broken down further into subcapabilities, as Denise Bedford shows, and then to operational- or functional-level knowledge resources (Milton & Lambe, 2020, p. 116).

The strategic knowledge areas approach does not provide a consistent framework of knowledge types that can be consistently applied across different domains or areas of practice. They simply state "we need to have knowledge of/about . . ." without stating the kinds of knowledge or how it is constituted and activated. They do not themselves provide the knowledge typology, though they can frame the knowledge investigation inquiry.

Getting from Strategic to Operational Knowledge

Matthew Loxton has proposed a way of getting to manageable components of knowledge at the operational level, from an analysis of strategic goals. He advocates identifying the business processes "which are individually necessary and collectively sufficient for their achievement" and then going down to the critical activities that are contained within those business process flows.

The knowledge audit kicks in at this point, driven by the question of how the agent in any critical activity knows how to perform the activity accurately. Loxton identifies three possible mechanisms: (a) hiring into the role, (b) training into the activity, and (c) providing knowledge aids to support performance of the activity.

Each knowledge mechanism has a corresponding inventory: (a) a recruitment inventory specifying the types of skills and experience required for the role, (b) a learning objectives inventory specifying the skills and measures of performance, and (c) a knowledge-base inventory describing the knowledge and information resources required for the performance of the task (Loxton, 2013a, 2013b).

Loxton's approach has the virtue of rendering the transition from strategic goals to the requisite operational knowledge more legible to managers. We know how to describe and manage recruitment, learning and development, and knowledge bases.

However, the model oversimplifies what we already know about many organizational knowledge environments. For a start, it assumes that all critical activities can be reduced to components of personal knowledge. The actions of the *team mind*, capabilities that are collective in nature and that cannot simply be characterized as the sum of individual capabilities, are ignored. The dimension of collective tacit knowledge (what a new hire needs to be inculturated into in order to be effective within the team and within the organization) is ignored. Let us look at this particularly vivid example from Nancy Dixon (2000):

> As it happens, three flute companies in the Boston area produce what are regarded by flutists as the best flutes in the world. All three companies—Haynes, Powell, and Brannen—have a common historical antecedent in the Haynes Company, founded in 1900. The flutes are hand-crafted by a series of workers who successively drill the tone holes in the tube, solder the key mechanisms, attach the pads, construct the head joint and embouchure hole, and polish, pack, and ship the completed flutes. Each craftsman is skilled in only certain steps of the process, and successive steps are often renegotiated between craftsmen when a developing flute does not have the right "feel." No two flutes are alike, yet flutists can easily differentiate a Powell flute from a Haynes flute by the way it plays. Each company produces flutes with a distinct quality or family resemblance. When craftsmen switch companies (e.g. from Haynes to Brannen), they find that they must retrain to learn the new feel. It is the particular common knowledge, learned from years of working at the Haynes company, that makes the Haynes flute unique; the same is true for Powell and Brannen. Each company's unique common knowledge is a critical factor in its success. (p. 12)

There are some key points here worth repeating because they are easily and often overlooked. First, an organization possesses capabilities that are not reducible to the knowledge of individuals (Kogut & Zander, 1997, p. 307). Second, this organizational knowledge can survive the coming and going of skilled and experienced individuals (Leonard & Sensiper, 1998, p. 122). Though it persists through time, because it is activated by a network of individuals working in concert it is still vulnerable to loss through the departure of a critical mass of "knowers" in key areas (as we saw in the NASA example). However, as long as it is constantly being activated through practice, it is retained in the organizational memory. Conversely, when that knowledge ceases to be practiced, it can be lost rather quickly (Nelson & Winter, 1982, p. 99; Szulanski, 2003, p. 20). Only part of this knowledge is procedural.

The Opacity of Strategic Knowledge

One of the great challenges in KM is in how to characterize and manage this collective knowledge. Indeed, it is sometimes considered so difficult that when an organizational capability has been achieved, the best strategy to transfer it is not to break it down and describe it in detail at all, but simply to "copy exactly" both the component practices and the physical environments in which the practices take place, and to use this replication as a means of helping the new, target employees organize themselves around the new practice, so that they can reconstruct the tacit personal knowledge necessary to make it work.

In much the same way, a novice will attempt to copy the master through formal drills and routines, without really understanding their importance or implication, until they have internalized the personal knowledge themselves (and they may never succeed). This is costly, but necessary, because in many situations the enactment of an organizational capability "is only partially understood at the source" (Winter & Szulanski, 2002, p. 208). This is what we referred to in chapter 13 as the "uncertain imitability" of organizational knowledge (Lippman & Rumelt, 1982).

Without a full understanding of how the capability is constituted, and if you copy selectively, you may be omitting critical elements that make it work. Only by blindly copying everything can you be confident you are capturing the core of what makes this practice work, and even then you will have to (re)construct tacit knowledge associated with the practice at the new site. Once internalized and perfected in terms of performance outcomes that are comparable to the source, *and only then*, can a group start experimenting with selectively editing portions of the practice and environment, to see if they can be optimized further.

We often fail to realize that our understanding of a collective capability we possess is imperfect. We rely on the two obvious sources of documentation and the knowledge of experts, but they are imperfect witnesses.

Documentation is often incomplete, and is abstracted from the implicit and tacit knowledge necessary to run a process and connect it with other processes successfully.

In theory, expert knowledge of a practice looks like an attractive source of testimony. In the real world, however, expert testimony turns out to be rife with blind spots and ignorance:

> The expert source's ignorance—of which she's generally unaware—can take a number of forms. Many details of the system are inevitably invisible to her. Some may be known to individual workers but not shared with higher-ups. Others may be tacit—learned on the job and well known but impossible to describe in a way that is helpful. Some may be secrets undisclosed because they make individual workers' jobs easier or because they run counter to an organization's formal work rules. Some represent "learning without awareness," adjustments that people make without being aware that they've made them. For example, hearing fluid moving through pipes may be a cue, not consciously recognized, that a process is operating correctly. Other unacknowledged characteristics may be hidden contextual factors related to, say, the design of equipment or even prevailing weather conditions. (Szulanski & Winter, 2002, p. 64)

The contributing factors that make organizational capabilities opaque include the following:

- Harry Collins's (2010) insights into the reasons why relational knowledge is kept implicit, and the "taken for grantedness" of socially held collective tacit knowledge can help to explain why we can be unaware of what we know.

- Another factor is what Ivan Illich (1981, chap. 5) called *shadow work*—that is, the background, unacknowledged tasks we have to do that are necessary to make organizational wheels turn. Illich was referring to the unacknowledged, unpaid "work" we do for a society driven by consumerism and industrial production, but it can equally refer to unacknowledged "invisible" work that takes place within organizations to bridge gaps in formal processes and roles. There is resistance to acknowledging it because then it might have to be measured and rewarded (Suchman, 1995; Star & Strauss, 1999; Allen, 2015).

- And finally, there may also be market-driven incentives to maintaining a causal ambiguity about how the knowledge of the organization combines to produce its unique capabilities. If this is kept mysterious, it is harder for competitors to copy (Baumard, 1999, pp. 218–220).

Even at the level of explicit knowledge, as we saw earlier, an organizational-level view often has poor visibility into the explicit knowledge resources of functional groups. Here is a typical example from the Swiss Nuclear Safety Inspectorate:

> Generally there is rather too much information than too little within an organization. However the information available is not in the required form. Much knowledge is stored unstructured in the offices of the experts and can therefore only be accessed with their aid. Since it is very expensive to compile and collate any unstructured information, it is absolutely important to identify the valuable knowledge of the organization. One must permanently assure that the necessary knowledge is present and that information no longer required is removed from the system. (Schwarz & Veyre, 2007, p. 16)

This is why Matthew Loxton's approach is likely to be too simplistic in all but the most mundane of organizational capabilities. In some ways it is also anachronistic and hearkens back to a simpler age. In the late eighteenth century, industrial spies routinely visited factories in the rapidly industrializing towns of England. They would make drawings or commit their observations to memory. You could observe processes and figure out how to replicate them.

At that time, an informed eye could learn a great deal about how to replicate a technology because the knowledge was embedded mainly in the machinery itself and in the processes for running the machinery, not in complex organizational routines around the technology. The British government of the time was aware of the vulnerability of its national competitive edge. Customs agents would inspect the possessions of foreigners leaving its ports and confiscate drawings, notes, machinery, or models that looked suspicious (or take bribes to let them pass). Britons seeking to travel overseas were restricted if they belonged to protected professions such as engineering.

And yet direct experience of working with the technology in a factory setting gave great advantages even then. The great pioneer of industrialization in the US, the Englishman Samuel Slater, had learned his trade in Jedidiah Strutt's textile mill in Milford, England, becoming an overseer by the age of twenty-one. In 1789 he fled the UK without drawings or machinery, concealing his trade from customs agents (he claimed to be a farmhand). Relying on his memory, he persuaded the Rhode Island industrialist Moses Brown to take him on as a partner, and after a year of tinkering with Brown's smuggled machinery, he got it working for large-scale textile production. He went on to become infamous in England as a technology pirate, and famous in the US for his business success (Ben-Atar, 2004, pp. 165–166).

The task of apprehending strategic capabilities in modern organizations—those that afford a strategic advantage—is much more complex now than in the newly industrializing eighteenth century, and this is reflected in the complexity of the organizations that deliver those capabilities. Strategic knowledge today is notoriously resistant to easy observation or imitability. In the early 1990s, Gordon Forward, the CEO of Chaparral Steel, famously claimed that he could show his competitors around his plants and not worry that they would be able to emulate his company's success (Leonard-Barton, 1992, p. 92). Andrew Campbell (1999) reports a similar reaction from a senior vice president at Emerson Electric Company:

> Many companies come to Emerson wanting to find out what we are doing and why it works. But often, the trip is wasted. Our process works for us because of the type of impact we are trying to have on the businesses and because of our CEO, Chuck Knight—how he likes to operate and his relationship and status with the divisions. Other companies can't duplicate that. When they try, they run the risk of turning their processes into ones that destroy value rather than create it. (p. 43)

This is because, as Szulanski (2003) put it, in the modern organization, "Practice is seen as fragmented, distributed and embedded in organizational routines" (pp. 20–21).

This fragmentation and scatter is contextually determined and is what gets in the way of emulation. In many cases, few people or no people hold the full picture (Leonard & Sensiper, 1998, p. 121). This is precisely the problem that NASA encountered when it tried to recover what it once knew about how to build the Saturn V rocket. In that case, *even the same organization* had problems diffusing (or harnessing on scale) its own knowledge over space and time (O'Dell & Grayson, 1998, pp. 16–17; Szulanski, 2003, pp. 22–23).

Andy Clark (1997, pp. 103–111) describes the challenge of moving from a description of operational-level activities to larger strategic capabilities in terms of three different mental models of explanation.

The first model is what he calls the *componential explanation*—where effects at a granular level do amplify and scale upward according to clearly defined and well-understood rules. This is the mental model underlying Matthew Loxton's approach. However, the componential explanation depends upon well-understood interactions between how the components interact and the capabilities of the whole system—for example, how a car or a television set works in relation to its parts. The relationship between operational knowledge resources and IC typologies or strategic capabilities does not mirror the workings of a car or television. We do not understand how the parts scale to the whole.

The second model is what Clark calls *catch and toss*, in which activity in one domain is described in one language, and activity in another domain is described in a completely different language, such as describing mental perceptions of the world (It's a warm day) and neurological explanations of how those perceptions are operationalized in the brain. These different explanation worlds are allowed to "peacefully coexist," and we do not bother ourselves about how things translate across the language-game boundaries. We "catch" a sensory perception of a summer's day and "toss" cognitive responses and actions back. This model works in situations of relatively equivalent scale and low-complexity differences between the two language worlds. This also clearly does not work for the gap between operational knowledge resources and large-scale strategic knowledge capabilities.

The third model is what Clark calls *emergent explanation*, in which the scale differences between the component level and the system level, and the degree of complexity in the system render it impossible to explain action at the system level in terms of extrapolation from the actions of its parts. He uses the example of applying heat to oil in a pan, which causes distinctive patterns of convection to occur. We know that heat is causing this, but an understanding of the individual oil molecules and their relative starting positions has no bearing on how a given molecule will behave in a convection roll.

The system effect is what Clark calls an *ensemble effect*, meaning that it is the whole system of parts interacting that produces distinctive and predictable effects, and those effects in turn have a reciprocal effect "downward" to modify the behaviors of the parts. Similar patterns can be seen in the behaviors of crowds—the main difference, of course, being that the people within a crowd are capable of self-actuation in the way that oil molecules are not. But in both cases, the descriptions at component level do not account for the effects at system level, as they do in the operation of a car, nor do component-level descriptions predict the reciprocal effects of the system on the components.

Another way of putting it is that (a) ensemble effects are agnostic to particular things but sensitive to types of things, and (b) ensemble effects are themselves constantly modifying or influencing the behaviors of particular things, which in turn have a recip-rocal effect on the ensemble. This seems much closer to the relationship between descrip-tions of operational knowledge resources and strategic capabilities (or broad IC types).

If a capability or a practice is an emergent effect of fragmented and distributed knowledge resources interacting in complex and mutually influencing ways and if it is an ensemble effect that is resistant to component-level description, then this explains why strategic capabilities are difficult to construct in a fully deliberate way, and why they are difficult to transfer deliberately to new environments and new people.

Some organizations simply give up on the challenge of transferring or modifying a rich capability and fall back instead on *thin* knowledge transfer, focusing on the transfer of explicit knowledge elements such as expertise directories, performance standards and statistics, and designs and specifications. They rely on their recipients to reverse engineer the rich collective knowledge behind them (Hislop, 2013, p. 54; Kasper et al., 2010).

Clearly, this is an easier strategy, but it might also be seen as a cop-out, particularly where there are high strategic stakes involved in the successful transfer, modification, or diffusion of a strategic capability. "Thin" knowledge does not in itself transfer or create a capability—it simply provides a superficial representation of what a capability looks like, as Lei Yijei's example of the failed Germany-China enterprise resource planning technol-ogy transfer showed (Lei, 2005). Or it can distract a management team by drawing them toward the appearance of a practice and away from actually creating value from their specific contexts. This is one of the risks in benchmarking (Campbell, 1999).

At face value the rapid acquisition of new capabilities through intellectual property theft might seem to provide a counterexample to this tale of difficulty and woe. The China of the late twentieth century was famous for its successful piracy of technologi-cal (strategic) capabilities. The role that China played in relation to the US ironically mirrored the role that the US played in relation to Britain in the eighteenth century.

Behind the scenes, however, this apparently rapid acquisition of capabilities has often involved serving long "apprenticeships" as joint-venture partners, contractors, outsourcees, or distributors to US manufacturers, in the course of which covert coun-terfeiting, imitation and reverse engineering through secret subsidiaries and personnel borrowing can be seen as systematic mechanisms for learning and "nonconsensual" knowledge transfer, operating alongside more legitimate knowledge-transfer avenues. Imitation of the directly observable is not enough: immersion in the target organization's structures and practices is necessary, sometimes taking decades (Minagawa et al., 2007). In effect, we need to "feel our way" into the ensemble effects that we desire.

Feeling Our Way

The acquisition of strategic capabilities takes commitment and time and is not simply the product of observation, inventory, and analysis. Organizations work very hard, and very deliberately, at building the kind of strategic capabilities that Pete Blaber described in his account of how the US forces established a forward operating base in the Persian Gulf (chapter 15).

This is why organizations find it surprisingly difficult to modify and adapt well-entrenched capabilities. Even the knowers do not fully know what they know, except in a diffuse and inexpressible way. Strategic capabilities are held together by a loose web of assets, not fully explicit routines, operating protocols, knowledge artifacts, knowledge integration and articulation mechanisms, and more finely drawn team capabilities, all producing emergent ensemble effects.

We feel our way toward capabilities of this nature by tasting and testing emergent effects, by finding ways of talking about the operational-level elements so that we can coordinate around them, and by adjusting in the direction of perceived improvements, as we ourselves are adjusted by the effects that we create.

Very similar organizations facing similar challenges in how to manage or adapt their strategic capabilities end up with very different outcomes. Only in retrospect do certain strategic bets turn out to look wise or foolish. But in the example below, the ability to self-describe through a knowledge audit appears to have been a critical factor in making a good strategic bet. While descriptions at the component level cannot predict effects at the system level, being able to describe the components, and experiment around their combinations, does seem to be useful in experimenting with emergent ensemble effects.

Case Study: Kodak, Fujifilm, and the Struggle to Manage Strategic Capabilities

Oliver Kmia (2018) has given an intriguing account of how two film companies, Kodak and Fujifilm, starting with very similar strategic capabilities and, facing very similar market challenges, ended up in two very different places: one (Kodak) defunct and the other (Fujifilm) thriving.

At the root of this difference in outcome was the mysterious capacity to configure and recombine in novel ways the underlying capabilities the organizations possessed—that is, what Kogut and Zander (1997) called *combinative capabilities*, "the intersection of the capability of the firm to exploit its knowledge and the unexplored potential of the technology" (p. 317). Both companies tried, but only one hit upon successful recombinations.

Prior to 2001 the bulk of revenue for both companies was from the manufacture and sale of color film and color processing. After that, with the advent of digital cameras and digital imaging, demand for film began to decline, slowly at first, and then precipitously. By 2010, demand was at less than 10 percent of the levels it had been at the start of the decade.

There was a twofold problem behind this shift. First, the manufacturing capabilities for color film production were extremely demanding, and had been very arduous to build up. They represented very high levels of sunk investment in facilities, expertise, research and development, and quality control. Second, because of the first issue, the barriers to entry were very high for competitors. This meant that between them, Kodak and Fujifilm had dominated the market for photographic film and had had for decades a safe and secure income. They were essentially extracting a very high rent from the market as a reward for the unique and difficult capabilities they had built up. Their entire business model was oriented around this, and the threat to this business model emerged so swiftly that it created a crisis of adaptation for both companies.

Why? Well, the technologies and the capabilities behind digital imaging are very different from film and print imaging. Film manufacture involves "film formation and high-precision coating . . . grain formation, function polymer, nano-dispersion, functional molecules, and redox control (oxidation of the molecule). Inherent in all these is very precise quality control" (Komori, 2015, p. 26).

Digital imaging was based on a very different and much more accessible technology base—the semiconductor. The technology was cheap and easy to build. "Suppliers selling components offered the technology to anyone who would pay, and there were few entry barriers. What's more, digital technology is modular. A good engineer could buy all the building blocks and put together a camera. These building blocks abstracted almost all the technology required, so you no longer needed a lot of experience and specialized skills" (Shih, 2016, p. 20).

So not only was the technology capability base different but so was the entire set of *soft capabilities* about how to engage with a market (barriers to entry, specialized vs. generalized players, relative ease of rent extraction, profit margins, degree of competition, pressures toward innovation, degree of sales and marketing effort required, cost-price ratios).

It was the soft capability challenge that killed Kodak. Seeing the shift to digital coming, it invested heavily and very quickly in a transition from film to digital-imaging technologies. But it could not make the transition to the entirely different business model and market engagement model. It was able to innovate and capture market share in digital imaging, but it was bleeding cash. And the film manufacturing business was drying up faster than the digital-imaging business could replace it in margin and volume (Kmia, 2018).

Fujifilm was encountering the same challenge. But Fujifilm also looked hard at how to extract rent from its heritage capabilities—the precision manufacture of thin, photosensitive films. It did sensible things like cutting costs by downsizing its traditional production facilities. But it also took a knowledge capitalization approach in relation to its existing specialist capabilities. It conducted a technology audit of its traditional capabilities and decomposed the seed technologies behind them. A technology audit is a very specialized kind of knowledge audit, looking at the underpinning knowledge capabilities for the development and deployment of a given set of technologies.

Having identified its seed capabilities, Fujifilm then prospected for emerging market opportunities beyond consumer imaging for those technology capabilities. It identified opportunities in (Kmia, 2018)

- pharmaceuticals (expertise in functional molecules and grain formation applied to radiopharmaceuticals),

- cosmetics (expertise in collagen behaviors, preserving sheen and elasticity, and slowing oxidation in film, as applied to human skin), and
- LCD screens (expertise in the precision manufacture of thin, flexible film for photosensitive panels for screens in TVs, phones, and personal-computing devices).

Both companies saw the digital revolution coming. By moving early into digital, both companies used diversification and the development of new capabilities to meet the competitive challenge. Neither company succeeded in adjusting its legacy soft capabilities to the digital-imaging market—that is, from a business and market engagement model based on high barrier to entry and high margins to one that served a low-margin, fast-moving, crowded mass market.

Only Fujifilm managed to create novel recombinations and opportunities for both their legacy technical capabilities and their legacy soft capabilities for market engagement. They did this by auditing and decomposing their existing specialized capabilities and then by creating novel combinations of capabilities for the niche, high-margin market opportunities they had identified.

The fact that organizations have imperfect knowledge of their own capabilities, combined with the uncertainty of imitability and control is why working top-down from strategic knowledge areas toward more granular typologies of knowledge is problematic, particularly if our purpose is a knowledge inventory audit.

At the strategic level, we just do not know fully what to look for, and we do not know what we are *not seeing* in the knowledge machinery and knowledge activity that underpins a strategic capability. We are looking at an ensemble effect of a complex system, not at a television set that can be taken apart and analyzed. Strategically, looking top-down, both Kodak and Fujifilm saw the transition to digital as the prime business driver. They saw imaging as their strategic capability. This did not help them figure out exactly what to do at the operational level.

It *seems* to make sense to identify strategic capabilities and goals first and then to infer or audit the knowledge required for those goals. And sometimes this may work out. But in practice, many of the components of that capability are not directly observable, and the collective *metaknowledge* that harnesses and knits these knowledge components together may resist easy analysis.

In short, audits organized around strategic capabilities, strategic goals, strategic decisions, or strategic problems all run the risk of missing important knowledge dependencies, or missing opportunities from unidentified knowledge resources currently available and in use in some part of the organization.

If Fujifilm had not done a middle-out audit of its existing capabilities and had only looked to strategic opportunities, it would have simply not seen those opportunities, unlikely as they were from a strategic, high-level point of view. Who would have thought of cosmetics as an opportunity unless they had looked deep inside themselves and realized that they had extensive knowledge of managing collagen behaviors?

Working middle-out, from the functional and operational knowledge that resides in the full spectrum of core activities of the organization, provides a more complete resource inventory, and a means to evaluate existing resources and the quality of resource utilization against strategic needs and opportunities. Strategic-level explanations and component-level explanations both need to be in play if we are to be able to experiment with the variables and different potential pathways of ensemble effects. When we frame our inquiry at a functional/operational level, as well as at a strategic level, we can start to identify meaningful and useful forms of collective knowledge to experiment with.

To illustrate the value of starting in the middle and why we see things differently when we do, let us revisit the three forms of collective knowledge identified by Achim Hecker (2012):

1. The set of shared knowledge and competencies that is taken for granted as part of the repertoire of a team or a functional group. No single member necessarily holds all of this knowledge, and there are substantial overlaps between individuals, but this repertoire is a bounded, known resource set that the group can call upon.

2. Knowledge that members of the group have about who knows what (Hecker calls this *complementary knowledge*). This serves to help group members navigate quickly to the holders of elements of the repertoire of shared knowledge in (1) above.

3. Knowledge embedded in artifacts shared by the group (Hecker calls this *artifact-embedded knowledge*). It provides easy reference to the more explicit, stable elements of what the group knows.

Now, while we can describe these three forms in a "thin" way at the organizational level (e.g., in competency maps, expertise directories, content inventories), these descriptions take on much more richness and become more actionable as we descend to a functional group level.

A directory of expertise does help us to identify who knows what, but it is expensive and difficult to maintain, and knowing who has what expertise does not in itself give us access to that expertise. What happens if the expert is a grumpy old man, nearing retirement, who has worked alone for most of his career and refuses to share with ignorant young whippersnappers who know nothing? (This situation was shared with us by a major bank a few years back.) A directory will not help solve that problem.

But within a functional team, what Hecker called complementary knowledge is an integral part of what it means to belong to a team. It is the implicit and tacit knowledge, which typically includes the working relationships that allow us to call on colleagues' knowledge when we need it. Looking at knowledge resources at this level does help to address practical accessibility problems, whereas "thin" organization-level way-finding resources do not.

"Thin" representations of what you know are abstracted from real situations and real applications. At the strategic level, a "thin" representation says your knowledge is in imaging. At the functional and team level, your representation says you know about how collagen works and how its properties can be sustained over time.

We have already observed that shared knowledge artifacts are typically structured and organized for easy access and use at the team level, whereas at the organizational level, collections of shared knowledge artifacts that have been created in other contexts are often opaque, confusing, or too generalized to be of use in the specific working contexts we need them in. Hecker's account of collective knowledge illustrates how much easier it is to characterize (and hence exert management action upon) knowledge resources at the functional as distinct from the organizational level.

Considerations for Working from Strategic to Operational Knowledge

We know from experience that it is tempting to start at the strategic level because it focuses our effort in the audit on what we think counts most. We run less risk of expending audit effort on operational knowledge resources that have little strategic value. If the Kodak and Fujifilm example was not convincing, here is a more mundane example of why this temptation can be problematic.

Case Study: Strategy as a Lens through Which to Inventory Knowledge

Several years ago, we were asked to review and validate an organizational taxonomy for a government agency. The taxonomy was intended to function as the organizing structure for an inventory of agencywide knowledge resources. It was constructed on the basis of the agency's mission, vision, and values, on the premise that the knowledge structure should follow the strategic direction of the organization. Since these resources were produced and managed by functional units, the levels below the mission vision and values were organized by function. So we had a strategy-based framework, further divided by functional areas.

We found that the knowledge resources at the working level were distributed unevenly across the taxonomy structure, with about half of the resources located in just one branch, and other branches very thinly populated. The organization's strategic view was not well matched to its functional division of labor—and this is understandable. Not everything that happens in an organization is strategic.

In relation to the way knowledge work was done, despite the organization of content by function, there were many significant knowledge resources in use on the ground that found no place in the taxonomy structure. The mission, vision, and values turned out not to predict very accurately the kind of knowledge resources used in practice on the ground.

The approach our client had used, of organizing knowledge resources top-down from an analysis of strategic goals, values, and then by business function was popular as a means of organizing corporate records in the records management professional community in the 1990s. It ran into problems similar to the ones we encountered: staff did not recognize or interpret the categories and organizing principles consistently, and they did not know how to assign their everyday working records to the scheme (Lambe, 2007, pp. 231–232).

> Strategic views are poor lenses for representing the full spectrum of organizational activities and knowledge resources.

Taxonomies can be considered types of knowledge maps and are often used to represent collections of knowledge resources. However, they are best developed as a result of an inventory audit of knowledge resources and not derived from evidence-free prior constructs. The audit is what provides evidence for the content and organization of the knowledge resource collection (Lambe, 2007, chap. 8; Perez-Soltero et al., 2009).

A taxonomy design based on an idealized view of the business (which is what a strategic view is) ends up representing only what can be attached to the components of that idealized view. Important knowledge areas are missed. Further, the strategic view represents the key elements of what an organization is supposed to be doing, as distinct from what it *actually* does, and this is also problematic: "it is what organizational members actually do that determines organizational capability and, ultimately, the performance of the organization" (Szulanski, 2003, p. 20). Finally, as we saw, it generates categories that are not naturalistic—they do not reflect the way that knowledge resources are viewed and used on the ground.

A purely goal-driven, forward-looking approach to how the resource collection is represented can also remove important historical knowledge from view. For example, when we identified the lack of a particular type of procurement activity in the proposed taxonomy, although other procurement activities were there, we were told, "Our internal auditors said that we had been over-using that method of procurement, and so we removed it." The taxonomy had been used as a mechanism for *managing activity* instead of *representing activity*, removing important and pertinent contextual knowledge about how things had been done in the past. The idealized view of how the knowledge resources *should be* had become dislocated from how they *actually were*.

At one level, this is a story about the relationship between a knowledge inventory and the taxonomy that represents it. More importantly, it illustrates the difficulties that arise when a top-down approach is taken to inventorying knowledge resources, scoped from high-level strategic views that are often partial, hold significant blind spots, inaccurately represent the way work is actually done, and imperfectly represent the knowledge resources actually available for exploitation and reuse.

To be clear, it is perfectly fine to determine knowledge needs and requirements from an analysis of strategic goals, objectives, decisions, and problems. It is also fine to audit knowledge that is considered strategic to the organization. However, this is not the best way to get to a systematic inventory of what actually exists, and the contexts in which it exists.

Strategic knowledge needs can legitimately be reviewed and identified in and of themselves. But to be truly useful, the assessment of strategic knowledge requirements should then be compared to what we know of *what actually exists* in order to determine how to meet those requirements.

Now, in the scoping of any audit there are going to be costs and benefits associated with taking any particular route. Against the value of comprehensiveness there is set the cost and effort involved in being comprehensive.

In our global survey of KM practitioners, almost half of the respondents stated that the biggest challenge in a knowledge audit was getting management and staff buy-in to spend the necessary time and effort to collect the baseline data.

But on the other side, a lack of comprehensiveness is a worry. Knowledge management expert Kate Pugh points out that "some audits are too narrow and prescribe point solutions to systemic problems." Christian De Neef observes that senior leadership and operational staff can have very different perceptions of knowledge use. Ian Fry of Knoco Australia makes the point that an audit can evolve based on what you discover in the audit, and priority areas can shift beyond those identified by senior leadership at the start (Lambe, 2017). Here are some considerations to bear in mind when evaluating this trade-off:

- *Systematic capability-mapping exercises*, such as that demonstrated in the Denise Bedford/Kent State approach, if they work down to the supporting operational and enabling capabilities, can economize on effort, especially if the capability maps enable one to focus on areas of particular strategic concern (or, in the Barnes and Milton case, key strategic knowledge areas). However, there is still a risk of missing important latent knowledge resources in the environment, particularly the nonobvious system-wide resources. Recall that in chapter 3 when we covered operational audits, we saw that processes and resources that cross functional (or organizational) boundaries are easily missed, and therefore carry more risk of error, mismanagement, and control. When we start with a strategic lens, we need to recognize that we do not get the value of a comprehensive knowledge inventory audit, and that we are instead conducting a narrower strategic knowledge audit with the limitations and risks that accompany it.

- *Functional-level audits* are another way of managing effort. If organization-wide support cannot be found, then inventory audits can be conducted at a functional level, department by department, depending on the support from those functional units. This approach is subject to the same constraints on insights into system-wide resources, synergies, and opportunities. Until you have covered a reasonable number of units, you can only show local (department level) insights and benefits, and because your sample is skewed, your view of enterprise KM needs and opportunities may not be representative of enterprise-wide needs, and it will not be easy to discern larger ensemble effects.

• *Snowball audits* are a way of expanding audits based on knowledge flow pathways discovered in the course of the audit. The snowball approach depends not merely upon inventorying knowledge resources but also on mapping knowledge flows. Let us say that in the course of an inventory audit with Department A you discover that they trade information with Department G. This is your warrant for expanding the audit to Department G. The snowball approach is a way of controlling the scope and scale of the audit based upon evidence collected as you go, and is a particularly useful way of auditing knowledge resources in environments where you do not have a full span of control—for example, when your audit covers different collaborating agencies and communities. However, this approach is time-consuming and is subject to scope creep, and it is difficult to show large-scale (system-wide) insights and benefits until you have covered a sufficient portion of the environment where knowledge is traded and needed.

• *Your choice of audit methods* can significantly influence the degree of effort and commitment required relative to the data you collect. For example, compared to mapping workshops involving representatives of work groups, interviews are more labor-intensive for the audit team (in their conduct and in their analysis) as well as for the ratio of respondent time to amount of data collected. The use of specialized software applications can speed up data collection and analysis. So the pain of comprehensiveness can be mitigated by the economy of methods and tools. These are assessments you must make, as long as you are conscious of the benefits and limitations of your choices.

*   *   *

Summary

In this chapter we reviewed the complex issues associated with analyzing and describing the different forms of organizational knowledge. Here is a summary of the main points:

1. At the organizational level, IC typologies do not function well for framing knowledge inventory audits. They are best fitted to creating narratives for internal sensemaking and for communicating with the market about how intangible assets are managed.

2. At the organizational level, typologies of strategic knowledge are based on idealized constructs and partial knowledge, not actual state of play.

3. Descriptions of strategic capabilities are descriptions of ensemble effects that are resistant to decomposition to an operational level. Similarly, it is not usually possible to extrapolate upward from an operational level knowledge inventory to strategic capabilities, except in the simplest of systems. In practice, much of organizational life is a dynamic interplay between operational explanations and strategic explanations. "Middle-out" approaches help to broker this interplay, and they can help us "feel our way" into better strategic capabilities.

4. Typologies of strategic knowledge can fail our comprehensiveness test for an inventory audit, and they may not represent knowledge types in ways that match the experience and perceptions of operational staff.

5. These typologies are more suited to strategic knowledge assessments and do not carry the same depth and breadth of insight as a full knowledge inventory audit.

20 Toward Integration: Typologies of Functional Knowledge

NOW I understand what knowledge management is.
—participant, knowledge-mapping workshop

We have seen that typologies of personal knowledge and organizational knowledge can help us to clarify what we need from an organizational knowledge inventory audit. Neither approach fully meets our needs. But they do illustrate the complexity of knowledge use in organizations. At several points in the previous chapters, we have seen that in the course of doing work and delivering value there are complex interactions between knowledge types: between knowledge resources at personal, team, and organizational levels, and between different forms of knowledge resources, whether explicit, implicit, or tacit.

Knowledge types are not "clean" or distinct in the ways they are deployed in practice. Reducing knowledge to the crude distinctions between tacit/explicit or personal/organizational, does not adequately characterize the way knowledge is used in the real world, which is "an interplay between tacit and explicit knowledge while it crosses boundaries of groups, departments, and organizations as people participate in work" (Fægri et al., 2010, p. 1120).

Toward an Integrated View: Using Matrices to Characterize Knowledge

So our task now is to try to achieve an integrative view, one that will meet our auditability criteria for reliable, robust, and reproducible inventory audits of organizational knowledge resources. One possible way of characterizing and understanding these interactions between more and less tacit, more personal and more collective, is to use matrices that consider the different ways in which knowledge types combine, and the different degrees to which they combine.

Gamble and Blackwell (2001) proposed a series of binary choices between declarative versus procedural, static versus dynamic, and abstract versus specific. In a three-dimensional matrix, you could look at eight different ways in which they could combine.

Conceptually, this is interesting, but for an inventory audit the matrix again fails our tests of observability, naturalistic distinctions, and actionability. The categories are simply too abstract to support reliable and consistent self-reporting of knowledge use at a functional or team level. How do you ask an engineer what a procedural-dynamic-abstract knowledge resource would look like?

Karl Wiig (1993, p. 153) used a more promising approach, with a matrix comprising *personal knowledge, shared expertise,* and *public knowledge* on the vertical axis and four types of knowledge on the horizontal axis, giving a grid of twelve potential combinations:

- *Factual knowledge*—broadly similar to declarative knowledge
- *Conceptual knowledge*—broadly similar to Zack's "know-why"
- *Expectational knowledge*—broadly similar to Nonaka's cognitive dimension of tacit knowledge comprising mental models, paradigms, and implicit rules
- *Methodological knowledge*—broadly similar to procedural knowledge but not in the very tacit sense of Ryle's original "know-how"

Wiig's matrix certainly looks as though it would help to capture functional knowledge areas (among others) at the level of specificity that we need. However, it is a complex matrix to implement in practice and therefore probably fails the naturalistic description test when exposed to responding managers across the organization.

It also does not fully represent the substantive differences in kind between a given knowledge type in persons, in groups, and in organizations. Conceptual knowledge of an individual is such a different phenomenon from conceptual knowledge of an organization that the use of the same term *conceptual* could easily mislead. It looks and feels like a framework that would be more appropriate to a skilled investigator than to group self-reporting. I have not been able to find evidence that it has been used extensively in knowledge auditing.

Moreover, while Wiig does acknowledge the existence of purely tacit knowledge in many places, this matrix in particular implies that all the knowledge to be inventoried using the framework is explicable to some degree. It therefore also fails the comprehensiveness test.

J.-C. Spender (1996a) described a matrix that combined the two dimensions of explicit versus implicit (which he uses as a synonym for tacit) on one side and individual versus collective on the other. He wanted to be able to differentiate the degree of managerial control that could be exerted and the ways that economic value that could be extracted.

Spender freely recognized that these were idealized types abstracted from the real situated contexts of work—that is, neither observable nor naturalistic.

He also recognized that the matrix was deficient in failing to capture the interactions between the types, and the fact that knowledge in action frequently contains aspects of several cells at once. Notwithstanding the limited purpose for which he intended it, other academic knowledge management (KM) researchers have attempted to use the matrix as a means of identifying organizational knowledge forms and types (Chua, 2002). It is not clear how this framework would work in real-world knowledge-mapping contexts.

Sidney Winter (1987, p. 170) described a more complex four-dimensional framework. Knowledge items could sit anywhere on the dimensions between the two poles:

- Tacit versus articulable—within which he differentiated teachable from nonteachable and not articulated from articulated
- Not observable in use versus observable in use
- Complex versus simple
- Element of a system versus independent resource

The model does appear quite comprehensive when compared against the typologies of personal knowledge discussed earlier. But Winter's matrix was intended to evaluate knowledge resources for their strategic importance and their relative accessibility to managerial intervention. It was not intended as a collection mechanism to drive an inventory audit.

In that sense Winters's model has some affinities with the late Max Boisot's I-Space (information space) framework. Boisot eschewed typologies altogether, and I believe he came closest to honoring the dialectical and multimodal nature of knowledge-in-use espoused by Ryle and Polanyi. His famous I-Space framework permitted the characterization of knowledge in two and sometimes three dimensions—namely, abstract versus concrete, undiffused versus diffused, and uncodified versus codified (Boisot, 1998; cf. also Nissen & Jennex, 2005).

Because (like Winter) the I-Space model simply describes dimensions and does not use a typology to delimit distinct cells in a grid, it was able to characterize knowledge use as fluid and mobile, taking on different affordances and constraints as it took on different positions along each dimension. Important as this was for understanding how to build KM capabilities that are appropriate to the complex nature of knowledge, the lack of a differentiated typology does not help us when we want to inventory knowledge stocks in use.

For both Winter and Boisot, the dimensionality *presupposes a prior method* for identifying and inventorying knowledge resources. Their frameworks were designed to characterize identified knowledge resources further in order to assess their strategic significance and drive appropriate managerial responses. In Boisot's (1998, pp. 230–231) case, the nature of the knowledge resources identified would depend heavily on the context of the knowledge-mapping activity: whether at the strategic level, at the competence level, or at a problem area to be addressed.

We can see then that the use of matrices has some analytical value. They can help to characterize, make sense of, and identify suitable actions to take upon knowledge resources, *once identified*.

Typologies of Functional Knowledge

There are several contenders for knowledge typologies organized around business functions. While the American Productivity and Quality Center (APQC) is a firm advocate of the tacit-explicit dualism, with an occasional nod toward implicit knowledge, when it comes to knowledge mapping in the field, it uses a couple of more fine-grained typologies in order to gather functionally useful data. In a 2005 APQC guide to knowledge mapping, Wesley Vestal (2005, pp. 9–10) differentiates between the following:

- *Social/cultural knowledge*—competency in working effectively within a given organizational culture, including the ability to build and maintain relationships and work collaboratively

- *Historical knowledge*—knowledge of the history of the organization, including past deals and practices

- *Human knowledge*—capabilities and skills of individual people

- *Functional knowledge*—the knowledge that is needed to perform a specific job function

This breakdown highlights several interesting areas of knowledge to consider—in particular, relationship-based knowledge, historical knowledge, and personal capabilities and skills. However, as a set of categories this does not provide a usable typology because the types can overlap. For example, in principle it could be argued that the APQC's "functional knowledge" could comprise any combination of the other three. If the types are not mutually exclusive, they cannot promise reliable and robust naturalistic distinctions. Ambiguities and overlaps always mean that different people will interpret and apply the types differently.

When it comes to producing detailed knowledge maps around key business functions, the APQC uses a slightly different typology (Vestal, 2005, pp. 40–48):

- Tacit expertise
- Competencies/learning needs

- Technical/functional knowledge
- Documented (explicit) knowledge
- Job/role-based (business process–based) knowledge

This is more satisfactory from a formal perspective, and it is evidently durable and relatively reliable, having been in regular use in multiple organizations as a standard APQC methodology for over a decade. It provides a differentiated breakdown on the scale between very tacit to very explicit forms of knowledge. The types represent relatively clear and naturalistic distinctions, although we imagine it might be important to highlight the distinctions between competencies, technical knowledge, and job-based knowledge to avoid ambiguities and divergent interpretations in use. It seems to pass our tests of observability and representing naturalistic distinctions, and in consequence it looks like it would support action planning.

However, it is not clear that it passes the comprehensiveness test. We cannot see how relationship-based knowledge and historical knowledge might be accommodated. There are some business functions, such as marketing, business development, and project management, that are extremely dependent on access to knowledge through relationships. Other business functions, such as policy advisory and infrastructure engineering, are heavily dependent on having access to historical knowledge of how things were done and decided in the past, going beyond the knowledge captured in formal explicit records. In addition, the typology does not seem particularly hospitable to the collective and metacognitive aspects of functional knowledge.

For the past twenty years, my company Straits Knowledge has been using a modified form of a typology first proposed by Dave Snowden, the ASHEN framework. Snowden's typology is as follows (Snowden, 2000c; Crane, 2016, p. xix):

- *Artifacts*—explicit knowledge and codified information in documents, data, and other artifacts
- *Skills*—competencies that can be trained and practiced and for which the performance can be measured, typically for routine tasks
- *Heuristics*—rules of thumb, ways of working, and other forms of implicit knowledge
- *Experience*—valuable tacit knowledge that has been gained through repeated, reflective practice over time, enabling the practitioners to be able to respond effectively to novel challenges as well as routine tasks
- *Natural talent*—special aptitudes or gifts that are unique to individuals and that cannot be transferred or learned, although they can be honed through developing associated skills and experience

The typology progresses along a continuum from most explicit to most tacit, expressing the more implicit and somatic (embodied) elements in between. Several of the elements were prefigured as different forms of knowledge input to organizational work as far back as 1982 by Richard Nelson and Sidney Winter (1982, p. 121)—notably, heuristics (described by Nelson and Winter as routines), skills, and experience; Nelson and Winter also add relationships.

In the course of using this typology, we made two modifications in the interest of greater comprehensiveness and greater clarity for respondent self-reporting. The first was to add relationship-based knowledge to the typology (for comprehensiveness), and the second was to reinterpret Snowden's "heuristics" knowledge type using the more naturalistic term "methods", which also accommodates the collective aspects of team knowledge. We call our framework the *Wheel of Knowledge* since we represent it in a circle in order to avoid any impression of linear progression. The elements we use are (Lambe, 2007, p. 194; Milton & Lambe, 2020, pp. 117–120)

- *documents and data*—following Snowden's *artifacts*—directly corresponding to explicit knowledge;

- *skills and competencies*—as described by Snowden. We see a correspondence here with Collins's somatic tacit knowledge, Hecker's shared knowledge, and Blackler's embodied knowledge;

- *method knowledge*—implicit routines, ways of working, and rules of thumb that have not been documented. To the extent they are documented, we also capture their complementary artifacts as *documents and data*. We see a correspondence here with the APQC's role-based knowledge, Collins's relational tacit knowledge, and Blackler's embedded knowledge;

- *relationships*—relationships of familiarity and trust that are necessary to gain access to other people's knowledge (internal or external to the organization) in order to perform key tasks effectively. This reflects the idea that we "store" knowledge in other people as well as in things (Sloman & Fernbach, 2017, pp. 5, 112–114, 120). We see a loose connection here with Collins's collective tacit knowledge, insofar as relationships help us negotiate and interpret different "knowledge worlds," and with Hecker's complementary knowledge, which helps us to seek help quickly from people who have the knowledge we need;

- *experience*—experience-based know-how and expertise, and/or historical knowledge of how things have been done in the past, elsewhere described as narrative knowledge (Wiig, 1993, p. 156);

- *natural talent*—as described by Snowden.

Figure 20.1 shows the framework in a "wheel" format, with selective examples given for a single business activity (securing a property for development) in a property development company.

The "wheel" format has some interesting advantages, although we happened on that format by chance. First, on the vertical axis it removes a strictly linear progression and helps us explain increasing degrees of tacitness and decreasing degrees of explicitness as we descend, without having to stipulate a strict sequence or hierarchy. It also accommodates the idea that the knowledge forms can interact.

Second, the diagonal left-right axis (figure 20.2) communicates the distinction between knowledge types more associated with collective team knowledge and requiring metacognitive skills (shared artifacts, shared implicit repertoires, and the complementary knowledge of other people engaged through networks and relationships) and the knowledge that is typically embedded more in individuals (skills, experience, natural talent).

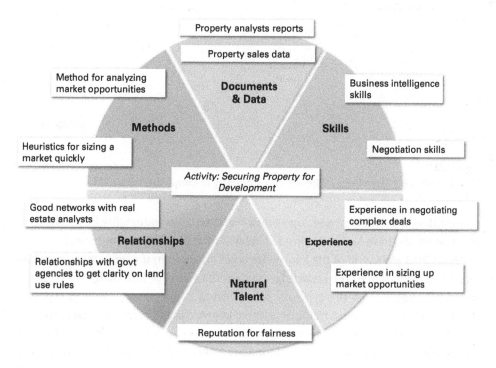

Figure 20.1
Worked example of knowledge resource types associated with a single business activity in a property development company.

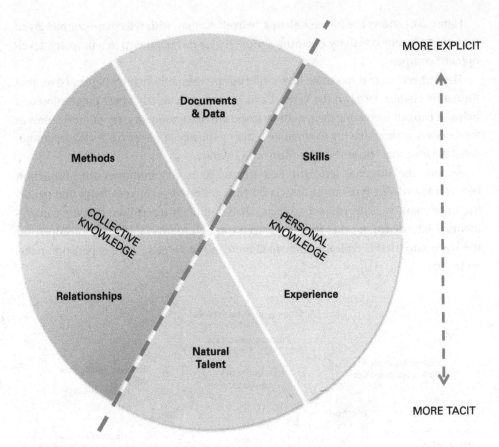

Figure 20.2
How the Wheel of Knowledge addresses the complexity of knowledge types.

How does this typology stack up against our criteria for auditability in an inventory audit, as we set them out in chapter 15? Table 20.1 analyzes its performance.

Figure 20.3 gathers all of the knowledge types discussed in the preceding three chapters into a single frame. The knowledge types in the Wheel of Knowledge are presented in bold. It suggests that this typology serves well as a functional knowledge typology, that can mediate an understanding of personal knowledge and organizational or strategic knowledge. It marks out key knowledge types in a spectrum from tacit to explicit and suggests that these types sit sensibly within the "universe" of types discussed in this book.

A caution: We should not delude ourselves that with this typology we have a "hard" categorization system that identifies objectively distinct knowledge types. There are potential overlaps and permeable boundaries between several of these types; for

Table 20.1

Auditability criteria for the Wheel of Knowledge framework

Criteria	Remarks
OBSERVABLE	*Observable* means there should be a way of helping staff in the organization to easily and consistently identify the knowledge resources they need for their work, either by direct observation or through proxies.

Of the six knowledge types, *documents and data* are the most easily observed in the enterprise. However, as we have noted, from an organization-wide perspective they can be subject to scatter and concealment, depending on the number of channels and mechanisms for storage, from the personal computers of individual staff, to shared folders and team site document libraries, to enterprise-wide applications. We start by asking functional teams what they use, for what activities, and then ask them to identify their locations. This gives us a clue as to where to go looking for a more thorough content audit.

Method knowledge is implicit knowledge and by definition not articulated unless you know where to go looking for it. In workshops we ask participants to think of the practice areas where new team members would need help, guidance, and on-the-job training. The learning curves of new staff are good indicators of the presence of method knowledge, since this form of knowledge represents the shared knowledge of a team accustomed to working with each other, evolved knowledge about how to perform an activity well, and knowledge routinized by the team (Gruenfeld & Fan, 1999). Once you know where it is, you can observe the practice, and document it or develop training support around it. Methods can be described as "How to . . ." perform a particular subtask within a major business activity of the workgroup. In some cases you might have a single activity with both a *document* knowledge resource (e.g., a procedure or a guideline) and a *method* knowledge resource closely associated with it (implicit knowledge of how to apply the procedure—e.g., when you can take shortcuts, when you cannot). Our guiding question is "When would you need to have somebody available to guide a new staff member in addition to the documented knowledge resources?"

Skills and competencies have good proxy descriptions in the way that you would define the job requirements for a particular role in a team or work group. Skills and competencies can be described in the same way you would describe a training course for that skills area.

Experience-based knowledge resources can also be associated with how you would frame job requirements, except that in the case of experience you would typically indicate how much experience would be required for this role, or how many cycles of a specific kind of activity need to be in place before you would judge that a person has enough experience to be put in charge. We explain that the difference between a skill and experience is that while a skill gives you the competency to perform fairly routine tasks to standard levels of performance, experience gives you the ability to deal with nonroutine situations quickly and effectively. Experience is often expressed as something that takes time to build and transfer and so we often ask respondents to indicate *how much* experience is required for that activity.

Relationships are elicited through the question "Who are the key persons or roles you need to interact with (or exchange knowledge with) in order to perform this activity?" It is relatively easy to identify that key relationships exist. Relationship knowledge reflects relationships of familiarity and trust, which enable concise, rich knowledge flows whenever required. If we have mutual familiarity (Hecker's complementary knowledge) *and* trust, then we can make concise ad hoc requests, be understood, and get what we need. If we do not have mutual familiarity, then we may not know who to ask, how to ask, and how to have our needs understood, and we may not get good answers. Familiarity and trust cannot be constructed or transferred mechanistically—these elements of strong knowledge relationships are built up incrementally over time and are uniquely dependent on the personalities involved and their interactions.

(continued)

Table 20.1
(continued)

Criteria	Remarks
	Natural talent refers to unique capabilities that cannot be transferred or learned. In this case we ask, "Where would you need to hire a headhunter (or keep one on retainer) because you have unique capabilities that are required? What are those capabilities that you are hiring for?" Because it is so bound up with special attributes of unique individuals, natural talent represents a risk to an organization and is not typically found in most operational business activities. If you see lot of natural talent knowledge resources mapped to fairly generic business activities, then this is an indication that you need to redirect the knowledge mappers toward what is more likely: specialized skills that can be trained, or special, deep insight and competencies that can be developed through experience.
NATURALISTIC	The framework does need to be explained (as we explain it above), and the initial knowledge inventorying and mapping activity using the framework needs to be facilitated to check for consistency of understanding. However, once explained and concept checked, we get reasonably consistent results across different groups and different organization types and industries. The resulting inventories and maps can be maintained and updated with relative ease. Participants can explain, discuss, and agree on the knowledge resources they use in the course of their work using this framework. All the knowledge types have easily observable indicators that can be translated into everyday organizational language—e.g., of bringing new staff up to speed, stipulating skills and experience requirements, maintaining key relationships and networks, and unique people requirements that call for special sourcing mechanisms.
	We can make reasonable predictions of what the overall shape of a knowledge map should look like for any given function. We have conducted more than thirty audits over the past twenty years, and we see consistent patterns for similar functions in different organizations. Highly structured functions such as finance, procurement, and internal audit tend to have a high dependency on documents and data and skills, and less dependency on undocumented method knowledge. Sales, marketing, and business development functions tend to have high dependency on relationships. Expertise-intensive functions such as engineering, especially in organizations with low turnover and long-serving staff, tend to have high dependencies (and risks) associated with experience-based knowledge resources. New organizations, or organizations with high turnover and subject to restructuring or constant change, tend to have high dependency on method knowledge compared to documents and data—they are constantly improvising and have not had time to stabilize their practice into explicit artifacts.
	The fact that these are consistent patterns across different organizations (or different groups inventorying the same organization in multiyear audit updates) suggests that the framework is robust in terms of generating common understandings and consistent reporting.
ACTIONABLE	Each knowledge type can be associated with clear management actions.
	Documents and data can be clearly associated with a wide range of information management solutions. This is not just about technology. Needs analysis will consider near and far transfer requirements and user-centered design processes, ensuring that content is written appropriately for its audience, and so on. Being tangible and explicit, these are the knowledge resources most amenable to managerial action.
	Method knowledge, once identified, can be observed and documented if needed. Teams can develop on-the-job training programs, and assign supervision or mentoring roles to help new staff get up to speed, and communities of practice can be helpful for allowing newer staff to observe how issues are dealt with.
	Skills and competencies, once identified, can be compared with the organization's training plan, or recruitment documentation, and considered in training needs analysis. Like documents and data, organizations usually have processes already in place to satisfy these needs.

Table 20.1
(continued)

Criteria	Remarks
	With *experience* we are moving further into tacit knowledge territory, and so KM actions become more specialized and technical. Context-sharing methods providing opportunities for guided observation can help people observe and build tacit knowledge in a directed fashion (e.g., job shadowing, mentoring and coaching, communities of practice, training, and sharing processes such as fishbowl discussions, knowledge cafés, and scenario-based learning). There are specialized interview techniques designed to identify the elements of what very experienced people know, compared to novices. These insights can be framed into learning artifacts and processes such as decision games, learning scenarios, and training curricula (Crandall et al., 2006; Lambe & Tan, 2008).
	Relationships can have different layers of action. First, we need to know who knows what, and there are several ways of representing that: expertise directories, tagging of contributors by expertise topics, and social network maps. Relationships can be cultivated through processes such as networking sessions, deliberate cross-fertilization in company-wide training programs, or sending staff to industry conferences and expos. Awareness is only the first step: relationships become knowledge resources when they have rich knowledge-carrying potential, and for that we need a panoply of relationships of mutual familiarity and trust. For this, again, we can co-opt many mechanisms, including team-building sessions, cross-posting of employees to work together on projects, drills and rehearsals (for unusual but high-impact events), and background relationship-building environments such as communities and networks of practice.
	Natural talent, by definition, is the hardest of all to manage and yet ironically the simplest. Because it is bound up with unique individuals, it automatically represents a risk. Any dependency on natural talent needs, first of all, close consideration to see whether it can be parlayed into some combination of specialized *skills and competencies*, *relationships*, or *experience*. If not, then we need mechanisms for finding the requisite natural talent in the market, we need to keep it happy for as long as possible, and we need to have backup plans in case we lose it suddenly.
	The typology helps us to become more deliberative and conscious about how we use the existing management mechanisms in our organization and it helps us decide which additional mechanisms we need to develop.
COMPREHENSIVE	Comprehensiveness relates to the typology as a whole, rather than the individual elements. Figure 20.3 shows our functional knowledge typology (*bold*) in the center column (functional/work group knowledge), showing how the knowledge types span the continuum between tacit, implicit, and explicit. The relative positions of the elements on the tacit-implicit-knowledge dimension are very approximate, but give some idea of how they position against the detailed personal and organizational knowledge types we have discussed in this section of the book. Different types of knowledge can legitimately sit on different places in the spectrum. For example, some skills and competencies can be relatively easy to reproduce and transfer (closer to implicit), or they can be highly difficult to reproduce and transfer, and might be closer to somatic, automatic knowledge (more tacit).
	The diagram shows that our typology covers a representative spread of knowledge types. With the guidance we give in introducing the framework about key distinctions, it is relatively good at capturing most major knowledge types experienced and used in the course of work, and the categories are hospitable to further drill downs at the personal knowledge level if necessary as part of our middle-out method of knowledge auditing. For example, our inventory of experience-based knowledge can be deepened through investigations of personal knowledge so that we can differentiate between anecdotal, historical, and narrative knowledge, and deep technical expertise; knowledge-carrying relationships can be explored to identify critical elements of internal complementary knowledge or external knowledge networks.
	And if needed, the knowledge types can be folded up into corresponding strategic capabilities, or intellectual capital "buckets," at the organizational level.
GRANULAR	The typology needs to identify knowledge resources at the right level of granularity so that gaps, opportunities, and risks can be identified in the context of work, and thereby lead to actionable insights at the operational level. Our observations on the naturalistic nature of the typology and the clarity of actionable insight for participants in the knowledge-mapping exercise suggests that this condition is met.

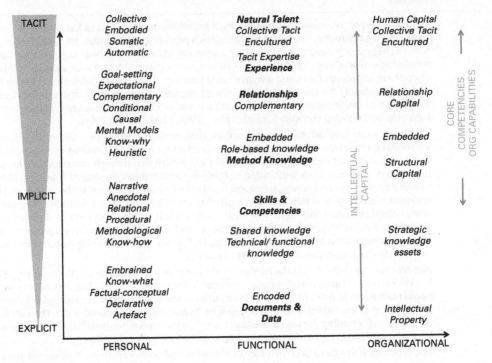

Figure 20.3
How the Wheel of Knowledge (functional) knowledge typology fares against a full spectrum of knowledge types.

example, at which point does a very specialized skill become better cataloged as experience? For a given activity that has been very explicitly documented and described as documents and data, there is often some residual method knowledge (e.g., as part of Collins's background collective tacit knowledge).

Experience can conceal several interesting distinctions between different knowledge subtypes that we would want to pick apart if we started to delve into the special knowledge of very experienced individuals. It could cover historical-narrative knowledge of how things have been done in the past, experiential knowledge that looks very much like an advanced, personal form of method knowledge (including heuristics and recipes for action), or very specialized technical knowledge that could be abstracted into a conceptual form as causal or conditional knowledge. Our use of a "wheel" to represent the typology (rather than a linear list) makes it easier to explain these kinds of interactions and overlaps.

But a hard categorization system was not our goal. For the purposes of a knowledge inventory audit, our goal is a very practical one, which is to have a typology that allows work groups to self-report consistently the knowledge they use in everyday work in ways that can be analyzed and compared on scale and in ways that allow those same groups to infer useful actions to take. As I have elsewhere said, with such a goal, pragmatism trumps purity (Lambe, 2007, p. 153). From a pragmatic point of view, our key questions are as follows:

- Does it work for work-group self-reporting? (Yes)
- Does it surface actionable insights for both work groups and organization? (Yes)
- Can ambiguities and overlaps be addressed easily? (Yes. Where it seems a knowledge area could encompass two or more types of knowledge—for example, partly but not fully documented—our advice is to capture all of the possible knowledge types that work in parallel. This gives a composite, rich picture of the knowledge at work there).

We have observed that the use of this typology corrects the bias toward just documenting explicit knowledge in depth, or toward the perceived need to "convert" tacit knowledge into explicit knowledge so that it can be managed. The typology has very strong heuristic and sensemaking power. Once the framework is grasped, and because it is framed against naturalistic contexts that people encounter every day in the work place, it becomes immediately obvious to respondents that different knowledge types require different kinds of management response. We have had people leaving knowledge-mapping workshops saying, "*Now* I understand what knowledge management is about."

The Effects of a Powerful Typology

At the beginning of chapter 15, I described a knowledge audit case study in a Scottish oil and gas company, where the use of a binary tacit-explicit typology produced highly detailed audit findings related to explicit knowledge resources, but rather abstract and generalized findings in relation to tacit knowledge, and nothing in between.

I want to contrast that now with the story of an audit we conducted for a property development company using the more differentiated Wheel of Knowledge typology, to illustrate what is possible when we meet our auditability criteria and get more granular views into knowledge in use.

Case Study: Going beyond the Obvious—a Knowledge Inventory Audit in a Property Development Company

ABC Properties is a very large, mature property development company spanning commercial, industrial, and residential developments. It is well established and has had an active KM program for about twenty years, with successive investments over that period in the use of information technology to solve knowledge capture and knowledge-sharing problems.

In recent years it had fallen prey to the common bias toward managing explicit knowledge (and to the belief that tacit knowledge has to be converted into explicit knowledge to be managed). Whenever it had run into a knowledge-sharing and access problem around a particular form of knowledge (e.g., engineering design, facilities management, estate management, rental yield management, land use planning), it would build a platform for that "knowledge."

By the time we were asked in to help the company with a knowledge audit and KM program review, we found a sophisticated but fragmented environment with specialized knowledge bases scattered across many specialized platforms, each with different governance, management, access, and labeling conventions.

When the company managers engaged us, they were interpreting their problem as a search and retrieval problem: either they needed a common taxonomy to bridge the knowledge resources across the different platforms or they needed a "better" search engine to help people find the resources wherever they were located. As it happened they had a pretty good search engine already. And as we discovered, their main problem was not even a common taxonomy problem (though their lack of consistency was a problem, and a taxonomy would be a part of the solution).

We helped them develop knowledge inventory maps across all the key functions of the organization, applying the Wheel of Knowledge typology. Through small-group interviews, we traced the existing knowledge and information flows between departments, whether tacit, implicit, or explicit. We published the resulting knowledge maps back to all the departments for their review, and we then asked each department when reviewing the maps to identify knowledge resources *in other departments* that would be useful to their own business activities. In this way we were able to trace *potential knowledge flows* as well as existing knowledge flows.

In parallel, we conducted a pain points analysis looking at pain points around operational knowledge and information use, a culture analysis looking at common behaviors around knowledge use (using an archetypes approach), and an information profile survey that looked at how the different departments worked with information and who they traded information with on a routine basis. In formal terms this was an inventory audit combined with a discovery review audit, using KM assessment instruments on pain points, culture, and information use. The combination of methods provided a rich picture of knowledge use, knowledge needs, and knowledge opportunities.

What we discovered was that the bulk of existing critical knowledge flows (some 80 percent) bypassed the formal knowledge-sharing platforms and took place through a wide and unmanaged variety of channels, including face-to-face, by telephone, by email, and via smartphone messaging apps. This surprised us because the organization evidently had a very mature information and knowledge-sharing infrastructure. The knowledge that was flowing through these informal channels included requests for explicit knowledge that was often officially contained on formal platforms, but a whole set of reasons conspired to nudge the flows into informal channels:

- The information was deeply buried and not easily accessible.
- The person asking did not have access rights to that platform.
- The information required was a small part of a more complex set of documentation that the inquirer did not know how to navigate.
- The inquirer did not know where the information was located.

- The inquirer needed some personal knowledge of the historical context behind some documented facts.
- To apply the information correctly, the inquirer needed experience-based knowledge involving somebody's judgment.
- The inquirer was asking for help to find somebody who knew something about the issue that was documented.

We found out in a set of narrative-based focus groups (anecdote circles) that the knowledge infrastructure was so complex that staff needed to have cross-organizational relationships (complementary knowledge) to get "close" to the location of a resource they needed, and they would then use their contacts to help them trace the "last mile" to the resource they needed in a form they could use. This requirement obviously disfavored newer staff who lacked internal networks.

In some cases the governance of the platforms was so tight that the staff who needed resources would not themselves have access rights and would need to find somebody who could give them access. If they got access, they might need help from somebody with contextual knowledge to navigate the complex material inside and interpret it. Because the company had a very long track record and staff who had been in place for many years, the staff often needed to know who knew the historical background to certain lease management policies that were in place, or who knew the history of a certain development or estate and why it had been developed a certain way. We were starting to get deep insight into the rich web of collective and personal knowledge that was being activated to navigate and exploit the shared information infrastructure.

We could not have achieved this depth of insight so quickly, if at all, with a binary explicit-tacit typology (or with a single audit instrument). With such a rich, visible array of tightly managed explicit knowledge resources, we would have missed the critical role of the cross-organizational relationship knowledge needed to navigate, interpret, and use the knowledge infrastructure, and we would have missed the significant business risks in depending on the long-serving "knowers" of (a) the knowledge resources in the platforms themselves and (b) the historical background of numerous projects, developments, estates, and customers.

At best, the tacit knowledge dependencies we would have gotten would have been the most obvious, which were the technical expertise areas their business depended on. Our typology enabled us to get considerably more differentiated and nuanced insights into the more implicit and tacit forms of knowledge, both personal and collective, beyond the most obvious.

One consequence of this insight was that when we did help the company develop a taxonomy, we developed one that was capable of describing the tacit and implicit knowledge exchange activity happening around and outside the formal platforms, as well as the content within those platforms. We were able to recommend collaboration mechanisms that would draw these knowledge-sharing questions and exchanges onto a common platform where they could be made visible, tagged, and available for reuse. Now, when somebody starts to ask a question, the taxonomy tag is picked up automatically, and prompts the inquirer with previous questions and answers on the same topic, as well as links to designated experts in that area—before they have even finished typing the question.

We have covered a lot of ground in this final section of the book. We have focused on how to operationalize an inventory audit, which is foundational to the other common forms of comprehensive knowledge audit.

We focused first on clarifying the metaphors we commonly use to describe knowledge, particularly those that hold some implications of value, ownership, and control. We then explored a number of different ways of describing and inventorying knowledge resources at the personal, functional, and organizational levels.

We found that the practice of inventorying knowledge stocks is a highly fragmented and contentious area with multiple competing schools of thought, some entrenched views, and multiple descriptive vocabularies, so it has been necessary to engage with the literature in some depth and to link to practical illustrations along the way.

My own view is that the most productive approach to an inventory audit is the "middle-out" approach, inventorying knowledge resources at the functional or team level, then exploring in greater depth specific areas of personal knowledge that emerge as interest areas, and then mapping upward against strategic knowledge needs in order to form conclusions about appropriate KM needs.

In the Wheel of Knowledge, I have proposed a functional knowledge typology that I believe is practical, accessible, and reliable as a framework for constructing actionable knowledge inventories.

*   *   *

Summary

In this chapter we focused on integrating the insights from our earlier analysis of the different approaches to describing knowledge into a typology that is relevant to an inventory of function or team-based knowledge resources. Here is a summary of the main points:

1. Some writers have used matrices to characterize and analyze different knowledge types. These are more useful for making sense of knowledge types after they have been identified, and for determining appropriate actions, but they do not function well as collection mechanisms for an audit.

2. We have identified a six-part typology of functional knowledge that meets our criteria of observable, naturalistic, actionable, comprehensive, and granular.

21 Conclusion: Possibilities

You don't really suppose, do you, that all your adventures and escapes were managed by mere luck, just for your sole benefit? You are a very fine person, Mr. Baggins, and I am very fond of you; but you are only quite a little fellow in a wide world after all!
—Tolkien (1966, chap. 19)

I would like to close this book with some principles and considerations to help you in the task of scoping and planning your knowledge audits.

Nine Principles to Plan By

1. Clarify your audit purpose, and work with your sponsors on clear descriptions of the needs driving the audit and what you would like to learn. Be open to using combined models of audit to meet the need. In the next section of this chapter, I will propose some different scenarios and suggest how they might be served by a combination of audit models. Chapter 4 provides a summary of audit models. Chapter 5 provides a summary of the types of phenomena you may be auditing.

2. Expect to use three or more independent evidence-collection methods or instruments. Your aim is to avoid the weaknesses of any single method by using methods that have different strengths so that you get complementary views on the knowledge landscape. Chapters 4 and 6 identify a number of different methods related to different audit areas of interest.

3. Describe and clearly communicate your chosen audit models to your sponsors and stakeholders. Distinguish what each audit model contributes, and do not claim greater authority for the process than it intrinsically holds. Explain what each audit method or instrument contributes to the overall findings. Be especially conscious of and cautious about the following:

(a) **Value audits:** Avoid cost-benefit audits if you can and explain why (chapter 13); try to keep these audits focused on the strategic value to be delivered by knowledge (chapter 19).

(b) **Assessment audits:** Avoid summative audits if you can, and be very cautious about how you use standards in knowledge-related audits (chapters 8–9). Ensure that contextual drivers and needs are adequately accounted for, and avoid giving the impression that there is a universal "best" way to do knowledge management (KM). We have taken the position that outside of the regulatory context, standards are most productively used to frame internal conversations within a formative audit.

4. Avoid using the term *knowledge assets* (and explain why) because of the confusion it can produce—*knowledge resources* or *knowledge/intellectual capital* or *strategic capabilities* are much less misleading (chapters 12–14).

5. Scale the complexity, participation requirements, and staging of the audit in ways that are appropriate to the audit needs and your level of support. It is generally better to pilot a well-defined and relatively complex audit approach within a very tight scope (e.g., single department) than to try a very lightweight audit collecting limited evidence across a broad population. Limited evidence means limited clarity on what needs to change. Consider that you may want to run some or all of the audit methods and instruments periodically to monitor progress and remain aligned with changing needs. Consider whether there is a need to use a consistent audit format over the life cycle of a KM road map plan (e.g., 5–10 years) so that you can monitor, measure, and evaluate progress (chapter 19).

6. Especially if you are conducting a discovery review or participative goal-setting audit, leave some flexibility in your audit plan to adjust the methods or instruments you use in case you make early discoveries that need further investigation (chapter 19).

7. If you are conducting an inventory audit, avoid overly simplistic typologies of knowledge (chapters 16–17). Use a range of knowledge types that reflect the naturalistic understandings of how knowledge is used in the work context. Test your typology against the literature and against your respondent base for consistency of understanding (chapter 20).

8. Document, describe, and compare your audit methodologies and approaches with other knowledge management professionals (it is possible to do this without compromising employer or client confidentiality; chapter 8).

Table 21.1

Audit suggestions for different scenarios

Scenario	Audit suggestions
1. You work for an industry membership body, and you are considering ways of helping members to compare their KM practices and learn from each other.	*Audit models:* • Assessment audit: benchmarking • Learning audit [future] *Instruments and methods:* • Standardized survey instrument adjusted to pick up challenges faced by the industry, covering KM enablers, KM processes, KM outcomes, KM challenges, and pain points. Use of KM standard possible (if contextualized). • Follow-up interviews with archetypal (for the industry) organizations and edge cases (beginners, repeated tries, mature). • Participatory learning events for the industry (e.g., workshops/conferences) focused on challenges being met and how; followed up by guidance paper incorporating feedback. • Consider regular tracking of industry KM activity using the same framework, and collecting periodic data on KM activity and business performance, for a periodic learning audit.
2. You work for a global multinational, and you want to build your collective KM capabilities by auditing KM practices across divisions and countries, as well as identify strategic centers of excellence.	*Audit models:* • Assessment audit: benchmarking • Discovery review audit • Inventory audit: focused on strategic knowledge areas • Value audit: asset capitalization *Instruments and methods:* • Standardized survey instrument/framework covering KM enablers, KM processes, KM outcomes, KM challenges, and pain points. Use of KM standard possible (if contextualized). • Participatory workshops to conduct sensemaking on the returns and to map strategic knowledge areas/capabilities and dependencies. • Participatory knowledge capitalization workshops to plan how strategic centers of excellence can be fostered and supported and deliver value to the organization at large. • Periodic participatory workshops to map capabilities in different countries around the strategic knowledge areas and to identify learning maps/plans to guide structured sharing and learning between countries.
3. You work for a large and distributed organization, and you want to enhance the sharing of key knowledge across organizational boundaries by improving your shared knowledge platforms and your collaboration and knowledge sharing processes.	*Audit models:* • Inventory audit: comprehensive mapping of knowledge resources using, e.g., Wheel of Knowledge typology • Discovery review audit

(*continued*)

Table 21.1
(continued)

Scenario	Audit suggestions
	Instruments and methods: • Participatory knowledge-mapping workshops and exposure of knowledge maps to identify knowledge resources in high demand for sharing. • Diagnostics frameworks/surveys for identifying pain points, cultural behaviors around sharing, enablers/disablers around KM processes, technology, and governance related to sharing. • Focus groups or participatory workshops to explore context-related differences and guide change planning. • Taxonomy development using knowledge maps and indicators of explicit high-demand knowledge resources in key domains. • Participatory planning workshops and pilots for sharing initiatives/platforms and their interrelations. • Monitor progress regularly using updates to knowledge maps and pain points as progress indicators.
4. You are part of a management team looking at a possible merger/acquisition/strategic joint venture. You want to assess compatibility with a number of other parties.	*Audit models:* • Participative goal-setting audit • Inventory audit: focused on strategic knowledge areas or using an intellectual capital typology with an assessment of knowledge maturity levels *Instruments and methods:* *Stage 1: shortlisting* • Content analysis from competitive intelligence sources and data from the prospective parties. • Participatory workshops to analyze, map, and compare strategic capabilities between yourself and your prospects, perform gap analysis, and analyze complementarity. *Stage 2: assess compatibility with finalists* • Culture analysis exercise using a recognition framework (e.g., personas) or survey to analyze cultural compatibility. • Diagnostics frameworks/surveys for enablers/disablers around KM processes, technology, and governance related to sharing. • Participatory workshops in dialogue with candidate to explore gaps, opportunities, and tasks.
5. You work in a new business function that is highly dependent on a few expert individuals who are trying to guide an inexperienced team. You have the mandate to stabilize and standardize the working processes so the department can operate sustainably into the future.	*Audit models:* • Inventory audit: focused initially on personal knowledge of experts, then on shared team knowledge requirements using a comprehensive typology, e.g., Wheel of Knowledge • Participative goal-setting audit

Table 21.1

(continued)

Scenario	Audit suggestions
	Instruments and methods: • Knowledge-mapping interviews or small group workshops to map expert knowledge using Cognitive Task Analysis (CTA) techniques. • Translate the personal knowledge maps into team operational knowledge maps using, e.g., Wheel of Knowledge typology. • Participatory workshops to enhance and refine the maps with the experts and the team to identify knowledge gaps and opportunities to create documented knowledge assets, stabilize method assets, and enhance the growth and transfer of skills, experience, and relationships. • Participatory workshops using a KM enablers framework to identify change tasks and plans.
6. You have been asked to help a rapidly growing start-up that suffers from high staff turnover. One of the reasons identified is the poor support given for new hires.	*Audit models:* • Discovery review audit • Inventory audit *Instruments and methods:* • Focus groups or anecdote circles with recent hires to get insight into new hire experiences and knowledge pain points, needs, and gaps. • Participatory knowledge-mapping workshops using, e.g., Wheel of Knowledge typology with team leads and with human resources (HR) to map knowledge resources available to support new hires and to identify the gaps illustrated from focus group findings. • Participatory workshops with team leads and with HR on how to meet the knowledge resource gaps and improve the onboarding process, including support for socialization, job knowledge, and information resource finding. • Devise measurement instrument based on focus group findings and change goals and use it as an evaluation instrument for new hires at the end of their onboarding process.
7. You work with a government-linked company that has traditionally provided training and advisory services to other agencies nationally and internationally. This function is now to be spun off and privatized as a consulting and training business.	*Audit models:* • Inventory audit: comprehensive knowledge resource mapping using, e.g., Wheel of Knowledge typology • Participative goal-setting audit *Instruments and methods:* • Participatory knowledge-mapping workshops to identify the key activities of the new company, the knowledge resources required for this new business, the knowledge resources that can be transferred from the parent company, and the knowledge gaps to be filled. • Participatory workshops using a KM enablers framework to identify change tasks and plans.

(*continued*)

Table 21.1
(continued)

Scenario	Audit suggestions
8. An external audit report has cited your organization for substantial legal and regulatory risk around records management—in particular, for poor records accessibility by people who make key decisions in the context of their work. The recommendation is to have an integrated knowledge management and records management system.	*Audit models:* • Assessment audit: Compliance or quality audit • Discovery review audit • Inventory audit: comprehensive mapping of knowledge types associated with key business activities using, e.g., Wheel of Knowledge typology *Instruments and methods:* • Content analysis of internal policies, guidelines, and standards relating to records and to documentation of activities and decisions. • Content analysis covering existing information systems. • Survey instrument and interviews using ISO standards for records management and for knowledge management systems. • Participatory workshops to examine findings, risks, and gaps and to determine priority areas. • Participatory knowledge resource mapping workshops in identified priority areas, focusing on, but not exclusively on, documented knowledge. • Participatory business and functional requirements workshops. • Development of harmonized policy for knowledge and records management. • Development and testing of a common taxonomy for records and knowledge resources using prior internal records classifications and knowledge maps as a basis. • Participatory workshops using a KM enablers framework to identify change tasks and plans.

9. Ensure that when providing for audit effort, you also provide for audit follow-up and the incorporation of audit findings into organizational planning (both strategic and operational) (introduction).

Different Scenarios, Different Audit Models

In Table 12.1 I provide some illustrative scenarios in which knowledge audits may help, together with some suggestions on audit approaches. These are by no means exhaustive, and my suggestions are not definitive.

Closing Words

I believe one of our greatest challenges in knowledge management is that of communication: first with our sponsors and stakeholders, and then with each other.

Our ability to communicate effectively, gather good evidence, and facilitate effective change depends on being able to set realistic expectations, compile and monitor measures of performance and effectiveness over time, and reflect and learn (a) with our stakeholders and sponsors and (b) with each other.

I hope this book is a contribution in that direction, and I wish you good fortune in your journeys.

References

Adam, E. E., Hershauer, J. C., & Ruch, W. A. (1981). Developing quality productivity ratios for public sector personnel services. *Public Productivity Review, 5*(1), 45–61.

Alasco, J. [pseudonym for Zbiegniew Domaniewski]. (1950). *Intellectual capitalism: A study of changing ownership and control in modern industrial society.* New York, NY: World University Press.

Alavi, M., & Leidner, D. E. (2001). Knowledge management and knowledge management systems: Conceptual foundations and research issues. *MIS Quarterly, 25*(1), 107–36.

Alexander, P. A., & Judy, J. E. (1988). The interaction of domain-specific and strategic knowledge in academic performance. *Review of Educational Research, 58*(4), 375–404.

Alias, D. F., Abbas, W. F., & Nordin, A. (2016). Knowledge sharing scenario capture: A case study in IT department of public higher education institution. *Journal of Advanced Management Science, 4*(6), 507–510.

Allen, D. (2015). *The invisible work of nurses: Hospitals, organisation and healthcare.* London, England: Routledge.

Amidon, D. M., & Dimancescu, D. (Eds.). (1988). *Managing the knowledge assets into the 21st century: Focus on research consortia. Proceedings from a conference at Purdue University April 28–29, 1987.* Cambridge, MA: Technology Strategy Group.

Anderson, J. R. (1976). *Language, memory, and thought.* Hillsdale, NJ: Lawrence Erlbaum.

Anderson, J. V. (1989). Technology and mindset: A model for generating new product and service ideas. *National Productivity Review, 6*(2), 111–124.

Andriessen, D. (2004). *Making sense of intellectual capital: Designing a method for the valuation of intangibles.* Amsterdam, Netherlands: Elsevier.

Andriessen, D. (2005, March 8). *Making profit from intellectual capital* [Conference presentation]. Intellectual Capital Conference, Jakarta, Indonesia.

Andriessen, D. (2006). On the metaphorical nature of intellectual capital: A textual analysis. *Journal of Intellectual Capital, 7*(1), 93–110.

Andriessen, D. (2008). Stuff or love? How metaphors direct our efforts to manage knowledge in organizations. *Knowledge Management Research and Practice*, *6*, 5–12.

Aravind, D., & Christmann, P. (2011). Decoupling of standard implementation from certification: Does quality of ISO 14001 implementation affect facilities' environmental performance? *Business Ethics Quarterly*, *21*(1), 73–102.

Argyris, C. (1977). Double loop learning in organizations. *Harvard Business Review*, *55*(5), 115–125.

Argyris, C. (2010). *Organizational traps: Leadership, culture, organizational design*. Oxford, England: Oxford University Press.

Arrow, K. J. (1962). The economic implications of learning by doing. *Review of Economic Studies*, *29*(3), 155–173.

Asiaei, K., Rezaee, Z., Bontis, N., Barani, O., & Sapiei, N. S. (2021). Knowledge assets, capabilities and performance measurement systems: A resource orchestration theory approach. *Journal of Knowledge Management*, *25*(8), 1947–1976.

Asian Development Bank. (2021). *Knowledge Management Action Plan, 2021–2025: Knowledge for a prosperous, inclusive, resilient, and sustainable Asia and Pacific*. Retrieved December 11, 2021, from https://www.adb.org/documents/knowledge-management-action-plan-2021-2025.

Ayinde, L., Orekoya, I. O., Adepeju, Q. A., & Shomoye, A. M. (2021). Knowledge audit as an important tool in organizational management: A review of literature. *Business Information Review*, *38*(2), 89–102.

Baber, C., & McMaster, R. (2016). *Grasping the moment: Sensemaking in response to routine incidents and major emergencies*. Abingdon, England: CRC Press.

Bailey, K. D. (1994). *Typologies and taxonomies: An introduction to classification techniques*. Thousand Oaks, CA: Sage.

Baker, M., Barker, M., Thorne, J., & Dutnell, M. (1997). Leveraging human capital. *Journal of Knowledge Management*, *1*(1), 62–74.

Baker, R. (1999). The role of clinical audit in changing performance. In R. Baker, H. Hearnshaw, & N. Robertson (Eds.), *Implementing change with clinical audit* (pp. 1–20). Chichester, England: John Wiley & Sons.

Baker, R., Hearnshaw, H., & Robertson, N. (Eds.). (1999). *Implementing change with clinical audit*. Chichester, England: John Wiley & Sons.

Barends, E., & Rousseau, D. M. (2018). *Evidence-based management: How to use evidence to make better organizational decisions*. London, England: Kogan Page.

Barnes, S., & Milton, N. (2015). *Designing a successful KM strategy: A guide for the knowledge management professional*. Medford, NJ: Information Today.

Barney, J. B., & Felin, T. (2013). What are microfoundations? *Academy of Management Perspectives, 27*(2), 138–155.

Barney, J. B., Ketchen, D. J., & Wright, M. (2011). The future of resource-based theory: Revitalization or decline? *Journal of Management, 37*(5), 1299–1315.

Barth, S. (2001). War management. *Knowledge Management*, October.

Barton, A. (1968). Bringing society back in: Survey research and macro-methodology. *American Behavioral Scientist, 12*(1), 1–9.

Bassellier, G., Benbasat, I., & Reich, B. H. (2003). The influence of business managers' IT competence on championing IT. *Information Systems Research, 14*(4), 317–336.

Baumard, P. (1999). *Tacit knowledge in organizations.* London, England: Sage.

Bavelas, A. A. (1950). Communication patterns in task-oriented groups. *Journal of the Acoustical Society of America, 22*, 725–730.

Bazerman, M. H., Loewenstein, G., & Moore, D. (2002). Why good accountants do bad audits. *Harvard Business Review, 80*, 96–102.

Be My Eyes (2018). corporate website retrieved from https://www.bemyeyes.com/ on 11 December 2021.

Becerra-Fernandez, I., & Sabherwal, R. (2010). *Knowledge management systems and processes.* Armonk, NY: M. E. Sharpe.

Becher, T., & Trowler, P. R. (2001). *Academic tribes and territories: Intellectual enquiry and the culture of disciplines* (2nd ed.). Buckingham, England: Open University Press.

Bedford, D. (2014, August 4). Presentation slides delivered via personal communication.

Bedford, D., Camp, M., Hein, D., Liston, T., Oxendine, J., & Testa, D. (2014). Developing an open source, adaptable and sustainable method for conducting knowledge management maturity modeling and assessment. In C. Vivas & P. Sequeira (Eds.), *The proceedings of the 15th European Conference on Knowledge Management, ECKM 2014:The Santarém School of Management and Technology, Polytechnic Institute of Santarém, Santarém, Portugal, 4–5 September 2014* (Vol. 1, pp. 111–119). Reading, UK: Academic Conferences and Publishing International.

Beer, S. (1966). *Decision and control: The meaning of operational research and management cybernetics.* London, England: John Wiley & Sons.

Ben-Atar, D. S. (2004). *Trade secrets: Intellectual piracy and the origins of American industrial power.* New Haven, CT: Yale University Press.

Bénézech, D., Lambert, G., Lanoux, B., Lerch, C., & Loos-Baroin, J. (2001). Completion of knowledge codification: An illustration through the ISO 9000 standards implementation process. *Research Policy, 30*(9), 1395–1407.

Beniger, J. R. (1986). *The control revolution: Technological and economic origins of the information society*. Cambridge, MA: Harvard University Press.

Benkard, C. L. (2000). Learning and forgetting: The dynamics of aircraft production. *American Economic Review, 90*(4), 1034–1054.

Bernstein, T. M. (1965). *The careful writer: A modern guide to English usage*. New York, NY: Free Press.

Berry, J. F., & Cook, C. M. (1976). *Managing knowledge as a corporate resource*. Washington, DC: US Department of Defense.

Beynon-Davies, P., & Williams, M. (Eds.). (2000, April 26–28). *Information systems—Research, teaching and practice. Proceedings of the 5th UKAIS Conference, University of Wales Institute, Cardiff, 26–28 April 2000*. New York, NY: McGraw Hill.

Bharadwaj, A. S. (2000). A resource-based perspective on information technology capability and firm performance: An empirical investigation. *MIS Quarterly, 24*(1), 169–196.

Blaber, P. (2008). *The mission, the men, and me: Lessons from a former Delta Force commander*. New York, NY: Berkley.

Black, J., Hashimzade, N., & Myles, G. (2012). *A dictionary of economics* (Oxford Quick reference, 4th ed.). Oxford, England: Oxford University Press.

Blackler, F. (1995). Knowledge, knowledge work and organizations: An overview and interpretation. *Organization Studies, 16*(6), 1021–1046.

Blegen, A. H. (1965). *Records management step-by-step*. Stamford, CT: Office Publications.

Bohm, D. (1996). *On dialogue*. London, England: Routledge.

Bohm, D., & Peat, F. D. (1987). *Science, order and creativity*. New York, NY: Bantam.

Bohn, R. E. (1994). Measuring and managing technological knowledge. *Sloan Management Review, 36*(1), 61–73.

Boisot, M. H. (1987). *Information and organizations: The manager as anthropologist*. London, England: Fontana Collins.

Boisot, M. H. (1998). *Knowledge assets: Securing competitive advantage in the information economy*. Oxford, England: Oxford University Press.

Bontis, N. (2001). Assessing knowledge assets: A review of the models used to measure intellectual capital. *International Journal of Management Reviews, 3*(1), 41–60.

Bontis, N. (Ed.). (2002). *World Congress on Intellectual Capital readings*. Boston, MA: Butterworth Heinemann.

Booth, A., & Haines, M. (1993). Information audit: Whose line is it anyway? *Health Libraries Review, 10*, 224–232.

Botha, A., Kourie, D., & Snyman, R. (2008). *Coping with continuous change in the business environment: Knowledge management and knowledge management technology.* Oxford, England: Chandos.

Bounds, S., Griffiths, D., & White, N. (2018). *Commentary and recommended edits to draft standard ISO 30401—Knowledge management systems—Requirements.* Retrieved December 11, 2021, from https://drive.google.com/file/d/13GMiKh7C7vMuG5gEYNfh7Hq0h1lrmGDk/view.

Bounfour A., & Edvinsson, L. (Eds.). (2012). *Intellectual capital for communities: Nations, regions and cities.* Amsterdam, Netherlands: Elsevier Butterworth Heinemann.

Bourdain, A. (2007). *Kitchen confidential: Adventures in the culinary underbelly* (Updated ed.). New York, NY: Harper Perennial.

Boyd, J. R. (1964). *Aerial attack study* (US Air Force Fighter Weapons School Document 50-10-6C). Nellis Air Force Base, NV: Air Force Fighter Weapons School.

Boyd, J. R. (1976). *Destruction and creation.* Fort Leavenworth, KS: US Army Command and General Staff College.

Boyd, J. R. (2018). *A discourse on winning and losing* (G. T. Hammond, Ed., Comp.). Maxwell Air Force Base, AL: Air University Press.

Boyes, B. (2018, April 6). *Implementing KM standard ISO 30401: Risks and opportunities.* RealKM. Retrieved December 11, 2021, from https://realkm.com/2018/04/06/implementing-km-standard-iso-30401-risks-and-opportunities/.

Brandes, S. D. (1976). *American welfare capitalism, 1880–1940.* Chicago, IL: University of Chicago Press.

Brien, R. H., & Stafford, J. E. (1968). Marketing information systems: A new dimension for marketing research. *Journal of Marketing, 32,* 19–23.

Bronk, R. (2009). *The romantic economist: imagination in economics* (Cambridge: CUP).

Brooking, A. (1996). *Intellectual capital* (London: International Thomson Business Press).

Brounstein, S. H. and Kamrass, M. eds. (1976). *Operations research in law enforcement, justice and societal security* (Lexington: DC Heath and Company).

Brown, J. S. and Duguid, P. (1998). Organizing knowledge. *California Management Review 40* (3): 90–111.

Brown, W. R. and Schaefermeyer, M. J. (1980). Progress in communication as a social science. In D. Nimmo (Ed.), *Communication Yearbook 4: An annual review published by the International Communication Association* (pp. 37–47). Piscataway, NJ: Transaction

BSI (2001). *PAS 2001:2001 Knowledge management.* London, England: BSI (British Standards Institute).

BSI (2003a). *Managing culture and knowledge: Guide to good practice* (British Standard No. PD 7501:2003). London, England: BSI (British Standards Institute).

BSI (2003b). *Guide to measurements in knowledge management: A guide to good practice* (British Standard No. PD 7502:2003). London, England: BSI (British Standards Institute).

BSI (2003c). *Introduction to knowledge management in construction* (British Standard No. PD 7503:2003). London, England: BSI (British Standards Institute).

BSI (2005a). *Knowledge management in the public sector: A guide to good practice* (British Standard No. PD 7504:2005). London, England: BSI (British Standards Institute).

BSI (2005b). *Skills for knowledge working: A guide to good practice* (British Standard No. PD 7505:2005).). London, England: BSI (British Standards Institute).

BSI (2005c). *Linking knowledge management with other organizational functions and disciplines: A guide to good practice* (British Standard No. PD 7506:2005). London, England: BSI (British Standards Institute).

Buchanan, S., & Gibb, F. (2008). The information audit: Theory versus practice. *International Journal of Information Management, 28*(3), 150–160.

Burford, S., & Ferguson, S. (2011). The adoption of knowledge management standards and frameworks in the Australian government sector. *Journal of Knowledge Management Practice, 12*(1), 1–12.

Burford, S., Kennedy, M., Ferguson, S., & Blackman, D. A. (2011). Discordant theories of strategic management and emergent practice in knowledge-intensive organizations. *Journal of Knowledge Management Practice, 12*(3),

Burk, C. F., & Horton, F. W. (1988). *Infomap: A complete guide to discovering corporate information resources*. Englewood Cliffs, NJ: Prentice Hall.

Burnett, S., Illingworth, L., & Webster, L. (2004). Knowledge auditing and mapping: A pragmatic approach. *Knowledge and Process Management, 11*(1), 25–37.

Burnett, V. (1961). Management's Tower of Babel. *Management Review, 50*, 4–11.

Burt, R. S. (2005). *Brokerage and closure: An introduction to social capital*. Oxford, England: Oxford University Press.

Callioni, P., Naismith, L., Halbwirth, S., Corcoran, C., Thomson, J., Hasan, H., & Handzic, M. (2004). KM standards: Developments in Australia. *Journal of Knowledge Management Research and Practice, 2*(1), 58–60.

Campbell, A. (1999). Tailored, not benchmarked: A fresh look at corporate planning. *Harvard Business Review, 77*(2), 41–50.

Cancer Genome Atlas Research Network. (2013). Integrated genomic characterization of endometrial carcinoma. *Nature, 500*, 1–7.

Canetti, E. (1962). *Crowds and power*. New York, NY: Viking Press.

Carnegie, D. (1936). *How to win friends and influence people*. New York, NY: Simon & Schuster.

Carpenter, S., & Rudge, S. (2003). A self-help approach to knowledge management benchmarking. *Journal of Knowledge Management, 7*(5), 82–95.

Čavalić, A., & Erkan, I. (2012, May 31–June 1). Knowledge maps and knowledge mapping: Literature review. In *Proceedings of the 3rd International Symposium on Sustainable Development* (pp. 373–380). Sarajevo, Bosnia and Herzegovina.

Cebrowski, A. K., & Garstka, J. J. (1998). Network-centric warfare: Its origin and future. *US Naval Institute Proceedings, 124*(1), 28–35.

CEN (2004). *CWA14924:2004: European guide to good practice in knowledge management.* Brussels: CEN (European Committee for Standardization).

Chambers, A., & Rand, G. (2010). *The operational auditing handbook: Auditing business and IT processes* (2nd ed.). Chichester, England: John Wiley & Sons.

Chandler Jr., A. D. (1977). *The visible hand: The managerial revolution in American business.* Cambridge, MA: Belknap Press.

Checkland, P. (1999). Systems thinking. In W. Currie & B. Galliers (Eds.), *Rethinking management information systems: An interdisciplinary perspective* (pp. 45–56). Oxford, England: Oxford University Press.

Checkland, P., & Poulter, J. (2007). *Learning for action: A short definitive account of soft systems methodology, and its use for practitioners, teachers and students.* Chichester, England: John Wiley & Sons.

Checkland, P., & Scholes, J. (1999). *Soft systems methodology in action.* Chichester, England: John Wiley & Sons.

Child, J., & Ihrig, M. (Eds.). (2013). *Knowledge, organization, and management: Building on the work of Max Boisot.* Oxford, England: Oxford University Press.

Choo, C. W., & Bontis, N. (Eds.). (2002). *The strategic management of intellectual capital and organizational knowledge.* Oxford, England: Oxford University Press.

Chua, A. (2002). Taxonomy of organisational knowledge. *Singapore Management Review, 24*(2), 69–76.

Cilliers, P. (2000). Knowledge, complexity, and understanding. *Emergence, 2*(4), 7–13.

Cissna, K. N., Eadie, W. F., & Hickson III, M. (2009). The development of applied communication research. In L. R. Frey & K. N. Cissna (Eds.), *Routledge handbook of applied communication research* (pp. 3–25). London, England: Routledge.

Clark, A. (1997). *Being there: Putting brain, body and world together again.* Cambridge, MA: MIT Press.

Collins, H. M. (1993). The structure of knowledge. *Social Research, 60*(1), 95–116.

Collins, H. M. (1997). Humans, machines, and the structure of knowledge. In R. L. Ruggles (Ed.), *Knowledge management tools* (pp. 145–163). Boston, MA: Butterworth Heinemann.

Collins, H. M. (2010). *Tacit and explicit knowledge.* Chicago, IL: University of Chicago Press.

Collis, D. (1996). Organizational capability as a source of profit. In B. Moingeon & A. Edmonson (Eds.), *Organizational learning and competitive advantage* (pp. 139–163). Thousand Oaks, CA: Sage.

Collison, C. J. (2018, January 4). *ISO 30401—KM standard draft available* [Online forum post]. SIKM Leaders Forum. Retrieved December 11, 2021, from https://sikm.groups.io/g/main/message/5541

Collison, C. J., Corney, P. J., & Eng, P. L. (2019). *The KM cookbook: Stories and strategies for organizations exploring knowledge management standard ISO 30401*. London, England: Facet.

Conklin, G. (Ed.). (1952). *Omnibus of science fiction*. New York, NY: Crown.

Connaghan, C. J. (1960). *An exploratory study of information needs of workers in an industrial organization* [Unpublished master's thesis]. University of British Columbia.

Cooperrider, D. L., Sorensen, P. F., Yaeger, T. F., & Whitney, D. (Eds.). (2001). *Appreciative inquiry: An emerging direction for organization development*. Champaign, IL: Stipes.

Corney, P. J., & McFarlane, K. (2018, September 25). *The new ISO standard for KM is coming*. Information Professional. Retrieved April 24, 2022, from https://www.cilip.org.uk/news/435197/The-new-ISO-Standard-for-KM-is-coming.htm

Crandall, B., Klein, G., & Hoffman, R. R. (2006). *Working minds: A practitioner's guide to cognitive task analysis*. Cambridge, MA: MIT Press.

Crane, L. (2016). *Knowledge and discourse matters: Relocating knowledge management's sphere of interest onto language*. Hoboken, NJ: John Wiley & Sons.

Crockett, M., & Foster, J. (2004). Using ISO 15489 as an audit tool. *Information Management Journal, 38*(4), 46–53.

Cronin, B. (Ed.). (1985). *Information management: From strategies to action*. London, England: Aslib.

Cross, R., & Parker, A. (2004). *The hidden power of social networks: Understanding how work really gets done in organizations*. Boston, MA: Harvard Business School Press.

Currie, W., & Galliers, B. (Eds.). (1999). *Rethinking management information systems: An interdisciplinary perspective*. Oxford, England: Oxford University Press.

Cyert, R. M., & March, J. G. (1963). *A behavioural theory of the firm*. Englewood Cliffs, NJ: Prentice Hall.

Daft, R. L., & Lewin, A. Y. (1990). Can organization studies begin to break out of the normal science straitjacket? An editorial essay. *Organization Science, 1*(1), 1–9.

Dahle, T. L. (1954). An objective and comparative study of five methods of transmitting information to business and industrial employees. *Communications Monographs, 21*(1), 21–28 (reprinted in W. C. Redding & G. A. Sanborn (Eds.), *Business and industrial communication: A source book* (pp. 310–322). New York, NY: Harper and Row.

Dattero, R., Galup, S. D., & Quan, J. J. (2007). The knowledge audit: Meta-matrix analysis. *Knowledge Management Research & Practice, 5*, 213–221.

Davenport, T. H. (1997). *Information ecology: Mastering the information and knowledge environment*. Oxford, England: Oxford University Press.

Davenport, T. H., & Prusak, L. (1998). *Working knowledge: How organizations manage what they know.* Boston, MA: Harvard Business School Press.

Davies, M. (2015). Knowledge—Explicit, implicit and tacit: Philosophical aspects. In J. D. Wright (Ed.), *International encyclopedia of social and behavioral sciences* (2nd ed., pp. 74–90). Oxford, England: Elsevier.

Davis, K. (1953). A method of studying communication patterns in organizations. *Personnel Psychology, 6,* 301–312.

Dean, A., & Kretschmer, M. (2007). Can ideas be capital? Factors of production in the postindustrial economy: A review and critique. *Academy of Management Review, 32*(2), 573–594.

DeLong, D. W. (2004). *Lost knowledge: Confronting the threat of an aging workforce.* Oxford, England: Oxford University Press.

Deming, W. E. (1982). *Out of the crisis.* Cambridge, MA: MIT Center for Advanced Educational Services.

Dennett, D. C. (1983). Styles of mental representation. *Proceedings of the Aristotelian Society, 83,* 213–226.

Derrida, J. (1981). *Dissemination.* London, England: Athlone Press.

Derry, G. M. (1967). Vital records programming. *Records Management Quarterly, 1*(4), 10–14.

DeWine, S., & James, A. C. (1988). Examining the communication audit assessment and modification. *Management Communication Quarterly, 2*(2), 144–169.

Dickson, G. W. (1981). Management information systems: Evolution and purpose. *Advances in Computers, 20,* 1–37.

Dieng-Kuntz, R., & Matta, N. (Eds.). (2002). *Knowledge management and organizational memories.* Boston, MA: Springer.

Dixon, N. M. (2000). *Common knowledge: How companies thrive by sharing what they know.* Boston, MA: Harvard Business School Press.

Dixon, N. M. (2018, February 16). The metaphor that leads organizations astray. *Conversation Matters.* Retrieved December 11, 2021, from https://www.nancydixonblog.com/2018/02/the-metaphor-that-leads-organizations-astray.html

Dockens, C. A. (1968). Records inventory and scheduling. *Records Management Quarterly, 2*(2), 21–24.

Douglas, M. (1986). *How institutions think.* Syracuse, NY: Syracuse University Press.

Dover, C. J. (1959). The three eras of management communication. *Journal of Communication, 9*(4), 168–172.

Dozier, D. M., & Hellweg, S. A. (1985, May 26). *A comparative analysis of internal communication and public relations audits* [Conference presentation]. Public Relations Special Interest Group, International Communication Association Annual Convention, Honolulu, HI, United States.

Druett, J. (2007). *Island of the lost: Shipwrecked at the edge of the world.* Chapel Hill, NC: Algonquin.

Dube, O. X. (2011). *Conducting a knowledge audit: The first step towards implementing a successful knowledge management initiative.* Saarbrücken, Germany: LAP Lambert Academic.

Dumay, J. C. (2010). A critical reflective discourse of an interventionist research project. *Qualitative Research in Accounting and Management, 7*(1), 46–70.

Durkheim, E. (1893). *De la division du travail social: Étude sur l'organization des societies supérieures.* Paris, France: Germer Bailliere.

Easterby-Smith, M., & Lyles, M. A. (Eds.). (2011). *Handbook of organizational learning and knowledge management* (2nd ed.). Chichester, England: John Wiley & Sons.

Eaton, J. J., & Bawden, D. (1991). What kind of resource is information? *International Journal of Information Management,* (11), 156–165.

Edelman, F. (1981). The management of information resources—A challenge for American business. *MIS Quarterly, 5*(1), 17–27.

Edvinsson, L., & Malone, M. S. (1997). *Intellectual capital: The proven way to establish your company's real value by measuring its hidden brainpower.* London, England: Piatkus.

Ellis, D., Barker, R., Potter, S., & Pridgeon, C. (1993). Information audits, communication audits and information mapping: A review and survey. *International Journal of Information Management, 13*(2), 134–151.

Eng, P. L., & Corney, P. J. (2017). *Navigating the minefield: A practical KM companion.* Milwaukee, WI: American Society for Quality Press.

Eppler, M. J. (2008). A process-based classification of knowledge maps and application examples. *Knowledge and Process Management, 15*(1), 59–71.

Ermine, J.-L., Boughzala, I., & Tounkara, T. (2006). Critical knowledge map as a decision tool for knowledge transfer actions. *Electronic Journal of Knowledge Management, 4*(2), 129–140.

Fægri, T. E., Dybå, T., & Dingsøyr, T. (2010). Introducing knowledge redundancy practice in software development: Experiences with job rotation in support work. *Information and Software Technology, 52*(10), 1118–1132.

Faris, R. E. L. (1947). Interaction of generations and family stability. *American Sociological Review, 12*(2), 159–164.

Farmer, T. (2002). *BSI position statement on standardization within knowledge management.* London, England: British Standards Institute.

Feather, J., & Sturges, P. (Eds.). (2003). *International encyclopedia of library and information science* (2nd ed.). London, England: Routledge.

Ferguson, S. (2006). AS 5037–2005: Knowledge management blueprint for Australian organizations? *Australian Library Journal, 55*(3), 196–209.

Ferguson, S., & Burford, S. (2009). Policies, standards and frameworks for managing knowledge—Exploring the use of the Australian Standard. In F. Papandrea & M. Armstrong (Eds.), *Record of the Communications Policy and Research Forum 2009* (pp. 47–55). Sydney, Australia: Network Insight.

Feynman, R. P. (1992). *Surely you're joking Mr Feynman! Adventures of a curious character as told to Ralph Leighton*. London, England: Vintage.

Firestone, J. M., & McElroy, M. W. (2003). *Key issues in the new knowledge management*. Amsterdam, Netherlands: Butterworth-Heinemann.

Foss, N. (Ed.). (1997). *Resources, firms and strategies: A reader in the resource-based perspective*. New York, NY: Oxford University Press.

Frank, R. (1972). Some uses of paronomasia in Old English scriptural verse. *Speculum, 47*(2), 207–226.

Frappaolo, C. (2006). *Knowledge management* (2nd ed.). Chichester, England: Capstone.

Fraser, R. C. (1982). Medical audit in general practice. *Trainee, 2*, 113–115.

Frazer, J. G. (1922). *The golden bough: A study in magic and religion*. London, England: Macmillan.

Frey, L. R., & Cissna, K. N. (Eds.). (2009). *Routledge handbook of applied communication research*. London, England: Routledge.

Fry, I. (2015, October 14). *Knowledge management and ISO 9001:2015*. RealKM. Retrieved December 11, 2021, from https://realkm.com/2015/10/14/knowledge-management-and-iso-90012015/

Gamble, P. R., & Blackwell, J. (2001). *Knowledge management: A state of the art guide*. London, England: Kogan Page.

Ganasan, A. B., & Dominic, D. D. (2011, November 23). *Knowledge audit made comprehensive thru 6 stages* [Conference presentation]. IEEE Research and Innovation in Information Systems International Conference.

Garfield, S. (2015, July 27). *Are you certifiable in knowledge management?* Medium. Retrieved December 11, 2021, from https://medium.com/@stangarfield/are-you-certifiable-in-knowledge-management-b4ee424ee632.

Gerstner, L. V. (2002). *Who says elephants can't dance? Inside IBM's historic turnaround*. New York, NY: HarperCollins.

Gherardi, S. (2006). *Organizational knowledge: The texture of workplace learning*. Malden, MA: Blackwell.

Gibbert, M., & Durand, M. (Eds.). (2007). *Strategic networks: Learning to compete*. Oxford, England: Blackwell.

Gibson, C. F., & Nolan, R. L. (1974). Managing the four stages of EDP growth. *Harvard Business Review*, January–February, 76–87.

Girard, J., & Girard, J. (2015). Defining knowledge management: Toward an applied compendium. *Online Journal of Applied Knowledge Management, 3*(1), 1–20.

Goldhaber, G. M. (1974). *Organizational communication*. Dubuque, IA: W. C. Brown.

Goldhaber, G. M. (1976, June). *The ICA communication audit: Rationale and development* [Conference presentation]. C.A.P. Convention, Kobe, Japan (compiled for the *Journal of the Communication Association of the Pacific*).

Goldhaber, G. M., Dennis III, H. S., Richetto, G. M., & Wiio, O. A. (1979). *Information strategies: new pathways to corporate power* (Englewood Cliffs, NJ: Prentice Hall).

Goldhaber, G. M., & Krivonos, P. (1977). The ICA communication audit: Process, status, critique. *Journal of Business Communication, 15*(1), 42–55.

Goldhaber, G. M., & Rogers, D. (1979). *Auditing organizational communication systems: The ICA communication audit*. Dubuque, IA: Kendall Hunt.

Gourlay, S. (2006). Conceptualizing knowledge creation: A critique of Nonaka's theory. *Journal of Management Studies, 43*(7), 1415–1436.

Gourova, E., Antonova, A., & Todorova, Y. (2009). Knowledge audit concepts, processes and practice. *WSEAS Transactions on Business and Economics, 12*(6), 605–619.

Graef, J. L. (1998). Getting the most from R&D information services. *Research Technology Management, 41*(4), 44–47.

Grant, K. A. (2007). Tacit knowledge revisited: We can still learn from Polanyi. *Electronic Journal of Knowledge Management, 5*(2), 173–180.

Grant, K. A., & Qureshi, U. (2006). *Knowledge management systems: Why so many failures?* [Conference presentation]. IEEE Innovations in Information Technology Conference, Dubai, United Arab Emirates.

Grant, R. M. (1996). Toward a knowledge-based theory of the firm. *Strategic Management Journal, 17*, 109–122.

Grant, R. M. (2002). The knowledge-based view of the firm. In C. W. Choo & N. Bontis (Eds.), *The strategic management of intellectual capital and organizational knowledge* (pp. 133–148). Oxford, England: Oxford University Press.

Graves, R. (1957). *Goodbye to all that*. London, England: Cassell.

Grey, D. (2004, August 13). *Posting patterns*. Knowledge at Work. Retrieved December 11, 2021, from http://denham.typepad.com/km/2004/08/posting_pattern.html.

Griffiths, D. (2011, August 7). The problem with "certified" KM training. *The knowledgecore's Blog*. Retrieved December 11, 2021, from https://theknowledgecore.wordpress.com/2011/08/07/the -problem-with-certified-km-training/.

Griffiths, D. (2012, July 7). The Borg have arrived! International Knowledge Management Standards and Accreditation Association. *The knowledgecore's Blog*. Retrieved December 11, 2021, from https://theknowledgecore.wordpress.com/2012/07/07/the-borg-have-arrived-international -knowledge-management-standards-and-accreditation-association/.

Griffiths, D. (2018, December 18). *Knowledge Management ISO 30401 (something rotten in the state of Denmark)*. K3-Cubed. Retrieved December 11, 2021, from https://web.archive.org/web/20180303062437/https://k3cubed.com/2017/12/18/knowledge-management-iso-30401-something-rotten-in-the-state-of-denmark/.

Griffiths, D., & Evans, P. (2010). Scaling the fractal plain: A general view of knowledge management. *International Journal of Knowledge and Systems Science, 1*(2), 1–14.

Griffiths, P. (2010). Where next for the information audit? *Business Information Review, 27*(4), 216–244.

Griffiths, P. (2012). Information audit: Towards common standards and methodology. *Business Information Review, 29*(1), 39–51.

Gruber, T. (1983). The operational audit: An integrated approach. *Internal Auditor, 40*(4), 39–41.

Gruenfeld, D. H., & Fan, E. T. (1999). What newcomers see and what oldtimers say: Discontinuities in knowledge exchange. In L. L. Thompson, J. M. Levine, & D. M. Messick (Eds.), *Shared cognition in organizations: The management of knowledge* (pp. 245–265). Mahwah, NJ: Lawrence Erlbaum.

Guimaraes, T., & Bond, W. (1996). Empirically assessing the impact of business process reengineering on manufacturing firms. *Gestão and Producão, 3*(1), 8–32.

Guin, W. (1952). Trigger tide. In G. Conklin (Ed.), *Omnibus of science fiction* (pp. 263–273). New York, NY: Crown.

Guthrie, J., Ricceri, F., & Dumay, J. (2012). Reflections and projections: A decade of intellectual capital accounting research. *British Accounting Review, 44*(2), 68–82.

Haas, G., & Zagat, H. (1957). Communicating on labor relations: A survey of company practices. *Personnel, 34*, 84–89.

Hackman, J. R. (2002). New rules for team building. *Optimize*, (July), 50–62.

Halbwirth, S., & Olsson, M. (2007). Working in parallel: Themes in knowledge management and information behavior. In S. Hawamdeh (Ed.), *Creating collaborative advantage through knowledge and innovation* (pp. 69–87). Singapore: World Scientific.

Hall, R., & Andriani, P. (1998). Analysing intangible resources and managing knowledge in a supply chain context. *European Management Journal, 16*(6), 685–697.

Hambelton, W. A. (1969). Vital records protection. *Records Management Quarterly, 3*(2), 27–31.

Handa, P., Pagani, J., & Bedford, D. (2019). *Knowledge assets and knowledge audits*. Bingley, England: Emerald.

Handzic, M., & Hasan, H. (2003). Continuing the knowledge management journey. In H. Hasan & M. Handzic (Eds.), *Australian studies in knowledge management* (pp. 522–555). Wollongong, Australia: University of Wollongong Press.

Handzic, M., Lagumdzija, A., & Celjo, A. (2008). Auditing knowledge management practices, a model and application. *Knowledge Management Research & Practice, 6*, 90–99.

Handzic, M., & Zhou, A. Z. (2005). *Knowledge management: An integrative approach.* Oxford, England: Chandos.

Hardesty, L. (2011, July/August). *The original absent-minded professor.* MIT Technology Review. Retrieved December 11, 2021, from https://www.technologyreview.com/s/424363/the-original -absent-minded-professor/

Hardin, R. (2009). *How do you know? The economics of ordinary knowledge.* Princeton, NJ: Princeton University Press.

Hargie, O., & Tourish, D. (Eds.). (2000). *Handbook of communication audits for organizations.* London, England: Routledge.

Hargie, O., & Tourish, D. (Eds.). (2009). *Auditing organizational communication: A handbook of research, theory and practice* (2nd ed.). London, England: Routledge.

Harorimana, D. (Ed.). (2009). *Cultural implications of knowledge sharing, management and transfer: Identifying competitive advantage.* New York, NY: IGI Global.

Harris, D. (Ed.). (1996). *Engineering psychology and cognitive ergonomics: Job design and product design.* Aldershot, England: Ashgate.

Hasan, H. (2004). Bottling fog: Conjuring up the Australian KM Standard. In *Proceedings of ACKMIDS 2004 (Australian Conference for Knowledge Management and Intelligent Decision Support): Organizational challenges for knowledge management, Melbourne, VIC, 29–30 November 2004* (pp. 100–112). Melbourne, Australia: Australian Scholarly.

Hasan, H. (2014, January 21). *ISO International Organization for Standards considering a standard for KM* [Online forum post]. ActKM discussion list (personal archive no longer available online).

Hasan, H., & Handzic, M. (Eds.). (2003). *Australian studies in knowledge management.* Wollongong, Australia: University of Wollongong Press.

Hasanali, F., Haytmanek, A., Leavitt, P., Lemons, D., & Newhouse, B. (2003). *Capturing critical knowledge from a shifting work force.* Houston, TX: American Productivity and Quality Center.

Hawamdeh, S. (Ed.). (2007). *Creating collaborative advantage through knowledge and innovation.* Singapore: World Scientific.

Heath, R. L. (Ed.). (2000). *Handbook of public relations.* Thousand Oaks, CA: Sage.

Hecker, A. (2012). Knowledge beyond the individual? Making sense of a notion of collective knowledge in organization theory. *Organization Studies, 33*(3), 423–445.

Heinlein, R. A. (1967). *The past through tomorrow.* New York, NY: G. P. Putnam's Sons.

Heisig, P. (2009). Harmonisation of knowledge management—Comparing 160 KM frameworks around the globe. *Journal of Knowledge Management, 13*(4), 4–31.

Helmreich, R. L., & Foushee, H. C. (2010). Why CRM? Empirical and theoretical bases of human factors training. In B. G. Kanki, R. L. Helmreich, & J. Anca (Eds.), *Crew resource management* (2nd ed., pp. 4–55). San Diego, CA: Academic Press.

Henczel, S. (2000). The information audit as a first step towards effective knowledge management: An opportunity for the special librarian. *Inspel, 34*(3/4), 210–226.

Henczel, S. (2001). *The information audit: A practical guide.* Munich, Germany: K. G. Saur.

Henderson, H. L. (1980). Cost effective information provision and the role for the information audit. *Information Management, 1*(4), 7–9.

Heywood, J. (1906). *The proverbs, epigrams, and miscellanies of John Heywood* (J. S. Farmer, Ed.). London, England: Early English Drama Society.

Hislop, D. (2013). *Knowledge management in organizations: A critical introduction.* (3rd ed.). Oxford, England: Oxford University Press.

Hislop, D., Murray, P. A., Shrestha, A., Syed, J., & Mouzughi, Y. (2018). Knowledge management: (Potential) future research directions. In J. Syed, P. A. Murray, D. Hislop, & Y. Mouzughi (Eds.), *The Palgrave handbook of knowledge management* (pp. 691–703). Cham, Switzerland: Palgrave Macmillan.

Hodges, D. C. (2000). *Class politics in the information age.* Urbana, IL: University of Illinois Press.

Holloway, J. L. (1980). *Rescue mission report.* Washington, DC: US Department of Defense, Joint Chiefs of Staff.

Holsapple, C. W. (Ed.). (2003). *Handbook on knowledge management: Knowledge directions* (Vol. 2). Berlin, Germany: Springer-Verlag.

Hong, S. (2012, January 10). *Minister: It's a flood, not ponding.* Asiaone News. Retrieved December 11, 2021, from https://www.asiaone.com/News/Latest+News/Singapore/Story/A1Story20120110-320827.html

Horton, F. W. (1974). *How to harness information resources: A systems approach.* Cleveland, OH: Association for Systems Management.

Horton, F. W. (1979). *Information resources management: Concept and cases.* Cleveland, OH: Association for Systems Management.

Horton, F. W., & Marchand, D. A. (1982). *Information management in public administration.* Arlington, VA: Information Resources Press.

Horvath, J. A. (2000). Working with tacit knowledge. In J. A. Woods & J. Cortada (Eds.), *The knowledge management yearbook, 2000–2001* (pp. 34–51). Woburn, CA: Butterworth-Heinemann.

Hsiao, R-L., Tsai, S. D. H., & Lee, C-F. (2006). The problems of embeddedness: Knowledge transfer, coordination and reuse in information systems. *Organization Studies, 27*(9), 1289–317.

Hsu, I-C., & Sabherwal, R. (2011). From intellectual capital to firm performance: The mediating role of knowledge management capabilities. *IEEE Transactions on Engineering Management, 58*(4), 626–642.

Hudson, W. J. (1993). *Intellectual capital: How to build it, enhance it, use it.* New York, NY: John Wiley & Sons.

Hutton, R. J. B., & Militello, L. G. (1996). Applied cognitive task analysis (ACTA): A practitioner's window into skilled decision making. In D. Harris (Ed.), *Engineering psychology and cognitive ergonomics: Job design and product design* (pp. 17–23). Aldershot, England: Ashgate.

Hylton, A. (2004). *The knowledge audit is first and foremost an audit* [White paper]. Retrieved April 24, 2022, from http://hosteddocs.ittoolbox.com/KAuditpaper.pdf.

IASB. (2007, February). *Information for observers: SAC Meeting. Conceptual framework phase B: Elements: Definition of an asset* (Agenda Paper 4A). Retrieved April 24, 2022, from downloaded from https://www.ifrs.org/content/dam/ifrs/meetings/2007/february/sac/conceptual-framework/ap4a-phase-b.pdf.

ICA. (2021). *About ICA*. Retrieved December 11, 2021, from https://www.icahdq.org/page/History

ICAEW. (2006). *Principles-based auditing standards*. London, England: Institute of Chartered Accountants in England and Wales.

IFRS. (2016). *Testing the proposed asset and liability definitions—Illustrative examples* [White paper]. IASB Meeting. Retrieved April 24, 2022, from https://www.ifrs.org/content/dam/ifrs/meetings/2016/october/iasb/conceptual-framework/ap10c-testing-proposed-asset-liability-definitions-illustrative-examples.pdf.

IFRS. (2019). *Documentation labels and implementation notes in Excel*. Taxonomy 2019. Retrieved April 24, 2022, from https://www.ifrs.org/content/dam/ifrs/standards/taxonomy/2019/documentation-labels-and-implementation-notes-in-excel.zip.

Ihrig, M., & MacMillan, I. (2013). The strategic management of knowledge. In J. Child & M. Ihrig (Eds.), *Knowledge, organization, and management: Building on the work of Max Boisot* (pp. 129–139). Oxford, England: Oxford University Press.

IKMSAA. (2018). Retrieved May 24, 2022, from https://www.linkedin.com/groups/4493906/ [closed group].

Illich, I. (1981). *Shadow work*. Boston, MA: Marion Boyars.

Inside Tucson Business. (2003, September 25). *Court notices*. Retrieved December 11, 2021, from https://www.insidetucsonbusiness.com/greenpoint-llc-vs-jorge-ramirez-diann-ramirez/article_40d1a8fe-9256-51cd-a9c0-c9cdde2bad8b.html.

Institute of Internal Auditors. (2021). *Elevating impact!* International Professional Practices Framework. Retrieved December 11, 2021, from https://na.theiia.org/standards-guidance/mandatory-guidance/Pages/Definition-of-Internal-Auditing.aspx

Isaacs, W. (1999). *Dialogue and the art of thinking together: A pioneering approach to communicating in business and in life*. New York, NY: Doubleday.

ISO. (2013). *New work item proposal: Knowledge management systems requirements*. Retrieved December 11, 2021, from https://share.ansi.org/shared%20documents/News%20and%20Publications/Links%20Within%20Stories/ISO%20NWIP%20-%20Knowledge%20Management%20Systems.pdf

ISO (2014). *Asset management: Overview, principles and terminology* (ISO Standard No. 55000:2014). Geneva, Switzerland: International Organization for Standardization.

ISO (2015). *ISO/IEC directives, part 1 consolidated ISO supplement—Procedures specific to ISO 6th edition*. Geneva, Switzerland: International Organization for Standardization.

ISO (2018a). *Guidelines for auditing management systems* (ISO Standard No. 19011:2018(E). Geneva, Switzerland: International Organization for Standardization.

ISO (2018b). *Knowledge management systems—Requirements* (ISO Standard No. 30401:2018). Geneva, Switzerland: International Organization for Standardization.

Itami, H. (1987). *Mobilizing invisible assets*. Cambridge, MA: Harvard University Press.

Jablin, F. M. (1980). Organizational communication theory and research: An overview of communication climate and network research. In D. Nimmo (Ed.), *Communication Yearbook 4: An annual review published by the International Communication Association* (pp. 327–347). Piscataway, NJ: Transaction.

Jacobson, E. W., & Seashore, S. E. (1951). Communication practices in complex organizations. *Journal of Social Issues, 7*, 28–40.

Jacques, R. (2000). Theorising knowledge as work: The need for a "knowledge theory of value." In C. Prichard, R. Hull, M. Chumer, & H. Willmott (Eds.), *Managing knowledge: Critical investigations of work and learning* (pp. 199–215). Basingstoke, England: Macmillan Press.

Jennex, M. E. (2006). Why we can't return to the Moon: The need for knowledge management. Editorial preface. *International Journal of Knowledge Management, 2*(1), i–iv.

Johannesen, L. (2008). Maintaining common ground: An analysis of cooperative communication in the operating room. In C. P. Nemeth (Ed.), *Improving healthcare team communication: Building on lessons from aviation and aerospace* (pp. 179–203). Aldershot, England: Ashgate.

Kamau, C. (2009). Strategising impression management in corporations: Cultural knowledge as capital. In D. Harorimana (Ed.), *Cultural implications of knowledge sharing, management and transfer: Identifying competitive advantage* (pp. 60–83). New York, NY: IGI Global.

Kanki, B. G., Helmreich, R. L., & Anca, J. (Eds.). (2010). *Crew resource management* (2nd ed.). San Diego, CA: Academic Press.

Kasper, H., Lehrer, M., Mühlbacher, J., & Müller, B. (2010). Thinning knowledge: An interpretive field study of knowledge-sharing practices of firms in three multinational contexts. *Journal of Management Inquiry, 19*(4), 367–381.

Kazoleas, D., & Wright, A. (2000). Improving corporate and organization communications: A new look at developing and implementing the communication audit. In R. L. Heath (Ed.), *Handbook of public relations* (pp. 471–478). Thousand Oaks, CA: Sage.

Keller, S. D. (2009). *The development of Shakespeare's rhetoric: A study of nine plays*. Tübingen, Germany: Francke Verlag.

Kendrick, J. W. (1961). Some theoretical aspects of capital measurement. *American Economic Review, 51*(2), 102–111.

Kerrigan, S., Heenan, C., Wang, H., Law, K. H., & Wiederhold, G. (2003, May 18–21). *Regulatory information management and compliance assistance* [Conference presentation]. National Conference on Digital Government Research, Boston, MA, United States.

Kim, W. C., & Mauborgne, R. (2015). *Blue ocean strategy: How to create uncontested market space and make the competition irrelevant* (Exp. ed.). Cambridge, MA: Harvard Business Review Press.

King, J. L., & Kraemer, K. L. (1988). Information resource management: Is it sensible and can it work? *Information & Management, 15*(1), 7–14.

Kish, J. L., & Morris, J. (1966). *Microfilming in business*. New York, NY: Ronald Press.Company

Klein, G. (1995). The value added by cognitive task analysis. *Proceedings of the Human Factors and Ergonomics Society Annual Meeting, 39*(9), 530–533.

Klein, G. (1998). *Sources of power: How people make decisions*. Cambridge, MA: MIT Press.

Klein, G. (2003). *Intuition at work: Why developing your gut instincts will make you better at what you do*. New York, NY: Currency Doubleday.

Klein, G. (2009). *Streetlights and shadows: Searching for the keys to adaptive decision making*. Cambridge, MA: MIT Press.

Klein, G. (2013). *Seeing what others don't: The remarkable ways we gain insights*. New York, NY: PublicAffairs.

Kling, R. (Ed.). (1996). *Computerization and controversy: Value conflicts and social choices* (2nd ed.). San Diego, CA: Academic Press.

KMCI. (2003, April 28). *KMCI position statement on KM standards and "certification" programs*. Retrieved December 11, 2021, from http://www.kmci.org/media/KMCI_Position_Statement .pdf.

Kmia, O. (2018, October 19). *Why Kodak died and Fujifilm thrived: A tale of two film companies*. PetaPixel. Retrieved December 11, 2021, from https://petapixel.com/2018/10/19/why-kodak-died -and-fujifilm-thrived-a-tale-of-two-film-companies/.

Knechel, W. R. (2013). Do auditing standards matter? *Current Issues in Auditing, 7*(2), A1–16.

Kogut, B., & Zander, U. (1993). Knowledge of the firm and the evolutionary theory of the multinational corporation. *Journal of International Business Studies, 24*(4), 625–645.

Kogut, B., & Zander, U. (1997). Knowledge of the firm, combinative capabilities, and the replication of technology. In N. Foss (Ed.), *Resources, firms and strategies: A reader in the resource-based perspective* (pp. 306–326). New York, NY: Oxford University Press.

Kolata, G. (2013, May 1). Cancers share gene patterns, studies affirm. *The New York Times*.

Komori, S. (2015). *Innovating out of crisis: How Fujifilm survived (and thrived) as its core business was vanishing*. Berkeley, CA: Stone Bridge Press.

Koontz, H., O'Donnell, C., & Weihrich, H. (1976). *Management* (8th ed.). Singapore: McGraw Hill.

Koulikov, M. (2011). Emerging problems in knowledge sharing and the three new ethics of knowledge transfer. *Knowledge Management and E-Learning, 3*(2), 237–250.

Krackhardt, D. (1992). The strength of strong ties: The importance of *philos* in organizations. In N. Nohria & R. G. Eccles (Eds.), *Networks and organizations: Structure, form, and action* (pp. 216–239). Cambridge, MA: Harvard Business School Press.

Kreps, G. L. (1980). A field experimental test and revaluation of Weick's model of organizing. In D. Nimmo (Ed.), *Communication Yearbook 4: An annual review published by the International Communication Association* (pp. 389–398). Piscataway, NJ: Transaction.

Kurtz, C. F., & Snowden, D. J. (2007). Bramble bushes in a thicket: Narrative and the intangibles of learning networks. In M. Gibbert & M. Durand (Eds.), *Strategic networks: Learning to compete* (pp. 121–150). Oxford, England: Blackwell.

Lakoff, G., & Johnson, M. (1980). *Metaphors we live by*. Chicago, IL: University of Chicago Press.

Lambe, P. (2005). Money, testosterone and knowledge management. *Straits Knowledge*. Retrieved December 11, 2021, from http://www.straitsknowledge.com/images/gallery/blog/Money_testos terone_and_km.pdf

Lambe, P. (2006, June 15). *Why KM is hard to do: Infrastructure, KM, and implementing change*. Green Chameleon. Retrieved December 11, 2021, from http://www.greenchameleon.com /uploads/Why_KM_is_hard_to_do.pdf

Lambe, P. (2007). *Organising knowledge: Taxonomies, knowledge and organization effectiveness*. Oxford, England: Chandos.

Lambe, P. (2011a). The unacknowledged parentage of knowledge management. *Journal of Knowledge Management, 15*(2), 175–197.

Lambe, P. (2011b, October 27–28). *The three tribes: Knowledge management, learning and intellectual capital—Towards a common agenda* [Conference presentation]. 8th International Conference on Knowledge Management, Intellectual Capital and Organizational Learning, Bangkok, Thailand.

Lambe, P. (2014). From the editor. Knowledge management: Connecting theory and practice [Special issue]. *Journal of Entrepreneurship, Management and Innovation, 10*(1), 3–5.

Lambe, P. (2017). Knowledge audits in practice: Report on a global survey of perceptions and experience. *Green Chameleon*. Retrieved December 11, 2021, from http://www.greenchameleon .com/gc/blog_detail/knowledge_audits_in_practice_report_on_global_survey

Lambe, P. (2018, January 4). *ISO 30401—KM standard draft available* [Online forum post]. SIKM Leaders Forum. Retrieved December 11, 2021, from https://sikm.groups.io/g/main/message/5544

Lambe, P., & Tan, E. (2008). *KM approaches methods and tools: A guidebook*. Singapore: Straits Knowledge.

Lauer, T. W., & Tanniru, M. (2001). Knowledge management audit—A methodology and case study. *Australasian Journal of Information Systems, 9*(1), 23–41.

Leahy, E. J. (1949). Modern records management. *American Archivist, 12*(3), 231–242.

Leavitt, H. J. (1951). Some effects of certain communication patterns on group performance. *Journal of Abnormal and Social Psychology, 46*, 38–50.

Leavitt, H. J., & Whisler, T. L. (1958). Management in the 1980's. *Harvard Business Review, 36*(6), 41–48.

Lee, A. (2017, 26 June) From braille to Be My Eyes – there's a revolution happening in tech for the blind. *Guardian.*

Lee, R. W. B., Yip, J. Y. T., & Shek, V. W. Y. (2021). *Knowledge risk and its mitigation: Practices and cases.* Bingley, England: Emerald.

Lei, Y. (2005). *The significance of situated context: Technology adaptation as an occasion of knowledge transfer* [Unpublished master's thesis]. National University of Singapore.

Lembcke, P. A. (1956). Medical auditing by scientific methods, illustrated by major female pelvic surgery. *Journal of the American Medical Association, 162*, 646–655.

Leonard, D., & Sensiper, S. (1998). The role of tacit knowledge in group innovation. *California Management Review, 40*(3), 112–132.

Leonard, D., Swap, W., & Barton, G. (2015). *Critical knowledge transfer: Tools for managing your company's deep smarts.* Boston, MA: Harvard Business Review Press.

Leonard, J. O. (1971). *A study of records management as an opportunity for information and cost controls* [Unpublished master's thesis]. Fairleigh Dickinson University.

Leonard-Barton, D. (1992). Core capabilities and core rigidities: A paradox in managing new product development. *Strategic Management Journal, 13*(Summer), 111–125.

Lev, B. (2001). *Intangibles: Management, measurement, and reporting.* Washington, DC: Brookings Institution Press.

Levantakis, T., Helms, R., & Spruit, M. (2008). Developing a reference method for knowledge auditing. In T. Yamaguchi (Ed.), *Practical aspects of knowledge management: 7th International Conference, PAKM 2008, Yokohama, Japan* (pp. 147–159). Berlin, Germany: Springer Verlag.

Levin, B. (2008, August). *Thinking about knowledge mobilization* [White paper]. Canadian Council on Learning and the Social Sciences and Humanities Research Council of Canada. Retrieved December 11, 2021, from http://en.copian.ca/library/research/ccl/knowledge_mobilization/knowledge_mobilization.pdf

Liebowitz, J., Rubenstein-Montano, B., McCaw, D., Buchwalter, J., Browning, C., Newman, B., & Rebeck, K. (2000). The knowledge audit. *Knowledge and Process Management, 7*(1), 3–10.

Lindsay, D. (2018). What progress on knowledge management systems—Requirements (BS ISO 30401). *K & IM Refer, 34*(1). Retrieved December 11, 2021, from https://referisg.wordpress.com/2018/03/28/what-progress-on-knowledge-management-systems-requirements-bs-iso-30401/

Lindstrom, L. (1990). Knowledge of cargo, knowledge of cult: Truth and power on Tanna, Vanuatu. In G. W. Trompf (Ed.), *Cargo cults and millenarian movements* (pp. 239–261). Berlin, Germany: Mouton De Gruyter.

Linger, H., Burstein, F., & Hasan H. (2005). Articulating knowledge work: The contributions of activity theory and task-based knowledge management. In G. Whymark & H. Hasan, *Activity as the focus of information systems research* (pp. 71–90). Eveleigh, New South Wales: Knowledge Creation Press.

Linstone, H. A., & Turoff, M. (1975). *The Delphi method: Techniques and applications.* Reading, MA: Addison-Wesley.

Lippman, S. A., & Rumelt, R. P. (1982). Uncertain imitability: An analysis of interfirm differences in efficiency under competition. *Bell Journal of Economics, 13*, 418–438.

Lis, A. (2014). Knowledge creation and conversion in military organizations: How the SECI model is applied within armed forces. *Journal of Entrepreneurship, Management and Innovation, 10*(1), 57–78.

Liyanage, S., & Jones, A. J. (2002). *Investing in knowledge capital: Management imperatives.* Singapore: Singapore Institute of Management.

Loughran, M. (2010). *Auditing for dummies.* Hoboken, NJ: John Wiley & Sons.

Loxton, M. H. (2012, July 4). *New LinkedIn KM group for standards & accreditation* [Online forum post]. SIKM Leaders Forum. Retrieved December 11, 2021, from https://sikm.groups.io/g/main/message/3120

Loxton, M. H. (2013a). A simplified integrated critical activity-based knowledge audit template. *Knowledge Management Research & Practice, 12*(2), 236–238.

Loxton, M. H. (2013b). *Knowledge auditing: An activity-based method for organizational success.* London, England: Ark Group.

MacGregor, D. (1960). *The human side of enterprise.* New York, NY: McGraw Hill.

Machlup, F. (1980). *Knowledge: Its creation, distribution, and economic significance: Knowledge and knowledge production* (Vol. 1). Princeton, NJ: Princeton University Press.

Machlup, F. (1984). *Knowledge: Its creation, distribution, and economic significance: The economics of information and human capital* (Vol. 3). Princeton, NJ: Princeton University Press.

Maier, R., & Remus, U. (2003). Implementing process-oriented knowledge management strategies. *Journal of Knowledge Management, 7*(4), 62–74.

Malhotra, Y. (Ed.). (2001) *Knowledge management and business model innovation.* Hershey, PA: Idea Group Publishing.

March, J. G., & Simon, H. A. (1958). *Organizations.* New York, NY: John Wiley & Sons.

Marchand, D. A., & Horton, F. W. (1986). *Infotrends: Profiting from your information resources.* New York, NY: John Wiley & Sons.

Marchand, D. A., Kettinger, W. J., & Rollins, J. D. (2001). *Making the invisible visible: How companies win with the right information, people and IT*. Chichester, England: John Wiley & Sons.

Marschak, J. (1968). Economics of inquiring, communicating, deciding. *American Economic Review, 58*(2), 1–18.

Martin de Holan, P. (2011). Organizational forgetting, unlearning and memory systems. *Journal of Management Inquiry, 20*(3), 302–304.

Martin de Holan, P., & Phillips, N. (2004). Remembrance of things past? The dynamics of organizational forgetting. *Management Science, 50*(11), 1603–1613.

Martinsons, M. G. (1988). Towards a tenable technology strategy. *Journal of Technology Management, 15*, 131–140.

Matta, N., Ermine, J. L., Aubertin, G., & Trivin, J-Y. (2002). Knowledge capitalization with a knowledge engineering approach: The MASK method. In R. Dieng-Kuntz & N. Matta, (Eds.), *Knowledge management and organizational memories* (pp. 17–28). Boston, MA: Springer.

Maximo, E. Z., Pereira, R., Malvestiti, R., & de Souza, J. A. (2020). ISO 30401: The standardization of knowledge. *International Journal of Development Research, 10*(6), 37155–37159.

Mayo, E. (1933). *The human problems of an industrial civilization*. New York, NY: Macmillan.

McCann, C., & Pigeau, R. (Eds.). (2000). *The human in command: Exploring the modern military experience*. Boston, MA: Springer.

McConnell, C., Brue, S., & Flynn, S. (2015). *Economics: Principles, problems, and policies* (20th ed.). New York, NY: McGraw Hill.

McDonough, A. (1963). *Information economics and management systems*. New York, NY: McGraw Hill.

McDowall, P. (2014). The rise and fall of exemplary practice in government: A case study of the learning and knowledge management program in the Treasury Board of Canada Secretariat (2000–2006). In L. Slater (Ed.), *Gaining buy-in for KM* (pp. 59–71). London, England: Ark Group.

McElroy, M. W. (2001). *KMCI issues statement on certification standards and accreditation*. Knowledge Management Consortium International. Retrieved December 11, 2021, from https://web
.archive.org/web/20021012223506/http://www.kmci.org:80/AboutUs/PressReleases/07-19
-01_cert_accred.htm.

Mentzas, G., Apostolou, D., Abecker, A., & Young, R. (2003). *Knowledge asset management: Beyond the process-centred and product-centred approaches*. London, England: Springer-Verlag.

Merali, Y. (2000). The organic metaphor in knowledge management. *Emergence, 2*(4), 14–22.

Mercer, P. (2007, February 17). *Cargo cult lives on in South Pacific*. BBC News. Retrieved December 11, 2021, from http://news.bbc.co.uk/2/hi/asia-pacific/6370991.stm

Merton, R. K. (1965). *On the shoulders of giants: A Shandean postscript*. New York, NY: Free Press.

Meyer, J. W., & Rowan, B. (1977). Institutionalized organizations: Formal structure as myth and ceremony. *American Journal of Sociology, 83*(2), 340–363.

Milton, N. (2015a, October 25). *Is it time for a knowledge management certification standard?* Knoco Stories. Retrieved December 11, 2021, from http://www.nickmilton.com/2015/10/is-it-time-for -knowledge-management.html

Milton, N. (2015b, November 6). *Is knowledge management certification counter-productive?* Knoco Stories. Retrieved December 11, 2021, from http://www.nickmilton.com/2015/11/is-certification -counter-productive.html

Milton, N., & Lambe, P. (2020). *The knowledge manager's handbook: A step by step guide to embedding effective knowledge management in your organization* (2nd ed.). London, England: Kogan Page.

Minagawa Jr., T., Trott, P., & Hoecht, A. (2007). Counterfeit, imitation, reverse engineering and learning: Reflections from Chinese manufacturing firms. *R&D Management, 37*(5), 455–467.

Mintzberg, H. (1994). *The rise and fall of strategic planning: Reconceiving roles for planning, plans, planners.* New York, NY: Simon & Schuster.

Moingeon, B., & Edmonson, A. (Eds.). (1996). *Organizational learning and competitive advantage.* Thousand Oaks, CA: Sage.

Moore, M. (2018, January 12). *ISO 30401—KM standard draft available* [Online forum post]. SIKM Leaders Forum. Retrieved December 11, 2021, from https://sikm.groups.io/g/main/message/5598

Moreno, J. L. (1934). *Who shall survive? A new approach to the problem of human interrelations.* Washington, DC: Nervous and Mental Disease Publishing Co..

Mouritsen, J., Johansen, M. R., Larsen, H. T., & Bukh, P. N. (2001b). Reading an intellectual capital statement: Describing and prescribing knowledge management strategies. *Journal of Intellectual Capital, 2*(4), 359–383.

Mouritsen, J., Larsen, H. T., & Bukh, P. N. (2001a). Intellectual capital and the "capable firm": Narrating, visualising and numbering for managing knowledge. *Accounting, Organizations and Society, 26*(7), 735–762.

Mullerbeck, E. (2014, January 17). *ISO International Organization for Standards considering a standard for KM* [Online forum post]. ActKM discussion list (personal archive no longer available online).

Murray, P. A. (2018). The domains of intellectual capital: An integrative discourse across perspectives. In J. Syed, P. A. Murray, D. Hislop, & Y. Mouzughi (Eds.), *The Palgrave handbook of knowledge management* (pp. 21–51). Cham, Switzerland: Palgrave Macmillan.

Nahapiet, J., & Ghoshal, S. (1998). Social capital, intellectual capital, and the organizational advantage. *Academy of Management Review, 23*(2), 242–266.

Nardi, B., & O'Day, V. (1999). *Information ecologies: Using technology with heart.* Cambridge, MA: MIT Press.

Nelson, R. R., & Winter, S. G. (1982). *An evolutionary theory of economic change.* Cambridge, MA: Harvard University Press.

Nemeth, C. P. (Ed.). (2008). *Improving healthcare team communication: Building on lessons from aviation and aerospace.* Aldershot, England: Ashgate.

Nevala-Lee, A. (2018). *Astounding: John W. Campbell, Isaac Asimov, Robert A. Heinlein, L. Ron Hub-bard and the golden age of science fiction.* New York, NY: Dey Street.Books

Niang, T. (2020). *Comment auditer un système de gestion des connaissances* [Presentation slides]. Dakar Yoff, Senegal: Afrique Communication.

Nichani, M. (2012). *Organizing digital information for others.* Singapore: Pebbleroad.

Nickols, F. (2000). The knowledge in knowledge management. In J. A. Woods & J. Cortada (Eds.), *The knowledge management yearbook, 2000–2001* (pp. 12–21). Woburn, CA: Butterworth-Heinemann.

Nimmo, D. (Ed.). (1980). *Communication Yearbook 4: An annual review published by the International Communication Association.* Piscataway, NJ: Transaction Books

Nissen, M. E., & Jennex, M. E. (2005). Knowledge as a multidimensional concept: A call for action. *International Journal of Knowledge Management, 1*(3), i–v.

Nohria, N., & Eccles, R. G. (Eds.). (1992). *Networks and organizations: Structure, form, and action.* Cambridge, MA: Harvard Business School Press.

Nonaka, I. (1991, November–December). The knowledge-creating company. *Harvard Business Review*, 96–104.

Nonaka, I., & Takeuchi, H. (1995). *The knowledge-creating company: How Japanese companies create the dynamics of innovation.* New York, NY: Oxford University Press.

NSPE. (1952). *How to improve engineering-management communications* (Executive Research Survey No. 1). Washington, DC: National Society of Professional Engineers.

Nystrom, P. C., & Starbuck, W. H. (1984). To avoid organizational crises, unlearn. *Organizational Dynamics, 12*(4), 53–65.

O'Dell, C., & Grayson, C. J. (1998). *If only we knew what we know: The transfer of internal knowledge and best practice.* New York, NY: Free Press.

Odell, J. (2018, November 27). A business with no end: Where does this strange empire start or stop? *The New York Times.*

Odiorne, G. S. (1954). An application of the communications audit. *Personnel Psychology, 7*(2), 235–243.

Omotayo, F. O. (2015, April 10). Knowledge management as an important tool in organizational management. *Library Philosophy and Practice* (Spring). Retrieved April 24, 2022, from https://digitalcommons.unl.edu/cgi/viewcontent.cgi?article=3330&context=libphilprac.

Oriel, S. L. (2003). From inventions management to intellectual capital measurement at the Dow Chemical Company: A 100+ year journey. In C. W. Holsapple (Ed.), *Handbook on knowledge management: Knowledge directions* (Vol. 2, pp. 489–500). Berlin, Germany: Springer-Verlag.

O'Riordan, J. (2005). *A review of knowledge management in the Irish civil service.* Dublin, Ireland: Institute of Public Administration.

Orna, E. (2004). *Information strategy in practice*. Aldershot, England: Gower.

Osono, E. (2004). The strategy-making process as dialogue. In H. Takeuchi & I. Nonaka (Eds.), *Hitotsubashi on knowledge management* (pp. 247–286). Singapore: John Wiley & Sons.

Owen, H. (1993). *Open space technology: A user's guide*. Kenosha, WI: Abbott.Publishing

Pa, N. C., Taheri, L., & Abdullah, R. (2012). A survey on approaches in knowledge audit in organizations. *Asian Transactions on Computers, 2*(5), 1–8.

Papandrea, F., & Armstrong, M. (Eds.). (2009). *Record of the Communications Policy & Research Forum 2009*. Sydney, Australia: Network Insight.

Parcell, G., & Collison, C. (2009). *No more consultants: We know more than we think*. Chichester, England: John Wiley & Sons.

Pariser, E. (2011). *The filter bubble: What the internet is hiding from you*. London, England: Viking.

Pascale, R. T., & Athos, A. G. (1982). *The art of Japanese management: Applications for American executives*. New York, NY: Warner.Books

Paulk, M. C., Curtis, B., Chrissis, M. B., & Weber, C. V. (1993). *Capability maturity model for software, version 1.1*. Pittsburgh, PA: Software Engineering Institute.

Penrose, E. T. (1959). *The theory of the growth of the firm*. Oxford, England: Basil Blackwell.

Perez-Soltero, A., Barcelo-Valenzuela, M., & Sanchez-Schmitz, G. (2009). Design of an ontology as a support to the knowledge audit process in organisations. *Journal of Information and Knowledge Management, 8*(2), 147–158.

Perkins, L. M. (1914). Schoolma'am and schoolmaster. *North American Review, 199*(698), 156–159.

Perry, D., & Mahoney, T. A. (1955). In-plant communications and employee morale. *Personnel Psychology, 8*, 339–346.

Pike, S., & Roos, G. (2011). Measuring and valuing knowledge-based intangible assets: Real business uses. In B. Vallejo-Alonso, A. Rodríguez-Castellanos, & G. Arregui-Ayastuy (Eds.), *Identifying, measuring, and valuing knowledge-based intangible assets: New perspectives* (pp. 268–293). Hershey, PA: Business Science Reference.

Polanyi, M. (1958). *Personal knowledge: Towards a post-critical philosophy*. Chicago, IL: University of Chicago Press.

Polanyi, M. (1966). *The tacit dimension*. New York, NY: Doubleday.

Powell, T. W. (2020). *The value of knowledge: The economics of enterprise knowledge and intelligence*. Berlin, Germany: Walter de Gruyter.

Power, M. (1997). *The audit society: Rituals of verification*. Oxford, England: Oxford University Press.

Prahalad, C. K., & Hamel, G. (1990, May–June). The core competence of the corporation. *Harvard Business Review*, 79–91.

Prichard, C., Hull, R., Chumer, M., & Willmott, H. (Eds.). (2000). *Managing knowledge: Critical investigations of work and learning*. Basingstoke, England: Macmillan Press.

Probst, G., Büchel, B., & Raub, S. (1998). Knowledge as a strategic resource. In G. Von Krogh, K. Ichijo, & I. Nonaka (Eds.), *Enabling knowledge creation: How to unlock the mystery of tacit knowledge and release the power of innovation* (pp. 240–252). Oxford, England: Oxford University Press.

Probst, G., Raub, S., & Romhardt, K. (2000). *Managing knowledge: Building blocks for success*. Chichester, England: John Wiley & Sons.

Pugh, K. B. (2011). *Sharing hidden know-how: How managers solve thorny problems with the knowledge jam*. San Francisco, CA: Jossey-Bass.

Quinn, A. V. (1979). The information audit: A new tool for the information manager. *Information Manager, 1*(4), 18–19.

Quinn, J. B., Anderson, P. and Finkelstein, S. (1996, March-April) 'Managing professional intellect: making the most of the best' *Harvard Business Review,* 71-80.

Ragab, M. A. F., & Arisha, A. (2013). Knowledge management and measurement: A critical review. *Journal of Knowledge Management, 17*(6), 873–901.

Ramanauskaitė, A., & Rudžionienė, K. (2013). Intellectual capital valuation: Methods and their classification. *Ekonomika, 92*(2), 79–92.

Raub, S., & Rüling, C-C. (2001). The knowledge management tussle—Speech communities and rhetorical strategies in the development of knowledge management. *Journal of Information Technology, 16,* 113–130.

Rechberg, I., & Syed, J. (2013). Ethical issues in knowledge management: Conflict of knowledge ownership. *Journal of Knowledge Management, 17*(6), 828–847.

Redding, W. C. (1964). The organizational communicator. In W. C. Redding & G. A. Sanborn (Eds.), *Business and industrial communication: A source book* (pp. 21–58). New York, NY: Harper and Row.

Redding, W. C. (1972). *Communication within the organization: An interpretive review of theory and research*. New York, NY: Industrial Communication Council.

Redding, W. C., & Sanborn, G. A. (Eds.). (1964). *Business and industrial communication: A source book*. New York, NY: Harper and Row.

Renaud, J., Lefebvre, A., & Fonteix, C. (2004). Improvement of the design process through knowledge capitalization: An approach by know-how mapping. *Concurrent Engineering, 12*(1), 25–37.

Repo, A. (1989). The value of information: Approaches in economics, accounting, and management science. *Journal of the American Society for Information Science, 40*(2), 68–85.

Ricceri, F. (2008). *Intellectual capital and knowledge management: Strategic management of knowledge resources*. London, England: Routledge.

Riley, R. H. (1976). The information audit. *Bulletin of the American Society for Information Science, 2*(5), 24–25.

Robertson, G. (1997). Information auditing: The information professional as an information accountant. *Managing Information, 97*(4), 30–35.

Robertson G., & Henczel, S. (2015, June 16). *Demystifying the information audit.* SLA Masterclass. Retrieved December 11, 2021, from https://www.sla.org/wp-content/uploads/2015/06/1650_Demystifying-the-Information-AuditHenczel.pdf

Roethlisberger, F. J., & Dickson, W. J. (1943). *Management and the worker.* Cambridge, MA: Harvard University Press.

Rogers, E. M. (2003). *Diffusion of innovations* (5th ed.). New York, NY: Simon & Schuster.

Roos, G., Bainbridge, A., & Jacobsen, K. (2001). Intellectual capital analysis as a strategic tool. *Strategy and Leadership, 29*(4), 21–26.

Roos, G., & Pike, S. (2007, May 3–4). *Intellectual capital research: a personal view* [Conference presentation]. IC-Congress 2007, INHOLLAND University of Professional Education, Haarlem, the Netherlands.

Roscher, W. (1878). *Principles of political economy* (Vol. 1). New York, NY: Henry Holt.

Rose, T. (2016). *The end of average: How we succeed in a world that values sameness.* New York, NY: HarperOne.

Rosenblueth, A., Wiener, N., & Bigelow, J. (1943). Behavior, purpose and teleology. *Philosophy of Science, 10*(1), 18–24.

Roth, S., & Carangal-San Jose, M. J. (2021, July 7). *Working towards a transformational knowledge management—Developing a knowledge management action plan at ADB* [Conference presentation]. KM Exchange Conference. Retrieved December 11, 2021, from https://www.mykmroundtable.org/uploads/3/8/2/6/38261647/6._km_exchange_2021_adb.pdf.

Rothberg, H. R., & Erickson, G. S. (2002). Competitive capital: A fourth pillar of intellectual capital? In N. Bontis (Ed.), *World Congress on Intellectual Capital readings* (pp. 94–103). Boston, MA: Butterworth Heinemann.

Rouse, J. (2001). Two concepts of practices. In T. R. Schatzki, K. Knorr Cetina, & E. Von Savigny (Eds.), *The practice turn in contemporary theory* (pp. 189–198). Abingdon, England: Routledge.

Rowland, T., Heal, C., Barber, P., & Martyn, S. (1998). Mind the "gaps": primary teacher trainees' mathematics subject knowledge. In *Proceedings of the British Society for Research in Learning Mathematics Day Conference at Birmingham* (pp. 91–96). Retrieved May 24, 2022, from http://www.bsrlm.org.uk/wp-content/uploads/2016/02/BSRLM-IP-18-12-16.pdf.

Rozental, D. (2013, January). ISO knowledge management certification: To be certified—Our personal perspective. *2Know Magazine.* Retrieved December 11, 2021, from http://www.kmrom.com/Site-En/Articles/ViewArticle.aspx?ArticleID=49

Ruggles, R. L. (Ed.). (1997). *Knowledge management tools*. Boston, MA: Butterworth Heinemann.

Rye, O. M. (1967). A shotgun wedding: Information storage and the computer. *Records Management Quarterly, 1*(4), 19–20.

Ryle, G. (1946). Knowing how and knowing that: The presidential address. *Proceedings of the Aristotelian Society New Series, 46*, 1–16.

Ryle, G. (1949). *The concept of mind*. London, England: Hutchinson.

Saetang, S. (2011). *Knowledge ownership, its influencing factors, and the relationships with knowledge sharing intentions in organizations: A comparative study between Thailand and the UK* [Unpublished doctoral thesis]. University of Manchester.

Sanborn, G. A. (1964). Communication in business: An overview. In W. C. Redding & G. A. Sanborn (Eds.), *Business and industrial communication: A source book* (pp. 3–26). New York, NY: Harper and Row.

Savić, D. (1992). Evolution of information resource management. *Journal of Librarianship and Information Science, 24*(3), 127–138.

Sbarcea, K. (2007, August 16). *Australian KM Standard* [Online forum post]. ActKM discussion list (personal archive no longer available online).

Sbarcea, K. (2010, April 2–3). *Overview of two knowledge management frameworks*. APO News. Retrieved May 24, 2022 from https://web.archive.org/web/20151015000914/http://www.apo-tokyo.org/productivity/114_prod.htm.

Scarborough, H., & Swan, J. (2001). Explaining the diffusion of knowledge management: The role of fashion. *British Journal of Management, 12*, 3–12.

Scarpignato, J. (2001). *Consumer warning about KM certification programs*. eKnowledge Center. Retrieved December 11, 2021, from https://web.archive.org/web/20010405215753/http://eknowledgecenter.com:80/consumer_warning_about_km_certif.htm.

Schaper, S. (2016). Contemplating the usefulness of intellectual capital reporting: Reasons behind the demise of IC disclosures in Denmark. *Journal of Intellectual Capital, 17*(1), 52–82.

Scharmer, C. O. (2009). *Theory U: Leading from the future as it emerges*. San Francisco, CA: Berrett-Koehler.

Schatzki, T. R., Knorr Cetina, K., & Von Savigny, E. (Eds.). (2001). *The practice turn in contemporary theory*. Abingdon, England: Routledge.

Schenk, M. (2006, January 26). *Disappearing Yahoo! groups*. Anecdote. Retrieved December 11, 2021, from https://www.anecdote.com/2006/01/disappearing-yahoo-groups/

Schopflin, K., & Walsh, M. (2019). *Practical knowledge and information management*. London, England: Facet.

Schramm, W. (1980). The beginnings of communication study in the United States. In D. Nimmo (Ed.), *Communication Yearbook 4: An annual review published by the International Communication Association* (pp. 73–82). Piscataway, NJ: Transaction.

Schumpeter, J. A. (1934). *The theory of economic development: An inquiry into profits, capital, credit, interest, and the business cycle.* Cambridge, MA: Harvard University Press.

Schwarz, G. F., & Veyre, J. C. (2007, June 18–21). *Implementing knowledge management at the Swiss Nuclear Safety Inspectorate (HSK)* [Conference presentation]. International Conference on Knowledge Management in Nuclear Facilities, Vienna, Austria.

Senior, N. W. (1836). *An outline of the science of political economy.* London, England: W. Clowes and Sons.

Serenko, A. (2021). A structured literature review of scientometric research of the knowledge management discipline: A 2021 update. *Journal of Knowledge Management, 25*(8), 1889–1925.

Serenko, A., & Bontis, N. (2009). Global ranking of knowledge management and intellectual capital academic journals. *Journal of Knowledge Management, 13*(1), 4–15.

Serenko, A., & Bontis, N. (2013a). Investigating the current state and impact of the intellectual capital discipline. *Journal of Intellectual Capital, 14*(4), 476–500.

Serenko, A., & Bontis, N. (2013b). The intellectual core and impact of the knowledge management academic discipline. *Journal of Knowledge Management, 17*(1), 137–155.

Serenko, A., Bontis, N., Booker, L., Sadeddin, K., & Hardie, T. (2010). A scientometric analysis of knowledge management and intellectual capital academic literature (1994–2008). *Journal of Knowledge Management, 14*(1), 3–23.

Shannon, C. E. (1949). Communication in the presence of noise. *Proceedings of the IRE, 37*(1), 10–21.

Shannon, C. E., & Weaver, W. (1964). *The mathematical theory of communication.* Urbana, IL: University of Illinois Press.

Shattuck, L. G., & Woods, D. D. (2000). Communication of intent in military command and control systems. In C. McCann & R. Pigeau (Eds.), *The human in command: Exploring the modern military experience* (pp. 279–291). Boston, MA: Springer.

Shelley, A. (2018, October 20). *Re: ISO 30401* [Online forum post]. SIKM Leaders Forum. Retrieved December 11, 2021, from https://sikm.groups.io/g/main/message/6092.

Sherman, A. J. (2012). *Harvesting intangible assets: Uncover hidden revenue in your company's intellectual property.* New York, NY: AMACOM.

Shewhart, W. A. (1939). *Statistical method from the viewpoint of quality control.* Washington, DC: The Graduate School, US Department of Agriculture.

Shiff, R. A. (1955a). A records-management credo. In H. W. MacDowell, ed., *Proceedings of the First Annual Conference on Records Management, September 20–21, 1954* (pp. 7–9). New York, NY: New York University Graduate School of Business Administration.

Shiff, R. A. (1955b). A technique to preserve the memory of business. *Office, 41*(1), 121–125, 186–188.

Shiff, R. A. (1965). Protect your records against disaster. *Harvard Business Review, 34*(4), 72–84.

Shih, W. (2016, Summer). The real lessons from Kodak's decline. *MIT Sloan Management Review*. Retrieved April 24, 2022, from https://sloanreview.mit.edu/article/the-real-lessons-from-kodaks -decline/

Simon, H. A. (1957). *Administrative behavior: A study of decision-making processes in administrative organization* (2nd ed.). New York, NY: Macmillan.

Simon, H. A. (1991). Bounded rationality and organizational learning. *Organization Science, 2*(1), 125–134.

Skyrme, D. J. (1998). *Measuring the value of knowledge: Metrics for the knowledge-based business.* London, England: Business Intelligence.Limited.

Skyrme, D. J. (2001, September). *I³ update no. 55: Knowledge digest*. Skyrme. Retrieved December 11, 2021, from http://www.skyrme.com/updates/digest.htm.

Skyrme, D. J. (2002). *KM standards: Do we need them?* Skyrme. Retrieved December 11, 2021, from https://www.skyrme.com/updates/u65_f1.htm.

Skyrme, D. J. (2007). *Knowing what you know and need to know: How to conduct a knowledge audit.* Newbury, England: David Skyrme.Associates.

Slater, L. (Ed.). (2014). *Gaining buy-in for KM*. London, England: Ark Group.

Sloman, S., & Fernbach, P. (2017). *The knowledge illusion: Why we never think alone.* New York, NY: Riverhead Books.

Smith, A. (1975). *An inquiry into the nature and causes of the wealth of nations.* (Vols. 1–2, R. H. Campbell, A. S. Skinner, & W. B. Todd, Eds.). Oxford, England: Oxford University Press.

Snowden, D. J. (1999). Storytelling: An old skill in a new context. *Business Information Review, 16*(1), 30–37.

Snowden, D. J. (2000a). The art and science of story or "Are you sitting uncomfortably?" Part 1: gathering and harvesting the raw material. *Business Information Review, 17*(3), 147–156.

Snowden, D. J. (2000b). New wine in old wineskins: From organic to complex knowledge management through the use of story. *Emergence, 2*(4), 50–64.

Snowden, D. J. (2000c) The ASHEN model: an enabler of action. *Knowledge Management, 3*(7), 14–17.

Snowden, D. J. (2002). Complex acts of knowing: Paradox and descriptive self-awareness. *Journal of Knowledge Management, 6*(2), 100–111.

Snowden, D. J. (2005). Stories from the frontier. *E:CO, 7*(3–4), 155–165.

Snowden, D. J. (2006a, August 30). *Standards and a trip on the Lego lake (with crocodiles)*. The Cynefin Co. Retrieved December 11, 2021, from https://thecynefin.co/standards-a-trip-on-the-lego -lake-with-crocodiles/.

Snowden, D. J. (2006b, October 29). *Seven approaches to complexity*. The Cynefin Co. Retrieved December 11, 2021, from https://thecynefin.co/seven-approaches-to-complexity/.

Snowden, D. J. (2012, July 8). *You can't create a craft by committee*. The Cynefin Co. Retrieved December 11, 2021, from https://thecynefin.co/you-cant-create-a-craft-by-committee/

Snowden, D. J., & Stanbridge, P. (2004). The landscape of management: Creating the context for understanding social complexity. *E:CO, 6*(1–2), 140–148.

Snyder, D. P. (1976). Computers, personal privacy, and the treatment of information as an economic commodity. In S. H. Brounstein & M. Kamrass (Eds.), *Operations research in law enforcement, justice and societal security* (pp. 304–315). Lexington, MA: DC Heath.

Spender, J.-C. (1996a). Making knowledge the basis of a dynamic theory of the firm. *Strategic Management Journal, 17*(2), 45–62.

Spender, J.-C. (1996b). Organizational knowledge, learning and memory: Three concepts in search of a theory. *Journal of Organizational Change Management, 9*(1), 63–78.

Spender, J.-C. (2008). Organizational learning and knowledge management: Whence and whither? *Management Learning, 39*(2), 159–176.

Spong, A., & Kamau, C. (2012). Cross-cultural impression management: A cultural knowledge audit model. *Journal of International Education in Business, 5*(1), 22–36.

Spradley, J. P. (1979). *The ethnographic interview*. Long Grove, IL: Waveland Press.

Stacey, R. D. (2000). The emergence of knowledge in organizations. *Emergence, 2*(4), 23–39.

Stacey, R. D., & Mowles, C. (2016). *Strategic management and organizational dynamics: The challenge of complexity to ways of thinking about organizations* (7th ed.). Harlow, England: Pearson.

Standards Australia. (2001). *Knowledge management: A framework for succeeding in the knowledge era* (Australian Standard No. HB 275–2001). Sydney, Australia: Standards Australia.

Standards Australia. (2003). *Interim Australian standard knowledge management* (Australian Standard No. AS 5037 (Int)-2003). Sydney, Australia: Standards Australia.

Standards Australia. (2005). *Knowledge management—A guide* (Australian Standard No. AS 5037–2005). Sydney, Australia: Standards Australia.

Standards Institution of Israel. (2011). *Knowledge management system* (Israel Standard No. SI 25006). Tel Aviv, Israel: Standards Institution of Israel.

Standfield, K. (2002). *Intangible management: Tools for solving the accounting and management crisis*. Amsterdam, Netherlands: Academic Press.

Star, S. L., & Strauss, A. (1999). Layers of silence, arenas of voice: The ecology of visible and invisible work. *Computer Supported Cooperative Work, 8*(1–2), 9–30.

Stark, R. J. (2009). *Rhetoric, science, and magic in seventeenth-century England*. Washington, DC: Catholic University of America Press.

Stevens, W. (1942). *Parts of a world*. New York, NY: Alfred A. Knopf.

Stewart, T. A. (1991). BRAINPOWER Intellectual capital is becoming corporate America's most valuable asset and can be its sharpest competitive weapon. The challenge is to find what you have—And use it. *Fortune Magazine, 123*(11), 44–50.

Stewart, T. A. (1998). *Intellectual capital: The new wealth of organizations*. London, England: Nicholas Brealey.

Stewart, T. A. (2001). *The wealth of knowledge: Intellectual capital and the twenty-first century organization*. New York, NY: Doubleday.

Stigler, G. J. (1976). The successes and failures of Professor Smith. *Journal of Political Economy, 84*(6), 1199–1213.

Stiles, C. C. (1915). Public Archives of Iowa. *Annals of Iowa, 12*, 14–60.

Stopford, Viscount, (1954). The measurement of clerical work. *O&M Bulletin, 9*(6), 40–45.

Storlie, C. (2010, November 3). Manage uncertainty through commander's intent. *Harvard Business Review*. Retrieved December 11, 2021, from https://hbr.org/2010/11/dont-play-golf-in-a-football-g

Suchman, L. (1995). Making work visible. *Communications of the ACM, 38*, 56–68.

Suchman, L. (1996). Supporting articulation work. In R. Kling (Ed.), *Computerization and controversy: Value conflicts and social choices* (2nd ed., pp. 407–423). San Diego, CA: Academic Press.

Sullenberger III, C. B. (2009). *Highest duty: My search for what really matters*. New York, NY: HarperCollins.

Sullivan, P. H. (2000). *Value-driven intellectual capital: How to convert intangible corporate assets into market value*. New York, NY: John Wiley & Sons.

Sussman, L. (1974). Perceived message distortion: Or, you can fool some of the supervisors some of the time . . . *Personnel Journal, 53*(9), 679–682.

Sveiby, K.-E. (1998, August). *Measuring intangibles and intellectual capital—An emerging first standard*. Sveiby. Retrieved December 11, 2021, from http://web.archive.org/web/20011219192016/http://www.sveiby.com/articles/EmergingStandard.html.

Sveiby, K.-E. (2001). *The intangible assets monitor*. Sveiby. Retrieved December 11, 2021, from http://web.archive.org/web/20011111043356/http://www.sveiby.com/articles/companymonitor.html.

Sveiby, K.-E. (2010). *Methods for measuring intangible assets*. Sveiby. Retrieved December 11, 2021, from http://web.archive.org/web/20110310125320/https://www.sveiby.com/articles/IntangibleMethods.htm.

Sveiby, K.-E., & Armstrong, C. (2004, September 2). *Learn to measure to learn!* [Speech transcript]. IC Congress, Helsinki, Finland. Retrieved December 11, 2021, from https://web.archive.org/web/20160512180508/http://www.sveiby.com/articles/measuretolearn.pdf.

Sveiby, K.-E., & Lloyd, T. (1987). *Managing knowhow: Adding value by valuing creativity*. London, England: Bloomsbury.

Sveiby, K.-E., & Risling, A. (1986). *Kunskapsföretaget*. Malmö, Sweden: Liber.

Swan, A. J. (2003). *An empirical framework for evaluating, implementing and managing a value-based supply chain strategy* [Unpublished doctoral dissertation]. University of Bath.

Swanstrom, E. C. (2001a). *What's new*. Innovation Management Institute. Retrieved December 11, 2021, from https://web.archive.org/web/20010402042233/http://metainnovation.com:80/

Swanstrom, E. C. (2001b). *Knowledge management partnership request for homeland security* [Online forum post]. e-gov.com message board. Retrieved December 11, 2021, from https://web.archive.org /web/20041127112552/http://www.unis-inc.com/security/knowledge_management_partnership _request_homeland_security_2.htm.

Swanstrom, E. C. (2001c). VOCKM. Retrieved December 11, 2021, from https://web.archive.org /web/20020606013452/http://www.nationalknowledge.org:80/retrieved.

Swanstrom, E. C. (2002, August 12). *ANSI KM and KE standards committees* [Online forum post]. Oasis Mailing List Archives. Retrieved December 11, 2021, from https://lists.oasis-open.org /archives/humanmarkup-comment/200208/msg00028.html.

Syed, J., Murray, P. A., Hislop, D., & Mouzughi, Y. (Eds.). (2018). *The Palgrave handbook of knowledge management*. Cham, Switzerland: Palgrave Macmillan.

Szulanski, G. (2003). *Sticky knowledge: Barriers to knowing in the firm*. London, England: Sage.

Szulanski, G., & Winter, S. (2002). Getting it right the second time. *Harvard Business Review, 80*(1), 62–69.

Takeuchi, H., & Nonaka, I. (Eds.). (2004). *Hitotsubashi on knowledge management*. Singapore: John Wiley & Sons.

Tarrant, R. (1969). Filing equipment standards. *Records Management Quarterly, 3*(1), 19–25.

Taussig, M. (1993). *Mimesis and alterity: A particular history of the senses*. New York, NY: Routledge.

Taylor, C. (1989). *Sources of the self: The making of the modern identity*. Cambridge, England: Cambridge University Press.

Teece, D. J. (Ed.). (1987). *The competitive challenge: Strategies for industrial innovation and renewal*. Cambridge, MA: Ballinger.

Teece, D. J. (1998). Capturing value from knowledge assets: The new economy, markets for know-how, and intangible assets. *California Management Review, 40*(3), 55–79.

Teece, D. J., & Al-Aali, A. (2011). Knowledge assets, capabilities and the theory of the firm. In M. Easterby-Smith & M. A. Lyles (Eds.), *Handbook of organizational learning and knowledge management* (2nd ed., pp. 505–534). Chichester, England: John Wiley & Sons.

Teece, D. J., Pisano, G., & Shuen, A. (1997). Dynamic capabilities and strategic management. *Strategic Management Journal, 18*(7), 509–533.

Teitel, A. S. (2011). *The lost art of the Saturn V*. Vintage Space. Retrieved December 11, 2021, from https://vintagespace.wordpress.com/2011/04/03/the-lost-art-of-the-saturn-v/.

Terlaak, A. (2007). Order without law? The role of certified management standards in sharing socially desired firm behaviors. *Academy of Management Review, 32*(3), 968–985.

Thayer, L. O. (1961). *Administrative communication*. Homewood, IL: Richard D. Irwin.Inc.

Thomas, J. A., Pierce, L. G., Dixon, M. W., & Fong, G. (2007). *Interpreting commander's intent: Do we really know what we know and what we don't know* [Conference presentation]. 2007 Command and Control Research and Technology Symposium: Adapting C2 to the 21st Century, Aberdeen, MD, United States. Retrieved December 11, 2021, from https://apps.dtic.mil/sti/pdfs/ADA481530.pdf .

Thompson, J. D. (1967). *Organizations in action: Social science bases of administrative theory*. New York, NY: McGraw Hill.

Thompson, L. L., Levine, J. M., & Messick, D. M. (Eds.). (1999). *Shared cognition in organizations: The management of knowledge*. Mahwah, NJ: Lawrence Erlbaum.

Tissol, G. (1997). *The face of nature: Wit, narrative, and cosmic origins in Ovid's* Metamorphoses. Princeton, NJ: Princeton University Press.

Tiwana, A. (2002). *The knowledge management toolkit: Orchestrating IT, strategy, and knowledge platforms* (2nd ed.). Upper Saddle River, NJ: Prentice Hall.

Toavs, D. V. (2004). *Pixelating policy: Visualizing issue transformation in real and virtual worlds* [Unpublished doctoral dissertation]. Virginia Polytechnic Institute and State University.

Tobin, P. K. J., & Snyman, R. (2004). World-class knowledge management: A proposed framework. *South African Journal of Information Management, 6*(3), a311. Retrieved April 24, 2022, from https://doi.org/10.4102/sajim.v6i3.311

Tolkien, J. R. R. (1966). *The hobbit, or there and back again*. London, England: George Allen and Unwin.

Tourish, D. (2019). *Management studies in crisis: Fraud, deception and meaningless research*. Cambridge, England: Cambridge University Press.

Tourish, D., & Hargie, O. (2000a). Communication and organizational success. In O. Hargie & D. Tourish (Eds.), *Handbook of communication audits for organizations* (pp. 3–21). London, England: Routledge.

Tourish, D., & Hargie, O. (2000b). Auditing communication to maximise performance. In O. Hargie & D. Tourish (Eds.), *Handbook of communication audits for organizations* (pp. 22–41). London, England: Routledge.

Trauth, E. M. (1989). The evolution of information resource management. *Information & Management, 16*, 257–268.

Trompf, G. W. (Ed.). (1990). *Cargo cults and millenarian movements*. Berlin, Germany: Mouton De Gruyter.

Tsoukas, H. (2000). Knowledge as action, organization as theory: Reflections on organizational knowledge. *Emergence, 2*(4), 104–112.

Tsoukas, H. (2005). *Complex knowledge: Studies in organizational epistemology.* Oxford, England: Oxford University Press.

Tuchman, B. W. (1962). *The guns of August.* New York, NY: Ballantine.Books

Ujwary-Gil, A. (2020). *Organizational network analysis: Auditing intangible resources.* New York, NY: Routledge.

Vallejo-Alonso, B., Rodríguez-Castellanos, A., & Arregui-Ayastuy, G. (Eds.). (2011). *Identifying, measuring, and valuing knowledge-based intangible assets: New perspectives.* Hershey, PA: Business Science Reference.

Vasconcelos, J., Kimble, C., & Gouveia, F. R. (2000). A design for a group memory system using ontologies. In P. Beynon-Davies & M. Williams (Eds.), *Proceedings of the 5th UKAIS Conference, University of Wales Institute, Cardiff, 26–28 April 2000.* New York, NY: McGraw Hill.

Vazsonyi, A. (1975). Information systems in management science: Data base management systems. *Interfaces, 5*(3), 47–52.

Vestal, W. (2005). *Knowledge mapping: The essentials for success.* Houston, TX: American Productivity and Quality Center.

Vílchez, V. F. (2017). The dark side of ISO 14001: The symbolic environmental behavior. *European Research on Management and Business Economics, 23*(1), 33–39.

Vivas, C., & Sequeira, P. (Eds.). (2014). *The proceedings of the 15th European Conference on Knowledge Management, ECKM 2014:The Santarém School of Management and Technology, Polytechnic Institute of Santarém, Santarém, Portugal, 4–5 September 2014* (Vol. 1). Reading, UK: Academic Conferences and Publishing International.

von Clausewitz, C. (1976). *On war* (M. Howard & P. Paret, Eds., Trans.) Princeton, NJ: Princeton University Press.

Von Krogh, G., Ichijo, K., & Nonaka, I. (Eds.). (2000). *Enabling knowledge creation: How to unlock the mystery of tacit knowledge and release the power of innovation.* Oxford, England: Oxford University Press.

Ward, V. (2010). Digging up the metaphors. *Inside Knowledge Magazine, 13*(8), 5–7.

Webb, S. P. (1998). *Knowledge management: Linchpin of change.* Abingdon, England: Aslib.

Webb, S. P. (2003). Information audit. In J. Feather & P. Sturges (Eds.), *International encyclopedia of library and information science* (2nd ed., pp. 252–254). London, England: Routledge.

Weber, F., Wunram, M., Kemp, J., Pudlatz, M., & Bredehorst, B. (2002, February 27). Standardisation in knowledge management—Towards a common KM framework in Europe. In *Proceedings of UNICOM Seminar: Towards common approaches and standards in KM.* Retrieved April 24, 2022, from

http://docplayer.net/45156781-Standardisation-in-knowledge-management-towards-a-common
-km-framework-in-europe.html.

Weick, K. E. (1969). *The social psychology of organizing*. Boston, MA: Addison-Wesley.

Weick, K. E., & Sutcliffe, K. M. (2001). *Managing the unexpected: Assuring high performance in an age of complexity*. San Francisco, CA: Jossey-Bass.

Welborn, L. (2006, August 22). Chat-room molester sentenced. *Orange County Register*. Retrieved December 11, 2021, from https://www.ocregister.com/2006/08/22/chat-room-molester-sentenced/

Wernerfelt, B. (1984). A resource-based view of the firm. *Strategic Management Journal, 5*(2), 171–180.

Wernerfelt, B. (1995). The resource-based view of the firm: Ten years after. *Strategic Management Journal, 16*, 171–174.

Whitehead, A. N. (1911). *An introduction to mathematics*. London, England: Thornton Butterworth.

Whymark, G., & Hasan, H. (2005). *Activity as the focus of information systems research*. Eveleigh, New South Wales: Knowledge Creation Press.

Wiener, L., & Mulvaney, M. (2008). Safeguarding children: Audit of staff knowledge. *Paediatric Care, 20*(4), 20–24.

Wiener, N. (1961). *Cybernetics or control and communication in the animal and the machine* (2nd ed.). Cambridge, MA: MIT Press.

Wiig, K. (1993). *Knowledge management foundations: Thinking about thinking. How people and organizations create, represent, and use knowledge*. Arlington, TX: Schema Press.

Wiig, K. (1995). *Knowledge management methods: Practical approaches to managing knowledge*. Arlington, TX: Schema Press.

Wiig, K. (2004). *People-focused knowledge management: How effective decision making leads to corporate success*. Amsterdam, Netherlands: Elsevier.

Wiio, O. A., Goldhaber, G. M., & Yates, M. P. (1980). Organizational communication research: Time for reflection? In D. Nimmo (Ed.), *Communication Yearbook 4: An annual review published by the International Communication Association* (pp. 83–97). Piscataway, NJ: Transaction.

Willard, N. (1993). Information resources management. *Aslib Information, 21*(5), 201–205.

Willekens, M., & Simunic, D. A. (2007). Precision in auditing standards: Effects on auditor and director liability and the supply and demand for audit services. *Accounting and Business Research, 37*(3), 217–232.

Williams, D. (2014). Models, metaphors and symbols for information and knowledge systems. *Journal of Entrepreneurship, Management and Innovation, 10*(1), 79–107.

Wilson, D. A. (1996). *Managing knowledge*. Oxford, England: Butterworth Heinemann.

Wilson, J. P., & Campbell, L. (2016). Developing a knowledge management policy for ISO 9001: 2015. *Journal of Knowledge Management, 20*(4), 829–844.

Wilson, T. D. (2002). The nonsense of knowledge management. *Information Research, 8*(1). Retrieved December 11, 2021, from http://informationr.net/ir/8-1/paper144.html.

Wilson, T. D. (2003). Information management. In J. Feather & P. Sturges (Eds.), *International encyclopedia of library and information science* (2nd ed., pp. 263–278). London, England: Routledge.

Winter, S. G. (1987). Knowledge and competence as strategic assets. In D. J. Teece (Ed.), *The competitive challenge: Strategies for industrial innovation and renewal* (pp. 159–184). Cambridge, MA: Ballinger.

Winter, S. G., & Szulanski, G. (2002). Replication of organizational routines: Conceptualizing the exploitation of knowledge assets. In C. W. Choo & N. Bontis (Eds.), *The strategic management of intellectual capital and organizational knowledge* (pp. 207–221). Oxford, England: Oxford University Press.

Woods, J. A., & Cortada, J. (Eds.). (2000). *The knowledge management yearbook, 2000–2001*. Woburn, CA: Butterworth-Heinemann.

Wright, J. D. (Ed.). (2015). *International encyclopedia of social and behavioral sciences* (2nd ed.). Oxford, England: Elsevier.

Yakhlef, A., & Salzer-Mörling, M. (2000). Intellectual capital: Managing by numbers. In C. Prichard, R. Hull, M. Chumer, & H. Willmott (Eds.), *Managing knowledge: Critical investigations of work and learning* (pp. 20–36). Basingstoke, England: Macmillan Press.

Yamaguchi, T. (Ed.). (2008, November 22–23). *Practical aspects of knowledge management: 7th International Conference, PAKM 2008, Yokohama, Japan*. Berlin, Germany: Springer Verlag.

Yates, J. (1989). *Control through communication: The rise of system in American management*. Baltimore, MD: Johns Hopkins University Press.

Yoder, D. (1952). Triple auditing employer-employee relations. *Business News Notes*, (2), 1–4.

Yoder, D., Heneman Jr., H. G., & Cheit, E. F. (1951). *Triple audit of industrial relations*. Bulletin 11, Industrial Relations Center. Minneapolis, MN: University of Minnesota Press.

Young, R., Payne, J., Milton, N., Latawiec, J., & Lambert, P. (2018, October 8). *Unlocking the value of knowledge* [Webinar]. London, England: British Standards Institute. Retrieved December 11, 2021, from https://realkm.com/2018/10/16/slides-and-recording-from-bsi-km-standard-webinar-now-available/.

Zack, M. D. (1999a). Developing a knowledge strategy. *California Management Review, 41*(3), 125–145.

Zack, M. D. (1999b). Managing codified knowledge. *Sloan Management Review, 40*(4), 45–58.

Zack, M. D. (2001). If KM is the solution, then what's the problem? In Y. Malhotra (Ed.), *Knowledge management and business model innovation* (pp. 16–36). Hershey, PA: Idea Group Publishing.

Index